The Fatimid Empire

THE EDINBURGH HISTORY OF THE ISLAMIC EMPIRES
Series Editor: Ian Richard Netton

Available or forthcoming titles

The Umayyad Empire
Andrew Marsham

The Abbasid Empire
Matthew Gordon

The Almoravid and Almohad Empires
Amira K. Bennison

The Seljuk Empire of Anatolia
Sara Yur Yildiz

The Great Seljuk Empire
A. C. S. Peacock

The Fatimid Empire
Michael Brett

The Mamluk Empire
Jo van Steenbergen and Patrick Wing

The Ayyubid Empire
Gerald Hawting

The Mongol Empire
Timothy May

The Ottoman Empire
Gokhan Çetinsaya

www.edinburghuniversitypress.com/series/ehie

The Fatimid Empire

Michael Brett

EDINBURGH
University Press

In memory of
John Wansbrough,
scholar and friend

Edinburgh University Press is one of the leading university presses in the UK. We publish academic books and journals in our selected subject areas across the humanities and social sciences, combining cutting-edge scholarship with high editorial and production values to produce academic works of lasting importance. For more information visit our website: edinburghuniversitypress.com

Edinburgh University Press Ltd
The Tun – Holyrood Road
12 (2f) Jackson's Entry
Edinburgh EH8 8PJ

Typeset in 11/13pt Adobe Garamond Pro by
Servis Filmsetting Ltd, Stockport, Cheshire
and printed and bound in Great Britain by
CPI Group (UK) Ltd, Croydon CR0 4YY

A CIP record for this book is available from the British Library

ISBN 978 0 7486 4077 5 (hardback)
ISBN 978 0 7486 4076 8 (paperback)
ISBN 978 1 4744 2151 5 (webready PDF)
ISBN 978 1 4744 2152 2 (epub)

Contents

Boxes

Illustrations

Figures

Maps

Introduction

The Question of Empire

'Neither holy, nor Roman, nor an empire.' Voltaire's disparaging description of the great mediaeval empire founded by Charlemagne and his Saxon successors on the eve of its extinction by Napoleon not only reveals the gap between the ideal and the reality, but identifies the elements of the ideal that had originally inspired its creation – religion, race and overrule. Race, in this empire of the Germanic barbarians who had overrun the western European portion of the Roman world, was sublimated into the succession to the Caesars who had conquered and ruled that world before reinventing their dominion in the name of Christ. Christianity, however, the first of the three religions in the Biblical tradition to emerge out of the post-exilic Judaism of the Second Temple, was closely followed after the destruction of the Temple at Jerusalem by Talmudic Judaism, and 600 years later by the third. A hundred and fifty years before Charlemagne, the Arabs, the last of the barbarians, overran Roman Syria and Egypt as well as Persian Iraq and Iran, and went on to conquer North Africa and Spain in the name of God. Like that of Charlemagne, the empire they created was founded on the basis of religion, race and overrule; the difference was that the race in question was that of the Arabs themselves, who took up their position as rivals rather than heirs of Rome. Their Emperors were the Caliphs or Lieutenants of God and His Prophet Muḥammad, first at Medina, then Damascus and finally Baghdad. Meanwhile, in the course of the seventh, eighth and ninth centuries, the faith preached by Muḥammad took shape as the religion of Islam, modelled not on the pattern of Christianity as a religion of sacraments administered by priests, but on that of Talmudic Judaism as a religion of divine law interpreted by scholars. But at the same time, the element of Messianism, common to all three religions, had not only thrown up a series of challenges for the right to rule the empire, most notably the revolution in 750 that had transferred the Caliphate from the Umayyads at Damascus to the ᶜAbbasids at Baghdad. It had begun to generate a rival version of the faith in which authority for the divine law rested not with the scholars but with a successor to the Prophet in his capacity as the source of revelation as well as leader of the community. That successor was held to be a member of the Prophet's family, but his descendants in line from his daughter Fāṭima and his son-in-law ᶜAlī had consistently failed to make good their claim, until by the end of the ninth century they had disappeared from view, to give rise to the expectation of the coming of a second Muḥammad out of the obscurity into which they had vanished. By the end of the century, that expectation came to a head in the crisis out of which, in 910, the Fatimid dynasty and empire was born in opposition to that of the ᶜAbbasids at Baghdad.

To call it an empire is to introduce this particular, indeed peculiar, combination of religion, race and overrule into the modern discussion of what the term might imply. The contrast between the ideal and the reality of the nation state, the standard political unit of the modern world, whose populations are regularly composed of different peoples rather than a single one, is at least partly responsible for the problem of deciding where to draw the line between the unitary state and Kipling's vision of empire as 'dominion over palm and pine', the rule of some metropolitan power over a heterogeneous collection of peoples and places assembled in the course of conquest and colonisation. The problem is apparent in the case of Great Britain and the British empire, the first a combination of at least four different peoples that subsequently extended to embrace the second, a vast miscellany of territories strung around the world. Apart from its lack of uniformity, what was missing from this evidently supranational entity was a rationale for its creation over and above the various economic and political objectives that brought it into being. Its justification after the event as the glorious achievement of a British race that had, with the help of God, brought it into being as an instrument of civilisation, was never particularly convincing. Unlike the Roman empire, which systematically pursued as well as proclaimed its civilising mission, it had neither the means, the time nor the inclination to draw its members into a similarly closely knit polity, in the manner of the United Kingdom at its heart. When it was rapidly obliged to reinvent itself in the middle of the twentieth century, it did so rather as a commonwealth of nations under the token presidency of the monarch, on the basis of shared values and interests rather than overrule. And with the secession of the bulk of Ireland, the United Kingdom itself began to break up on the same principle of home rule.

By contrast, when the Roman empire reinvented itself, it did so in the name of a universal faith that sanctified it as the empire of God on earth. In the imperial moment of the early Middle Ages, such a faith inspired the creation of the Holy Roman Empire in western Europe out of the Frankish and German kingdoms, and still more so the rapid conquest by the Arabs of a truly enormous area, the territory of an empire that formed God's government of the world. It is a little ironic, therefore, that when both of these empires began, like the British empire, to break up under the impossibility of maintaining central control of their various provinces, the outcome should be a commonwealth solution in which the role of the Emperor as the representative of God preserved him as the nominal suzerain of his erstwhile subjects. This was particularly striking in the case of the ᶜAbbasid Caliphs of Baghdad, who after 200 years had lost all power even in Iraq, but continued to be recognised by the monarchs of Islam as the authority for their rule. Such recognition was the only means at their disposal to preserve what little remained of their dominion when they were challenged by the Fatimids for the right to rule Islam.

Despite their messianic zeal, however, the Fatimids were not able to repeat the exploits of the original Arabs, nor that of the ᶜAbbasids themselves, in conquering the bulk of the territories that now constituted the lands of Islam. The culmination of the revolution that brought them to power in North Africa was their acquisition of Egypt and Syria, a nuclear state that served as their equivalent of Great Britain, a composite base from which to pursue their imperial ambition. The aim of further conquest was then largely abandoned in favour of a similar drive for recognition by the sovereigns of the Muslim world, a means to displace their ᶜAbbasid rivals as the legitimate rulers of a Muslim commonwealth centred upon Cairo. To win such recognition, the Fatimids not only laid claim to the Caliphate in the main line of descent from Muḥammad, Fāṭima and ᶜAlī, the trio at the root of the holy family of Islam, but still more to the Imāmate, the supreme authority for the faith as well as the government of the community. Such a claim had been abandoned by the ᶜAbbasids; in western Europe it was reserved to the Pope rather than the Emperor. But it lay at the heart of the Fatimid empire and its complicated history, as the dynasty transferred itself from North Africa to Egypt, and its mission to rule the world separated out into the tasks of governing the lands it controlled, of winning recognition for itself elsewhere in the Muslim world and of developing a doctrine and a following of true believers in its mission. Some 150 years after the inception of this mission, the religious and political opposition it generated turned into a counter-revolution that not only changed the face of the Islamic, and indeed the mediaeval world, but eventually disposed of the dynasty itself.

The Question of the Fatimids

In following this trajectory of rise, decline and fall over a period of almost 300 years from 910 to 1171, the problem for the historian is to combine these strands into a single story that does not break down, as it usually does, into episodes in the histories of North Africa, Egypt and Ismāᶜīlism, the branch of Shīᶜite Islam that the Fatimids established. This breakdown is not simply because the Fatimids did indeed play an important part in all these different histories, but because the sources fall into two quite separate groups, the North African and the Egyptian, both of which are coupled with a third, the doctrinal literature of the sect. For the most part, the secondary literature has in consequence lost sight of the empire as a whole, to the extent that up to now it has only been treated in its entirety by Heinz Halm in his three-volume work, *Das Reich des Mahdi*, translated as *The Empire of the Mahdi*; *Die Kalifen von Kairo*; and *Kalifen und Assassinen*.[1] Paul Walker's *Exploring an Islamic Empire* summarises its history in ninety pages before turning to a discussion of the sources.[2] Brett's *The Rise of the Fatimids*[3] stops at the end of the tenth; Farhat Dachraoui's *Le Califat Fatimide au Maghreb*,[4] like Halm's *Empire of the Mahdi*, deals only with the North African period to 973. In Egypt, Walker's *Caliph of Cairo* discusses the reign of al-Ḥākim[5] and Thomson's *Politics and Power in Late Fatimid Egypt* covers the reign of al-Mustanṣir.[6] Elsewhere, the fragmentation of the subject is apparent in *The Cambridge History of Egypt*,[7] where the imperial dimension is treated separately from the state in Egypt. In general histories of the Arabs and Islam, from Hitti's *A History of the Arabs*[8] through Bernard Lewis's *The Arabs in History*[9] and Hugh Kennedy's *The Prophet and the Age of the Caliphates*[10] to *The New Cambridge History of Islam*,[11] the Fatimids appear as a postscript to the empire of the Umayyads and ᶜAbbasids as the founders of an independ-

1 H. Halm, *Das Reich des Mahdi. Der Aufsteig der Fatimiden* (Munich, 1991), trans. M. Bonner, *The Empire of the Mahdi* (Leiden, 1996), *Die Kalifen von Kairo* (Munich, 2003), *Kalifen und Assassinen* (Munich, 2013).

2 P. E. Walker, *Exploring an Islamic Empire. Fatimid History and its Sources* (London and New York, 2002).

3 M. Brett, *The Rise of the Fatimids. The World of the Mediterranean and the Middle East in the Tenth Century* CE (Leiden, 2001).

4 F. Dachraoui, *Le Califat Fatimide au Maghreb (296–365H./909–975 JC.)* (Tunis, 1981).

5 P. E. Walker, *Caliph of Cairo al-Ḥākim bi-Amr Allah, 996–1021* (Cairo, 2009).

6 K. Thomson, *Politics and Power in Late Fatimid Egypt. The Reign of Caliph al-Mustansir* (London and New York, 2016).

7 C. F. Petry (ed.), *The Cambridge History of Egypt*, vol. 1, *Islamic Egypt, 640–1517* (Cambridge, 1998).

8 P. K. Hitti, *A History of the Arabs. From the Earliest Times to the Present* (London and New York, from 1937).

9 B. Lewis, *The Arabs in History* (London, 1950).

10 H. Kennedy, *The Prophet and the Age of the Caliphates* (London and New York, 1986).

11 *The New Cambridge History of Islam*, vol. 1, ed. C. F. Robinson, *The Formation of the Islamic World, Sixth to Eleventh Centuries*; vol. 2, ed. M. Fierro, *The Western Islamic World, Eleventh to Eighteenth Centuries* (Cambridge, 2010).

ent Egyptian state. In Farhad Daftary's *The Ismāᶜīlīs*[12] the emphasis is on their role in the evolution of their adherents into the sectarian communities of today. Meanwhile, in histories of North Africa, from Georges Marçais, *La Berbérie musulmane et l'Orient au Moyen Âge*,[13] through Brett and Fentress, *The Berbers*,[14] to, once again, *The New Cambridge History of Islam*, they appear as contributors to regional histories of the Maghrib and the Mashriq, the Muslim West as distinct from the Muslim East.

To a large extent, this is because the Fatimids *per se* have attracted attention relatively recently: the above list of studies of their empire are, with few exceptions, all publications of the last forty years. As rulers of Egypt in particular, they have profited from the general growth of the subject of Islamic history, in which Egypt has figured prominently on the strength of the available sources, witness the ongoing series of conference publications under the title of *Egypt and Syria in the Fatimid, Ayyubid and Mamluk Eras*.[15] But the rise to prominence of the Fatimids themselves stems from the study of Ismāᶜīlism and its literature, which began in the 1930s with the pioneering work of Wladimir Ivanow and entered the mainstream of scholarship in 1959 with the publication of the first of Wilferd Madelung's many studies. Since 1977 it has enjoyed the institutional support of the Institute of Ismaili Studies, whose research and publications have been directed by Farhad Daftary, the author of *The Ismāᶜīlīs*, published in 1990 as the first comprehensive account of their history and subsequently revised. It is the recovery of the literature of the sect, including the pronouncements of the Fatimids themselves, which has added that extra dimension to the study of the dynasty, and made possible the study of their empire as a religious as well as a political and administrative exercise.

It has, on the other hand, created its own problems, with paradoxical consequences that stem from the doctrinal character of the literature in question. This is predicated not simply upon a belief in the Imāmate as the necessary instrument of God's guidance of the community, but upon its corollary, a belief in the unbroken continuity of this Imāmate in a direct line of succession to the Prophet. For the historical veracity of this article of faith before the advent of the Fatimids, however, there is nothing to confirm the versions given out by the dynasty, its sectarian successors and its enemies. This has

[12] F. Daftary, *The Ismāᶜīlīs. Their History and Doctrines*, 2nd edn (Cambridge, 2007).

[13] G. Marçais, *La Berbérie musulmane et l'Orient au Moyen Âge* (Paris, 1946).

[14] M. Brett and E. Fentress, *The Berbers* (Oxford, 1996).

[15] U. Vermeulen et al., *Egypt and Syria in the Fatimid, Ayyubid and Mamluk Eras*, Proceedings of the International Colloquium (CHESFAME) at the Universities of Leuven and Gent, series 1995 ff., Leuven.

not only created an inconclusive argument over the origins of the Fatimids. Belief in the previous continuity of their line has retrospectively imposed a narrow sectarian perspective upon an imperial enterprise designed to establish the Imāmate as the true form of the faith, one that endorses rather than contradicts the understanding of the Fatimid project as the vain attempt of a divergent minority to rule over the consensual majority of Muslims. As their place in history, this was assigned to them, implicitly or otherwise, by the Arab generalists of the post-Fatimid period, beginning with Ibn al-Athīr, in whose *Kitāb al-kāmil fī᾿ l-ta᾿rīkh* the political history of the dynasty is scattered across the years in the annual record of events throughout the Muslim world. It was agreed by Ibn Khaldūn in his *Muqaddima* when he denounced the Fatimids as heretical extremists, but ones who were indeed the descendants of the Prophet that they claimed to be, since otherwise their success in winning the support required to found such a long-lasting dynasty would be inexplicable. Such an understanding of their history as yet another dynasty built on the strength of the *ᶜaṣabiyya* or solidarity of its followers agrees very well with our own understanding of the revolution that brought them to power, but not with that of the dynasty itself; from its point of view, the distinction between the doctrine and the genealogy separates the inseparable. But the distinction finds a perverse echo in Stanley Lane-Poole's *A History of Egypt in the Middle Ages*, first published in 1901, when it was still possible to regard their revolution as the work of unscrupulous fraudsters trading on the gullibility of simple tribesmen.[16] Subsequent scholarship may have relegated this preposterous explanation to some historiographical dustbin, but as the disconnected treatment accorded to the dynasty in the plan of *The New Cambridge History of Islam* makes clear, it has not yet gone far enough to consider the Fatimids for a major role in the history either of Islam or of the world of which Islam was a part, not least as having been responsible in some measure for the crisis of the eleventh century that divides the first from the second volume.

The Argument

In 'ᶜAbbasids, Fatimids and Seljuqs', Chapter 22 of *The New Cambridge Medieval History*, vol. IV, part 2, together with the relevant chapters in *The New Cambridge History of Islam*, I have made the case for such a role.[17] It is

16 S. Lane-Poole, *A History of Egypt in the Middle Ages* (London, 1901), 2nd edn 1913, pp. 94–5.

17 M. Brett, 'ᶜAbbasids, Fatimids and Seljuqs', in D. Luscombe and J. Riley-Smith (eds), *The New Cambridge Medieval History*, vol. 4, part 2 (Cambridge, 2004), pp. 675–720; 'Egypt', *The New Cambridge History of Islam*, vol. 1, pp. 541–80; and 'The Central Lands of North Africa and Sicily', ibid., vol. 2, pp. 48–65.

a thesis developed in the following narrative, which takes up the theme of empire in the way that the Fatimids themselves conceived it, as the dynasty pursued its claim to govern the empire of Islam in succession to the Prophet in his dual capacity, on the one hand as leader of the community and on the other as source of revelation. That is to subordinate their Dawla, the state that they actually created in the three centuries of their career, to their Daᶜwa, or Calling, an English translation of their Arabic whose ambiguity nicely conveys the double sense of their summons to the faithful to believe in their divine mission, and their own summons by God to their divinely appointed task. It will do so on the basis of four closely related premises. The first is that the formation of Islam over the first centuries of its existence was a matter of convergence as well as divergence, as elements of Christianity and Judaism, rabbinical and Roman law, and Greek philosophy were all adduced to explicate the meaning of the revelation to Muḥammad and give a doctrinal character to the disputes within the community that broke out within thirty years of his death. The second is the argument advanced in *The Rise of the Fatimids*, my account of the dynasty in the first century of its existence, that in the case of the Fatimids such a convergence served to unite a disparate collection of believers and beliefs in a doctrine that now passes under the name of Ismāᶜīlism. The third is that the controversy which that doctrine engendered at the hands of an aggressive monarchy was instrumental in completing the present broad division of Islam between Sunnism and Shīᶜism, as its opponents were obliged to take up their theological positions in reply to the challenge. The fourth is that the theocratic principle of government by a ruler possessed of religious as well as political authority was not unique either to the Fatimids or to Islam, but was common to the Byzantine empire and to Christian Europe in various ways of which the Fatimid doctrine of the Imām-Caliph was an extreme example. How that principle worked itself out in practice is the story of their empire.

The Sources

It is a story obviously dependent upon the available sources, to which the most comprehensive introduction is provided by Paul Walker's *Exploring an Islamic Empire.*[18] The threefold division of the Fatimid enterprise between the dynasty's consecutive political careers in North Africa and Egypt, and the evolution of its mission, corresponds to a similar but even more complicated division in the sources. These are not only specifically North African, specifically Egyptian, and specifically doctrinal, but are divided between the

[18] See above, n. 2.

works of the dynasty itself and its adherents; those hostile to the dynasty and its claims; and the broad range of Islamic historiography, the annals and histories of cities, countries and the Islamic world, including the histories of the Christian churches of Egypt. Crucially, moreover, they are divided between the contemporary and the subsequent, all the more important because it is the later compilations from the thirteenth century CE onwards that preserve in various degrees many of the contemporary sources that have not otherwise survived. This is true of the only two such complete histories of the dynasty, those of the fifteenth-century Yemeni Idrīs ᶜImād al-Dīn and the Egyptian al-Maqrīzī, also from the fifteenth century. Idrīs was an Ismāᶜīlī, the head of the community in the Yemen, which had kept the faith of the Fatimids after the demise of the dynasty, to the extent of preserving its literature as a record of the sacred history of the Imāmate, from its inception down to Idrīs's own day. In drawing on that literature for his own history of the Imāmate, in the final three volumes of his seven-volume work, the *ᶜUyūn al-akhbār*, he has preserved a great deal that otherwise would have been lost or remained inaccessible.[19] Al-Maqrīzī, on the other hand, was a historian of Egypt, albeit one so interested in the Fatimids that in his *Ittiᶜāẓ al-ḥunafāʾ* he compiled an annalistic chronicle of the dynasty from its beginnings in North Africa.[20] As an Egyptian, he was unfamiliar with the North African period, but as an Egyptian, he drew on an Egyptian tradition beginning with al-Kindī's *Wulāt waʾl-quḍāt* or *Governors and Judges*,[21] which was continued by Ibn Zūlāq into the Fatimid period, and thereafter by a succession of Fatimid and post-Fatimid authors. These begin with al-Musabbiḥī in the early eleventh century,[22] and continue to al-Muḥannak in the mid-twelfth, when they are followed by Ibn al-Maʾmūn and Ibn al-Ṭuwayr in the second half of the century, and by Ibn Muyassar 100 years later. The works of al-Musabbiḥī and his successors are largely lost, but supply al-Maqrīzī with the bulk of

[19] Idrīs ᶜImād al-Dīn, *ᶜUyūn al-akhbār wa funūn al-āthār*, vols 1–7, ed. Maḥmūd Fakhūrī et al. (Damascus, 2007–12); vol. 5 and part of vol. 6, dealing with the North African period, ed. M. al-Yaᶜlāwī) as *Taʾrīkh al-khulafāʾ al-fāṭimiyyūn biʾl-Maghrib* (Beirut, 1985); vol. 7, ed. A. F. Sayyid with P. E. Walker and M. Pomerantz as *The Fatimids and their Successors in the Yemen* (London, 2003). The section covering the life of al-Muᶜizz has been translated by S. Jiwa, *The Founder of Cairo* (London, 2013).

[20] Al-Maqrīzī, *Ittiᶜāẓ al-ḥunafāʾ bi akhbār al-aʾimma al-fāṭimiyyīn*, 3 vols, ed. J.-D. al-Shayyāl and M. H. M. Aḥmad (Cairo, 1967–73); 4 vols, ed. A. F. Sayyid (London, 2010). The section dealing with the conquest of Egypt down to the death of al-Muᶜizz has been translated by S. Jiwa, *Towards a Shiᶜi Mediterranean Empire* (London, 2009).

[21] Al-Kindī, *Governors and Judges of Egypt*, ed. R. Guest (Leiden and London, 1912).

[22] Al-Musabbiḥī, *Tome quarantième de la Chronique d'Égypte de Musabbiḥī*, 2 vols, ed. A. F. Sayyid and Th. Bianquis (Cairo, 1978).

his information. For the twelfth century, this information is supplemented by the surviving portions of the history compiled by his fourteenth-century predecessor Ibn al-Furāt.[23] These Egyptian authors are complemented by the fourteenth-century Moroccan historian Ibn ᶜIdhārī al-Marrākushī, whose *Kitāb al-bayān al-mughrib* is a history of North Africa and Spain, the first volume of which covers the history of North Africa down to the end of the eleventh century.[24] Thus it includes the Fatimid period and that of their Zirid successors, in other words the history of their empire in the Maghrib. The section on the Fatimids is drawn from the Andalusian historian ᶜArīb ibn Saᶜd, writing from the hostile viewpoint of the rival Umayyad Caliphate at Cordoba. It is nevertheless the principal source for their North African career. The Zirids, on the other hand, had their own chroniclers in their secretary al-Raqīq and his successors Ibn Sharaf and Abūᵓl-Ṣalt, who between them provide the substance of the narrative in the *Bayān*, and thus the backbone of the history of the dynasty in H. R. Idris's *La Berbérie orientale sous les Zīrīdes*.[25]

The corpus of literature produced by the Fatimids themselves is centred on a cluster of works produced in the mid-tenth century, after they had secured their hold on the Maghrib and before their conquest of Egypt. At their heart is the *Daᶜāᵓ im al-Islam*, or *Pillars of Islam*, the doctrine of the Imāmate and its definition of the Sharīᶜa, the divine law, produced by the Qāḍī al-Nuᶜmān on the authority of the Imām-Caliph al-Muᶜizz.[26] The accompanying works are similarly doctrinal in character, but as contributions to a body of such literature they are of wider historical value, whether like al-Nuᶜmān's *Kitāb al-majālis waᵓl-musāyarāt* they recount the sayings and doings of the Imām-Caliph,[27] or like the *Sīrat al-Ustādh Jawdhar* they detail the workings of government,[28] or like al-Nuᶜmān's *Iftitāḥ al-daᶜwa wa ibtidāᵓ al-dawla* they narrate the previous history of the foundation of the dynasty from the standpoint of the mid-tenth

[23] Ibn al-Furāt, *Taᵓrīkh al-duwal waᵓl-mulūk*; the passages of information not found elsewhere have been edited and translated by Fozia Bora, 'The Mamluk historiography of the Fatimids reconsidered: Ibn al-Furāt's *Taᵓrīkh al-duwal waᵓl-mulūk*, DPhil thesis, University of Oxford, 2010.

[24] Ibn ᶜIdhārī al-Marrākushī, *Kitāb al-bayān al-mughrib*, vol. 1, ed. G. S. Colin and É. Lévi-Provençal, *Histoire de l'Afrique du Nord de la conquête au XIe siècle* (Leiden, 1948).

[25] H. R. Idris, *La Berbérie orientale sous Zīrīdes* (Paris, 1962).

[26] Al-Qāḍī al-Nuᶜmān, *Daᶜāᵓim al-Islām*, ed. A. A. A. Fyzee (Cairo, 1951–61).

[27] Al-Qāḍī al-Nuᶜmān, *Kitāb al-majālis waᵓl-musāyarāt*, ed. Ḥ. al-Faqī, I. Shabbūḥ and M. al-Yaᶜlāwī (Tunis, 1978).

[28] Al-Jawdhārī, *Sīrat al-Ustādh Jawdhar*, ed. M. K. Ḥusayn and M. A.-H. Shaᵓīra (Cairo, 1954); ed. and trans. H. Haji as *Inside the Immaculate Portal* (London, 2012).

century.[29] After the move of the dynasty to Egypt, this immediacy is largely lost to the Iranian authors who take over from the Imām-Caliphs and their entourage. Thus al-Naysābūrī early in the eleventh century writes of the necessity of the Imāmate for the faith; of the duties of the *dāʿī*, or caller, the missionary who takes the place of the Imām at the head of some distant community; and problematically of the Imāmate in *satr*, or concealment, before the appearance of the Mahdī.[30] His contemporary al-Kirmānī continued in the same Iranian tradition of philosophical theology,[31] which was carried further by his successor al-Shīrāzī in the middle of the century. Al-Shīrāzī was nevertheless exceptional as a narrator of the part he played in the politics of the period;[32] but with him and his fellow Iranian Nāṣir-i Khusraw the line of these authors comes to an end as the Iranians branched away from the Fatimids under a breakaway Imāmate. The Yemenis eventually followed suit, but meanwhile the Fatimid connection generated the last surviving work of Fatimid literature, the *Sijillāt al-mustanṣiriyya* or letters of the Imām-Caliph al-Mustanṣir to the Yemen in the second half of the eleventh century.[33]

The *sijillāt* or sijills, from the Latin *sigillum*, or seal, were documents of the Fatimid chancery, and are of major importance from both the religious and the political point of view. With the disappearance of the Fatimid archives, however, they have survived for the most part only as copies of the originals, either, in this case, for their religious character as utterances of the Imām, or in the case of the fifteenth-century *Ṣubḥ al aʿshā* of al-Qalqashandī, for their merit as examples of chancery practice in a work that also includes material on the Fatimid hierarchy.[34] The principal exception is the group of ten privileges mostly granted to the monks of St Catherine's monastery in Sinai, and published by Stern under the title *Fāṭimid Decrees*.[35] These are supplemented

[29] Al-Qāḍī al-Nuʿmān, *Iftitāḥ al-daʿwa wa ibtidāʾ al-dawla*, ed. F. Dachraoui (Tunis, 1975); trans. H. Haji as *Founding the Fatimid State. The Rise of an Early Islamic Empire* (London, 2006).

[30] Al-Naysābūrī, *Ithbāt al-imāma*, ed. and trans. A. Lalani as *Degrees of Excellence. A Fatimid Treatise on Leadership in Islam* (London, 2009); *Risāla al-mujāza al-kāfiya fī ādāb al-du ʿāt*, ed. and trans. V. Klemm and P. E. Walker as *A Code of Conduct. A Treatise on the Etiquette of the Fatimid Ismaili Mission* (London, 2011); *Istitār al-imām*, ed. W. Ivanow in *Bulletin of the Faculty of Arts, University of Egypt*, vol. 4, part 2 (1936), pp. 93–107, trans. W. Ivanow in *Ismaili Tradition Concerning the Rise of the Fatimids* (London, 1942), pp. 157–83.

[31] Cf. P. E. Walker, *Ḥamīd al-Dīn al-Kirmānī: Ismaili Thought in the Age of al-Ḥākim* (London, 1999).

[32] *Sīrat al-Muʾayyad fīʾl-Dīn dāʿī al-duʿāt*, ed. M. K. Ḥusayn (Cairo, 1949, repr. Beirut, 1996).

[33] *Al-Sijillāt al-mustanṣiriyya*, ed. A.-M. Mājid (Cairo, 1954).

[34] Al-Qalqashandī, *Ṣubḥ al aʿshā fī ṣināʿat al-inshāʾ* (Cairo, 1912–38).

[35] S. M. Stern, *Fāṭimid Decrees* (London, 1964).

by an assorted group of documents from the Genizah collection, published by Khan under the title of *Arabic Legal and Administrative Documents in the Cambridge Genizah Collections*.[36] They come from the Cairo Genizah, a vast assortment of manuscripts of the North African Jewish community in the Egyptian capital. Deposited in their synagogue, these have enabled the reconstruction of everyday life in Fatimid Egypt, most notably by Goitein in *A Mediterranean Society*.[37] Documentation of a different kind is provided by the dynasty's coinage, catalogued by Nicol in *A Corpus of Fāṭimid Coins*.[38] The style and legends of the gold coins, the dīnārs, are statements of the dynasty's claims to the Imāmate and Caliphate, which are matched by the numerous inscriptions on buildings, woodwork and so on recorded by Wiet in 'Matériaux pour un Corpus inscriptionum arabicarum'[39] and by Sayyid in *La Capitale d'Égypte jusqu'à l'époque fatimide*.[40] These are the subject of an informative study by Bierman in *Writing Signs; the Fatimid Public Text*.[41] The relevant buildings themselves are described by Sayyid in *La Capitale*, and those in North Africa by Lézine in *Mahdiya: recherches d'archéologie islamique*.[42] Sayyid's work is an essay in reconstruction going back to that other indispensable work of al-Maqrīzī, his voluminous *Khiṭaṭ*, or 'Places', which besides its topography contains a large quantity of other historical information.[43] Meanwhile, the impressive art and architecture of Fatimid Egypt is comprehensively illustrated by Bloom in *Arts of the City Victorious*,[44] and in *L'Égypte Fatimide: son art et son histoire*, edited by Marianne Barrucand,[45] and is put in its wider context in *Egypt: Faith after the Pharaohs*, ed. C. Fluck et al. (2015), the catalogue of the exhibition under that name at the British Museum.[46] The life that animated the city thus created by the dynasty is described by

36 G. Khan, *Arabic Legal and Administrative Documents in the Cambridge Genizah Collections* (Cambridge, 1993).

37 S. D. F. Goitein, *A Mediterranean Society*, 6 vols (Berkeley, CA, 1967–93).

38 N. D. Nicol, *A Corpus of Fāṭimid Coins* (Trieste, 2006).

39 G. Wiet, 'Matériaux pour un Corpus inscriptionum arabicarum, part 1, Égypte, vol. 2', *Mémoires de l'Institut français d'archéologie du Caire*, 52 (1929–30).

40 A. F. Sayyid, *La Capitale d'Égypte jusqu'à l'époque fatimide (al-Qāhira et al-Fustāt): essai de reconstitution topographique* (Beirut and Stuttgart, 1998).

41 I. A. Bierman, *Writing Signs; the Fatimid Public Text* (Berkeley and Los Angeles, CA, 1998).

42 A. Lézine, *Mahdiya: recherches d'archéologie islamique* (Paris, 1965).

43 Al-Maqrīzī, *Al-Khiṭaṭ* (Būlāq, 1853).

44 J. M. Bloom, *Arts of the City Victorious. Islamic Art and Architecture in Fatimid North Africa and Egypt* (New Haven, CT and London, 2007).

45 M. Barrucand (ed.), *L'Égypte Fatimide: son art et son histoire* (Paris, 1999).

46 C. Fluck et al. (eds), *Egypt: Faith after the Pharaohs* (London, 2015).

Sanders in *Ritual, Politics and the City in Fatimid Cairo*,[47] and by Cortese and Calderini in *Women and the Fatimids in the World of Islam*.[48]

The size and importance of the Christian communities of Egypt make their own literature a necessary supplement to the Muslim sources, beginning with *History of the Coptic Patriarchs of Alexandria*[49] and including the *Taʾrīkh* of al-Anṭākī[50] and *History of Churches and Monasteries* by Abūʾl-Makārim Jirjis, formerly attributed to Abū Ṣāliḥ the Armenian.[51] Yaḥyā was an Orthodox, Melkite Christian from Antioch rather than an Egyptian Copt, who moved in court circles at al-Qāhira before returning to his home town in 1014. Antioch at the time was ruled from Constantinople, but Yaḥyā's career illustrates the Syrian dimension of the Fatimid empire and the importance of Syrian sources, among them the *Dhayl taʾrīkh Dimashq* of the twelfth-century Damascan chronicler Ibn al-Qalānisī.[52] Such works feed into the universal histories of the following centuries, beginning with the thirteenth-century *Kāmil fīʾl-taʾrīkh* of Ibn al-Athīr. In this the history of the Fatimids is itemised year by year in the midst of events from across the Muslim world, losing its identity in the process. With its religious and political claims to the Imāmate and Caliphate generally dismissed by the prevalent Sunnī historiography of this later period, it was left to the thoughtful Ibn Khaldūn in the *Muqaddimah* or preface to his own universal history to comment that the Fatimids must have been the descendants of the Prophet that they claimed to be, since otherwise the success of their appeal would be inexplicable.[53] However justified, it is a remark that places the dynasty firmly at the heart of the struggle for power and authority in Islam that came to a head in the 300 years of its career.

47 P. Sanders, *Ritual, Politics and the City in Fatimid Cairo* (Albany, NY, 1994).

48 D. Cortese and S. Calderini, *Women and the Fatimids in the World of Islam* (Edinburgh, 2006).

49 *History of the Coptic Patriarchs of Alexandria*, ed. and trans. B. T. A. Evetts et al., 3 vols (Paris, 1901; Cairo, 1943–59, 1968–70).

50 Yahyā ibn Saʿīd al-Antākī, *Taʾrīkh*, parts 1 and 2, ed. and trans. I. Kratchkovsky and A. Vasiliev, *Patrologia Orientalia*, 18 (1924), pp. 690–833, and 23 (1932), pp. 347–520; part 3, ed. and trans. I. Kratchkovsky, F. Micheau and G. Troupeau, *Patrologia Orientalia*, 47 (1997), pp. 373–559. See also J. H. Forsyth, 'The Byzantine-Arab Chronicle (938–1034) of Yaḥyā ibn Saʿīd al-Antākī', PhD dissertation, University of Michigan (Ann Arbor, MI, repr., 1977).

51 Abūʾl-Makārim Saʿdallah Jirjis, *Taʾrīkh al-kanāʾis waʾl-adyira*, ed. and trans. B. T. A. Evetts (Oxford, 1895), under the title *Churches and Monasteries of Egypt*, attributed to Abū Ṣāliḥ the Armenian.

52 Ibn al-Qalānisī, *Dhayl taʾrīkh Dimashq*, ed. H. F. Amedroz (Leiden and London, 1908).

53 Ibn Khaldūn, *The Muqaddimah*, trans. F. Rosenthal, 3 vols (London and Henley, 1986), vol. 1, pp. 41–6.

1

The Coming of the Mahdī

Revolt in the East

The First Centuries of Islam

The Fatimids came to power in 910 on the crest of a wave of expectation of the coming of the Mahdī, the Rightly Guided One, a second Muḥammad of the line of ᶜAlī who would restore the true faith and bring in the reign of justice before the end of the world. They did so at the outset of what Adam Mez described in cultural terms as the Renaissance of Islam, what Maurice Lombard called the Golden Age of its economy and what Hugh Kennedy has characterised politically as the Muslim Commonwealth, the collection of states into which the old Arab empire disintegrated.[1] All three are aspects of the growth of society in the lands conquered by the Arabs in the seventh and early eighth centuries, on the basis of the common market economy that had developed in this intercontinental realm from the Atlantic to Central Asia and India, and reached out beyond its borders to the Far East and sub-Saharan Africa. New crops diffused across the region and cultivated with the aid of irrigation had added a summer season to the agricultural year;[2] new as well as old cities had become major centres of industry and long-distance trade. Their growth had seen the development of the Muslim community from a conquering army into a civilian population which by the tenth century was well under way to becoming a majority of the population as a whole. In the process the Arabs of that army had, as Ibn Khaldūn put it in his *Kitāb al-ᶜIbar*, melted away into the peoples they had conquered, to be replaced by a further generation of tribesmen on the desert fringes of

[1] A. Mez, *The Renaissance of Islam*, trans. S. Kh. Baksh and D. S. Margoliouth (Patna, 1937); M. Lombard, *The Golden Age of Islam* (Amsterdam, Oxford and New York, 1975); H. Kennedy, *The Prophet and the Age of the Caliphates* (London and New York, 1986), ch. 7.

[2] Cf. A. M. Watson, *Agricultural Innovation in the Early Islamic World* (Cambridge, 1983).

this new world.[3] Their language, by contrast, had established itself as the universal language of literacy and learning, government and commerce, not only as the language of the Sharīᶜa, the divine law, with its multiple applications to daily life. In the cities, centred around the mosque which had taken the place of the old Roman forum, the scholars of the divine law spoke for a population conscious of its Islamic identity; meanwhile, they belonged to an intelligentsia that cultivated the arts and the sciences, from literature and philosophy to medicine and horticulture. That intelligentsia staffed the offices of government, an institution whose political and administrative development out of the original leadership had already generated the large and growing literature surveyed by Ann Lambton under the heading of state and government.[4]

The contrast in that literature between the ideal and the reality was a further reflection of the way in which the Muslim community within the Arab empire had evolved into a civilian population alongside the dwindling number of its non-Muslim subjects. In principle, the Caliph, the Amīr al-Muᶜminīn, or Commander of the Faithful, and by extension his provincial deputies, whether or not they had made themselves effectively independent, was just that – the military leader of the community and the defender of its faith, who ruled the empire on its behalf. However, as the community was transformed from an army into a populace, and the faith was formulated as the law of God for the regulation of its way of life, his role as a ruler as well as a commander was more clearly defined as the duty to live by that law and to enforce it through the appointment of a *qāḍī*, or judge, with himself as the judge on appeal. But since the authority for this law had passed into the hands of the scholars who had elaborated its precepts, there had appeared within this apparently seamless fabric of jurisdiction a distinction in government between the religious and the political that corresponded to the more formal distinction in contemporary Christendom between church and state. It was formulated, if at all, in the scholarly doctrine of *siyāsa sharᶜīya*, or lawful policy-making, whereby the monarch was entitled to act outside the law in the practical affairs of government, if only to preserve the state and therefore the community from dissolution. But it took physical shape in the separation of the mosque from the palace, which in the manner of the Round City built in the middle of the eighth century by the first ᶜAbbasid Caliphs at Baghdad,

3 Ibn Khaldūn, *Kitāb al-ᶜIbar*, ed. Hūrīnī, 7 vols (Būlāq, 1284H/1867), vol. 6, pp. 2–6; passage translated in A. Cheddadi, *Ibn Khaldūn. Peuples et nations du monde*, 2 vols (Paris, 1986), vol. 2, pp. 419–27, and in W. M. De Slane, *Histoire des Berbères*, 2nd edn, ed. P. Casanova, 4 vols (Paris, 1925), vol. 1, pp. 1–5.

4 A. K. S. Lambton, *State and Government in Medieval Islam* (Oxford, 1981).

came to be located in new royal residences outside the *amṣār*, the so-called garrison cities that had been the original capitals of the empire. In their separation of the prince from the people, these residences went back to the palace of the Roman Emperor Diocletian at Split; in contrast to the civilian and mainly Muslim populations grouped around the mosque at the centre of the original cities, their inhabitants belonged to a household army of servants, soldiers and secretaries, not all of whom were necessarily Muslim, and in the case of both servants and soldiers, had come to be recruited in large measure from outside the empire – Turks, Greeks, Slavs, sc. Europeans and Sudanese, all foreign to the people they ruled.

In his conduct of government, the prince at the head of this personal and professional army then acted in two capacities. On the one hand, as leader of the community he attended its weekly celebration in the mosque, where the Friday prayer was offered in the name of the Caliph, and as defender of the faith ensured its keeping of the divine law through the appointment of the *qāḍī*, while standing ready to rouse it and lead it in war upon the infidel enemy. On the other, as heir to the previous empires of the Romans and Persians, he headed a tax-collecting regime that had initially been devised for the great non-Muslim majority of the conquered, for the benefit of the conquerors. By the eighth century, however, it had come to embrace the growing Muslim population, with only partial regard for its taxation according to the law. His government, in fact, was of the late Roman and Byzantine type described by Hartmann in *The Early Mediaeval State* as Oriental as distinct from Occidental, one in which the state enjoyed the paramount and inalienable right to tax the land in cash and kind, irrespective of its occupants.[5] To some extent this right was accommodated by the law, and from the tenth century onwards it achieved a measure of philosophical respectability with the appearance in the literature of the pseudo-Aristotelian *Secretum Secretorum*, or *Sirr al-asrār*, in which the responsibility of the prince for justice generated a circular proposition roughly rendered as 'no justice without the army; no army without taxes; no taxes without wealth; no wealth without justice'.[6] Even given the licence of *siyāsa sharᶜīya*, there was nevertheless wide scope in such a regime for fiscal oppression, social inequality and opposition on religious grounds from a Muslim population torn between the ideal and the reality.

[5] I. M. Hartmann, *The Early Mediaeval State. Byzantium, Italy and the West* (London, 1949); cf. Brett, *Rise of the Fatimids*, pp. 423–4.

[6] Cf. Ibn Khaldūn, *The Muqaddimah*, trans. F. Rosenthal, 2nd edn, 3 vols (New York, 1967; repr. London and Henley, 1986), vol. 1, pp. 81–2, and vol. 2, frontispiece; also Lambton, *State and Government*, pp. 136–7.

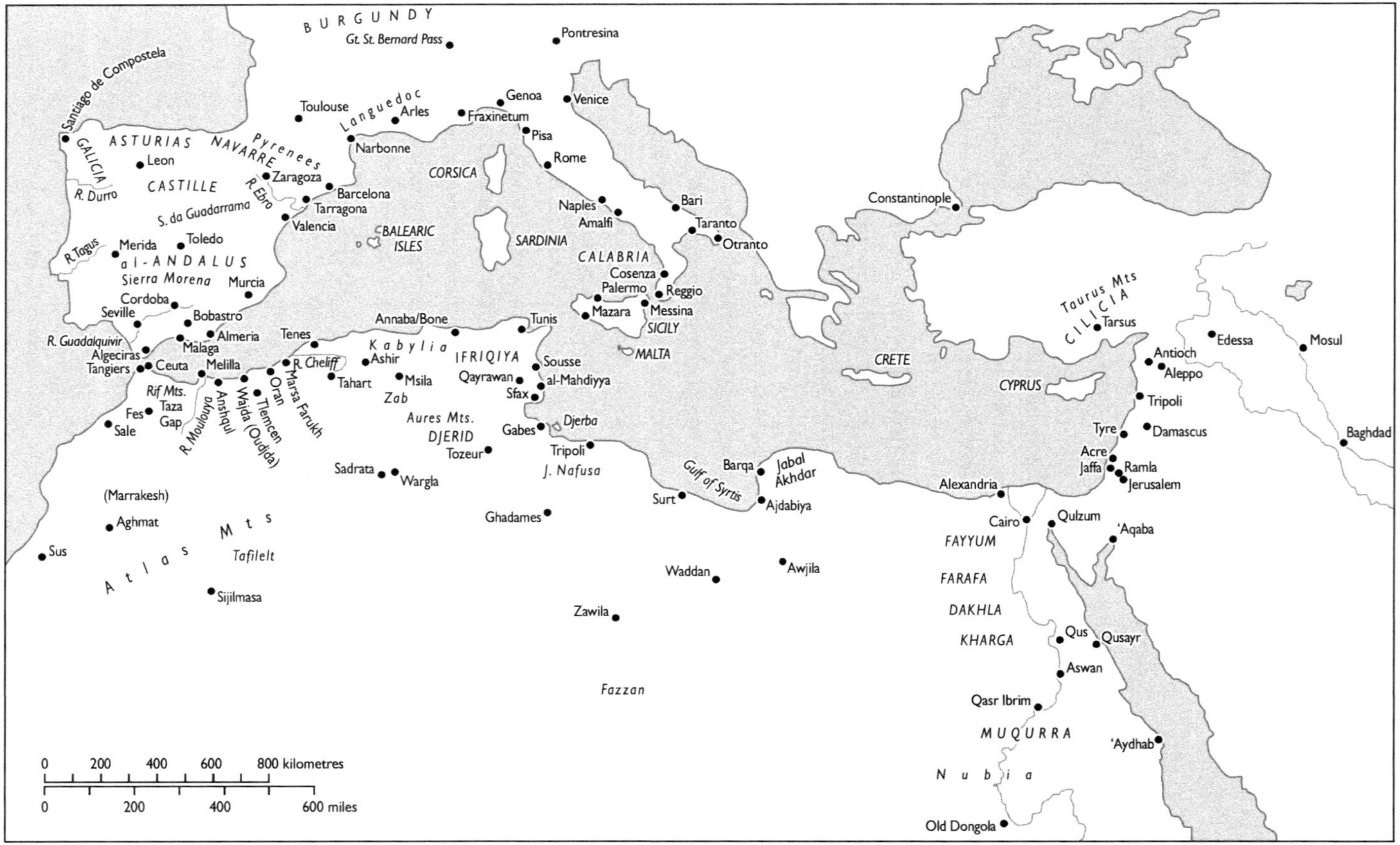

Map 1.1 The Mediterranean World

The Crisis of Shī^c^ism

By the end of the ninth century, long before Ibn Khaldūn in the fourteenth century denounced the evils of excessive taxation, such oppression had combined with religious discontent to reveal the dark side of the expansion of Islamic civilisation in 'the revolt of Islam', the name given by Bernard Lewis in *The Arabs in History* to the messianic unrest that culminated in the appearance of the Fatimids.[7] They did so in the political context of an empire that was finally losing the battle to retain control of its provinces, one that had begun in the middle of the eighth century with the overthrow of the Umayyads by the ᶜAbbasids. That overthrow had been a spectacular success for the opposition on religious grounds to a regime whose unpopularity had illustrated only too well the difficulty of both leading and taxing a growing community resentful of its exclusion from power. But it had entailed the loss of the western outliers of the empire in Spain and North Africa, while the transfer of the capital from Damascus to Baghdad, from Syria to Iraq, had been followed by successive experiments in provincial devolution. While the Muslim population had continued to grow and to take on separate provincial identities, those experiments had been crippled in the course of the ninth century by crises at the centre. The unity that was with difficulty restored in the first half of the century after the long civil war over the succession to the Caliph Hārūn al-Rashīd in 809 was never to be recovered in the second half, after the decade of anarchy that followed the murder of al-Mutawakkil in 861. The Iranian east and north was then largely lost to the Ṣaffārids of Sistan, the Sāmānids of Transoxania and the local dynasties of the Caucasus and Elburz which are listed by Bosworth in *The New Islamic Dynasties*,[8] while Egypt and Syria fell to the Ṭūlūnids, a dynasty founded by a Turkish governor who seized control of their revenues from the *ᶜāmil*, or tax collector. In the 870s and 80s Aḥmad ibn Ṭūlūn made himself effectively independent at a time when the ᶜAbbasids were not only menaced with invasion by the Ṣaffārids, but threatened with extinction by the rebellion of the Zanj in southern Iraq. In that rebellion, 'the revolt of Islam' came to the surface with the claim of its leader, ᶜAlī ibn Muḥammad, to descent from the Prophet's son-in-law and fourth Caliph ᶜAlī, and his proclamation as the Mahdī at his headquarters, al-Mukhtāra, the Chosen City.

The Zanj rebellion took its name from the black slaves of East African origin employed on the salt flats around Basra, but it attracted other malcontents, including Arab Bedouin, with its promise to turn slaves into slave-owners,

[7] B. Lewis, *The Arabs in History* (London, 1950), ch. VI.
[8] C. E. Bosworth, *The New Islamic Dynasties* (Edinburgh, 1996).

poor into rich. It was a sign of the times that, given the progressive disintegration of the original empire, it remained local, without the wide appeal that had brought the ᶜAbbasids to power. But it belonged with the ᶜAbbasids to the same revolutionary strand that ever since the murder of ᶜAlī in 661 and the fall of the Caliphate into the hands of the Umayyads, had looked for a Caliph from the house of the Prophet. The ᶜAbbasids, who reckoned their descent from the Prophet's uncle, claimed to have met that demand; but their claim had been consistently rejected by the Shīᶜa, the Party of ᶜAlī, whose adherents continued to maintain the claim of his descendants to the leadership of the community against both the Umayyads and the ᶜAbbasids. Those descendants were in turn divided between the progeny of his two sons by the Prophet's daughter Fāṭima, Ḥasan and Ḥusayn. The offspring of Ḥasan had indulged in sporadic rebellions down to the end of the eighth century; since the death in battle of Ḥusayn in 681, however, his line had developed into a dynasty of its own, one that remained politically quiescent as far as its claim to the Caliphate was concerned, but which came to be considered by its followers as a line of hereditary Imāms in succession to the Prophet as the representative of God on earth. The line lasted down to the death of the eleventh, Ḥasan al-ᶜAskarī, in 874, but the problem posed by his death had meanwhile been anticipated in controversy over the succession to the sixth of these Imāms, Jaᶜfar al-Ṣādiq, who died in Iraq in 760. For whatever reason, there were those who considered that the line had then ended with a seventh Imām who had gone into hiding, either to return one day to claim his inheritance, or against the time when one of his descendants would 'arise with the sword' to vindicate the right of ᶜAlī to the succession to the Prophet. Among these so-called Seveners, the identity of this Seventh Imām was disputed, but by the end of the ninth century was widely held to be Jaᶜfar's grandson, Muḥammad ibn Ismāᶜīl. By then, however, this Muḥammad had been joined after the death of Ḥasan al-ᶜAskarī by a second, an infant son who had likewise vanished into obscurity as the Twelfth Imām whose return was expected by his followers, the Twelvers, at some point in the future. His disappearance in 874 was a major event, one that helped bring to a head the millenarian expectation of the coming of a second Muḥammad as the Qāʾim or Mahdī, He Who Arises as the Rightly Guided One, sent by God to bring in the final age of the world. In that expectation, the legitimist and revanchist claims of the house of ᶜAlī, what might be called an ᶜAlid Jacobitism, flowed together with this Muḥammadan messianism to provide a historical identity for this apocalyptic figure at his second coming.[9]

[9] Cf. M. Brett, 'The Mīm, the ᶜAyn, and the making of Ismāᶜīlism', *Bulletin of the School of Oriental and African Studies* 57 (1994), 25–39, and Brett, M., *Ibn Khaldūn and the Medieval Maghrib*, Variorum Series (Aldershot, 1999), no. III.

The revolt of the Zanj was finally crushed in 883 by the forces of the Caliphate as the first step towards the reconstitution of its empire, only to be succeeded by the appearance of the Qarāmiṭa or Carmathians, a name of unknown origin applied to a number of revolutionary communities and movements known mainly from external sources that are both hostile and dubious. Two contemporaries, al-Nawbakhtī[10] and al-Ṭabarī,[11] the one a Twelver Shīʿite who anticipated the return of his own Muḥammad, the son of Ḥasan al-ʿAskarī, the other great historian of Islam at Baghdad, together with the anti-Fatimid Akhū Muḥsin writing 100 years later in Syria, tell of one or possibly two communities or movements located once again in southern Iraq. On the one hand these believed in the return of Muḥammad ibn Ismāʿīl to reveal a new law known only to his representatives in the twelve 'islands' of the world; on the other they followed a messianic prophet who preached as John the Baptist in the name of Christ, with twelve agents like the twelve apostles, and generally believed in free love, licentiousness, the killing of infidels and the capture of their women. But whoever these Carmathians were, and whatever they believed, no Mahdī arose in the region after the suppression of the Zanj, where the peasantry revolted around the year 900 only in response to official persecution. The preaching ascribed to them by al-Ṭabarī in the name of Christ is nevertheless echoed in the name of John the Baptist, Yaḥyā ibn Zakariyyā/Zakrūyā/Zikrawayh, which is attributed to the Lord of the She-Camel, the leader of a Bedouin invasion of Syria in 902 who took the messianic name of Muḥammad ibn ʿAbd Allāh. After his death in battle in 903, his place as the Mahdī was taken by his brother, the Lord of the Mole or Birthmark, who was captured and horrendously executed at Baghdad by an ʿAbbasid regime that was, with reason, thoroughly alarmed by the rising, all the more since the Bedouin invaded Syria and Iraq once again in 906 under the Mahdist leadership of Zikrawayh, the putative father of the two Lords. Meanwhile, the name Carmathian came to be attached to the successful rising of one Abū Saʿīd al-Jannābī in Bahrayn, the Gulf region of Arabia on the fringe of the ʿAbbasid empire. Following his victory over the ʿAbbasids in 900, Abū Saʿīd ruled over his own utopian state at al-Ḥasāʾ/al-Aḥsāʾ near Hofuf in Saudi Arabia until his murder in 913, after which his return was awaited by his followers. As the Messiah or Mahdī in person, however, he may have executed a missionary from the Yemen, a country far beyond the reach of the ʿAbbasids, where in 906 two preachers

[10] Al-Nawbakhtī, *Firaq al-Shīʿa*, ed. H. Ritter, *Die Sekten de Schiʾa* (Istanbul, 1931); trans. M. J. Mashkour, *Les sectes Shiites*, 2nd edn (Tehran, 1980).

[11] Al-Ṭabarī, *Kitāb al-rusul waʾl-mulūk*, ed. M. J. de Goeje, *Annales*, 16 vols (Leiden, 1879–1901); trans. *The History of al-Ṭabarī*, ed. E. Yar-Shater, 38 vols (New York, 1985–).

of the coming of the Mahdī, who had raised their own armies from the tribal population, came into conflict. While ᶜAlī ibn al-Faḍl, allegedly the junior, overran most of the country, his senior, Ibn Ḥawshab, was forced back into the mountains, while he himself claimed to be the Mahdī in person. Unlike the Carmathians of Bahrayn, however, their state-building foundered after both of them died around 915, leaving Ibn Ḥawshab's community to survive in isolation. Nevertheless it had lasting consequences, since it was an emissary of Ibn Ḥawshab in the 890s who preached the revolution in North Africa that brought the Fatimid Mahdī to power in 910, at the end of a long journey from Syria.[12]

The Problem of Fatimid Origins

This spectacular achievement is the climax of the story from the point of view of the empire that was born in this way. The Whig interpretation of history that is invited by this Mahdī's success is certainly matched by his dynasty's own view of its rise to power as the predestined triumph of the true representatives of God on earth. The place of the Fatimid Mahdī and his preaching in this range of messianic insurgency, however, is by no means clear, depending upon the position ascribed to his lineage in the spectrum of belief in a Seventh Imām, and the role that is attributed to it in the fomentation of these uprisings. The descent of that lineage from Muḥammad, ᶜAlī and Fāṭima is essential to the beliefs of Ismāᶜīlism today, while its continuity in some shape or form following the death of Muḥammad ibn Ismāᶜīl, the Seventh Imām, is the paradigm for the modern account of the origins of the dynasty set out by Farhad Daftary in *The Ismāᶜīlīs*.[13] This is to the effect that Muḥammad ibn Ismāᶜīl was succeeded by a clandestine line of Ḥujja-s, his 'Proofs', or representatives. Located first at Aḥwaz in Khuzistān to the east of Basra, and then at Salamiyya in Syria, these preached his eventual return. From the 870s onwards, however, significantly after the death of Ḥasan al-ʾAskarī and the occultation of the Twelfth Imām, missionaries functioning as *duᶜāt* (sing. *dāᶜī*), 'callers', were sent out to Iraq, Iran, Arabia, the Yemen, India and North Africa, to preach an imminent return. But in 899 their mission was thrown into disarray at the accession to the leadership of one who declared himself to be the Mahdī, the latest in a line of Imāms in succession to Muḥammad ibn Ismāᶜīl, whose time had now come to claim the Caliphate.

12 Cf. Brett, *Rise of the Fatimids*, pp. 49–72.

13 F. Daftary, *The Ismāᶜīlīs. Their History and Doctrines*, 2nd edn (Cambridge, 2007), pp. 87–136. Cf. also the articles by Wilferd Madelung in *Encyclopaedia of Islam*, 2nd edn, s.v. Ismāᶜīliyya, Ḳarmaṭī, Hamdān Ḳarmaṭ and H. Halm, *The Empire of the Mahdi* (Leiden, 1996), pp. 5–88.

This was ᶜAbd Allāh, the founder of the dynasty-to-be, who was promptly rejected in Iraq and Iran by a major section of the movement led by the Dāᶜī Ḥamdān Qarmaṭ and his brother ᶜAbdān. Although Ḥamdān disappeared and ᶜAbdān was murdered, the mission in the name of Muḥammad ibn Ismāᶜīl survived notably in Iran, while ᶜAbd Allāh was obliged to flee from Salamiyya, first to Egypt and finally to Sijilmāsa in southern Morocco, to await the success of the revolution brought about by the Dāᶜī Abū ᶜAbd Allāh in Ifrīqiya.

This version has been long in the making, ever since Bernard Lewis, in *The Origins of Ismāᶜīlism*, envisaged two parallel lines of Imām in the 100 years or so of clandestinity between the death of Muḥammad ibn Ismāᶜīl and the manifestation of the Mahdī: the one *mustaqarr*, or genuine, the actual descendants of Muḥammad, the other *mustawḍaᵓ* or substitute, acting on behalf of the true line to preserve it in hiding against the day of its revelation. ᶜAbd Allāh, the Mahdī, was the last of this line, preparing the way, in John the Baptist fashion, for his successor Muḥammad, the Qāᵓim, with whom the true line entered into its kingdom.[14] Lewis's hypothesis is the first of successive attempts to make sense of the conflicting reports in the sources surveyed by Daftary,[15] the problem with which is that virtually none are contemporary. In origin, they date from the middle of the tenth century, from a time when the Fatimids in North Africa were relaunching their appeal in readiness for the conquest of Egypt; and they are invariably apologetic and polemical, for and against the dynasty's claims. The actual contemporary sources, al-Nawbakhtī and al-Ṭabarī, make no specific mention of the Mahdī and the revolution in North Africa. One provides a list of those who held a variety of beliefs in a Seventh Imām, the other refers to him only vaguely, as a rebel called Ibn al-Baṣrī who launched the first Fatimid attack upon Egypt in 914. Al-Nawbakhtī does indeed speak of a secession of the Carmathians from a group called the Mubārakites, who believed in the survival of a line of descendants from Muḥammad ibn Ismāᶜīl rather than in his return,[16] but with no further details. Of the Fatimid sources, even the *Sīrat Jaᶜfar*, the reminiscences of the Mahdī's personal servant who accompanied him on his journey from Salamiyya, belongs to the mid-tenth century corpus of dynastic literature, dictated as it was to an amanuensis and written down after the arrival of the dynasty in Egypt.[17] Like the rest of that corpus, it is partial in

[14] B. Lewis, *The Origins of Ismāᶜīlism: a Study of the Historical Background of the Fāṭimid Caliphate* (Cambridge, 1940).

[15] Daftary, *The Ismāᶜīlīs*, pp. 99–107.

[16] Al-Nawbakhtī, *Firaq al-Shīᶜa*, pp. 71–6; *Les sectes Shiites*, pp. 86–91.

[17] *Sīrat Jaᶜfar*: text published by W. Ivanow, in *Bulletin of the Faculty of Arts of the Egyptian*

both senses of the word, giving only a fraction of a story which it fails to clarify. The descent of the Fatimids from Muḥammad ibn Ismāᶜīl, which was spelled out for the first time towards the end of the century in the *Istitār al-Imām*, or Concealment of the Imām, by the Iranian *dāᶜī* al-Naysabūrī, is at variance with the Mahdī's own declaration in letter(s) written to the Yemen shortly after his accession, that he was descended from ᶜAbd Allāh, the eldest son of Jaᶜfar al-Ṣādiq.[18] On the subject of the mission and its history, there is no mention of Ḥamdān Qarmaṭ and ᶜAbdān and their quarrel with him at his accession. It is ironic, therefore, that the story in which they appear should depend upon the black legend of Fatimid origins perpetrated by one Ibn Rizām at Baghdad around the middle of the tenth century, and elaborated by Akhū Muḥsin at Damascus in the 980s.[19]

While denouncing the Carmathians as libertines who preach and practise the reverse of all morality and law, these authors, as quoted in later works, pour scorn on the Fatimids as impostors. This accusation, the source for Lane-Poole's dismissive reference to their origins in his *History of Egypt*,[20] is in fact a parody of the various stories about the Mahdī's ancestry which, as his letter to the Yemen shows, were current among the faithful from the time of his appearance, and continued to recur in the literature of the dynasty and its Ismāᶜīlī successors. While prompting the various modern attempts to establish his identity from Lewis onwards, these make clear that this was as much of a problem for the Fatimids as it is for us.[21] It was important not simply because, in the ᶜAlid tradition of Shīᶜism, his genealogy was required as proof of his claim. In the Muḥammadan tradition of messianism, his fulfilment of the prophecy of an end to history at his coming was conditional upon the validity of his succession to the Imāmate of his predecessors. The question on the one hand masked, but on the other hand brought into focus, a whole set of beliefs that by the end of the ninth century were predicated upon the idea of the Seventh Imām. They are enunciated in three tracts

University, IV (1936), 107–33; trans. Ivanow, *Ismāᶜīlī Tradition Concerning the Rise of the Fatimids* (London, 1942), pp. 184–223, and by M. Canard, 'L'autobiographie d'un chambellan du Mahdi Obeid-Allah le Fatimide', *Hespéris*, XXXIX (1952), 279–329.

18 *Istitār al-Imām*: text published by W. Ivanow, in *Bulletin of the Faculty of Arts of the Egyptian University*, IV (1936), 93–107; trans. Ivanow, *Ismāᶜīlī Tradition*, pp. 157–83; A. Hamdani and F. de Blois, 'A re-examination of al-Mahdī's letter to the Yemenites on the genealogy of the Fatimid Caliphs', *Journal of the Royal Asiatic Society* (1983), 173–207. The text, reconstructed from memory by Jaᶜfar, son of the Dāᶜī Ibn Ḥawshab in the Yemen, may summarise two or more originals.

19 For these authors and their writings, see Daftary, *The Ismāᶜīlīs*, pp. 8–9.

20 See Introduction, n. 16.

21 Cf. Brett, *Rise of the Fatimids*, pp. 34–6.

attributed to the Fatimid missionaries in the Yemen, Ibn Ḥawshab and his son Jaᶜfar, all of which anticipate the coming of the Mahdī and thus predate his appearance: the *Kitāb al-rushd waʾl-hidāya*, or Book of Righteousness and True Guidance; the *Kitāb al-ᶜālim waʾl-ghulām*, or Book of the Teacher and the Pupil; and the *Kitāb al-kashf*, or Book of Revelation.[22] Taken out of the Fatimid context in which they have been transmitted, both the Book of Righteousness and the Book of Revelation might be taken to await the appearance of the Mahdī under the name of Muḥammad as some apocalyptic return of a once and future king; the Book of the Teacher, on the other hand, makes clear that he is already biding his time in the world – a man, in other words, the latest of a line. But in either case, they predict an end to the sequence of seven cycles through which the world has passed since its creation, each introduced by a Prophet who has revealed a law presided over by the seven Imāms who have succeeded him. The eighth of these Imāms has become the Prophet of the subsequent cycle who has revealed a new law that had been concealed behind that of his predecessor, until it too was superseded by the manifestation of the next.[23] The time has now come for the final act in a cosmic design embedded in a cosmological myth of creation, in which the universe has emanated from the Deity in a downward progression from the divine word of command running out into the succession of Prophets, which will eventually bring the world to an end.[24]

Sevener Eschatology

At the beginning of the tenth century, the widespread expectation of the coming of a second Muḥammad as the seventh successor to the Prophet in the line of ᶜAlī, who would bring in the final age of the world, was associated with a cosmogony and cosmology at the root of a historical scheme of Seven Ages of the world in Seven Cycles of Seven Prophets each followed by Seven Imāms.

At the head of this cosmic scheme, God, the Creator, has the Will and the Word: Kun, i.e. Be. From Kun come the two primordial principles, Kūnī, the Throne or Essence, and Qadar (Power), the Footstool or Form.

22 *Kitāb al-rushd* and *Kitāb al-ᶜālim*, trans. W. Ivanow, *Studies in Early Persian Ismailism*, 2nd edn (Bombay, 1955), chs 2–4; *Kitāb al-ᶜālim*, ed. and trans. J. W. Morris, *The Master and the Disciple* (London and New York, 2001); *Kitāb al-kashf*, ed. R. Strothmann (London, New York and Bombay, 1952).

23 Cf. Brett, *Rise of the Fatimids*, pp. 120–4.

24 Ibid., pp. 117–20, with reference to H. Halm, *Kosmologie und Heilslehre der frühen Ismāᶜīlīya* (Wiesbaden, 1978).

From Kūnī spring the Seven Heavens, and from Qadar the Twelve Signs of the Zodiac, which together compose the Cosmos.

From Kūnī and Qadar, meanwhile, come Jadd (Fate), Fatḥ (Beginning) and Khayāl (Spirit), corresponding to the three angels, Jibrāʾīl, Mīkāʾīl and Isrāfīl, who mediate between the spiritual and the material world of humanity.

Below them, the seven letters of Kūnī and Qadar, K-Ū-N-Ī-Q-D-R, stand at the head of the sacred history of the world as the Seven Archetypes of the Seven Prophets: Adam, Nūḥ (Noah), Ibrāhīm (Abraham), Mūsā (Moses), ʿĪsā (Jesus), Muḥammad and the Muḥammad who is yet to come.

Each of these Prophets is a Nāṭiq, or Speaker, of a Revelation which is Ẓāhir, or Patent, deriving from Qadar, the ultimate Ẓāhir, or Form, while in receipt of a Bāṭin, a Hidden Doctrine deriving from Kūnī, the Inner Essence. Each Prophet is then followed by Seven Imāms who carry on his Revelation. The first of these is Ṣāmit, or Silent, the Asās, or Foundation, of the line, while the last becomes the next Nāṭiq, with whom the Hidden Doctrine of his predecessor becomes the next Revelation.

In this scheme, Muḥammad is the Sixth Prophet, whose Ẓāhir, or Patent Revelation, is the Qurʾān and the Sharīʿa, or Divine Law, while ʿAlī is the Ṣāmit and Asās the first of the subsequent Imāms. Of these, the Seventh and Last is still to come as the Mahdī/Qāʾim, with whom the Bāṭin, or Hidden Doctrine, of Muḥammad and ʿAlī will become the Seventh and Last of God's revelations to the world.

The expectation that this Messiah would be Muḥammad ibn Ismāʿīl, the grandson of Jaʿfar al-Ṣādiq, the Sixth Imam of the line of ʿAlī, was maintained in Iran down to the middle of the tenth century. The Carmathians at the end of the ninth century were retrospectively accused of abandoning the Sharīʿa for licentiousness as if the Seventh and Last Prophet had arrived. In Ifrīqiya, the Fatimid Mahdī Abd Allāh denounced such *ghuluww*, or excess, on the part of those who hailed him as the bringer of the New Age. Instead, in his letter to the Yemen, he disassociated himself from the Apocalypse of the Last Days, and declared it his mission to restore the rule of Islam to the rightful successors of Muḥammad and ʿAlī in a line of as many Imāms as God intended, irrespective of the actual number Seven. His son nevertheless bore the name Muḥammad and the title of the Qāʾim, the One Who Arises (at God's Command). The apocalyptic victory ascribed to him over the rebel Abū Yazīd, cast in the role of the Dajjāl, or Antichrist, enabled his son and successor Ismāʿīl al-Manṣūr, the Conqueror, confidently to proclaim the triumph of the dynasty, while the claim of al-Manṣūr's son al-Muʿizz to be the Seventh Imām in succession to the previous Seventh,

Muḥammad ibn Ismāᶜīl, enabled him to win over to the Fatimids the Iranians who looked for the return of this Muḥammad, and consolidate the majority of these various Seveners into the community and creed that now passes under the name of Ismāᶜīlism.

Cf. Brett, *The Rise of the Fatimids*, pp. 117–24, 112–14, 203–5.

Such a scheme, in which the Nāṭiq, or Speaker, of the Ẓāhir, or Open Law, was succeeded by the Ṣāmit, the Silent Keeper of the Bāṭin, the Hidden Law, in his capacity as the first of the Imāms of the cycle, ran into disagreement when matched against the names in the Islamic and particularly the Shīᶜite record. Who the Prophets had been; whether Muḥammad had been the Seventh and the Last or only the Sixth; and whether or not the Sharīᶜa was the final Law, were questions further complicated by the role ascribed to ᶜAlī as the Waṣī, or Trustee of the Prophet, and the dispute over the relationship between the Seventh Imām and the coming Mahdī in the obscurity of the ninth century. Illustrated by the Books of Righteousness, Revelation and the Teacher, the various answers combine with the argument over the ancestry of the Fatimid Mahdī to preclude any clear answer to the questions of who he actually was, who or what his predecessors may have been and the extent to which they were responsible for the outbreak of Mahdism following the suppression of the Zanj and their Mahdī with the name of ᶜAlī ibn Muḥammad. The insistence of the Fatimid Mahdī in his letter(s) to the Yemen that all names were in some measure a disguise may well be an admission that we are dealing with personae rather than with the persons themselves, whoever they may have been. The Mahdī himself appears in the account of his servant Jaᶜfar as a wealthy and well-educated gentleman at the head of a genteel household, who may well have belonged to the Shīᶜite elite which throughout the ninth century had been in and out of favour with the ᶜAbbasids. That there was some kind of revolutionary conspiracy associated with the leadership at Salamiyya is evident from the risings in the Yemen and North Africa. Given the range of beliefs in a Seventh Imām and the variety of expectations of the Mahdī, however, it is unlikely that it can account for the whole range of revolt at the time. Those of the Zanj and the Carmathians of Bahrayn seem to have been wholly independent; those that had the name of Zikrawayh in common helped to drive the Fatimid Mahdī from Salamiyya. The task for this Mahdī at his appearance in North Africa in 910 was to win for himself and his dynasty the recognition of this gamut of messianists on the strength, above all, of his evident success.

Revolution in the West

The Maghrib

'The Sun of God shall rise in the West.' This prophecy of the coming of the Mahdī, which was recorded, inevitably after the event, by the Qāḍī al-Nu^{c}mān in the *Iftitāḥ al-da^{c}wa wa ibtidā$^{\circ}$ al-dawla*, the Opening of the Mission and the Beginning of the Dynasty,[25] placed the event in the Maghrib, the Muslim West, as distinct from the Mashriq, the Muslim East. Comprising North Africa, Sicily and Spain, this had largely broken away from the empire of the ^{c}Abbasids in the second half of the eighth century, following the rebellion of the Berbers in 740 and the ^{c}Abbasid revolution in 750. The first had anticipated the second, contributing to the overthrow of the Umayyads in a revolt against Arab dominance that swept away the government of Damascus at Qayrawān (Kairouan) in modern Tunisia. The rebels were the Berbers, the largely tribal inhabitants of the mountains, valleys and deserts from Morocco to Tripolitania and the Fezzan, whom the Arabs had named the Barbar, the barbarians of Classical Antiquity who spoke neither Latin nor Greek. They spoke instead the languages that are now called Berber and classified as a branch of Afro-Semitic. The Arabs classified them rather as a race in line of descent from Noah, one that they considered to have been pagan but which was now considered Muslim on the strength of its submission to the Arabs in the course of conquest from 670 to 710. The conquest had in fact lain largely within the *limes*, the southern frontier of the Roman empire, which excluded a good half of this newly designated nation. But within those limits, the Berbers had been variously subjected to a tribute, most notably in slaves, but at the same time recruited into the Arab armies for the conquest and settlement of Spain that began in 711. The resentment fostered by the contradiction between their incorporation into the ranks of the rulers of the empire and their taxation as its subjects was focused by the demand of the dissident movement known as Khārijism for a Caliph who should be the best Muslim rather than a faithless Arab. Their rebellion threw up a number of pretenders, and failed to match the advance of the ^{c}Abbasids from the east; but it left the Maghrib permanently divided between Ifrīqiya, the old Byzantine province of Africa comprising eastern Algeria, Tunisia and Tripolitania; the old Roman Mauretanias in northern Morocco and western Algeria; and al-Andalus or Muslim Spain. Ifrīqiya became effectively independent of Baghdad in 800, when Ibrāhīm ibn al-Aghlab was admitted as a

[25] Al-Qāḍī al-Nu^{c}mān, *Kitāb iftitāh al-da^{c}wa wa ibtidā$^{\circ}$ al-dawla*, ed. W. el-Qadi (Beirut, 1970); trans. H. Haji, *Founding the Fatimid State: the Rise of an Early Islamic Empire* (London, 2006).

hereditary monarch in return for recognition of the Caliph as his suzerain. But it was surrounded from west to south by a vast Khārijite domain centred on Tāhart in western Algeria and Zawīla in the Fezzan, loosely headed by the Rustamids, a dynasty of Iranian origin under whom the Ibāḍī school of Khārijism developed into a separate branch of Islam. Still further west, northern Morocco was taken over by the Idrisids, descendants of Hasan rather than Ḥusayn ibn ᶜAlī in flight from the ᶜAbbasids, who founded the city of Fes. Meanwhile, in the fall-out from the ᶜAbbasid revolution, al-Andalus had been taken over by a refugee Umayyad prince and his dynasty.

This was the political framework for the growth of an Islamic society with the development of trade and communications from east to west and north to south, from Egypt to al-Andalus and across the Sahara to the central Sudan around Lake Chad and the western Sudan around the Niger bend and the Senegal. It was carried out through the colonisation of the routes by Muslim settlers in Muslim cities, large and small, that proliferated around the nodes of the original conquest: Tripoli, Qayrawān, Tlemcen and Tangier, and the major foundations in the aftermath of the Berber rebellion: the Kharijite cities of Tāhart and Sijilmāsa and the Idrisid city of Fes. Such cities, with their Muslim princes, mosques and markets, acted as magnets for the population of their regions, whether Latin Christian or Berber, and as the agents of its Islamisation, politically, socially and, increasingly, religiously.[26] Under the Aghlabids in the ninth century, Ifrīqiya took the process much further, becoming a major princely state, an equally major centre of Islam in the form of the Mālikite school of law, and an imperial power that undertook the conquest and colonisation of Byzantine Sicily. The conquest of Sicily, which began in 827 and dragged on for the rest of the century, was the culmination of a struggle on the part of the dynasty to defeat a rebellious Arab army and landholding Arab aristocracy, which ended in victory with the prince ensconced with a slave army in a palace city outside Qayrawān. Qayrawān itself developed into a large and prosperous metropolis with a monumental Great Mosque and a reservoir for water from the hills, becoming under the great jurist Saḥnūn the centre of a combative Islam. But it had a rival in Tunis, which had taken the place of the Roman and Byzantine capital of Carthage; a port for the conquest of Sicily in Sousse; an outlier in Tripoli, and in between the important coastal cities of Sfax and Gabes, and the inland city of Gafsa. This urban and agricultural society of the Tunisian coast and hinterland made Ifrīqiya into a hub of Mediterranean as well as

[26] Cf. M. Brett, *Ibn Khaldūn and the Medieval Maghrib*, no. I, 'The Islamisation of Morocco from the Arabs to the Almoravids'; II, 'Ifriqiya as a market for Saharan trade from the tenth to the twelfth century'.

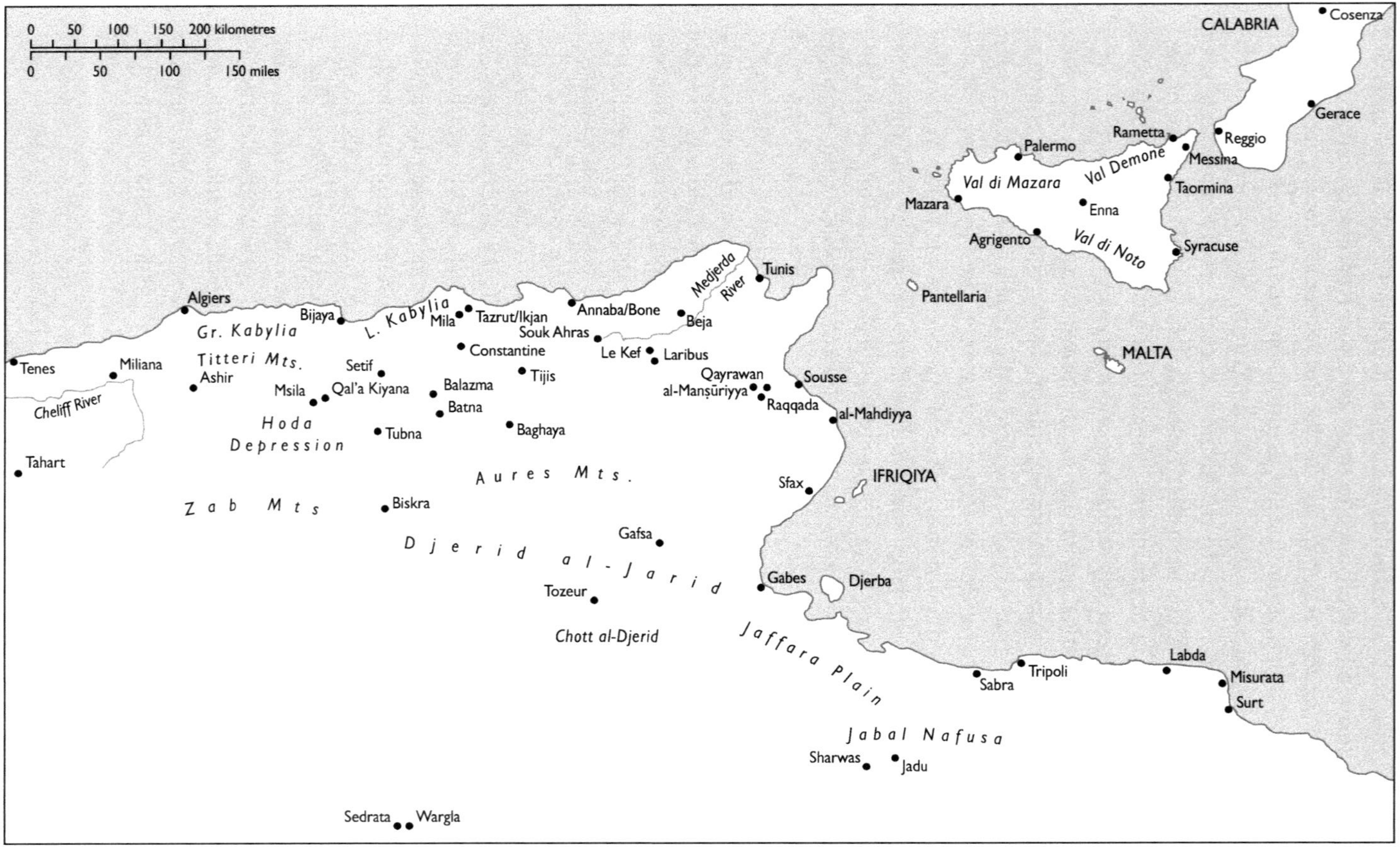

Map 1.2 Ifrīqiya

Saharan trade, while a vigorous Muslim population continued to grow, and the native Christians became a dwindling minority alongside the commercial community of the Jews.

South of Gabes and Gafsa, however, Ifrīqiya embraced the margin of the desert in the oases of the Djerid and the hills of the Jabal Nafūsa, home to a Christian population in the Djerid, but more importantly to an Ibāḍī Berber population living halfway between Rustamid Tāhart and Zawīla in the Fezzan. Its political and religious loyalties were not those of the regime at Qayrawān, although the trans-Saharan trade in slaves and gold that was developing out of the two Khārijite capitals drew it into the market economy of Ifrīqiya. Meanwhile, to the west of Qayrawān, the hills rose up into the mountains and high plains of eastern Algeria, across which ran the routes to Spain through Tāhart and Idrisid Fes. It was partly the prospect of a challenge to Baghdad from an ᶜAlid prince at Fes that had given Ibrāhīm ibn al-Aghlab his independence as the champion of Baghdad in the Maghrib, and turned this western region of his domain into a frontier province under a military governor at Ṭubna. Strategically situated at the meeting-place of the route from Qayrawān across the high plains to the north of the Aures mountains and the route coming around them to the south through the oasis of Biskra in the Djerid, Ṭubna commanded the main route to the far west that ran along the northern edge of the Hodna depression. Meanwhile, the wide corridor formed by the high plains between the massif of the Aures and the ranges of Kabylia that lined the Mediterranean coast was garrisoned by Arab militias that kept in check the Berbers of the mountains, much as the Romans had done before. The Berbers of Kabylia were the Kutāma, the Ucutumani of Antiquity, who seem not to have participated in the great Khārijite rebellions, but who had nevertheless been drawn into the ambience of Islam and its state at Qayrawān, much as they had been drawn into the ambience of Rome. In this position they exemplified what Ernest Gellner called marginal tribalism, governing themselves while recognising the values of the wider society, and pitting the right that it represented against the wrong that it did in the attempt to bring them under its control. The values of their own society were epitomised in a remarkable passage of the *Iftitāḥ*, which reports the answers of the Kutāma to the questions put to their pilgrims at Mecca by Abū ᶜAbd Allāh, the Fatimid *dāᶜī* who won them for the cause:

> 'Who is in command of your affairs?'
> 'Each man of us is his own master, although each tribe has its elders, and advisers in matters of (religious) conduct, to whom we take our disputes; and whoever loses must accept the judgement against him, or suffer the wrath of the whole community.'

'Are you in fact a single people?'
'We are certainly all Kutāma, although divided into various tribes, clans and families.'
'And are you close to each other?'
'Yes, there is no great distance between us.'
'But are you united?'
'No; we fight each other and then make peace, and make peace with one group while we fight another. That's our way.'
'Do you unite if a foreign enemy attacks?'
'No-one has ever made it necessary, because of our numbers and the fastness of our land.'[27]

This catechism, the reverse of the questioning of the master by the seeker after knowledge in the Book of the Teacher and the Pupil, not only conforms to Ibn Khaldūn's description of the self-reliant tribesman infused with *ᶜaṣabiyya*, or fierce loyalty to kith and kin, but confirms the findings of modern anthropology as set out by Evans-Pritchard in *The Sanūsī of Cyrenaica*,[28] and agrees more particularly with the study of Kabyle society in the years after the French conquest of Algeria by Emil Masqueray, *Formation des cités chez les populations sédentaires de l'Algérie*. This goes on to describe the way in which a tribal politician could rise from a position of influence to one of power by the elimination of rivals within his own clan, and the waging of successful war upon others.[29] Not elicited by the questions of the *dāᶜī*, this feature of tribal behaviour became the key to his success in transforming this stateless society into one obedient to the command of a military and religious dictator, an embryonic state. Such mobilisation of the *ᶜaṣabiyya* of a tribal society depended, as Ibn Khaldūn said, upon the call of faith; but as he also observed, without the *ᶜaṣabiyya* inherent in its tribal structure, the call would have come to nothing.[30] Why in this case the mobilisation succeeded as it did depended upon the Ifrīqiyan situation of the Kutāma and their willingness to be persuaded as much as upon the call itself. Like the Kharijites before them, the Kutāma were yet another Berber people inspired to organise themselves into God's chosen people in the manner of the Arabs before them, in defiance of His official representatives and their regime. John Wansbrough's com-

[27] As quoted in M. Brett and E. Fentress, *The Berbers* (Oxford, 1996), p. 6.
[28] E. E. Evans-Pritchard, *The Sanūsī of Cyrenaica* (Oxford, 1949).
[29] E. Masqueray, *Formation des cités chez les populations sédentaires de l'Algérie. Kabyles du Djurdjura, Chaouia de l'Aouras, Beni Mezab* (Paris, 1886). Reprinted with Introduction by F. Colonna (Aix-en-Provence, 1983). Cf. esp. pp. 116–21, and Brett, *Rise of the Fatimids*, ch. 4.
[30] Ibn Khaldūn, *The Muqaddimah*, vol. 1, pp. 305–6, 322–7.

ment, 'that the propaganda in this particular case should have been Ismāᶜīlī is historically, but not phenomenologically, relevant',[31] puts their response into the perspective of the growth of Islam: the religion, the society and the state, to include the tribal peoples within and without the original Arab empire, to explosive effect.

The Triumph of the Dāᶜī

For the way in which this came about, the *Iftitāḥ al-daᶜwa wa ibtidāᵓ al-dawla* of the Qāḍī al-Nuᶜmān is in remarkable contrast to the inconclusive miscellany of sources for the genesis of the Fatimids in the East. Written half a century after the event by the spokesman of the dynasty who was instrumental in the renewal and reformulation of its propaganda, it is inevitably apologetic, moulded to meet the criteria of a hereditary Imāmate and Caliphate from which the apocalyptic aspect of the Mahdī has largely disappeared. It is in this way that his line is represented at the outset as the true alternative to the defunct succession of the Twelvers, and in conclusion as the reality behind the mistaken expectations of a new Revelation. In between, however, is an account of the mission of Ibn Hawshab to the Yemen, and more particularly a detailed narrative of the achievement of the revolution in Ifrīqiya by the emissary sent from the Yemen on the strength, apparently, of the intelligence gathered at Mecca. Behind the account of the mission to the Yemen there is a lost *Sīra*, or biography, of Ibn Hawshab, perhaps by his son Jaᶜfar, who emigrated to Ifrīqiya. There is no known source for the account of the revolution, but given its hagiographic character, replete with prophecy, the detail is such that al-Nuᶜmān must have had some first-hand narrative available, some second *Sīra* of Abū ᶜAbd Allāh himself.[32] As reported in the *Iftitāḥ*, the exchange between the Dāᶜī and the Kutāma pilgrims at Mecca must be a literary device, but one that goes on to evoke the uneasy relationship with the Aghlabid regime in the region. The fortress cities of Mila and Setif in the mountains to the north and Balazma at the foot of the Aures to the south of the high plains are described as the seats of lords owing only nominal allegiance to Qayrawān. These were the commanders of the Arab *jund*, or militias, relegated to these outposts in the west by the Aghlabids, and still rebellious in the reign of Ibrāhīm II, a prince with the reputation of an Ivan the Terrible as a paranoid champion of the people against the nobility, who had massacred the guardsmen of his predecessor, and built for himself the new palace city of Raqqāda with a new slave army of Blacks. The 890s, when Abū ᶜAbd Allāh arrived among the

[31] J. Wansbrough, 'On recomposing the Islamic history of North Africa', *Journal of the Royal Asiatic Society* (1969), 161–70, at 168.

[32] Cf. Halm, *Empire of the Mahdi*, p. 102, n. 153.

Kutāma with the pilgrims returning from Mecca, was a decade of insurrection and repression that saw the massacre of the Arabs at Balazma, a revolt at Tunis and defeat of the Kharijites of the Jabal Nafūsa, culminating in 902 with a major expedition to complete the conquest of Sicily, which ended with his death at Cosenza in Calabria at the end of the year.[33] The rebellion being hatched by the Dāᶜī, however, was ignored as it played itself out with a *hijra* in the manner of the Prophet from Ikjān under the protection of the Saktān clan to his own Medina at Tāzrūt under the protection of the Ghashmān. His following grew on the strength of an oath of secrecy and fidelity, but not simply on the strength of his call to prepare the coming dawn. His preaching was a catalyst for the outbreak of clan rivalries, in which, in the manner described by Masqueray, his allies and their enemies fought for supremacy. Those enemies allied with the Arabs at Mila; and it was only with the capture of Mila in 902, in the year of Ibrāhīm II's departure for Sicily, that Abū ᶜAbd Allāh finally gained the upper hand over the Kutāma. His capture of Mila finally provoked an expedition from Qayrawān, but in the midst of a murderous succession crisis following the death of Ibrāhīm II, this came to nothing, and with the capture of Setif in 904 the conquest of Ifrīqiya had begun.[34]

Whatever Abū ᶜAbd Allāh may have owed to the pursuit of clan rivalries by the shaykhs of the Kutāma, the opportunity for power and wealth that he offered to those who accepted him came at the price of his dictatorship as head of an organisation in which the Kutāma were divided into seven regiments under a staff of *muqaddam*-s, or commanders, and *duᶜāt*, or missionaries, the shaykhs or personnel of this nascent state. At the same time they were ruthlessly disciplined, punished by ostracism or execution by their relatives to take away the bloodguilt in a regime of terror under which, says the *Iftitāḥ*, they were united, whatever their motives, as brothers in virtue and devotion to the cause, a prime example of tribal *ᶜaṣabiyya* put to the use of faith. Drilled in the expectation of the Mahdī, they were made custodians of the fifth portion of any booty taken, his due as supreme commander which was set aside to await his coming. Meanwhile, the Dāᶜī was sending messages to the Mahdī himself, whom he had never met, but who was on his way to the west. For this the principal source is the *Sīra* of Jaᶜfar al-Ḥājib, the memoirs of the Mahdī's personal servant.[35] Written up in Egypt years after Jaᶜfar's death, they belong to the mid-century corpus of Fatimid literature, but have the merit of describing a plausible human being, an aspect of this

33 Details in M. Talbi, *L'Émirat Aghlabide, 184–296, 800–909. Histoire politique* (Paris, 1966), pp. 271–322, 519–28.

34 Full details in Talbi, *L'Émirat Aghlabide*, and Halm, *Empire of the Mahdi.*

35 See n. 17 above.

man of destiny that was perhaps one way in which the dynasty wished him to be remembered. He left Salamiyya, a relatively safe haven from the ᶜAbbasids in Ṭūlūnid Syria, in the crisis of the invasion of the country by the Lords of the She-Camel and the Mole in 902–3, perhaps in response to rumours of his imminent appearance. He was welcomed in Egypt by the *dāᶜī* Abū ᶜAlī, but left in 905 when the ᶜAbbasid armies, who had taken back Syria after the suppression of the uprising, recovered Egypt from the last of the Ṭūlūnids at the beginning of the year. The expectation of his entourage that he would go to the Yemen to declare himself was then deceived. Parting company with his chief Dāᶜī Fīrūz, who left for the Yemen to join the rival cause of ᶜAlī ibn al-Faḍl, he set out for the Maghrib, as in retrospect he was of course destined to do in foreknowledge of the outcome. Urged to do so by Abū ᶜAbd Allāh, he was accompanied by the Dāᶜī's brother Abūʾl-ᶜAbbās. Travelling through Tripoli, he continued on through the Kharijite territory of the Djerid to Sijilmāsa, the twin of Tāhart as the seat of a second Kharijite dynasty, Ṣufrī instead of Ibāḍī. Situated in the Tafilelt, an oasis to the south-east of the Moroccan Atlas, Sijilmāsa was equally a centre of trans-Saharan trade, at the head of a route to the Niger and Senegal. There in this remote but affluent centre of commerce, after a journey of perhaps eight months, the Mahdī settled at with his household and belongings to await developments in Ifrīqiya.

For Abū ᶜAbd Allāh, the year had been decisive with the rout of a joint Aghlabid force composed of troops from Qayrawān and Ṭubna as it advanced towards Mila at a place called Kayūna/Kabūna. Declared by the *Iftitāḥ* to be the first victory of the Mahdī, who received the news at Sijilmāsa, it opened the way to the conquest of Ifrīqiya that began in the following year, 906, with the taking of Ṭubna. This essential move to secure the west before the advance on Qayrawān served also to eliminate the last of the Kutāma opponents of the Dāᶜī, who had taken refuge in the fortress. At the same time it provided the occasion for the first public pronouncement of the revolution, the abolition of all illegal taxes in favour of the Sharīᶜa, the law of the Prophet. It was an impeccable reply to the invective of Qayrawān, which contained all the charges of charlatanry and licentiousness familiar from the later descriptions of the Carmathians in the Mashriq. But that invective made no mention of the Mahdī, or of the hoarding of the fifth of the booty at Tāzrūt for his future use, simply proclaiming the holy war upon such iniquity.[36] After Kayūna, however, there was no stopping the advance. In 907 the capture of the fortresses of Balazma, Bāghāya and Tījis drove the Aghlabids from the high ground of eastern Algeria to take up a final defensive position in the defile of al-Urbus

[36] Cf. Brett, *Rise of the Fatimids*, pp. 95–7.

(Laribus, Lorbous) east of Le Kef in Tunisia, on the main route to Qayrawān. There they were overwhelmed and massacred in 909 by the Kutāma at the head of what had become a vast insurrection, a righteous slaughter of the wicked that left the Aghlabid Amīr Ziyādat Allāh III with no choice but flight to Egypt. Qayrawān, and by extension the rest of his dominions, was granted *amān* or *pax*, 'peace', in return for its submission – the basis in Islamic law of the relationship between conqueror and conquered. Ensconced in the palace of Raqqāda, Abū ᶜAbd Allāh then set about restoring law and order with the prevention of further pillage, the maintenance of the existing administration under new governors sent out to the provincial cities, and the enforcement of strict morality. The changes that declared the nature of the revolution were to the symbols of authority: the call to prayer, the coinage and the formula that served as a signature on the Dāᶜī's seal: 'Completed is the Word of your Lord'.[37] In this interval before the discovery of the Mahdī and the revelation of his identity, his coming was anticipated in the invocation of the holy family of Muḥammad, ᶜAlī, Ḥasan, Ḥusayn and Fāṭima in the call to prayer, and in the inscription on the coinage: 'The Ḥujja of God is victorious; His enemies are scattered'. With the regime in place, three months later Abū ᶜAbd Allāh departed with his army, in June 909, to fetch the man himself from Sijilmāsa.

Leaving a Kutāma, Abū Zakī, together with his brother Abūᵓl-ᶜAbbās in command at Raqqāda, Abū ᶜAbd Allāh passed through Tāhart, where he suppressed the Rustamid dynasty and installed a Kutāma governor, to reach Sijilmāsa in August. Its Midrarid ruler fled, the city was ransacked but the Mahdī found and presented to the troops as 'my lord and yours, oh ye faithful'. This was the term employed in the Caliphal title of Amīr al-Muᵓminīn, or Commander of the Faithful, but one that in the language of the dynasty designated the true believers in the Imām as distinct from the mass of Muslims. The corresponding presentation of the troops to their new lord, dressed in the finery he had kept for the occasion, then served not only as an acknowledgement of his Caliphate but also as a recognition of their status as an elite, the *Awliyāᵓ*, or Friends of God. At the same time a letter to be read from the pulpit at Qayrawān announced the discovery of the Ḥujja, or Proof of God, His Friend, the Son of His Messenger and Commander of the Faithful. Returning eastwards, the triumphant procession passed through Ikjān to collect the fifth in the keeping of the shaykhs, before reaching Qayrawān in January 910 to be met by the townsfolk. The *amān* was duly renewed, and the Mahdī rode into Raqqāda in splendid array, Abū ᶜAbd Allāh in front, his son Muḥammad behind. The proclamation that followed announced his titles to be used in the

[37] Qurᵓān VI: 115.

formula of prayer after the invocation of Muḥammad, ᶜAlī, Ḥasan, Ḥusayn and Fāṭima and the Imāms of his progeny: Your, sc. God's, ᶜAbd or Servant, Your Caliph or Deputy, al-Qāʾim, He Who Arises to command Your worshippers in Your land, ᶜAbd Allāh, Abū Muḥammad, the Imām, al-Mahdī biʾllāh, He Who is Rightly Guided by God, Commander of the Faithful in succession to his fathers, Your Caliphs, al-Rāshidūn al-Mahdiyyūn, the Orthodox and Rightly Guided, who judged in fairness in accordance with the Truth. It went on to proclaim his mission: to conquer the world to East and West, in accordance with God's promise, from sinful rebels.

The Accession of the Mahdī

In those titles lay not only his immediate problem but that of his dynasty, and by extension the whole difficulty with its origins and its role in the wave of messianism on which it came to power. In advancing the legitimist claim of a descendant of ᶜAlī to the Caliphate, they are quite different from the Ḥujja, or Proof of God, and the Son of the Messenger of God hailed by the Dāᶜī in his despatch from Sijilmāsa, just as the Ḥujja of God is different from the Ḥujja of the hidden Imām in the Daftary version of Fatimid origins. As an assertion of an uninterrupted succession of heirs to the government of Islam, they were reinforced in these titles by the name that he took at his accession: ᶜAbd Allāh, Abū, or Father, of Muḥammad. This was the very reverse of Son of the Messenger of God, but one that ensured that in his son the prophecy would be fulfilled, that the Mahdī/Qāʾim would bear the name of the Prophet, Muḥammad ibn ᶜAbd Allāh. Thereby the Jacobitism of the ᶜAlids was seamlessly blended with the tradition of Muḥammadan messianism into the principle of the new dynasty. But it took the place of quite a different expectation on the part of the Dāᶜī, one that may be suspected not only in the titles he had employed in the despatch from Sijilmāsa, but in the report of a previous conversation with him at Qayrawān. This was by Ibn al-Haytham, an Ifrīqiyan scholar won over to the cause by Abū ᶜAbd Allāh in yet another series of questions and answers, but writing once again long after the event in the middle of the century, when the dynasty was moving towards the acceptance of Muḥammad ibn Ismāᶜīl as the crucial link in its chain of descent from the Prophet. What he wrote, nevertheless, was that when asked, the Dāᶜī had declared that the Mahdī was indeed Muḥammad ibn Ismāᶜīl, who had indeed born the name of the Prophet on the understanding that the father in this case was Ismāᶜīl son of Abraham, the father of the race.[38]

[38] Ibn al-Haytham, ed. and trans. W. Madelung and P. E. Walker (2000), *The Advent of the Fatimids. A contemporary Shiᶜi Witness* (London and New York, 2000): text pp. 55–6, trans. p. 107.

According to Ibn al-Haytham, the Dāʿī's statement followed his exposition of the sequence of seven Prophets and seven Imāms in the course of the conversation, and might be explained by his ignorance of the man himself before the meeting at Sijilmāsa. It was nevertheless precisely this belief that the Mahdī was concerned to deny in the letter(s) that he subsequently sent to the Yemen, to the community of Ibn Ḥawshab, the Dāʿī who had sent Abū ʿAbd Allāh to Ifrīqiya in the first place. Its attribution to Abū ʿAbd Allāh not only heightens the uncertainty regarding the role of Salamiyya in 'the revolt of Islam', but anticipates the dénouement of the relationship between the Mahdī and the man who brought him to power in the assassination of both the Dāʿī and his brother Abūʾl-ʾAbbās a year later.

The assassination was a repetition of the fate of Abū Muslim, the architect of the ʿAbbasid revolution, who had likewise produced a monarch from nowhere who refused to be a figurehead. The story in the *Iftitāḥ* is of a conspiracy to assassinate the Mahdī hatched by Abū ʿAbd Allāh's two lieutenants, Abū Zakī at the head of the shaykhs of the Kutāma, who was resentful of the Mahdī's appropriation of the wealth stored at Ikjān, and his brother Abūʾl-ʾAbbās. Abūʾl-ʾAbbās appears as the instigator, a man learned in the Bāṭin, the esoteric doctrine of the Mahdī, who had indeed known the man himself beforehand, but who had been corrupted by the taste of power in his brother's absence, and now cast doubt on his identity. When the Mahdī refused the Dāʿī's suggestion that he be left in command of the Kutāma, Abū ʿAbd Allāh fell in with the plot, which failed when the Mahdī perceived what was afoot, the two brothers were speared by loyal Kutāma, and Abū Zakī and his cronies were executed. It is clear that clan loyalties were once again involved in the exploitation by the Mahdī of continuing rivalry within the body politic of the Kutāma. But it is equally clear that his position was more generally at stake. To maintain the continuity of the revolution, he granted the Dāʿī an honourable burial as a loyal servant who had been led astray, praying for him more in sorrow than in anger. But he was immediately confronted with a rebellion of the Kutāma back in the hills in favour of a boy declared to be the true Mahdī, in receipt of a new revelation which, as was said of the Carmathians, permitted all kinds of licentiousness. Its suppression required an expedition by the Mahdī's son, Abūʾl-Qāsim Muḥammad, now formally designated as the Qāʾim, the Mahdī's successor, with the title of Walī ʿAhd al-Muslimīn.

But neither the play on names, which gave the name of the Prophet to the Mahdī's son, nor that on numbers, were at an end. In the *Iftitāh*, Abū ʿAbd Allāh is given the personal name of Ḥusayn ibn Aḥmad, while Abūʾl-ʿAbbās is called Muḥammad ibn Aḥmad. But in the Mahdī's letter(s) to the Yemen, the first of these names is attributed to his own natural father, while the second is given to his predecessor in the Imāmate. In such a context, where names invest persons with personae, the agnomen Abū ᶜAbd Allāh would designate the Dāᶜī as the father of the Mahdī under his regnal rather than his proper name. In the letter(s), that name was claimed to be ᶜAlī as distinct from Saᶜīd, which would have been his name in the line of Imāms prior to his manifestation. The association of the name Abūʾl-ᶜAbbās with that of Muḥammad ibn Aḥmad is less clear; the Mahdī declared himself to be the son of his predecessor in the sense of the Bāṭin, the hidden sense of the law that might have been expected to emerge with the Mahdī as a fresh Revelation, and in which Abūʾl-ᶜAbbās was said to be learned. It may be that the stigmatising of Abūʾl-ᶜAbbās served as a repudiation of this apocalyptic expectation, while in the persona of Abū ᶜAbd Allāh, the Dāᶜī himself served as a reassurance to the faithful that they had not been deceived. Given that the faithful in question were in the Yemen, from which the Dāᶜī had set out on his mission to preach, if Ibn al-Haytham is to be believed, the second coming of Muḥammad ibn Ismāᶜīl as the Seventh and last Imām, this is certainly consonant with the Mahdī's evident purpose, which was to disabuse the addressees of any such idea. All previous Imāms have been Muḥammads, while Ismāᶜīl was the pseudonym of ᶜAbd Allāh, eldest son of Jaᶜfar al-Ṣādiq and ancestor of the ᶜAbd Allāh who has now arisen as the Mahdī. This ᶜAbd Allāh is quite different from the Great Mahdī, a fearsome figure who will come at the end of time. Instead he is the first of a line of *mahdī*-s from the family of the Prophet, which has now been established as the dynasty destined to rule until that final day. And as for the number seven, it refers like the days of the week to seven steps through which the Imāms of each cycle have passed, irrespective of their actual number.

As recorded by Jaᶜfar son of Ibn Ḥawshab, the letter(s) of the Mahdī to the Yemen serve as an apology for the revolution in the West, which had cost the life of the missionary sent by Ibn Ḥawshab. Given the underlying doctrinal issue and its fatal outcome, the episode may well be the reality behind the story of the quarrel back in 899; it is inherently unlikely that there should have been two such quarrels over the identity of the Mahdī within a dozen years of each other. The Yemenis, at least, appear to have been convinced. But while the letter(s) may have been addressed to a remote constituency for its eyes only, they contain a manifesto for the entire world. Doctrinally as well as politically, the murderous outcome of the affair was of critical importance not only for the establishment of the dynasty in Ifrīqiya, but for its pursuit of empire.

2

The City of the Mahdī

The Takeover of the Revolution

In Ibn ᶜIdhārī's *Bayān al-mughrib*, a fourteenth-century history of North Africa and Muslim Spain, the Mahdī's regnal name of ᶜAbd Allāh is rendered as ᶜUbayd Allāh, or Little Servant of God.[1] The text is extensively based for this period on the work of an Andalusian chronicler, ᶜArīb ibn Saᶜd, writing in the second half of the tenth century under the rival Caliphate of the Umayyads at Cordoba. The diminutive, as it were little Napoleon or little Hitler, was evidently employed by the opponents of his dynasty from an early date, and passed into the mainstream of Arabic historiography, to be repeated as late as the 1980s by Kennedy in *The Prophet and the Age of the Caliphates.*[2] Its success is a measure of the ultimate eclipse of the dynasty he founded, but its appearance in the tenth century is a sign of the opposition aroused by his takeover of the revolution accomplished by his Dāᶜī, and the seriousness of his threat to carry it to the world. The obstacles in his way were correspondingly formidable. The letter(s) to the Yemen that followed the assassination of the agent who had brought him to power in Ifrīqiya were a token of the need to prove himself to a doubtful world of radical revolutionaries; the greater challenge was to convince the great majority of schoolmen who practised the law in the name of other founders than a Shīᶜite Imām. Both tasks were bound up with the political imperative to demonstrate his title by manifest success in the exercise of the power he had so determinedly seized: in mastering the Kutāma; in securing his hold on Ifrīqiya and its Sicilian colony; and in pursuing the goal on which his credibility rested, the conquest of the world to East and West. All of these were interrelated; and a matter of urgency if the new dynasty were ever to begin to realise its messianic vision of a worldwide community restored to its rightful religion under its rightful rulers.

1 Ibn ᶜIdhārī al-Marrākushī, *Kitāb al-bayān al-mughrib*, vol. 1, *Histoire de l'Afrique du Nord de la conquête au XIe siècle*, ed. G. S. Colin and E. Lévi-Provençal (Leiden, 1948).
2 H. Kennedy, *The Prophet and the Age of the Caliphates.*

That vision gave its own peculiar twist to the structural problem of government in the kind of state that had grown out of the Arab conquests. The problem is identified by Kennedy in his description of what he calls the Muslim commonwealth, in the pivotal chapter of *The Prophet and the Age of the Caliphates*.[3] It was the need to pay the army of soldiers, servants and secretaries out of the taxes of the subject, a need that was subordinated in Ibn Khaldūn's wheel of state to the need for justice. Justice in principle, but not necessarily in practice, meant government in accordance with the Sharīᶜa, the law of Islam, a requirement that was in turn subordinated to the dynamic role of the Muslim monarch as the leader of the people in God's holy war. For the Mahdī, who had arisen with the sword to claim the birthright of the Prophet's heirs, that war was the campaign to sweep away the ᶜAbbasids and take their place at the head of Islam. But while all these requirements had with difficulty been met in the single army into which the Kutāma had been formed for the purpose of conquest, their satisfaction in Ifrīqiya ran into the systemic opposition between army and people, tax collectors and taxpayers, which was sharpened by the opposition between believers and non-believers in the Mahdī's cause, and complicated by the division within the new government between the incoming Kutāma and the personnel of the previous regime in charge of the administration. That division was further complicated by the position of the prince as an outsider to both of them, a state of affairs that was by no means settled by the assassination of the Dāᶜī, for which the Mahdī had turned to one faction of the Kutāma to eliminate the man who had welded them together. All these factors combined after the murder to test the determination and ability of the Mahdī to bend his new dominion to his ambition.

The common denominator was the Kutāma, the Mahdī's indispensable asset, but at the same time a liability and a threat. They were naturally patronised by the Mahdī, who licensed them to celebrate his arrival in the kind of finery in which he garbed himself in contrast to the simplicity of the Dāᶜī's dress; in a society in which clothes were an essential element of ceremony, and ceremony was an essential demonstration of authority and power, such display was an affirmation of the Caliphate he claimed. But the licence the Kutāma claimed as his Friends to lord it over his subjects provoked these to rebel, from Tāhart in the west through Qayrawān to Tripoli in the east, even while they themselves rebelled in Kabylia in the wake of the assassination, on behalf of a Mahdī of their choosing. Tāhart rebelled and was recaptured in 911; but at Qayrawān it was the turn of the Old Palace, that is, the previous fortress city of the Aghabids before the move to Raqqāda. This had retained its garrison

[3] Ibid., pp. 200–11.

as well as the offices of the administration; when fighting broke out with the Kutāma, it was an armed rising that had to be put down, to be followed a year later by a massacre of Kutāma in Qayrawān itself. More serious was the victory over the rebels in Kabylia, nominally accomplished in 912 by the Mahdī's son, Abū'l-Qāsim Muḥammad al-Qā'im, but in fact by Ghazwiyya, the killer of the Dā'ī, who was appointed the govern the whole of the Zab, the western province of Ifrīqiya, while his brother Ḥubāsa was given command of the south and east, the Djerid and Tripolitania. The appointment of the two brothers was no doubt a political calculation, in that it rewarded these newly powerful allies among the Kutāma with their own fiefdoms while removing them from the capital. The danger that these two ambitious warlords nevertheless posed for the Mahdī was paradoxically averted only by the failure of his first attempt to carry the revolution to the East. The rebellion at Tripoli was put down in 913 by a second expedition by Abū'l-Qāsim at the head of an army commanded by Ḥubāsa, which then advanced on Egypt. Supported by the fleet that the Mahdī had inherited from the Aghlabids, Ḥubāsa had no difficulty in occupying first Barqa in Cyrenaica and then Alexandria by August 914, where he was joined by Abū'l-Qāsim for an advance upon the Egyptian capital Fusṭāṭ at the head of the Delta. But by then 'Abbasid reinforcements had arrived from Syria, to be followed by Mu'nis al-Muẓaffar, the commander-in-chief at Baghdad. Defeated at Fusṭāṭ, in 915 the expedition retreated to Alexandria and finally to Ifrīqiya, where the kingmakers Ḥubāsa and Ghazwiyya were both put to death, to the Mahdī's great satisfaction. As the final act in the struggle begun by the Dā'ī in Kabylia to defeat the clannish opposition to his dictatorship, their execution allowed the Mahdī to appoint men of his own choosing to command the Kutāma, turning the Friends of God into the standing army of the dynasty.

The Takeover of the State

The Mahdī completed his takeover of the Aghlabid dominions with the subjection of Sicily in the next two years. In the seventy-five years since the initial invasion of the island in 827 to the death of Ibrāhīm II in 902, its conquest had proceeded in fits and starts, leaving the Byzantines still with a foothold in the north-east corner of the island at Taormina. Muslim settlement had taken place mainly in the west of the island, leaving the Christian Greek population still in the majority. The slowness of this conquest and occupation may be explained by the intermittent character of the dynasty's commitment to campaigning on the island, partly by the relatively small numbers of immigrants, but partly because the sea was more attractive than the land. Palermo, the new capital of the island, had quickly developed into a major port and base for the corsairs who raided the coasts of both Italy and the Balkans, joining Tunis and Sousse in a flourishing maritime activity that not only linked the island to North Africa, but extended westwards to Spain and eastwards to the Levant. Meanwhile, its contribution to the Aghlabid fleet had made Ifrīqiya into the major naval power on display in the armada that had sailed to Egypt with the ill-fated expedition of 914–15. Close though the relationship was between Sicily and their original homeland, however, the colonists had quickly acquired a Sicilian identity, which set them against subsequent immigrants from Ifrīqiya as well as government interference.[4] Thus the first governor sent to claim the island for the Mahdī had been expelled in 912, and his place taken by one Ibn Qurhub, who declared for the ᶜAbbasids, and in 914 ravaged the Ifrīqiyan coast. He was surrendered in 916 by the Sicilians in hope of independence in exchange for submission; but with the fall of Palermo in 917 to an army of occupation, they were both defeated and disarmed, and brought to heel.

Meanwhile, in 916, the Mahdī had begun the construction of his own fortress city of al-Mahdiyya on a mile-long peninsula jutting out from the coast to the south of Sousse (see Map 2.1). Its narrow neck was closed off with a massive gate and a fortified mosque that served as a corner tower in a perimeter wall. Along from this mosque on the south side was an arsenal for the construction of warships, and still further along a harbour enclosed by the wall, whose entrance was defended by two towers linked by a chain. On a hill in the middle stood two palaces on either side of a central square, one facing west for the Mahdī and the other facing east for his son, the Qāᵓim; both are long gone, but certainly, like the Umayyad palace of Madīnat al-Zahrāᵓ at Cordoba and what is known of the Fatimid palaces at al-Qāhira in Egypt, they centred on a throne room, called an *īwān*, for official receptions. On that analogy they would have contained or been surrounded by the offices, residences and quarters of an extended household of family and domestics, high and low. The complex probably included the chancery but not the treasury, which was located down by the mosque, most probably together with the mint. The mosque itself, a fortress like the mosque at Sousse, built by the Aghlabids to defend the harbour of their naval base, was the Great Mosque of the city. Like that of Sousse, it was a rectangle which, like all others of the period, at Qayrawān, Tunis and Cordoba, for example, contained a prayer hall and a courtyard, oriented to the south rather than in the direction of Mecca; the slight deviation to the east was required by the site. But unlike those of Qayrawān and Cordoba, it was not a centre for the population of a civilian city, but a complement to the palace of the representative of God on

[4] Cf. Talbi, *L'Émirat Aghlabide*; A. Metcalfe, *The Muslims of Medieval Italy* (Edinburgh, 2009), pp. 10–43.

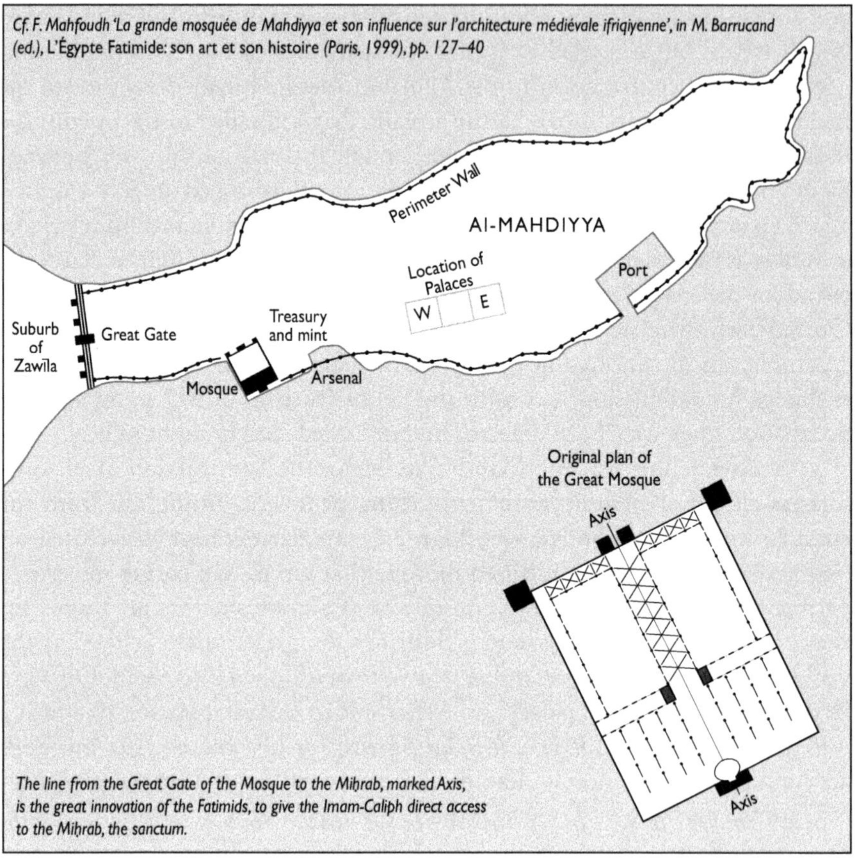

Map 2.1 Al-Mahdiyya

earth, for whom it provided a monumental entry into His presence through the arch of a porch tower on the axis of the Mihrab in the far wall of the prayer hall (see Fig. 2.1). Meanwhile, it served a very practical purpose. As usual in the towns and cities of the period, including Qayrawān, rainwater was collected in cisterns, of which two were in the corner towers of the mosque's façade, while a vaulted reservoir was built by its side; at some stage, as previously at Qayrawān and subsequently at Cordoba and Madīnat al-Zahrāʾ, this was fed by an aqueduct from an external source. Outside was the suburb of Zawīla, where the Kutāma of the garrison lived with their families, side by side with the Black slave troops recruited from the trans-Saharan slave trade through Zawīla in the Fezzan.[5]

[5] The Fatimid city has been surveyed and described by A. Lézine, *Mahdiya: recherches d'archéologie islamique* (Paris, 1965).

Figure 2.1 The Great Mosque of al-Mahdiyya.

The Great Mosque of al-Mahdiyya, whose monumental porch, aligned with the Mihrab of the prayer hall, was designed to give the Imām-Caliph a ceremonial entrée into the presence of God. At the same time the building was a fortress which served as a bastion in the angle of the perimeter wall of the city, where the wall turned inland from the southern coast to run across the neck of the peninsula.

Such a relocation of the seat of government in a grand new monumental city was the typical gesture of a monarch seeking in this case to emulate his rival in Baghdad, but radical in the lengths to which it went to do so. Both in its site and in its massive fortification, this city of the Mahdī took to an extreme of seclusion the removal of the prince from the people in palatial residences away from the capital cities, while as the White City it took its stance in opposition to the Black of the ᶜAbbasids, in whose direction the peninsula pointed with the threat of its fleet. In so doing, it gave a new purpose to the empire that the Aghlabids had created by land and sea. The continued recruitment to the corps of Black troops inherited from the previous dynasty followed the practice of the Aghlabids, who from the beginning had relied upon such a force of *ᶜabīd*, or slaves, to dominate the Arabs of the *jund*. Under the new dynasty, these now counterbalanced not only the Arabs but the Kutāma. Still more important were the White slaves, the Ṣaqāliba or Slavs, procured as previously mainly from the Balkans by the slave raiding and trading of the corsairs of Ifrīqiya and Sicily. These now served in the palace, either as guardsmen whose officers eventually came to command the army in the field, or crucially as eunuchs in the personal service of the two princes. These domestics supplemented and eventually replaced the four comrades of the Mahdī on his journey from the East as lieutenants of the prince in the execution of his commands and the direction of the administration. Thus Jaʿfar al-Ḥājib, the diarist of the flight to Sijilmāsa, was superseded by al-Ustādh, or 'Mister' Jawdhar, the confidential servant of the Qāʾim, whose own posthumous memoirs record the career of an indispensable minister to three successive Caliphs.[6] It was their loyalty and their competence that made the new regime so very effective.

It could not, on the other hand, function as it did without the performance of the *kuttāb* (sing. *kātib*), the professional secretaries upon whose literacy, numeracy and familiarity with the operation of the various *dīwān*-s, or offices, of the administration the edifice of government depended. They formed a class that had developed into an aristocracy of the pen in ʿAbbasid Iraq, whose prestige and abilities made their members welcome elsewhere in the world of Islam. Thus two such emigrants with the epithet al-Baghdādī served in succession as chief secretaries to the last Aghlabids and first Fatimids with the title of al-Kātib. The second of these, Abū Jaʿfar Muḥammad, was their chancellor, a minister who sat in audience with the Caliph, with responsibility for the letters and documents that were the instruments of government, and for the related service of the *barīd*, 'the post', which doubled as an intelligence agency on the watch for subversion. As befitted a state that, in Hartmann's Oriental manner, lived to tax and taxed to live, however, much the largest employer of the class was the Treasury, housed at al-Mahdiyya in the Dār al-Muḥasabāt, or Counting House, by the Great Mosque. Apart from the Sikka, the Mint, this contained four departments: the Bayt al-Māl, or Public Treasury; a Dīwān al-Kharāj, or Board of Revenue; a Dīwān al-Ḍiyāʿ, or Office of Estates; and a Dīwān al-ʿAtāʾ, or Board of Pay. The apparent simplicity of the arrangement disguises what was certainly a complicated system, in which *kharāj* stood not only for the tax on land, levied on the basis of fiscal registers, but for the *jizya*, or poll tax, payable by non-Muslims, and the various taxes on trade in particular that went under the name of *mukūs* (sing. *maks*), impositions not permitted by the law. *Ḍiyāʿ*, meanwhile, referred to the estates confiscated from the Aghlabids, which provided the new monarch with a large patrimony. As for *ʿaṭāʾ*, salaries, these could only be paid out of central funds to those resident in the capital; elsewhere they

6 *Sīrat al-Ustādh Jawdhar*, ed. M. K. Ḥusayn and M. A. Shaʿīra (Cairo, 1954), trans. M. Canard, *Vie de l'Ustadh Jawdhar* (Algiers, 1958).

could only be paid out of local revenues that never reached the treasury, even if they entered into the accounts of the Dīwān al-Kharāj and the Dīwān al-Ḍiyāᶜ. To keep the whole system as far as possible under control, its oversight was entrusted to a minister or ministers from the household, beginning with one of the Mahdī's attendants from Salamiyya, al-Khazarī, and continuing in the reign of the Qāᵓim with the eunuch Jawdhar. And as far as it was possible to be, it appears to have been efficient to the point of being oppressive and correspondingly unpopular.[7]

The Role of the Qāᵓim

The Mahdī took up residence in his new city in 921, to receive his son the Qāᵓim on his return from a second, more prolonged, but equally unsuccessful attempt to conquer Egypt. Here was a country which, after its recovery by the ᶜAbbasids from the last of the Ṭūlūnids in 905, following their victory over the Carmathians in Syria, had reverted to the status of a province with a small garrison under a Turkish governor, but one that was by no means docile. A long history of unrest dated back to the beginning of the eighth century; from the middle of the ninth, it had been affected by the messianism of the period – revolts by ᶜAlid pretenders that were only finally suppressed by Aḥmad ibn Ṭūlūn, and Shīᶜite sympathies worked on by those agents of the Mahdī who had helped him on his way to the West, and who now agitated in favour of his conquest of the country. Meanwhile, an Egyptian patriotism behind the revolt of an Egyptian officer, Ibn al-Khalīj, in 905–6, resented the return of the ᶜAbbasids, making it politic for their commander-in-chief Muᵓnis to withdraw from the country after forcing the retreat of the Qāᵓim in 915. The religious divide was apparent when in response to Fatimid propaganda, slogans in praise of the three Caliphs before ᶜAlī: Abū Bakr, ᶜUmar and ᶜUthmān, were painted on the doors of the Mosque of ᶜAmr, the Great Mosque of the capital Fusṭāṭ, now Old Cairo; crowds demonstrating their support with the approval of the chief of police were dispersed by troops.[8] When, after the reconquest of Barqa in 917, the Qāᵓim once again occupied Alexandria in 919, the government was in crisis. His second invasion was a more substantial attempt to conquer the country en route, as he declared, to Iraq; it failed yet again because, with the previous campaign in mind, the planning was too methodical, and whatever moment there had been was lost. Abūᵓl-Qāsim waited at Alexandria for the fleet to arrive in 920 and sail up

[7] Cf. F. Dachraoui, *Le Califat fatimide au Maghreb, 296-362/909-973* (Tunis, 1981), pp. 323–64.

[8] Cf. Brett, *The New Cambridge History of Islam*, vol. 1, pp. 562–4; *Rise of the Fatimids*, pp. 56–7, 146–7.

the Rosetta branch of the Nile in company with the army. But when it did, it was caught by the wind on a lee shore, most probably in Aboukir Bay, where it was destroyed by the ᶜAbbasid fleet from Cilicia as Nelson destroyed that of Napoleon at the Battle of the Nile in 1798. There was, moreover, time for Muᵓnis to arrive yet again from Iraq, and take up a defensive position at Gizeh across the river from Fusṭāṭ. The Qāᵓim himself moved down from Alexandria into the Fayyum, the large floodplain in the desert to the south-west, from where he occupied the Valley to the south of the capital. For a year there was confrontation without conflict, until the stalemate was broken by the Cilician fleet, which first retook Alexandria, and then allowed Muᵓnis to advance upstream to the point from which he could invade the Fayyum. The Qāᵓim retreated across the desert to Barqa with great loss along the largely waterless route before returning to Ifrīqiya.[9] He had behaved in Egypt as its ruler, and had he conquered it would surely have remained there as ruler of the East while his father ruled the West. As it was, the retrospective apology for these two successive failures was attributed to the Mahdī by the Qāḍī al-Nuᶜmān in the closing pages of the *Iftitāh*, an epilogue to the saga of the Dāᶜī which brings the story down to his own day, and again on the authority of the great-grandson of the Mahdī, the Imām-Caliph al-Muᶜizz, in his record of the latter's pronouncements, the *Kitāb al-Majālis waᵓl-Musāyarāt*. The Mahdī, he says, sent the Qāᵓim twice to Egypt in the full knowledge that it would only be conquered by one of his descendants, solely as a proof of the Daᶜwa, the Summons of God's representatives to the world. The evident disappointment overshadowed the one important gain. Barqa remained in Fatimid hands as an eastern outpost of the new empire, a base from which Egypt continued to be raided, and one that fifty years later enabled its final conquest.

The descendant in question turned out to be al-Muᶜizz himself, anticipating his own triumph with this gloss upon the past. Long before his final success, however, the terms that he eventually dictated to the Egyptians had been anticipated in the title conferred upon the Qāᵓim in his capacity as heir to the Caliphate, that of Walī ᶜAhd al-Muslimīn, 'Keeper of the Covenant of the Muslims'. *ᶜAhd*, meaning covenant, pact or treaty, had long been employed by the ᶜAbbasids in the designation Walī ᵓl-ᵓAhd for the appointed successor to the throne. But in this case the covenant is not that of the monarch with his heir, but that of the Muslim community with its ruler. It was in fact a title that had been used by the ᶜAbbasids on coins minted in Khurāsān for the third of their Caliphs, al-Mahdī, before his accession.[10] The ᶜAbbasid

[9] Cf. Halm, *The Empire of the Mahdi*, pp. 206–13.

[10] Cf. M. L. Bates, 'Khūrāsānī revolutionaries and al-Mahdī's title', in F. Daftary and J. W. Meri (eds), *Culture and Memory in Medieval Islam* (London and New York, 2003), p. 295.

precedent was all the more remarkable since the ᶜAbbasid prince, with the name of Muḥammad ibn ᶜAbd Allāh, was already designated as the Mahdī, just as the Fatimid Mahdī's son was already the Qāᵓim. The parallel is with the ᶜAbbasids' own messianism; the titulature is part of the Fatimids' own attempt to take over the Caliphate in the form created by their opponents. Its meaning for the Fatimids themselves became clear in the middle of the century in the *Daᶜāᵓim al-Islam*, or *Pillars of Islam*, the definitive statement of the doctrine of the dynasty by the Qāḍī al-Nuᶜmān,[11] and was articulated in the ᶜAhd, or covenant, with the people of Egypt concluded at the time of its conquest in 969.[12] That covenant rested upon a distinction between those who believed in the Imām and the mass of those members of the community who did not. While both were Muslim, submitted to God and regulated by His law, only the former could be regarded as Muᵓminūn, or Faithful, the original term for the followers of the Prophet that survived in its original sense in the Caliphal title of Amīr al-Muᵓminīn, or Commander of the Faithful. Fifty years earlier, when granted the title of Walī ᶜAhd al-Muslimīn, the Qāᵓim had been nominally entrusted by the Mahdī with the keeping of the obligation incumbent upon the whole of the community to obey its rightful lord. For that purpose he was accorded the right to correspond in his own name, while the further title of Sword of the Imām envisaged the conquest that would turn that obligation into reality.[13] But in Ifrīqiya, where this grand plan was first put to the test, its enforcement in practice ran into difficulty as the Mahdī endeavoured to steer a course between the apocalyptic expectations of the believers on the one hand and the doctrinal hostility of the non-believers on the other.

The Conflict with the Schoolmen

The course itself was set out in principle in the letter(s) to the faithful in the Yemen, in which Muḥammadan messianism was subordinated to ᶜAlid legitimism for the purpose of a dynasty destined to rule indefinitely over a world restored to the rightful successors of the Prophet. If the Yemenis appear to have been convinced, the rising on behalf of a second Mahdī which greeted the assassination of the Dāᶜī revealed the strength of the current of radical messianism that surfaced as the Qāᵓim retreated from Egypt in 921. In that year, the Mahdī finally had some 200 *ghulāt*, or extremists, arrested, executed or imprisoned for life for the sin of *ghuluww*, 'excess', in other words for the antinomian licentiousness attributed to the Carmathians

[11] Al-Qāḍī al-Nuᶜmān, *Daᶜāᵓim al-Islam*, ed. A. A. A. Fyzee, 2 vols (Cairo, 1951–61).

[12] See Chapter 3.

[13] Cf. Brett, *Rise of the Fatimids*, pp. 143–4.

of Iraq, which probably extended to the deification of the Mahdī. Reported in the *Bayān* from the outside standpoint of Umayyad Cordoba, the episode fed the black legend of the Fatimids cultivated by their opponents of the Mālikī school and preserved in the *Riyāḍ al-Nufūs* of Abū Bakr al-Mālikī, hagiographical biographies of its followers compiled in the second half of the eleventh century, in which the Mahdī is alleged to have gone down on all fours, covered in a sheepskin and bleating like a sheep as a sign of emancipation from the law.[14] The story is evidence of the sharp conflict that developed between the Mahdī and the Mālikī *ᶜulamāᵓ*, or scholars, as he endeavoured to impose his authority upon his new subjects, and in the process found himself involved in the sectarian rivalries of the schoolmen that dated from the previous century.

The rivalry was between the Mālikī majority, belonging to the *madhhab*, or school, of the eighth-century Meccan jurist Mālik ibn Anas, and the substantial Ḥanafī minority, who belonged to the school of the equally eighth-century Kufan jurist Abū Ḥanīfa. This was the school in favour with the ᶜAbbasids and thus with their Aghlabid lieutenants, but in the middle of the ninth century it had lost its predominance in Ifrīqiya with the appointment of the great Mālikī jurist Saḥnūn to the supreme position of Qāḍī of Ifrīqiya. His appointment came in the wake of the *miḥna*, the attempt by the Caliph al-Maᵓmūn to impose the doctrine of the created as distinct from the uncreated Qurᵓān upon the jurists of the empire. It had been an unsuccessful attempt to assert the supreme authority of the Caliph for the faith at a time when the definition of the law as the law of God had reduced his legal competence to that of an administrator and adjudicator in cases of last resort. The violence of the persecution was matched in Ifrīqiya by the violence of the opposition, when after the abandonment of the *miḥna* Saḥnūn had his predecessor flogged to death. With his appointment the juridical establishment moved from closeness to the dynasty to a critical distance as the Mālikites asserted themselves at the expense of the Kufans, as the Ḥanafites were known.[15] In the revolutionary years leading up to the overthrow of the dynasty by the Dāᶜī, the opposition between them was exacerbated by the appointment of a Ḥanafī as Qāḍī of Ifrīqiya, and by the subsequent appeal to the Mālikites for their support by the last Aghlabid Amīr. It was perpetuated with the arrival of the Dāᶜī, when the Kufans went over to the new regime, and one of their number, al-Marwarrūdhī, was appointed Qāḍī. It would appear that among them were those, like Ibn

[14] Abū Bakr al-Mālikī, *Riyāḍ al-Nufūs*, ed. al-Bakkūsh, 3 vols (Beirut, 1981), vol. 2, pp. 503–6. Cf. Brett, *Rise of the Fatimids*, pp. 156–7.

[15] Cf. Talbi, *L'Émirat Aghlabide*, pp. 231–40.

al-Haytham, who were, or at least claimed to be, Shīᶜites of the Iraqi kind, followers of the known successors of Jaᶜfar al-Ṣādiq who enjoyed considerable influence in ᶜAbbasid society. The desertion of the ᶜAbbasids by these schoolmen for the cause of the new dynasty pointed to the continuing fluidity of religious and political loyalties that promised well for the success of the Fatimid Daᶜwa in its bid to take over the direction of Islam. In Ifrīqiya itself, meanwhile, their recruitment to the cause was crucial to the success of the Mahdī in taking over the country.

The reverse of the coin was the hostility of the Mālikites, who found themselves not only out of office, but the victims of persecution by the victorious Ḥanafites and targeted by the Mahdī's own *miḥna*, the enforcement of conformity to the new forms of worship that he introduced to proclaim the authority of the new dynasty as rulers of Islam. The persecution began with al-Marwarrūdhī, the Qāḍī appointed by the Dāᶜī, and probably for that reason dismissed and executed along with Ghazwiyya and Ḥubāsa in the final purge of the revolutionary regime. The reform of the judicature that followed saw his Kufan successor as Qāḍī of Qayrawān, Qāḍī of Ifrīqiya, ranked below the Qāḍī of the palace city of al-Mahdiyya, the Kutāma jurist Aflaḥ al-Malūsī, while retaining responsibility for the administration of justice by his subordinates throughout the country. These were not only the *quḍāt* of the provinces but holders of the post of *ḥākim* (pl. *ḥukkām*), officers who had grown in competence under the Aghlabids to deal with cases involving sums up to 100 gold dīnārs, complaints of injustice and trading in the market. Under the Fatimids the *ḥākim* became a formidable figure, with the powers of the whip and the sword 'to command the right and forbid the wrong', the injunction known as the *ḥisba*.[16] At the highest level, the rights and wrongs in question consisted in observance or non-observance of the ritual innovations that proclaimed the supremacy of the dynasty at the head of the community in the formula *Hayy ᶜalā khayr al-ʾamal* or 'Come to the best of works', employed in the call to prayer; in variations in the number of prostrations; in alterations to the forms of prayer, including the obligation to curse the enemies of the Imām; and in the beginning and ending of the fast of Ramadan by astronomical calculation rather than by sighting of the new moon. For failure to conform, or for arguing against the dynasty, Mālikites suffered legendary punishment: hanging up by one hand in the sun until dead; throwing in the sea; cutting out of the offending tongue; stripping and whipping. Such incidents may have been few and far between, but their stories are symptomatic

[16] Cf. Brett, *Rise of the Fatimids*, p. 155; Dachraoui, *Califat fatimide*, pp. 416–21. From *hisba* comes the term *muḥtasib* for the market inspector, and more generally for a censor of morals.

of an opposition to the Mahdī that may have been rooted in the politics of Ifrīqiya but was nevertheless indicative of the wider obstacles in the way of winning Islam to the dynasty's side. In Ifrīqiya itself, it is clear that the balance to be struck between ruler and subject was still experimental.

The Advance to the West

If the opposition of the Mālikites represented the long-term threat of juridical resistance to the claims of the dynasty, a more immediate threat was posed by the Khārijites and the tribal populations with which they were associated to the south and west of Ifrīqiya. The Khārijites, the product of that first wave of religiously inspired revolt by the Berbers against Arab imperialism in the middle of the eighth century, took their name of 'goers-out, rebels' from those who had seceded from the army of ᶜAlī in his confrontation with his rival Muᶜāwiya, the founder of the Umayyad dynasty, at Ṣiffīn in 657, and had gone on to murder him in 661. Out of these secessionists came the bands and groups of terrorist insurgents and religious separatists who went under the names of Azraqites, 'Blues', Ṣufrites, 'Yellows' and Ibāḍites, 'Whites', whose common denominator was the call for the best Muslim to be Caliph. In the Maghrib, this had been a call for the various pretenders who had wrecked any unity there may have been in the revolt of the Berbers against the Umayyads, and any hope of a successful revolution, but one that had nevertheless produced the Ibāḍī dynasties at Zawīla and Tāhart in the Fezzan and western Algeria, and a Ṣufrī dynasty at Sijilmāsa in south-eastern Morocco. With the adherence of extensive tribal confederations, these dynasties had grown rich through the development of trans-Saharan trade, and throughout the ninth century represented a major alternative to the Arab empire as a form of Islamic government for the lands and peoples largely beyond the old Roman pale. In fostering the conviction underlying the original revolt, that of the Berbers as superior to the Arabs in the purity of their faith, the Ibāḍites in particular had nevertheless become exclusive, sectarians who cultivated their own school of law in vigorous arguments over the Imāmate of the Rustamid dynasty at Tāhart.[17] The Rustamids together with the Midrarids of Sijilmāsa had both been overthrown by the Dāᶜī in his expedition to fetch the Mahdī from Sijilmāsa; but while this put an end to the Khārijite realm of the previous century, it was only the beginning of the Fatimid attempt to incorporate its peoples into the empire they had in mind.

[17] Cf. E. Savage, *A Gateway to Hell, a Gateway to Paradise. The North African Response to the Arab Conquest* (Princeton, NJ, 1997).

Khārijism, Mahdism and the Umayyads

The teleological focus of the Qāḍī al-Nuᶜmān in the *Iftitāḥ al-daᶜwa*, upon the success of Abū ᶜAbd Allāh in winning the Kutāma for the cause of the Fatimid Mahdī, excludes the prevalence of such revolutionary preaching in North Africa and al-Andalus as well as in the East. Abū Yazīd, when he rose against the Qāᵓim in 940, was heir to the revolt of Berbers against the Umayyad Caliphate at Damascus in the mid-eighth century, which had resulted in the installation of the Ibāḍī Imāmate at Tāhart. Abū Yazīd himself was in denial of that Imāmate as a usurpation of the leadership of the community by a hereditary dynasty, and all the more in revolt against that of the Fatimids. But as the Ṣāḥib al-Ḥimār, or Man on a Donkey, he placed himself in the messianic tradition of the Fatimids themselves. Coming after the appearance of the Fatimid Mahdī, his own messianism was a retort to that of the Fatimids, but one that belonged to a much wider tradition of Mahdism in the Muslim West, one that went back in the first instance to the risings of the ᶜAlids against the ᶜAbbasids in the eighth century. In 789 Idrīs I, brother of the self-proclaimed Mahdī Muḥammad al-Nafs al-Zakiyya, killed by the ᶜAbbasids in 762, was welcomed by the Berbers at Walīla/Volubilis, the former Roman capital of Mauretania Tingitana, only to be assassinated before he could mount his own challenge to the ᶜAbbasids. Ten to twenty years later, however, his son Idrīs II went on to found al-ᶜAliyya, the city of ᶜAlī, on the site of Fes; to issue a coinage with the inscription 'Muḥammad is the Messenger of God and the Mahdī is Idrīs ibn Idrīs'; and probably to style himself Amīr al-Muᵓminīn. Meanwhile on the Atlantic plains of Morocco appeared the Barghawāṭa, a militant Berber community which in the ninth century looked back to its foundation in the eighth by Ṣāliḥ, a self-styled prophet armed with a Berber Qurᵓan. Leaving his son to preserve his doctrine and fight all those who did not accept it, Ṣāliḥ had left for the East with the promise that he would return when the seventh king ascended the throne, having declared himself to be the Great Mahdī who would appear at the end of time to combat the Dajjāl. This was the story of origin behind the claim of his grandson Yūnus, perhaps the real founder of the community in the ninth century, to be a prophet in his own right, with his own Berber scripture. At the beginning of the tenth century Ḥā-Mīm, a second Ṣāliḥ, appeared among the Ghumāra to the south of Tetuan, the most prominent of a variety of such upstarts responding in their own way to the messianic and apocalyptic strain in Islam.

It was the same story in al-Andalus, where the mixture of Muslims, Christians and Jews generated in the literature of all three communities a sense of the apocalypse. With the approach of the millennium in AD 1000, the Mozarabs, or Arabised Christians, produced illustrated commentaries on the Apocalypse of St John. Much earlier, the same sense of impending doom had been focused on the Umayyad dynasty at Cordoba. Founded by the Umayyad prince ᶜAbd al-Raḥmān, who had entered Spain in 755 in flight from the massacre of his kinsfolk by the ᶜAbbasids, by the beginning of the tenth century the state ruled by his successors was on the verge of collapse. In the mountains to the south of Cordoba, the role of his contemporary Abū ᶜAbd Allāh in Ifrīqiya was played by Ibn Ḥafṣūn, a *muwallad*, or Islamised and Arabised but otherwise underprivileged Spaniard. The ascetic al-Sarrāj, 'the Saddler', became his envoy preaching the messianic cause across the peninsula; in the north, he succeeded in inciting the rebellion in 900 of Ibn al-Qiṭṭ, a member of the Umayyad family who claimed to be the Mahdī and announced the coming of the Final Hour. Ibn al-Qiṭṭ was killed in battle with the northern Christians, but Ibn Ḥafṣūn went from strength to strength, contacted by Abū ᶜAbd Allāh as the *qāʾim*, or riser, against the Umayyads. He died in 917, but not until 928 did his fortress of Bobastro fall to ᶜAbd al-Raḥmān III, who after his accession in 912 had gradually restored the power of the Umayyad dynasty. Bobastro was then refortified to serve, much like al-Mahdiyya in retrospect, as a refuge against the coming of the Dajjāl. Just as in Ifrīqiya, however, where the victorious Ismāᶜīl assumed the regnal title of al-Manṣūr, the Victorious, the fall of Bobastro opened the way for ᶜAbd al- Raḥmān to claim for himself the title and role of Amīr al-Muʾminīn, Caliph under the equivalent name of al-Nāṣir, the Conqueror. He claimed it on the basis of God's evident favour, but at the same time as a necessary counter to the pretentions of the Fatimids. As al-Hādī, the True Guide, he was then of a stature to confront his rivals on equal terms as the champion of an alternative, Mālikite Islam, and, equally to the point, to capture Ceuta in 931 and conduct his proxy war with the Fatimids through the Berber tribesmen of North Africa. Mahdism, meanwhile, survived both Umayyads and Fatimids to achieve its greatest triumph in the Maghrib in the twelfth century with the Mahdī of the Almohads, Ibn Tūmart and his Caliph ᶜAbd al-Muʾmin.

Cf. M. Garcia-Arenal, *Messianism and Puritanical Reform. Mahdis of the Muslim West* (Leiden, 2006), Introduction and chs 1, 3 and 6.

The difficulty of the attempt was immediately apparent in 911, when Tāhart revolted. Although it was immediately retaken, the Kutāma governor and the *dāᶜī* appointed by Abū ᶜAbd Allāh to implant the revolution in this capital of a rival Islam were replaced by a tribal chieftain of the region, Maṣāla ibn Ḥabūs. While the Khārijite community in the city emigrated into the Sahara to carry on its commerce in the oasis of Sadrāta, this very different appointment aimed to recruit to the Fatimid cause the warrior nomads whose tribes had clustered around the Rustamids at Tāhart and cooperated with them in their long-distance trade. The recruitment of these nomads was the most immediate way to advance that cause, harnessing their energies for a drive to the west that matched the drive to the east. But the tribes that passed under the name of the Zanāta were divided among themselves. As a chieftain of the Miknāsa to the west of Tāhart, Maṣāla was an obvious choice to spearhead that drive westwards through Tlemcen into northern Morocco; but it pitted him, and the Fatimids, against Muḥammad ibn Khazar, a chieftain of the Maghrāwa in the region of Tāhart itself. Ibn Khazar had been instrumental in the revolt of Tāhart, and been obliged to submit, but remained a latent opponent astride the vital route out of Ifrīqiya. Some ten years later, the conflict became open. In 921–3 northern Morocco was overrun by Maṣāla, and Sijilmāsa retaken from its Midrarid dynasty. The Idrisids, the Ḥasanid princes who had colonised the old Roman Mauretania Tingitana since the arrival of their founder as a refugee from the ᶜAbbasids at the end of the eighth century, were evicted from their capital Fes, and their land of little city states[18] placed under the overlordship of Mūsā ibn Abīᵓl-ᶜĀfiya, a cousin of Masāla. But the prospect of a powerful Fatimid viceroy ruling the west from Tāhart ended in 924 with the death of Maṣāla at the hands of Ibn Khazar.

To restore the situation, a major operation was called for, whose outcome was a change of strategy in the context of a radical change in the strategic position in the Muslim West. In 927–8 the Maghrāwa felt the full force of the Mahdī's formidable military machine: Kutāma Berbers, Whites and Blacks, cavalry and infantry, all under the command of the Qāᵓim. It was an expedition bent not only on the subjugation of the nomads, but on the westward extension of Ifrīqiya through the conquest of the hill country north and south of the route to Ṭāhart. In this it was successful: the route was secured with the foundation of Masīla (M'sila) in place of Tubna as the capital of the Zāb, some fifty miles further to the west. With the appointment of ᶜAlī ibn Ḥamdūn al-Andalūsī, a stalwart of the cause since the days of the Dāᶜī, it became the headquarters of a powerful provincial dynasty in command of the western frontier.[19] It did not, however, achieve its aim

18 Cf. M. Brett, 'The Islamisation of Morocco from the Arabs to the Almoravids', in *Ibn Khaldun and the Medieval Maghrib*, no. I.

19 Cf. M. Canard, 'Une famille de partisans, puis d'adversaires, des Fatimides en Afrique du

of eliminating Ibn Khazar, who remained at large. Tāhart continued to be held for the Fatimids by Maṣāla's brother and eventually his nephew; but still further west the inclusion of northern Morocco within the empire of the Mahdī was blocked by the intervention of Cordoba. The Mahdī had come to power in Ifrīqiya at a low point in the fortunes of the Umayyad dynasty in Spain; discontent within al-Andalus, coupled with invasions by the Christians to the north, had reduced the sway of the Amirate to little more than Cordoba itself. But even as the Mahdī was building his empire in Ifrīqiya, the Umayyad Amīr ᶜAbd al-Raḥmān III was steadily bringing the country back under his control, until in 929 he proclaimed himself Caliph with the title of al-Nāṣir, 'the Victorious'. The challenge was not so much to the ᶜAbbasids as to the Fatimids, in a contest for supremacy in the western Mediterranean. In 931 he took Ceuta to establish a bridgehead across the Straits, while Mūsā ibn Abīᵓl-ᶜĀfiya, the Mahdī's lieutenant in northern Morocco, went over to his side. For tribal allies in the west, the Fatimids turned instead to the Talkāta, a hill people like the Kutāma in the Titteri range to the south of Algiers. In 936 their chieftain Zīrī ibn Manād was helped by the Qāᵓim to build the citadel of Ashīr, a mountain stronghold that not only commanded the route from Masīla to Tāhart, but the way to the sea down the valley of the Cheliff.[20] Overlooking the pastures of the Maghrāwa, it secured the extension of Fatimid power as far as Tāhart, while setting the scene for endless frontier warfare on behalf of the two empires between the Zanāta and the Ṣanhāja, that other Berber race to which the Talkāta were reckoned to belong. Punctuated from time to time by triumphant but ephemeral Fatimid sorties into northern Morocco, that warfare continued for the rest of the century to mark the boundary of Fatimid imperialism in the west.

The Vanishing of the ᶜAbbasid Empire

In 936, the Qāᵓim was two years into his reign as successor to the Mahdī. At his death in 934, Abū Muḥammad ᶜAbd Allāh, al-Mahdī biᵓllāh, guided by the grace of God, had failed to follow in the footsteps of the ᶜAbbasids in 750, winning for himself the universal empire for which he had arisen as the sun of God in the west. By dint of ceaseless aggression, he had nevertheless created a formidable empire of his own by land and sea in the central

Nord', in G. Marçais, *Mélanges d'histoire et d'archéologie de l'Occident musulman*, 2 vols (Algiers, 1957), vol. II, pp. 33–49.

20 For Zīrī and the dynasty he founded, see H. R. Idris, *La Berbérie orientale sous les Zīrīdes. Xe–XIIe siècles*, 2 vols (Paris, 1962); for Ashīr, cf. M. Brett, 'Ashīr', *Encyclopaedia of Islam*, 3rd edn.

Mediterranean, stretching over some 1,300 miles from Tāhart to Barqa in Cyrenaica, and across the Malta channel to Sicily. If this was driven by the conviction of his destiny, the ideology that sustained that conviction was yet to be settled. As the Mahdī, ʿAbd Allāh had struggled to shake off the apocalyptic expectations of the revolution that had brought him to power, proclaiming instead the birthright of the descendants of the Prophet to the government of Islam. The notion of a Bāṭin, or final revelation, concealed beneath the surface of the Ẓāhir, or open doctrine of the Islamic law, had correspondingly become the doctrine of the Imāmate, of the divine understanding possessed by the one person in each generation appointed to maintain the continuity of God's message to the world. That in turn conferred on the Imām of the time the title to the Caliphate, which had finally been claimed by the Mahdī for himself and his line. The proof as distinct from the proclamation of that title lay in its vindication by the successful achievement of universal empire. While the revolution in Ifrīqiya had made a dramatic start, the failure to conquer Egypt had necessitated an apology in the shape of a deferral of the dynasty's destiny, to await its accomplishment by an eventual successor. That successor should have been the Mahdī's son, the Qāʾim, the one who bore the name of the Prophet, Muḥammad ibn ʿAbd Allāh, as required in the messianic tradition. Not only, however, did he fail, as Imām and Caliph, to rise to the challenge; his reign ended in disaster.

The failure is perhaps to be traced to his *kunya*, the name by which he is commonly called prior to his accession, Abūʾl-Qāsim, 'Father of (his eldest son) Qāsim'. Qāsim himself, however, appears only twice in the record, once to the effect that he had written to his father on campaign in the west in 927–8, to say that the Mahdī was about to proclaim one of his other sons as heir; the news would have caused the father to break off the pursuit of Muḥammad ibn Khazar and return to al-Mahdiyya. Much later, the Qāʾim's grandson, al-Muʿizz, declared that the accursed Qāsim was the cause of all the (unspecified) trouble within the family. Whatever the truth, the Qāʾim's son has otherwise disappeared, never to be proclaimed heir, as might have been expected, with the title of Wālī ʿAhd al-Muslimīn. Whatever his fate, the elimination of a favourite son from the succession may explain the transformation of the militant Sword of the Imām into the reclusive Caliph who, after his accession, never left his palace, and certainly never publicly proclaimed a successor. He was supposedly in perpetual mourning for the Mahdī; the effect, however, was to lose the initiative of the revolution at home and abroad at a time when the world around was changing.[21]

[21] Cf. Brett, *Rise of the Fatimids*, pp. 163–4.

In 908, as the Dāʿī prepared for his final assault upon Qayrawān, the ʿAbbasid empire entered what proved to be the last phase of its existence as a state. The death in that year of the last of the strong monarchs who had over the previous thirty years defeated the Zanj and recovered Egypt and Syria from the Tulunids was followed by the accession of one who left the government to the Men of the Pen. These, the secretaries of state, were divided into rival factions, and were themselves reliant upon the army under the command of Muʾnis al-Muẓaffar, the commander-in-chief who had repulsed the attempted conquest of Egypt by the Qāʾim in 914 and 919–21. The crisis developed in the 920s, when a corrupt and impoverished regime faced the invasions of Iraq by the Carmathians of Baḥrayn, who in 930 notoriously carried off the sacred Black Stone from the Kaaba at Mecca. If the threat of the Carmathians was not as serious as that of the Zanj, it nevertheless precipitated a struggle for power that culminated in 936 in the takeover of a bankrupt state by Ibn Rāʾiq, a military commander at the head of a fresh army. But he in turn was only the first of several to compete for control, until the competition came to an end in 945, and the empire was partitioned between the Shīʿite Buyids or Buwayhids, a dynasty from the mountains of Daylam to the south of the Caspian, who annexed Baghdad to their dominions in western Iran; the Arab Ḥamdanids at Mosul and Aleppo in northern Iraq and Syria; and the Turkish Ikhshīdids in Egypt and central and southern Syria. The ʿAbbasid Caliph became a ruler in name only under the protection of the Būyids, his sole function to confer the authority of the Caliphate upon these usurpers of his power.

None of this turned to the immediate advantage of the Fatimids. Baghdad passed into the hands of the Būyids at a time when al-Mahdiyya itself was in the throes of a crippling rebellion, the victim of a second wave of messianic fervour that threatened to do away with the Mahdī's dynasty in the same way that the first had abolished the Aghlabids. That the dynasty should find itself in such a predicament was a measure of the distance travelled by the regime away from the apocalyptic expectations of the revolution that had brought it to power. Despite the efforts of the Mahdī to present himself as the founder of a dynasty rather than the instrument of some final revelation, those expectations had not died away, and resurfaced at his death in the brief appearance at Tripoli of a new messiah, Muḥammad ibn Ṭālūt. Under the Qāʾim such messianism persisted in opposition to a monarchy remote in its coastal fortress, without the panache to justify its taxation. The reign began with a second major expedition of the Fatimid forces under their Slavonic generals into northern Morocco in 935, a show of strength to be followed in 936 by the foundation of Ashīr as the answer to challenge of Cordoba. But those were the years in which the disarray of Baghdad had left Egypt to the squabbles of its factious soldiery: the Mashāriqa, or Turkish Easterners, and the Maghāriba, or Westerners, probably Berbers and possibly Blacks. When the Mashāriqa under a newly arrived Turkish governor, Muḥammad ibn Ṭughj, defeated the Maghāriba, these retreated to Barqa to appeal to al-Mahdiyya. In 936 the Qā᾽im sent troops for an expedition that once again briefly occupied Alexandria before withdrawing. It was a venture that certainly demonstrated the continued vitality of Fatimid designs upon the country as a gateway to the East. But as an opportunistic intervention in the affairs of Egypt, it cannot be compared with the determined invasions of 914 and 919–21. It was moreover followed in 937 by a major revolt of the Ifrīqiyan colony in Sicily on the part of a quarrelsome population of different origins united by opposition to direct rule from across the water. As a war for independence, or at least a measure of self-government, it exposed the whole problem of empire at a time when all over the Mediterranean and Europe, local populations were growing up to manage their own affairs. The revolt was only put down in 941 after four years of destructive warfare that saw a spate of refugees in Byzantine territory.[22]

The Man on a Donkey

Ideology may have been absent from the Sicilian revolt, but infused a far more dangerous opposition on the mainland. On the southern borders of Ifrīqiya, the Khārijite Berber population of the oases of the Djerid and the hills of the Jabal Nafūsa had lost their Rustamid Imām with the fall of Tāhart, but neither their faith nor their commercial livelihood. Strengthened by the foundation of Sadrāta in the desert by the refugees from Tāhart, they had continued to trade across the Sahara with the Bilād al-Sūdān, or Land of the Blacks. Meanwhile, they had continued to live under their own version of the law, taught by their own shaykhs, at odds with the doctrine of the Mālikite schoolmen of Qayrawān, and most certainly with the pretensions of the Fatimids to the Imāmate and Caliphate. That opposition was particularly acute in the case of the Nukkārī-s, a sect within a sect that had opposed the hereditary claims of Rustamids to the Imāmate in favour of the election of the Imām. A product of this lively sectarian society, Abū Yazīd Makhlad ibn Kaydad is said to have been born of a black slave mother to a merchant father at Tādmakka on the far side of the desert, whence his soubriquet of Black Ethiop, al-Ḥabashī al-Aswad. But as a follower of the blind seer Abū ᶜAmmār, he became in his fifties an outspoken teacher and preacher in the Djerid, falling foul of the Fatimid authorities. Rescued from prison,

[22] Cf. A. Metcalfe, *The Muslims of Medieval Italy* (Edinburgh, 2009), pp. 49–53.

in 937 he retreated into the Aures massif to preach a holy war to the mountain tribes of the Hawwāra, as Abū ᶜAbd Allāh had done to the Kutāma. Denounced in the subsequent tradition of his fellow Ibāḍī-s as an enemy of God, he nevertheless assumed the title of Shaykh al-Muslimīn, or Patriarch of the Muslims. Over the next seven years he formed the tribesmen into a horde that in 944 came down from the hills to sweep all before them on the road to Qayrawān. Riding on a donkey, in true messianic fashion, with the soubriquet of Ṣāḥib al-Ḥimār, or Lord of the Donkey, he appealed to his followers on the strength of the old Khārijite doctrine, which in the East was ascribed to the Carmathians, that the lives, property and womenfolk of other Muslims were forfeit to the true believers. By October he was at Qayrawān, where he executed the Fatimid commander and the Fatimid Qāḍī, and killed in battle the Slavonic general Maysūr al-Fatā at the head of the relieving army. Accepted by the Mālikite jurists of the city as their leader in the holy war upon 'the Imām of the Unbelievers', he exchanged the rags of an ascetic for the robes of royalty, and the donkey for a horse, while gold coins were struck in his name. Leaving his old master Abū ᶜAmmār to rule at Qayrawān, and appointing his four sons provincial governors, he and his swollen horde laid siege to al-Mahdiyya in January 945.[23]

Al-Mahdiyya, however, proved to be impregnable; the isolation of the Qāᵓim turned out to be his salvation. His alleged confidence in his foreknowledge of Abū Yazīd's failure was justified when a disappointed army of besiegers began to melt away from its core of Hawwāra faithful. In the hope of bringing the Andalusian fleet to complete the blockade, Abū Yazīd had sent to Cordoba to offer his submission to the Umayyad Caliph, but too late for it to sail that year. The siege was finally lifted in September, when Abū Yazīd fell back on Qayrawān to revert to his rags and his donkey. Still in control of the heart of Ifrīqiya, despite revolts at Tunis and elsewhere and the advance of ᶜAlī ibn Ḥamdūn from Masīla in the west, he returned to the offensive in January 946, laying siege to Sousse, the one city to have succeeded in breaking away from his dominion. But once again he was thwarted, by the Aghlabid fortifications of this old naval base for the conquest of Sicily, and the siege dragged on until it was broken in May by a concerted attack, by land and sea, from al-Mahdiyya some forty miles down the coast. At the news, Qayrawān rose against Abū ᶜAmmār, forcing Abū Yazīd to take up his position outside the city to await the Fatimid riposte. It proved to be the beginning of the end.

[23] For the detail of the campaign, see Halm, *The Empire of the Mahdi*, pp. 298–325; more briefly, Brett, *Rise of the Fatimids*, pp. 165–70.

That the tables had turned in this way was entirely because of the death of the Qāʾim a week before the expedition to Sousse, and the accession of his son. In his Memoirs, Ismāʿīl's right-hand man, the Slavonic eunuch Jawdhar, claimed that Ismāʿīl's designation by his father as his heir had been a secret entrusted only to him by the Qāʾim, which was to be made public only at his death. This would certainly be in accord with the theory of Imāmate, passed by such designation from father to son, and as such is accepted by Paul Walker as the first recorded instance of the practice after the exceptional case of the Qāʾim, the Mahdī under another name.[24] But given the murky fate of Qāsim, the Qāʾim's firstborn and natural successor, the story looks suspiciously like a fabrication to legitimise a palace coup effected by Jawdhar on behalf of his master, one that left all his uncles and brothers under arrest. Whatever the truth, the succession certainly went to the right man for the job, one who instantly went on to the offensive as his father had once done in his capacity as Walī ʿAhd al-Muslimīn and Sword of the Imām, to the extent of addressing the news of his victory at Qayrawān to his dead father at al-Mahdiyya. The victory that he won outside the city in June 946 he won on the battlefield, riding beneath the parasol that betokened the presence of God's appointed, and wielding the sword of his ancestor ʿAlī, the legendary Dhūʾl-Fiqār, God's proof of the dynasty to the world. The final breakthrough came in August, when Abū Yazīd was finally driven away westwards. From the October through to August 947, he was pursued by Ismāʿīl in person, in flight through the Djerid and the Saharan Atlas to a final refuge in the mountains to the north of the Zāb. Besieged for three months in the Qalʿa Kiyāna, he died of his wounds after the fortress was stormed. While still live, he was reproached for his error by the victor; after his death, the corpse was flayed, the skin stuffed and the grisly trophy paraded in mock finery through Qayrawān and al-Mahdiyya. Thus triumphant, Ismāʿīl finally assumed the Caliphate under the title of al-Manṣūr, the Victorious.

24 P. E. Walker, 'Succession to rule in the Shiite caliphate', *Journal of the American Research Center in Egypt*, 32, 1995, 239–64, reprinted in his *Fatimid History and Ismaili Doctrine*, Variorum Series (Aldershot, 2008), no II.

3

The Conquest of Egypt

The Relaunch of the Dynasty

In life, Abū Yazīd had brought the Mahdī's dynasty to the brink of destruction; in death he was a godsend, in both senses of the word. He had not only delivered the dynasty from the fading charisma of the Qā᾽im, and created the opportunity for it to begin its career all over again. For the purpose of that resurrection, he was cast in the role of the Dajjāl, the Antichrist destined to conquer the world before the final triumph of the Mahdī. In the flowering of literature to which that resurrection gave birth, the history of the dynasty was written around this apocalyptic event, which, like the failure to conquer Egypt, had been foreseen by both the Mahdī and the Qā᾽im in their supernatural wisdom. Al-Mahdiyya, said the Qādī al-Nuᶜmān in his *Iftitāh*, had been built as a refuge for the dynasty from the great enemy, and a citadel from which the whole world would then be conquered. As propaganda for the cause, it scarcely mattered that the lesser apocalypse, the *Zuhur*, or appearance, of the Fatimids in the here and now, had been conflated with the greater apocalypse at the end of the world, an identification that the Mahdī himself had been anxious to disclaim. What did matter was that the appearance of the new sovereign with the title of al-Manṣūr bi-Naṣr Allāh, The Victorious, or The Conqueror, with the Help of God, could be represented as the dynasty's second and final *zuhur* after its passage through this second eclipse.[1] What remained to be seen was the success of this representation in giving fresh credence to the dynasty as it renewed its bid for the hegemony of Islam. The success of that bid, however, was crucially dependent upon the policies pursued by the new regime to win the acceptance of the Muslim world not only by persuasion, but through the deeds that would demonstrate in practice the validity of its claim. Two sides of the same coin, both lines of attack were vigorously followed up by al-Mansūr and his son and successor al-Muᶜizz.

[1] Cf. Brett, *Rise of the Fatimids*, pp. 170–5.

They began with the victory itself, a triumph in the eyes of the world whose significance as a proof of God's favour was spelled out in the panegyric of Aḥmad al-Marwarrūdhī, the son of the former Qādī of Qayrawān Muḥammad al-Marwarrūdhī, executed in 916.[2] His eyewitness account, as the Qāḍī of Ismāᶜīl's army, began the efflorescence of writing that over the next thirty years created the canon of Fatimid doctrinal literature, setting out the doctrine of the Imāmate and exemplifying its operation in narratives of the doings and sayings of the Imām-Caliphs.[3] In that canon, it served the particular purpose of validating the succession of Ismāᶜīl to the Imāmate in the absence of any public endorsement by his father: al-Marwarrūdhī himself becomes the crucial witness who recognises the light of prophecy in his master when Ismāᶜīl drops a spear and compares it to the staff thrown down by Moses to confound the wizards of Pharaoh.[4] By contrast, in a letter written by him to the eunuch Jawdhar, the agent of his accession at al-Mahdiyya, those male relatives under house arrest in the fortress city were described as monkeys and pigs, a Qur'ānic transformation visited upon those who deviated from the true faith. Whatever discord had been sown in the family by the wretched Qāsim was thus physically suppressed, leaving the conqueror of the Dajjāl to appear in public as the undoubted successor to the Mahdī-Qā'im and undisputed head of state. Thus vindicated, under his new title of al-Mansūr, Ismāᶜīl could begin the dual task of cultivating rather than simply inviting the recognition of his dynasty by the Mālikite jurists of Qayrawān as a first step towards universal acceptance of his overlordship of Islam, while resuming the conquest of empire that would make that acceptance good.

As a symbol of his triumph, he founded a new palace city outside Qayrawān, to which he transferred his residence from al-Mahdiyya. Its name, al-Ṣabra al-Manṣūriyya, 'Victorious Endurance', epitomised not only his personal triumph, but the resolution that had enabled the dynasty to survive and the quality that would ensure its permanence. As a great public work, meanwhile, it was more than a dramatic reversal of past policy and a statement of confidence in the new era. The return of the dynasty to the metropolis after its removal to al-Mahdiyya was a powerful gesture to its citizens, one that in material terms meant an access of prosperity with the employment generated by the construction of the new city, and the expenditure of a wealthy court. Its conspicuous consumption was on display in its ritual pomp and ceremony,

[2] Al-Marwarrūdhī is the most probable author of the otherwise anonymous eyewitness account of Ismāᶜīl's campaign: cf. Halm, *The Empire of the Mahdī*, pp. 313, 320.

[3] Cf. Brett, *Rise of the Fatimids*, pp. 176–7.

[4] Ibid., pp. 177–8.

Figure 3.1 Painted drawing of the marble relief of the Imām-Caliph with flute player from al-Manṣūriyya in Bardo Museum, Tunis. © Michael Brett.

The carving from the palace city of the Fatimids outside Qayrawān shows the Caliph in regal posture, wearing the three-peaked bonnet crown, holding a drinking vessel and clad in a robe with bands of *ṭirāz* embroidery on the sleeves. He is attended by a musician, evidence of the importance of music in the daily life of the court.

when the Imām-Caliph rode out under the parasol that proclaimed his majesty. So conspicuously neglected by the Qāʾim, its round of theatrical performance was vital to the public perception of the monarch as Commander of the Faithful, the leader of the community (see Fig. 3.1). What amounted in these ways to a colossal bribe was meanwhile matched by a major concession, the appointment of a Mālikite as Qāḍī of Qayrawān alongside the Fatimid Qāḍī of Ifrīqiya installed in the palace of al-Manṣūriyya. Something like the old harmony between dynasty and city, which had been cultivated in much the same way by the Aghlabids in the middle of the previous century, was thereby restored. The iron fist in this velvet glove was the surveillance of a city so recently in revolt, made possible by the close proximity of the head of state. The rapprochement of prince and people in the capital of the empire, however, was not simply a matter of expediency. Almost literally, it laid the foundations of a policy of government for the whole of the Islamic world in the empire-to-be.

In the provinces of the empire that was, it was a question of suppressing the lawlessness following the breakdown of the state in the great rebellion. While the sons of Abū Yazīd were hunted down, the shape which that empire had begun to take under the Qā'im was completed with the confirmation of Zīrī ibn Manād at Ashīr and Ja'far son of 'Alī ibn Ḥamdūn at Masīla as viceroys of the western marches, and a final settlement of the Sicilian problem. In 948 the third strong man of the dynasty, the Arab Ḥasan al-Kalbī, governor of Tunis, was sent to suppress yet another revolt at Palermo, and recover from the Byzantines the tribute that they had ceased to pay as Danegeld for the cessation of piratical raids. No sooner was this done, however, than the Byzantines entered into an alliance with Cordoba, one that incidentally led to the Byzantine mosaics which are the splendour of the mihrab of the Great Mosque of Cordoba. As the Andalusians took possession of Tangier as well as Ceuta, and the Greeks built up their forces in Calabria, the threat of war on two fronts was averted by Ḥasan's pre-emptive crossing of the Straits of Messina, to win a victory which obliged Byzantium to make peace in 952. Hasan himself remained in Sicily as its viceroy, repeating in effect the achievement of his master at Qayrawān in creating a monarchy for the island, round which a restive population could be rallied. But that was in 953 on the eve of the death of al-Manṣūr, a sick man who was obliged to leave the realisation of his design to his young son and successor Ma'add, with the title of al-Mu'izz li-Dīn Allāh, 'Mighty for the Religion of God'.

The Formulation of the Law

The regnal title was a declaration that the new Imām-Caliph was the supreme defender of the faith on behalf of all Muslims. As such, it was a declaration in keeping with the new tolerance of the differing schools. As far as his title to this Imāmate and Caliphate was concerned, however, the question of the succession, which the Qā'im had left mired in controversy, was still not settled according to rule. Although the youthful Ma'add had accompanied his father as the ostensible heir, at al-Manṣūr's death he relied upon the indispensable Jawdhar to keep his relatives imprisoned in al-Mahdiyya while he himself followed his father's example in keeping the death secret. Instead, like his father before him, he went on campaign as the Sword of the Imām, in his case a token gesture that took him only as far as the outpost of Laribus on the route to the west, before handing over command of the expedition into the Aures mountains to Buluggīn ibn Zīrī, son of the lord of Ashīr. It nevertheless qualified him on his return to announce the death of his father and reveal himself as the new sovereign. With this third, symbolic instance of the waging of war by the ruler-to-be, the precedent set by the Qā'im on his Egyptian campaigns was well on the way to becoming a necessary qualification for the succession, the proof by which the rightful heir was known. As Sword of the Imām, however, the Qāʾim had enjoyed the formal designation by the Mahdī as Walī ᶜAhd al-Muslimīn, a designation that he himself had failed to confer on any of his sons. It was an omission rectified in the literature composed in the course of this new age, most notably by the Qādī al-Nuᶜmān, the principal author in whose works the subsequent doctrine of the dynasty is grounded. In his *al-Urjūza al-mukhtāra*, or Favourite Poem, in defence of the dynasty's claim to the Imāmate he employs a variety of expressions for the appointment of ᶜAlī as the Prophet's successor, and still more in the *Iftitāḥ* to describe in general rather than specific terms the designation of al-Muᶜizz by his father. Among them, however, one in particular stands out in the *Urjūza*, where the Qāʾim is said to have been designated by the Mahdī, not as Walī ᶜAhd al-Muslimīn, but as *walī ᶜahdihi*, or keeper of his, the Mahdī's, covenant, in a phrase that recalls the ᶜAbbasid term Walī ʾl-ᶜAhd for the appointed heir. As employed by al-Nuᶜmān, however, it refers not merely to the choice of an heir, but to the charge that is laid upon the heir appointed by the incumbent Imām to maintain the sacred office entrusted by the first Muḥammad to ᶜAlī, the first of the line. Recurring elsewhere in the literature, not least in the conflicting reports of the designation of Ismāᶜīl by the Qāʾim, the phrase invests the succession to the Imāmate with the formality required of such a crucial event, however it may have come about in practice. In the circumstances surrounding the accession of al-Muᶜizz, it is nevertheless overridden in the *Iftitāḥ*, where the *ᶜahd* in question becomes a charge conferred directly by God upon the new Imām. Just as it was for al-Manṣūr in the account of al-Marwarrūdhī, so for in the account of the Qāḍī al-Nuᶜmān: the divine choice is apparent in the amazing ease with which his young master has taken charge of both Daᶜwa and Dawla, the mission and the empire.[5]

However easily he may have done so, there is no doubt that on both counts, al-Muᶜizz was the monarch who oversaw the systematic reformulation of the dynasty's messianism as a scriptural creed, and refounded the state with the conquest of Egypt and its occupation as the seat of the dynasty for the next 200 years. The creed itself was divided as before into the Ẓāhir and the Bāṭin, the open and the hidden sense of the Daᶜwa, the appeal of the Imām. But the hazy promise of a new and final law brought out of concealment by a second Muḥammad, which the Mahdī had been at pains to reject, was now conclusively superseded by a doctrine of the law of the Prophet, validated from generation to generation by what might be called the apostolic succession of Imāms of the line of ᶜAlī. The formulation of this legal creed as the

[5] Ibid., pp. 180–4.

Ẓāhir, or open doctrine of the dynasty, was of a piece with the toleration of the Mālikite version of the law through the appointment of a Mālikite Qādī at Qayrawān – a coming to terms with the great achievement of the past 300 years, the elaboration and validation of the law of Islam by what might be called the rabbinical succession of innumerable scholars in their traditional schools. Necessary as such an accommodation may have been to establish the credentials of the dynasty in its drive to assume the headship of the community, it was quite impossible for such a gigantic task to be performed all over again by the Fatimid Imām and his adherents. But it was certainly possible to rebrand the result of previous scholarship on the authority of the Imām, stamped by certain distinctive rulings that proclaimed its source, to produce a definitive statement of the dynasty's position. That task was performed for al-Muᶜizz by his Chief Qādī at al-Manṣūriyya, Abū Ḥanīfa al-Nuᶜmān ibn Muḥammad, invariably known as the Qāḍī al-Nuᶜmān, in his *Daᶜāʾim al-Islam*, or *Pillars of Islam*, the centrepiece of an *oeuvre* that formed the canonical basis of the Fatimid creed.[6]

The Doctrine of the Law

By the ninth century the law of Islam had taken shape as the Law of God, covering in its divine perfection every aspect of human behaviour. Revealed to humanity in the Qurʾan and the sayings and doings of His Prophet, his Sunna, or Custom, it was interpreted as best they could by the followers of the various schools, whose traditional doctrines went under the name of a founding father. Of these by the end of the century there were four: Mālikī, Ḥanafī, Shāfiᶜī and Ḥanbalī; the Jaᶜfarī school of the Twelver Shīᶜites was still in the process of formation on the authority of traditions from the first six Imāms. This scholarly law had escaped definition by the Umayyad and ᶜAbbasid Caliphates; the latter's claim to doctrinal authority had ended in the middle of the century with its failure to impose the doctrine of the created as distinct from the uncreated Qurʾan. Failing such authority, the responsibility of the monarch for the law came down to its administration, by the Qāḍī or by himself in consultation with the jurists. The task for the Fatimids in the following century was then to stamp their own authority on this growing body of law which they had not formulated but which they claimed to authorise in their wisdom as successors to the

6 Al-Qādī al-Nuᶜmān, *Daᶜāʾim al-Islam*, ed. A. A. A. Fyzee, 2 vols (Cairo, 1951). For his extensive *oeuvre*, see S. A. Hamdani, *Between Revolution and State. The Path to Fatimid Statehood* (London and New York, 2006).

Prophet. It was a task accomplished in the reign of al-Muᶜizz by the Qāḍī al-Nuᶜmān in collusion with his sovereign.

Al-Nuᶜmān was an Ifrīqiyan jurist won for the Fatimid cause, who compiled a vast collection of traditions from Muḥammad and the first six Shīᶜite Imāms as the scholarly basis for a Fatimid version of the law. His *Īḍāḥ*, or Exposition, however, is largely lost, and never gave rise to a Fatimid school of law to match the others. Instead, the Fatimid doctrine of the law was spelt out in his *Daᶜāᵓim al-Islām*, or *Pillars of Islam*, a relatively short work whose longest section offers a proof of the Imāmate as the sole authority for the Law of God. By definition this was single, the different doctrines of the various schools were *ipso facto* false and only the version in the following chapters, which al-Muᶜizz himself had authenticated, was true. To the usual five pillars of faith, prayer, *zakat*, or alms tax, fasting and pilgrimage were added ritual purity and *jihād* to make them up to the sacred number seven, while faith, *īmān*, has become *walāya*, devotion and submission to the Imām of the time – a confirmation of the distinction between the *muᵓminūn*, the truly faithful, and the *muslimūn*, those who had only submitted to God. The call to prayer included the Shīᶜite formula '*Hayy 'alā khayr al-ᶜamal*' ('Come to the better work'); the number of required prostrations was changed; and the beginning and ending of the fast of Ramadan depended on astronomical calculation rather than the sighting of the new moon – stipulations that required the worshipper to acknowledge the pre-eminence of the Imām-Caliph. From these seven primary obligations stemmed the more detailed account of the law, one that was notably different from the works of the schools, in that the approval given by the Imām dispensed with the apparatus of quotations required to justify their conclusions. On the other hand, its prescriptions themselves were for the most part those of the schools, with a preference for Shīᶜite rulings and only a few novelties, for example in the matter of female inheritance, reflecting the status of Fāṭima in the ancestry of the dynasty. There was, in other words, no alternative for the Fatimids to giving their approval for the Sharīᶜa, the law as it had evolved over the past 300 years. As to its application by the dynasty, there was some attempt to insist that *qāḍī*-s of whatever school ruled in accordance with its particular stipulations, while in response to a request from the Yemen, al-Ḥākim referred the questioner to the *Daᶜāᵓim*. But there was no further development or elaboration of its points of law; nor was there any systematic collection of the rulings based upon it by, in the first instance, the descendants of al-Nuᶜmān who succeeded him as Qāḍī to the dynasty down to the middle of the eleventh century. As an exposition of the law, the *Daᶜāᵓim* remained *sui generis*.

Cf. Brett, *Rise of the Fatimids*, pp. 187–95.

Al-Nuᶜmān himself was the son of one of those scholars who had rallied to the Mahdī on his arrival, like the younger al-Marwarrūdhī a member of the second generation of these adherents, and by far the most outstanding. Having made his career in the dynasty's service, he now brought to fruition the task that the Mahdī had set their côterie, of presenting to the world a credible doctrine of the Imāmate as the authority for the Sharīᶜa, the law of Islam. The *Daᶜāʾim* itself had been long in preparation; already in the time of the Mahdī al-Nuᶜmān had made an immense collection of legal *ḥadīth*, or traditions, ascribed to the Prophet and his family down to Jaᶜfar al-Sādiq, the Sixth Imām, in his *Kitāb al-Īdāh*, or Book of Exposition. Drawn from the common stock of Shīᶜite scripture, such traditions equally contributed to the jurisprudence of an emerging Twelver Shīᶜite school of law in Iraq, variously called the Jaᶜfarī or Imāmī; for al-Nuᶜmān, they were materials towards the formation of a Fatimid equivalent. In a series of shortened versions of the *Īdāḥ* composed over the next twenty-five years, he came close to doing just that in a work simply entitled *Kitāb al-Ikhtisār*, The Abridgement (of the authentic legacy of the Imāms of old). Dating from the reign of al-Muᶜizz, this was the immediate predecessor of the *Daᶜāʾim*, the work in which his efforts culminated around the year 960.[7] Written at the behest of al-Muᶜizz, and approved by him at every step in its composition, it stakes its claim to distinction in the Pillars of the title. With the addition of ritual purity and holy war to the usual five – the profession of faith, prayer, almsgiving, fasting and pilgrimage – these are now seven, the number of the Prophets and Imāms in the dynasty's history of divine revelation. The outcome of that history is then spelled out in the profession of faith, the first of the Pillars, in which belief in the Imām is added to the requisite belief in God and His Messenger.[8] So important is this belief that *īmān*, faith, becomes *walāya*, devotion to the Imām of the time and obedience to his *wilāya*, his power and authority. Only those who make this equation are truly *Muᶜmin* as well as *muslim*, faithful as well as submitted to God. All are nevertheless required to conform in public to the signature prescriptions of the dynasty for prayer and fasting, beginning with the Shīᶜite call to prayer, 'Come to the better work', altering the usual number of prostrations, commencing and ending the fast of Ramadan by astronomical calculation rather than sighting of the new moon, and inserting a controversial request for divine aid against the opponents of the Imām.

What is then surprising is the meagre treatment of all the other subjects

[7] Cf. I. K. Poonawala, 'Al-Qādī al-Nuʿmān and Ismaᶜili jurisprudence', in F. Daftary (ed.), *Medieval Ismaᶜili History and Thought* (Cambridge, 1996), pp. 117–43.

[8] *The Book of Faith*: *Daᶜāʾim al-Islam*, section on Imāmate, trans. A. A. A. Fyzee (Bombay, 1974).

covered by the law, which by this time offered a comprehensive prescription for every human activity, from the highest to the lowest, from the worship of God to elementary hygiene. What is so briefly set out in the *Daᶜāʾim* is a range of stipulations drawn with little variation from those of the traditional schools. The differences between these schools over a law of God that was single by definition were held up as proof of their inadequacy by contrast with the unique knowledge possessed by the Imām. Despite its claim to authenticity, however, the account of that knowledge offered by the Qādī al-Nuᶜmān was yet another version of the rules and regulations worked out by the schoolmen over the previous centuries in their effort to infer the heavenly perfection of the divine original from the evidence of the Qurʾān and Traditions of the Prophet. In this it was comparable to the *Risāla* of Ibn Abī Zayd, a summary of Mālikite doctrine composed in Ifrīqiya at the end of the century.[9] Where they differed was in their application. The *Risāla* was a practical introduction to an ongoing corpus of case law composed of the opinions or *fatwa*-s offered by *muftī*-s or jurists of recognised authority, and the judgements of *qādī*-s in their courts, such as are represented in monumental collections like the *Miᶜyār al-muʾrib* of the sixteenth-century al-Wansharīshī.[10] It was a contribution, in other words, to the practice of law in the community, a practice that was beginning to take the same shape in the Jaᶜfarī school of Twelver Shīᶜism. The *Daᶜāʾim*, on the other hand, may have summarised a previous history of lawgiving by the Mahdī and his successors, but never gave rise to a comparable school with a comparable literature. The reason was the Imām, whose absence in Twelver Shīᶜism necessitated the appearance of jurists to act in his name, but whose presence for al-Nuᶜmān and his successors precluded any reference to any other authority. Since it was clearly impossible to refer to the Imām at every turn, the Fatimid *qādī* presumably exercised his own judgement; but whatever his rulings, they were not recorded. The bulk of the *Īdāh* has not survived; and the *Daᶜāʾim* had no successor.[11]

The Creation of Ismāᶜīlism

Whatever its usefulness for the Fatimid judiciary, the *Daᶜāʾim* was a powerful statement of the dynasty's position on the law, the essence of the faith for the vast majority of the community, with which it was imperative to engage.

9 Ibn Abī Zayd al-Qayrawānī, *La Risāla*, ed. and trans. L. Bercher (Algiers, 1974).

10 Al-Wansharīshī, *Miʾyār al-muʾrib*, 13 vols (Rabat: Ministry of Culture and Religious Affairs, 1981–3).

11 Cf. A. A. A. Fyzee, *Compendium of Fatimid Law* (Simla, 1969), pp. xlviii–l; Poonawala, 'Al-Qāḍī al-Nuᶜmān and Ismaᶜili jurisprudence', pp. 131–2; Brett, *Rise of the Fatimids*, pp. 192–5.

From that position, al-Nuᶜmān was able to dispute with the Mālikites on his doorstep in and around the Great Mosque of Qayrawān, on both the *usūl*, or sources of the law, in the Qurᵓān and Sunna, or Custom, of the Prophet variously recorded in the ḥadīth, or traditions, of his doings and sayings, and its *furūᶜ*, or branches, the derivations that likewise varied from school to school. Such disputation was a measure of the new willingness of the dynasty to engage with its subjects, one that the Qāḍī al-Nuᶜmān celebrated in his *Kitāb al-Majālis waᵓl-Musāyarāt*, or Book of Sessions and Excursions, an account of the sayings and doings of al-Muᶜizz, in particular in the course of his audiences and rides abroad. For the faithful these were the materials for a Sunna, or Custom, of the Imāms on the analogy of that of the Prophet, one that never became a formal source of law, but certainly a source of edification.[12] For the historian the *Majālis* illustrates the operation of government at the personal as well as the institutional level. Fulfilling the role of the Caliph as the fount of justice, al-Muᶜizz invited written petitions, handed in either formally, when he sat in audience, or informally, when he was out riding. The hospitality that he meanwhile extended to his household and his guests among the faithful at al-Manṣūriyya will certainly have trickled down to a wider populace. Between the rooted objections of the Mālikites to his pretensions and the exaltation of his divine authority by al-Nuᶜmān, such cultivation of the image of the ideal ruler seems to have earned him a measure of popularity.

For a monarch whose ambitions extended far beyond the borders of Ifrīqiya to the empire of Islam, however, it was necessary to look beyond the parochial politics of his capital city for a following in the heartlands of Islam. For that it was necessary to reach out beyond the Mālikites and their fellow schoolmen, the Ḥanafites, Shāfiᶜites and Hanbalites, who were beginning to think of themselves collectively as Sunnī, or followers, of the Custom of the Prophet in contrast to the Shīᶜites, for whom the Custom of the Prophet was maintained by their Imāms. The rise of such a sectarian consciousness was in opposition to that of Shīᶜism as a political and intellectual force. In this confrontation, what was important for the Fatimids was to win over the Shīᶜites themselves, a broad spectrum ranging from the Zaydī-s, for whom the Caliphate belonged to the descendant of ᶜAlī strong enough to seize it, to the Twelvers with their Hidden Imām, and the assortment of Seveners whom the Mahdī had left behind in the East in continued expectation of a second coming. The Zaydī-s had already carved out for themselves a state on the Caspian and a second in the Yemen under their own Imāms in the millenarian fervour at the end of the ninth century. The Yemen they had conquered from Ibn Hawshab and ᶜAlī ibn al-Fadl,

[12] Al-Qāḍī al-Nuᶜmān, *Kitāb al-Majālis waᵓl-Musāyarāt*, 2nd edn, M. al-Yaᶜlawī (Beirut, 1997).

the agents of Salamiyya who had despatched the Fatimid Dā^{c}ī Abū ^{c}Abd Allāh to the Maghrib. But having driven the Da^{c}wa away into the mountains, their threat to the Fatimids was localised. The Twelvers, on the other hand, who had finally resigned themselves to the *ghayba*, or absence, of their Expected Imām in some otherworldly state, were not only much more central to al-Mu^{c}izz's designs, but potentially amenable to the offer of an Imām in person in place of the mysterious Muḥammad al-Muntazar. In the *Iftitāḥ al-Da^{c}wa*, composed at this time by al-Nu^{c}mān, the mission to the Yemen begins when Ibn Ḥawshab, bewildered by the disappearance of the Twelfth Imām, happily encounters the predecessor of the Fatimid Mahdī on the bank of the Euphrates, and recognises him as the true Imām. To the Seveners, meanwhile, the offer was of an Imām in line of descent, not as in the case of the Mahdī from ^{c}Abd Allāh, but from Muḥammad ibn Ismā^{c}īl. This appeal to all those who had continued to believe in the second coming of this Seventh Imām in line from ^{c}Alī was more than a question of genealogy. In reckoning al-Mu^{c}izz to be the seventh Imām in succession to this forefather of the dynasty, it cast him as the Second Seventh in the line, not simply the true Imām, but the one whose coming they had awaited.[13] The believers in question were for the most part Iranian. The Carmathians of Iraq with their miscellany of messiahs had largely faded away, leaving only the Carmathians of Bahrayn to maintain themselves like the Zaydī-s, as followers of their own Mahdī under their own Imāms.

The Iranians in question are indiscriminately labelled Carmathian by the principal source for their history, the *Siyāsat-nāma* of the Seljuk Wazīr Niẓām al-Mulk in the second half of the eleventh century. As used by its author, a principal opponent of the Fatimids and all their works at a crucial stage in the interrelated history of the dynasty and Islam, the term is synonymous with Bātinī in an account that extends the conspiracy theory of Fatimid origins to cover the whole spectrum of messianisms from the ninth century onwards. Rather than schismatics who had broken away from the Da^{c}wa at Salamiyya, however, the Iranians he denounced are best considered as belonging separately within the range of Sevener beliefs and believers. As the Wazīr described it, their history in the first half of the tenth century was certainly their own and quite distinctive.[14] Like the Twelver Shī^{c}ites in government in Iraq, they

[13] Cf. Brett, *Rise of the Fatimids*, pp. 199–205, with reference to the seminal article by Wilferd Madelung, 'Das Imāmat in der frühen ismailitischen Lehre', *Der Islam*, XXXVII (1961), 43–135, specifically 86–101.

[14] Niẓām al-Mulk, *Siyāsat-nāma*, trans. H. Darke, *The Book of Government, or Rules for Kings* (London, 1960), pp. 213–38; cf. S. Stern, 'The early Ismā^{c}īlī missionaries in North-West Persia and in Khurāsān and in Transoxania', in S. Stern, *Studies in Early Ismā^{c}īlism* (Jerusalem and Leiden, 1983), pp. 189–233.

moved in court circles, engaged in converting the miscellany of princes who had sprung up in Iran as the old empire fell apart, rather than preaching revolution. The mountains around the Caspian, where the Zaydī-s had made their state, had a long history of dissidence and Shīʿite leanings. When warlords in quick succession made their capital at Rayy near Tehran, they welcomed the Dāʿī Abū Hātim al-Rāzī until the third such warlord, Mardāvīj, drove him out c. 933. At Bukhara, meanwhile, at the much more important court of the Sāmānids, a major dynasty that had risen to power in Transoxania and Khurāsān, the preaching was carried on by the equally proselytising al-Nasafī until his execution in 943. Thereafter it fell to their successor, Abū Yaʿqūb al-Sijistānī, to recognise a line of Imāms in the interval before the second coming of Muḥammad ibn Ismāʿīl. More particularly, he envisaged al-Muʿizz himself, not by name but as the seventh in the line, a Qāʾim ruling by the law prior to the final arrival of Muḥammad himself as the Qāʾim proper.[15] For al-Muʿizz such recognition was not only a major coup that turned the largest community of Seveners into the largest and most influential group of his followers. It transformed the Daʿwa itself by substituting the respectable philosophy of Neoplatonism elaborated by al-Sijistānī and his predecessors for the fanciful myth of creation that had lain behind the sequence of the seven Prophets and the seven Imāms.

The myth had supplied the frame for the scheme of successive revelations, successive laws, each of which constituted the Bātin, or Hidden Doctrine, of the previous age before its disclosure as the Ẓāhir, or Open Doctrine, of its time. In maintaining against all apocalyptic expectation that the Open Doctrine of their age was the Sharīʿa, or Law of the Prophet, the Fatimids had equated its Hidden Doctrine with the Imām's inspired knowledge and understanding of God's ways. This concept of a continuous revelation playing upon the scriptural revelation of the Qurʾān and ḥadīth, or authentic tradition, had defined the Sharīʿa as the Open Doctrine of Islam in the Qāḍī al-Nuʿmān's *Daʿāʾim al-Islām*. It was now taken to endorse a cosmology in which the Imām occupied a pivotal position between heaven and earth as well as between God and man. The cosmology itself pitted reason against revelation, in the sense that it derived from the works of Greek philosophy translated into Arabic in the previous century. Where Neoplatonism proposed to bridge the gap between the perfect unity of God and the imperfect multiplicity of His creation through successive emanations of Intellect and Soul, Aristotelianism invested the life of the world

[15] Cf. P. E. Walker, *Early Philosophical Shiism. The Ismaili Neoplatonism of Abū Yaʿqūb al-Sijistānī* (Cambridge, 1993), pp. 16–18; Halm, *Empire of the Mahdī*, pp. 379–80; Brett, *Rise of the Fatimids*, pp. 205–6.

with the principles of growth, feeling and, in the case of humanity, reason. That reason then enabled the philosopher to comprehend the rational nature of God's universe through its affinity with the Active Intelligence that had brought the multiplicity of the world into existence. In such a scheme, the supreme wisdom vouchsafed to the Imām placed him at the pinnacle of such human understanding of the cosmos. In this way the Bāṭin, or Hidden Doctrine, of the Imāmate was fleshed out into a comprehensive account of God's creation dependent, like the Open Doctrine of the Sharīᶜa, upon the enlightenment of the Imām.[16] With such a theology, and the recognition by al-Sijistānī and the Seveners of Iran of an Imām who claimed descent from Muḥammad ibn Ismāᶜīl, Ismāᶜīlism and its community came into existence as a creation of the Fatimids, a form of Islam that has survived to the present day.[17]

The Development of the Mission

For al-Muᶜizz, Ismāᶜīlism in this sense and under this name did not exist; it was not simply a form of Islam, but Islam itself, the basis on which he turned his attention to the winning of its empire in the new age that had dawned with the defeat of the Dajjāl, the Antichrist. Politically, that age had indeed dawned, not simply with the triumph in Ifrīqiya, but with the transformation of the landscape of the Muslim world that had been accomplished by the abolition of the ᶜAbbasid empire in all but name in 945. In the Muslim commonwealth that then took the place of the old Arab empire,[18] the salient features from the Fatimid point of view were the takeover of Iraq by the Būyids and of Egypt and the bulk of Syria by the Ikhshīdids. The Būyids were the most successful of those warlords of the mountains of northern Iran, three princes from the region of Daylam who by the time of al-Manṣūr's victory in Ifrīqiya had divided central and southern Iran and central and southern Iraq between them. Ruling in the name of their protégés the ᶜAbbasids, they took from them their honorific titles as upholders of their Dawla, or state; but their sympathies seem to have been Shīᶜite, potentially amenable to the approach of missionaries working in the manner of al-Rāzī and al-Nasafī on behalf of the Fatimids. The Ikhshīdids, on the other hand, were a Turkish dynasty descended from a captain in the army of the Tūlūnids at the beginning of the century, and whose founder, Muḥammad ibn Ṭughj, had acquired the princely title of al-Ikhshīd after he took power in Egypt in 935. But at his death in 946, the government passed into the hands of a regent for his two

[16] Cf. Walker, *Early Philosophical Shiism*, and Brett, *Rise of the Fatimids*, pp. 210–15.
[17] Cf. Brett, *Rise of the Fatimids*, pp. 215–19.
[18] For its description, see Kennedy, *The Prophet and the Age of the Caliphates*, p. 200ff.

sons, the black eunuch Abūʾl-Misk Kāfūr, who as their Ustādh, or Tutor, ruled in their name for the next twenty years. With this return to independence, Egypt was once again a powerful state, although one which, unlike the province invaded by the Qāʾim some forty years earlier, was now isolated.

The Būyids had their own agenda; while ruling in the name of the ᶜAbbasids, they took the old Persian title of Shahanshah, King of kings, to establish their independence. Thanks to the irrigated agriculture of the Nile Valley and Delta and its revenues, Ikhshīdid Egypt was a prime example of what Kennedy has called the *ghulām* (pl. *ghilmān*) state, after the term 'youth', 'slave' given to the Turkish soldiery of the ᶜAbbasids and their successors.[19] Whatever its other pretensions, such a state was geared to the payment of its army, upon which the regime depended for its survival. Failure to do so in Iraq had in Kennedy's opinion brought down the ᶜAbbasids; it is significant that from this time on the need to do so was incorporated into the many 'Mirrors for Princes' that described both good and bad government, in the circular maxim that held the monarch responsible for justice: no justice without the army; no army without taxation; no taxation without wealth; no wealth without justice.[20] In Egypt, Kāfūr was himself a military man in command of the army of his master Muḥammad ibn Ṭughj, but one who neither sought to enlarge the Ikhshīdid share of the old empire, nor throughout the 950s was obliged to defend it against a competitor. The aggressive Ḥamdānid dynasty in Aleppo was engaged in holy war with the Byzantines to the north. In 951 the Carmathians of Bahrayn returned the Black Stone they had taken from the Kaaba at Mecca in 930, and in exchange for a subsidy did not interfere with the pilgrimage to the Holy Places, of which the Ikhshīdids were the official guardians. A Nubian invasion from the south was repelled, while al-Muᶜizz was for the time being taken up with the threat of the Umayyads in North Africa and the Byzantines in Spain.

As this new patchwork of states settled into place in the ᶜAbbasid East, therefore, the expansion of the Fatimid Dawla, or empire, into the heartlands of Islam was for the moment delayed. That of the Daᶜwa, the mission, on the other hand, was energetically pursued. Whether or not the recognition of the Fatimid Imām by the Seveners who looked for the return of Muḥammad ibn Ismāᶜīl had been actively sought, it certainly led to their organisation into correspondents of the Imām and agents of his campaign to take over the government of Islam. As their representatives travelled to Ifrīqiya to submit their questions and receive his answers, so they were drawn into a

[19] Ibid., pp. 206–10.

[20] See the discussion in M. Brett, 'State formation and government', in M. Fierro (ed.), *The New Cambridge History of Islam*, vol. 2, pp. 549–53.

worldwide community of local activists on his behalf. Such questions and answers were the common practice of the mediaeval world, on the basis of which legal, philosophical and theological treatises were composed in Islam and Christendom, and administration conducted in response to requests and petitions. The *Majālis* of the Qāḍī al-Nu^cmān is an example of the literary genre, from which comes an instance of the practice in the development of the Da^cwa. Presumably founded by emissaries from the Yemen around the beginning of the century, the community at Multan in the Punjab came to al-Mu^cizz's attention when he was asked to resolve a dispute over a *dā^cī* who had converted the Muslim ruler of the city, but then tolerated the persistence of non-Islamic beliefs. Al-Mu^cizz replied in favour of the complainants, whose leader then solicited his explanation of the faith and his claim to the Imāmate, together with his permission to destroy the great Hindu idol in this predominantly Hindu city. Permission granted, congratulations and battle flags were sent in 965 when the deed was declared done and a mosque built on the spot, together with a request that the heads of the fallen idol be sent to him to incite the zeal of the faithful throughout the world.[21] Announcements of such triumphs in letters to the believers were an important feature of the dynasty's propaganda. But al-Mu^cizz himself appears to have been enthused by this particular event, suggesting as it did in the run-up to the conquest of Egypt that the fulfilment of God's promise was at last at hand.

The Return to Conquest

By 965, the situation in the Mediterranean and in Egypt in particular had changed in his favour. Ten years of warfare by land and sea had brought victory over the Umayyads in North Africa and the Byzantines in Sicily and southern Italy. Raids and counter-raids by the Fatimid and Umayyad fleets upon Almeria and the coast of Ifrīqiya in 955–6, provoked by the capture of a Fatimid ship sailing from Sicily to al-Mahdiyya by an Umayyad vessel sailing back from Alexandria, were less important than the major expedition in 958–60 that reversed the gains made by Cordoba in northern Morocco and western Algeria in the years following the rebellion of Abū Yazīd. Joined by the forces of Ja^cfar ibn ^cAlī ibn Ḥamdūn at Msila and Zīrī ibn Manād at Ashīr, the expedition was an impressive exercise in organisation, significantly under the command of a *kātib*, or secretary, rather than a soldier, Jawhar al-Siqlabī, 'the Slav', a member of the monarch's household elite. The Umayyads retained their foothold across the Straits at Ceuta and Tangier, which they had occupied in 951; otherwise their suzerainty over this buffer zone was lost, replaced for the time being by

[21] Cf. Brett, *Rise of the Fatimids*, pp. 396–9; Halm, *Empire of the Mahdī*, pp. 385–92.

that of the Imām-Caliph in this impressive display of his might. There was no question of annexation; Tāhart, which had passed in and out of Fatimid control over the past half century, was assigned to Zīrī ibn Manād to complete the defence of the western frontier of the Fatimid realm. In disposing of the Umayyad threat, the expedition took its place in the broader scheme of empire, compensating in the first instance for the failure of successive attempts by the Kalbid brothers Ḥasan and ᶜAmmār to invade Byzantine Calabria from Sicily in 957 and 958. The tables were only turned some four years later, when the capture of the Byzantines' Sicilian capital of Taormina in 962 followed in 963 by the siege of Rametta, their last possession on the island, provoked a Byzantine expedition that was overwhelmingly defeated in 964–5. This was more of a propaganda than a strategic victory for al-Muᶜizz, but of immense importance in the context of his design upon Egypt.

It was in fact his response to the reconquest of Crete by the Byzantines in 960, some 140 years after it had been lost to Muslims from Alexandria. Al-Muᶜizz was too late to come to its rescue, but emerged as the champion of Islam at the expense of Kāfūr in Egypt, as Crete proved to be the first blow struck by the aggressive new Emperor Nicephorus Phocas. That did not prevent the conclusion of a mutually advantageous peace in 967, which enabled both rulers to concentrate on Syria and Egypt respectively. By then the Ikhshīdids were in trouble. In the early 960s the Nubians advanced down the Nile into Upper Egypt, where they may have remained for three years. Further north, the onset of low Niles and shortages from 963 onwards led to Bedouin invasions down the western side of the Valley and Delta. In 964 the Carmathians of Baḥrayn under their new Imām Ḥasan al-Aᶜṣam invaded Ikhshīdid Syria together with their Bedouin tribal allies, who plundered the pilgrimage from Damascus in 966. Ikhshīdid impotence was compounded by the destruction of a fleet sent to prevent the Byzantine capture of Cyprus in 965. Most importantly, the death of the second of Kāfūr's Ikhshīdid protégés in 966 left the eunuch as head of state with no obvious successor when he died in 968. The disappearance of this 'black stone', as the Fatimids called him, was the moment for which al-Muᶜizz had waited. By January 969 the expeditionary army was gathered at al-Manṣūriyya; in Egypt itself his agent Ibn Naṣr, no covert subversive but a prominent merchant, was putting him forward not as a conqueror but as the strongest candidate for a vacant throne; his justification in the eyes of the world was the defence of Islam as Nicephorus Phocas advanced to the capture of Antioch.

The expedition, once again under the command of Jawhar al-Ṣiqlabī, was an immense logistical enterprise to which all the resources of Ifrīqiya had been dedicated; its failure was out of the question. Its preparation emerges from the *Life* of Jawdhar, the indispensable lieutenant of al-Mansūr and al-Mu^c^izz, now an old man but still very much in charge of the business of government.[22] Composed in Egypt after his death, the work includes, yet again, a set of questions and answers, those put to his masters in matters of administration, together with their replies. The reason for the compilation was clearly pious; but the result is the nearest thing to an archive to survive from a regime whose official records, whatever they may have been, have not been preserved, in common with those of mediaeval Islamic states in general. It illustrates very clearly the complicated relationship between revenues, rulers and the commercial economy from which the state derived the means for the expedition. On the principle that the land belonged to the state and was subject to its taxation, the costs of government were met in practice by the extensive conversion of its rights into rewards for its servants or the allocation to them of specific incomes for their purposes. The practice was open to systematic abuse, which al-Mu^c^izz could only lament as a necessary evil, and which Jawdhar in consultation with his master could only mitigate when a provincial governor, for example, who was expected to pay himself as well as the costs of his administration out of taxation, had clearly overstepped the mark. That was equally the case when the personnel of the regime were granted estates, and the taxation of the land became a rent to the estate holder. Such grants, on the other hand, were not hereditary, and we find Jawdhar seeking approval to use the income from an estate that had fallen vacant for the expenses of the palace. Such arrangements meant that the income of the Treasury was residual, and may have amounted, according to the contemporary traveller and geographer Ibn Ḥawqal, to no more than 700,000–800,000 gold dīnārs. But they also meant that an immense amount of disposable wealth was in the hands of the members of government, from the monarch downwards. That wealth was invested, in property and in commerce. Not only had Jawdhar been commissioned by Ismā^c^īl at his accession to look after the commercial dealings with which the new Imām-Caliph had previously supported his family. He himself had grown very rich, with among other things a business in shipping and timber from Sicily with which he could supply the navy, and a fortune that he offered to donate to the cause of Egypt. Ifrīqiya under the Fatimids had indeed become a hub of trade, not only in the Mediterranean but across the Sahara on the strength of its exports of ceramics and textiles, and its demand for imports, including the gold of the western Sudan. Of the routes across the desert that the Kharijites had developed, from Sijilmāsa to the Niger bend; from the Niger bend into Ifrīqiya;

[22] Al-Jawdharī, *Sīrat al-Ustādh Jawdhar*, ed. M. K. Husayn and M. A. Sha^c^ira (Cairo, 1954); trans. M. Canard, *Vie de l'Ustādh Jawdhar* (Algiers, 1958); ed. and trans. H. Haji, *Inside the Immaculate Portal* (London, 2012).

and from the central Sudan through the Fezzan to Tripoli, the last was of strategic as well as commercial importance for the Egyptian venture. While turning Tripoli into a major and very lucrative port, it made allies rather than enemies of the Kharijites who controlled it, and were in a position to threaten the route along the coast.[23]

That route was well prepared with the digging of wells and the establishment of depots for the supply of the host when it set out under Jawhar's command. The cost had been enormous. While insisting that so sacred an enterprise could only be financed out of revenues permitted by the law, al-Muᶜizz complained to Jawdhar that money was running out of the Treasury like water, as accountancy was no doubt overlooked in the rush to complete, prices went up and pockets were lined. He himself had made over his personal fortune to the venture, to the value, it was said, of 24 million dīnārs. When the time eventually came, Jawhar was sent on his way in a ceremony where only he and al-Muᶜizz were on horseback, a plenipotentiary viceroy entrusted with the authority of the Imām-Caliph to take over the realm of Egypt in his name. So great a responsibility, in which absolute discretion was conditional upon absolute obedience of the slave to the master, may have been spelled out for his benefit in a text that the Qāḍī al-Nuᶜmān included in the *Daᶜāʾim al-Islām*. This, like the *Siyāsat-nāma* of the Wazīr Niẓām al-Mulk, belongs to the genre of Mirrors for Princes, treatises on good and bad government addressed to real or imagined monarchs. It is a version of a letter purporting to have been addressed by ᶜAlī to a provincial governor, which sets out the ideal of a ruler rising above all classes of his subjects, and dealing with them as he was in duty bound, with due regard for their welfare. The addressee in this case, described as one of humble birth, a critic of kings who has become a king himself and must avoid the mistakes of kings, fearing death, has been identified as either the Dāᶜī Abū ᶜAbd Allāh or the Mahdī himself, apostrophised by the Dāᶜī. But it may have been incorporated into the *Daᶜāʾim* precisely because it was used or reused to remind Jawhar of his onerous duty in the task ahead. It was certainly consonant with the terms on which he accepted the submission of the Egyptians, and envisaged the principles upon which the Fatimids set out to govern their new dominion.[24]

The Takeover of Egypt

Festina lente: it is a measure of the care taken to ensure its success, as well as the slowness imposed by the size of the host with its baggage train of

[23] For this political economy, cf. Brett, *Rise of the Fatimids*, pp. 243–66.

[24] Cf. Brett, *Rise of the Fatimids*, pp. 137–9; Halm, *Empire of the Mahdī*, pp. 162–3; and now S. A. Hamdani, *Between Revolution and State*, pp. 125–8.

pack animals, herds of cattle and flocks of sheep, that it took the expedition three months, from February to May, to arrive at Alexandria. When finally encamped at the entrance to Egypt, its multitude was compared to the pilgrimage at Arafat, come at God's command for God's purpose. Having lived in expectation of its arrival, the caretakers of the Ikhshīdid regime sent to request the terms of the *amān*, the safe-conduct offered by the Imām-Caliph and his representative in return for their surrender. They were in no position to resist. Ja^c^far ibn al-Furāt, the Wazīr who headed the regime as regent for the infant prince Ahmad ibn ^c^Alī al-Ikhshīd after Kāfūr's death, had been deserted by Shamūl, the commander of the army, who had decamped to Syria, and by Ya^c^qūb ibn Killis at the treasury, who had fled to Ifrīqiya to take service with al-Mu^c^izz. The troops of the Ikhshīdiyya, the Turks recruited by Muḥammad ibn Ṭughj; the Kāfūriyya, or Black guards, recruited by Kāfūr; and the regiments of Slavs or Greeks, were unpaid and mutinous. Abū Ja^c^far Muslim, the Naqīb, or head of the Ashrāf, the important nobles claiming membership of the family of the Prophet, remained an ally, but his brother ^c^Abd Allāh, known as Akhū Muslim, the governor of Syria, had successfully resisted the attempt to depose him, allying himself with the Carmathians, who had invaded the country in the autumn of 968. It was to Abū Ja^c^far that the Wazīr nevertheless turned to lead a delegation composed of three such Ashrāf, together with the Qāḍī of the Egyptian capital, his subordinates and the Fatimid agent Aḥmad ibn Naṣr, to the meeting with Jawhar. The Ashrāf and the Naqīb who verified their ancestry were a new phenomenon in the Muslim world; over the past half century, the bulk of those who claimed descent from ^c^Alī had abandoned any claim to the Caliphate and Imāmate in favour of high social status and collective authority. In principle the Fatimids were numbered among them, which is why their leaders were chosen as mediators to greet Jawhar's arrival. On the other hand they were not Ismā^c^īlī, either genealogically or religiously, and were politically wary of Fatimid pretensions. They remained to be persuaded.[25]

As the envoy come to take over the government of their country in the name of his master, Jawhar was reassuring but firm towards them. The *amān*, or act, which he presented to the delegation for signature offered a comprehensive guarantee of life, property and position, given in the name of a monarch whose declared aim was to defend the land of Islam; to secure the pilgrimage to Mecca; to wage holy war upon the infidel; and to bring back peace and prosperity with the abolition of illegal taxes, the restoration of good money and the upkeep of mosques. A provisional guarantee of freedom of worship

[25] Cf. Brett, *Rise of the Fatimids*, pp. 297–300.

was given, but all in return for a binding commitment to total and perpetual obedience to the representative of God on earth. Such a commitment was more than merely political. The *Amān* that Jawhar offered was declared to be the *Amān* of God Himself, while the *ʿAhd*, or agreement, to which both he and the Egyptians were now irrevocably committed was His inviolable *Mīthāq*, or covenant, with His people. It was indeed none other than the *ʿAhd al-Muslimīn*, the commitment of the community to Islam that was embedded in the Qāʾim's title of Walī ʿAhd al-Muslimīn. Invoked for this purpose by Jawhar, acting in the same capacity as the Qāʾim before him on behalf of his master, its political implications were fundamental. By this compact between God and the Egyptians which the Fatimid envoy had concluded, these were placed under His *Dhimma*, or protection, as provided for them by the Imām-Caliph al-Muʿizz li-Dīn Allāh, the rightful successor to the Prophet with whom the original compact was made. As a concept, the Dhimma of God enters into the so-called Constitution of Medina, a collection of rules governing the relationship between the believers and their allies ascribed to the Prophet in his *Sīra*, or biography, and reappears on the authority of ʿAlī in the *Daʿāʾim* of the Qāḍī al-Nuʿmān. In both, it applies to the Muslim community, which may then extend it to non-Muslims living under Muslim rule. This is the sense in which the term is more narrowly and more commonly employed to designate such Christians, Jews and Magians as Ahl al-Dhimma or Dhimmī, as indeed it is in the text of the Amān. But in the context of the Fatimid conquest of Egypt, Jawhar's employment of the term to designate the Muslims themselves harks back once again to the ʿAbbasids, who identified their rule with the Dhimma of God on coming to power in 749. More importantly, it picks up on the notion contained in the Mirror attributed to ʿAlī in the *Daʿāʾim*, of a monarch rising above his subjects, to adumbrate a new relationship between the new monarchy and its new subjects in a new order of the world. Under a dynasty that distinguished between Muslims who believed in the Imām and Muslims who did not, the Dhimma of God was the prescription for a benevolent despotism of universal application.[26]

It remained to put the agreement into effect. Crowds in the capital Fusṭāṭ demonstrated against it and had to be reassured by the head of the delegation, Abū Jaʿfar Muslim, on his return. More importantly, the regiments of the Ikhshīdiyya and Kāfūriyya took up positions on the island of Roda in the Nile opposite the city to defend the crossing of the river. But the Nile was low, and Jawhar's Kutāma swarmed across to drive them off, killing many of their commanders. Despite such resistance, Jawhar renewed the Amān, and

[26] Ibid., pp. 300–3.

was introduced to the Wazīr Ja^cfar ibn al-Furāt and his colleagues by the Fatimid agent Ahmad ibn Nasr. Across the river, Jawhar was welcomed by the populace as he rode in procession through the city to camp in the Garden of Kāfūr two or three miles to the north. Beyond the site of Aḥmad ibn Ṭūlūn's palace city, destroyed except for its mosque by the ᶜAbbasids when they recovered the country in 905, this summer retreat was already chosen as the site of the Fatimids' own royal city, al-Muᶜizziyya al-Qāhira, the Victorious City of al-Muᶜizz. At the Great Mosque of ᶜAmr in the centre of Fustāt, the prayer was offered in the name of the Imām-Caliph. Back in Ifrīqiya, the event was celebrated by the court poet Ibn Ḥāniᵓ, who looked forward to the imminent conquest of Baghdad. In Egypt, it was commemorated with the issue of a gold coin, whose legends, inscribed on both sides within the three concentric circles that characterised the Fatimid dīnār, spelled out in succession the sequence of God, His Messenger Muḥammad, his Executor ᶜAli and finally al-Muᶜizz, His Imām and His Caliph. The construction of the new palace city began with the laying out of a *muṣallā*, or prayer ground, within a rectangle about three-quarters of a mile square. It proceeded with the utmost urgency in readiness for the arrival of the monarch himself four years later, in 973. Meanwhile, there was trouble, as triumph turned to near disaster.

Egypt itself was still in the grip of a shortage of grain and revenues in the aftermath of low Niles and confusion following the death of Kāfūr, with food prices high, state income low, the currency debased after years of inflation and brigandage in the countryside. Pairing himself with the Wazīr Ibn al-Furāt for the indispensable duty to receive petitions, and his own people with senior members of the administration, Jawhar with difficulty managed to put good money in place of bad, and grain that had been hoarded was forced onto the market. The *kharāj*, or land tax, in effect the tax on the grain harvest, was raised, possibly doubled; but although the flood of the Nile returned to normal levels in the summer of Jawhar's arrival, such an increase could only take effect after the harvest in the spring. The immediate shortfall was at least mitigated by the confiscation of the estates of the Ikhshīdiyya and Kāfūriyya, those whose revenues were allocated to their upkeep as well, presumably, as the personal estates of their commanders, and by higher taxation of trade. Ikhshīdid commanders who had submitted rather than fled were sent south into the Valley to deal with robbers, but the one sent to suppress the rebellion of the textile town of Tinnīs in the eastern Delta joined its revolt against the new taxation until it was suppressed. Such problems were relatively minor in a country with a long tradition of central administration. It was quite another matter when it came to Syria, a very different country of disparate peoples, regions and cities overseen by the Ikhshīdids from Damascus and held in the north by the Ḥamdānids at Aleppo.

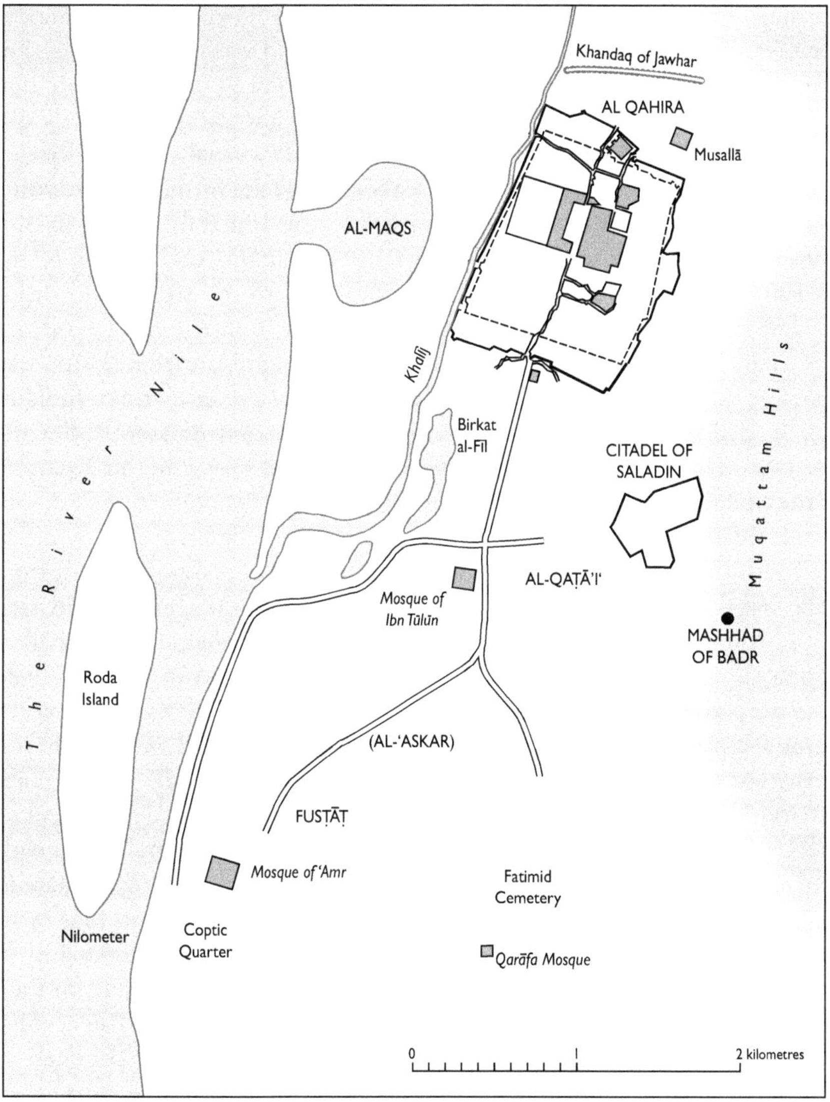

Map 3.1 Cairo

While asserting the Fatimid claim to the whole of the Ikhshīdid dominion, the invasion of Syria in 970 aimed to do far more in the cause of empire. Headed by the Kutāma general Ja[c]far ibn Falāḥ, its immediate objective was to depose the Ikhshīdid governor of the province, the Ikhshīdid prince Ḥasan, and overcome the remnants of the Ikhshīdiyya who had fled from Egypt. This was easily accomplished; both Ramla and Tiberias were taken, and Damascus was abandoned by Hasan's ally, the former commander-in-chief

Shamūl, who returned to a welcome in Egypt by Jawhar. But Damascus itself resisted after its delegates were mistreated, and was punished by exemplary executions of leading citizens. Such opposition by a citizen body that could field its own militia in its own defence was a warning of the very different character of Syria from Egypt, geographically, socially and politically. Where Egypt was nothing if not the Valley and Delta of the Nile, running from south to north through the desert, Syria was zoned from west to east, from the Mediterranean littoral across the mountains and valleys of the Jordan and Orontes to the plains running out into the steppe and desert beyond. Socially, the line of cities along the coast from Ascalon to Antioch was parallelled inland by the line from Bosra through Damascus, Homs and Hama to Aleppo. Between them the population of the hills and mountains was divided by religion as well as habitat into a variety of Sunnīs, Shīᶜites and Christians, not to speak of the Fatimid faithful surviving the departure of the Mahdī from Salamiyya. Out to the east, the Bedouin confederations of the Kilāb, the Kalb and the Ṭayy controlled the desert fringe, while in the south the coastal plain of Palestine, with the city of Ramla inland from Jaffa, was the corridor to and from Egypt. Politically, the Umayyad division of the country from north to south into Junds, or tribal armies, based at Qinnaṣrīn south of Aleppo, at Homs, at Damascus and in Palestine, had been perpetuated after the fall of the dynasty, when Syria lapsed into the status of a province of one empire or another. Briefly united by the Ṭūlūnids at the end of the ninth century, its partition in the middle of the tenth between the Ikhshīdids at Damascus and the Hamdānids at Aleppo elevated the Umayyad division to the dynastic level, where the geopolitical divide was emphasised by the Iraqi origins and connections of the Ḥamdānids. In this disparate country, the kind of centralised administration that made Egypt into a state for the taking by Jawhar was absent. The individuality of its cities, each with its own economy in its own environment, made for their autonomy under whatever regime was imposed from above.[27] The acquisition of Antioch by the Byzantines in the year of the Fatimid conquest of Egypt not only exemplified but promoted their differences from each other. Damascus itself, although the Ikhshīdid capital, was in fact a city state whose citizens were in partnership with their ruler. Making enemies of the Damascans was a mistake on the part of Jaᶜfar that put an end to the Fatimid onrush, which after the Ikhshīdids had been swept aside set out to carry the Syrians with it in holy war upon the Byzantines at Antioch.

The Ḥamdānid prince Sayf al-Dawla, who had taken over Aleppo as his

[27] Ibid., pp. 308–11.

share of the ʿAbbasid empire in the mid-940s, had waged a long and fruitless holy war against an unrelenting Byzantine advance upon Cilicia and northernmost Syria down to his death in 967. In 962 Aleppo itself was taken and briefly occupied; significantly it was the citizens who negotiated the Byzantine withdrawal. The Muslim frontier he had defended then collapsed, and the Muslim population was driven out of lands originally settled in the eighth century. In 969 Antioch was taken and Aleppo was again occupied and made tributary to Constantinople. In fulfilment of al-Muʿizz's pledge to defend Islam against this assault, which had been a prime justification for the conquest of Egypt, the submission of Damascus in October 970 was followed by the despatch of Jaʿfar's *ghulām* Futūḥ to raise the districts of Palestine for the holy war. There was an enthusiastic response but no success before the advance on Antioch was called off in June 971 as Jaʿfar at Damascus turned eastwards to face a new enemy. In response to the appeal of the fugitive leaders of the Damascan resistance, a formidable coalition of Arab tribesmen and defiant Ikhshīdid *ghilmān* had been put together by the Carmathians of Bahrayn. Electing to encounter this horde in the desert, Jaʿfar himself was killed as his army was surrounded and destroyed in the August. A month later, reinforced by yet more Arab tribesmen from Transjordan, the Carmathian Imām Ḥasan al-Aʿṣam entered an Egypt that was almost defenceless. Occupying the eastern Delta before moving on Fusṭāṭ, however, he gave Jawhar the time to build a ditch and wall to the north of the city from the river to the west to the Muqattam cliffs to the east. An amazing feat, which required the mobilisation of the entire population, it served its purpose in the December, halting the Carmathian advance and allowing Jawhar's improvised army to rout the invaders in battle outside the gates. At the approach of a relieving force from Ifrīqiya, al-Aʿṣam fled back into southern Syria. That Jawhar was able to rally the inhabitants of Fusṭāṭ in this way was a tribute to the success of his conduct of the mission with which he had been entrusted, in contrast to Jaʿfar's failure at Damascus. Syria, where the Carmathians remained, was nevertheless lost apart from Ramla, the capital of Palestine, which was recovered in May of the following year, 972. The *élan* of al-Muʿizz's great expedition had been lost as it came up against the political realities of the Mashriq in this post-ʾAbbasid era. From Ifrīqiya, on the other hand, the view remained good. As Jawhar struggled to restore the revenues of Egypt and to cope with rebellion in Upper Egypt and continued discontent in the eastern Delta, the Imām-Caliph prepared to set out for a golden future in the palace city that Jawhar was so urgently building for him.

4

The Constitution of the State

The Emigration from Ifrīqiya

Even more than the expedition of Jawhar, the removal of the sovereign and his family, including the coffins of his ancestors, together with his extended household of ministers, troops and domestics, and not least his treasure, over the 1,500 miles from the capital of Ifrīqiya to the capital of Egypt, was a feat of administration that testified to the competence of the government that had emerged from its victory over the Dajjāl. Largely organised by the indispensable Jawdhar, who continued to keep the 'monkeys and pigs' of the monarch's wider family securely out of the way, the enterprise took shape as a huge ceremonial procession. Its size was nevertheless strictly controlled: written permission was required to join, with passes controlled at checkpoints along the way. Accompanied by the fleet sailing out of Tripoli along the coast, the host moved majestically from reception to reception along the way; one at least, at Ajdābiya, was held in a palatial throne room built for the occasion. Compelling the homage of citizens and tribesmen, these not only marked the triumphal progress of the Imām-Caliph towards his destiny as ruler of the world; more mundanely, they served to secure the vulnerable lifeline between Ifrīqiya and Egypt. Still more to the point, at its departure from al-Manṣūriyya in the autumn of 972 the procession left behind an Ifrīqiya equally carefully converted from the seat of empire into a province. The length of time this required explains, quite as much as the Carmathian invasion of Egypt, the delay in setting out. The problem was immediately apparent in Sicily, from which the Kalbids, the family whose members had recovered the island for al-Manṣūr and proceeded to expel the Byzantines, had been recalled at the end of 969 to command fleet and army for the move to Egypt; it was one of them, the Kalbid Ḥasan ibn ᶜAmmār, who led the force sent to expel the Carmathians in 971, and who remained there as a grandee of the regime. In their absence, government of the island was left in the hands of another Jawdhar, a freedman of the family, who lacked the necessary charisma to prevent an outbreak of fighting as old enmities resurfaced in their absence. Order was only restored on the return of the Kalbid Abūᵓl-Qāsim ᶜAlī, sent back to the island to resume the headship of its communities as a Sicilian monarch ruling on behalf of the Caliph. The moral was not lost on al-Muᶜizz, who informed Jawdhar that he lacked the necessary following to be left in charge of Ifrīqiya after his own departure. For that, a figure who could command obedience in his own right was required.

Ifrīqiya, however, was not Sicily; and the choice of a lieutenant to take it in hand was not straightforward, given the need to leave the business of government in the hands of a competent administrator while entrusting the defence of the realm to a warrior prince. With Sicily assigned to the Kalbids, and Zīrī ibn Manād still very much the tribal chieftain at Ashīr, the only person capable of acting in both capacities was Jaᶜfar ibn ᶜAlī ibn Ḥamdūn, the governor of the Zāb at Masīla. But he was accused by Jawdhar of withholding the taxes of the Zāb, and as an Andalusian by origin, of harbouring an agent of Cordoba. He was, moreover, at odds with Zīrī ibn Manād at Ashīr; and when summoned to al-Manṣūriyya in April 971, fled westwards to join the Maghrāwa, the tribal allies of Cordoba, who had spearheaded a fresh Umayyad offensive after Jawhar's departure for Egypt. The Maghrāwa had been worsted by Zīrī's son Buluggīn, but in alliance with Jaᶜfar returned to the attack, killing Zīrī in battle at Tāhart. While Jaᶜfar went on to a ceremonial welcome at Cordoba, Zīrī's death was avenged by Buluggīn at the end of the year with the aid of troops sent by al-Muᶜizz. Taking Jaᶜfar's place at Masīla, Buluggīn was then the only possible choice of viceroy for the whole of Ifrīqiya after the departure of the Imām-Caliph a year later. When the time came, the doyen of the old secretarial families of Ifrīqiya and head of the Treasury, Abū Mudar Ziyādat Allāh, was put in charge of the administration at Qayrawān as Buluggīn's subordinate, while Buluggīn himself was ennobled under a new name: Sayf al-Dawla (Sword of the State) Abūᵓl-Futūḥ (Man of Many Victories) Yūsuf. To complete his investiture, the procedure followed at Jawhar's departure was reversed; it was now the lieutenant who accompanied the sovereign en route towards Tripoli. On taking his leave of the Imām-Caliph, however, Buluggīn returned to the west rather than take up his new command at al-Manṣūriyya. Within a year or two, he had replaced the elderly Ziyādat Allāh with his own nominee from the administrative class, ᶜAbd Allāh ibn Muḥammad al-Kātib, the Secretary. In 977–8 his dominion was rounded off with the return of Tripoli to Ifrīqiyan administration, after it had served its purpose in the conveyance of al-Muᶜizz to Egypt. But for the moment the government continued to be divided between Qayrawān and Ashīr, two separate spheres of competence reflecting the long-standing difference between the regions.

The Break with the Past

The consequences of this major devolution of authority for the constitution of the empire took time to work themselves out. Meanwhile, al-Muᶜizz arrived in Egypt to the same reception at Alexandria and Fustāt that had greeted Jawhar, masterminded this time by Jawhar himself before he was ceremonially relieved of his command. Entering into his new capital, he took up residence in the palatial city created for him by his deputy. Built on the pattern of al-Mahdiyya, with a greater and eventually a lesser palace on either side of a north-south thoroughfare between gates that exist today, the Bāb al-Futūḥ and the Bāb Zawīla, al-Qāhira was more than merely stone, brick and mortar. Together with its Great Mosque, al-Azhar (see Fig. 4.1), it stood for his arrival not only as ruler of Egypt but as the ruler of Islam and the world, in fulfilment of the destiny prepared by the rising of the Mahdī and the defeat of the Dajjāl.

That arrival as the Second Seventh in line from ᶜAlī is epitomised in the story that when challenged by a member of the Ashrāf, the nobles of the Prophet's family, to prove his claims, he half drew his sword, saying 'here is my pedigree', and threw down gold coins, saying 'here are my proofs'. The sword was claimed to be the sword of ᶜAlī, and the coins bore the names of Muḥammad and ᶜAlī, with the appropriate legends. They had indeed been minted for that very purpose, to a new and distinctive design in concentric circles that spelled the message out.[1] But the story as told in a later source is anti-Fatimid, designed to show the monarch up as an impostor who had fought and bribed his way to power.[2] And it takes the reader back to the downside of this triumph, the opposition that greeted the installation of the dynasty in Egypt. Located in Syria, this manifested itself almost immediately in a scornful rejection by the Carmathian Ḥasan al-Aᶜṣam of al-Muᶜizz's summons to return to Fatimid allegiance, followed by a renewed Carmathian invasion of Egypt in 974. The defeat of that invasion by ᶜAbd Allāh, al-Muᶜizz's son and heir, drove Ḥasan from Syria as well as Egypt, and allowed the Fatimids to reoccupy Damascus. But if this ended the threat of an ᶜAlid challenge to the dynasty on the part of the dissident Akhū Muslim and his Carmathian ally, it

[1] Cf. S. Anwar and J. L. Bacharach, 'Shīᶜism and the early Dinars of the Fatimid Imām-caliph al-Muᶜizz li-dīn Allāh (341–365/952–975): an analytic overview', *Al-Masāq*, 22 (2010), 259–78.

[2] For this anecdote, see Brett, *Rise of the Fatimids*, pp. 325–6; Halm, *The Empire of the Mahdi*, p. 353, speculates that the antique sword described by the Qādī al-Nuᶜmān as short, pointed and two-edged, purloined from the ᶜAbbasid treasury in Baghdad, may have been an old Roman *gladius*.

did not do away with the hostility of an important section of the Ashrāf. Some ten years later at Damascus, Akhū Muḥsin, one of their number who claimed descent from Muḥammad ibn Ismāᶜīl, put into its final form the black legend of Fatimid origins perpetrated by Ibn Rizām in the middle of the century. His polemic came at a time when the Fatimids themselves, having proved themselves by their deeds, were finally making public a full version of their ancestry. Al-Muᶜizz's summons to al-Aᶜṣam to return to the allegiance of his predecessors rested on the premise of his appeal to all Seveners, that all of them had originally belonged to the faithful following of the Imāms in *satr* or concealment. At the beginning of the next century, and with official approval, the Iranian *dāᶜī* al-Naysabūrī listed the names of these Imāms in his *Istitār al-Imām*, or Concealment of the Imām. Even in Ismāᶜīlī sources, however, the notion of a substitute line of Imāms, which the Mahdī had been at pains to deny in his letter to the Yemen, rumbled on as the fire behind the smoke of Akhū Muhsin's tale of impostors. That tale became a starting point for a fresh round of polemic in the following century, long after the death of al-Muᶜizz and the hope he may have entertained of a speedy advance upon Baghdad.

Egypt had in fact proved fatal for him and his Ifrīqiyan entourage. Jawdhar had died on the way at Barqa; Ibn Hāniᵓ, the poet who anticipated the conquest of Baghdad, had been murdered there on the beach. The Qāḍī al-Nuᶜmān died a year later in 974, and Jaᶜfar ibn Manṣūr al-Yaman perhaps in 976. ᶜAbd Allāh, the son and heir who had routed the Carmathians, died early in 975, and al-Muᶜizz himself at the end of the year, aged only forty-four, to be succeeded by a younger son, Nizār. Once again there had been no public designation. ᶜAbd Allāh had evidently been preferred to his elder brother Tamīm, but Nizār may have been indicated only by the feeble instruction to hear the petitions of the people. He effectively proclaimed himself by riding out under the *miẓalla*, or umbrella, the jewelled shield on the point of a lance that betokened the Imām-Caliph, and offering the prayer for the Feast of Sacrifice under the regnal title of al-ᶜAzīz biᵓllah, Mighty by God. But if there was no crisis of succession, there was a climax, the consummation of the break with the Ifrīqiyan past that is signalled in the literature by the substitution of Egyptian for Maghribī sources. The great burst of literary output for which al-Muᶜizz had been largely responsible came to an end with the posthumous composition of the memoirs of Jawdhar and Jaᶜfar al-Ḥājib; the story of Ifrīqiya was taken up by the chroniclers of the Zīrids, the descendants of the lords of Ashīr. That of the dynasty in Egypt was recorded by a series of annalists close to the court whose works have not for the most part survived except in later compilations, of which by far the most important are those of the fifteenth-century Egyptian historian al-Maqrīzī. His *Ittiᶜāẓ al-ḥunafāᵓ*, or Cautionary Tales of the Ancestors, is a complete

Figure 4.1 The prayer hall of the Mosque of al-Azhār. Photo: Bernard O'Kane.

The original mosque of al-Qāhira, al-Azhār takes its name, 'the Radiant', from the epithet of Fatima, the mother of the dynasty. Renovated and remodelled over the centuries, its Fatimid core is no longer visible, but the building itself, and its name, is a permanent legacy of the dynasty to posterity.

history of the dynasty, flanked by the huge topography that goes under the abbreviated title of *al-Khitat*, the Places (of Egypt), and the numerous biographies of his *Kitāb al-muqaffā*.[3] His account of the dynasty's Ifrīqiyan past

[3] Al-Maqrīzī, *Itti*ᶜ*āẓ al-hunafā*ʾ *bi-akhbār al-a*ʾ*imma al-Fātimiyyīn al-khulafā*ʾ, 3 vols, ed. J.-D. al-Shayyal and M. H. M. Ahmad (Cairo, 1967–73); 4 vols, ed. A. F. Sayyid (London, 2010); section on the reign of al-Muᶜizz trans. S. Jiwa, *Towards a Shi*ᶜ*i Mediterranean Empire* (London, 2009); *Kitāb al-mawā*ᶜ*iẓ wa*ʾ*l-i*ᶜ*tibār fi dhikr al-khitāt wa*ʾ*l-āthār (Khiṭāṭ)* (Bulaq, 1853); ed. G. Wiet, first 4 vols only (Cairo, 1911); autograph MS, ed. A. F. Sayyid (London, 1416/1995); *Kitāb al-muqaffā*, extracts ed. M. Yalaoui (Beirut, 1987).

is nevertheless cursory and second-hand, a mere preliminary to the narrative of its Egyptian career based on his Egyptian sources. Instead, the dynasty's own record of those previous years was compiled and transmitted by the devotees of the Daʿwa rather than the chroniclers of the Dawla. With these it ended in the Yemen long after the end of the dynasty in the *ʿUyūn al-akhbār*, or Choice Reports, of the fifteenth-century *dāʿī* Idrīs ʿImād al-Dīn, a seven-volume history of the Daʿwa from the Prophet onwards.[4] The two traditions certainly interlocked, as the pronouncements of the dynasty that the faithful preserved helped to mould the tale told by the chroniclers. But their subject is the doings of the Caliphate rather than the proofs of the Imāmate advanced in the previous literature by the Qāḍī al-Nuʿmān and his contemporaries.

The Entry into the ʿAbbasid Inheritance

Such a concern with the affairs of state reflected the political achievement of the dynasty in moving from the periphery into the heart of the Muslim world. But at the same time it exposed the extent to which the dynasty had entered into the affairs of a world whose unity it aimed to restore. The partition of that world between the successor states of the ʿAbbasid empire was the outcome of a long period of regional growth away from the central control once exercised by Damascus and Baghdad. Having benefited from and promoted such growth in the Maghrib for its imperial purpose, the dynasty now found itself doing the same in the Mashriq. But in taking advantage of the break-up of the old empire to acquire the Ikhshīdid share of its territory, the Fatimids took their place in the system they sought to overthrow. The rhetoric of an imminent march upon Baghdad to complete their triumph did not survive the euphoria of the conquest. As their advance into Syria ground to a halt, the building of al-Muʿizziyya al-Qāhira, the Victorious City of al-Muʿizz, signalled the intention to settle in Egypt as the seat of their empire and the base of their mission. In so doing, they settled into the ways of the post-imperial world they wished to rule.

In Egypt itself, those ways did indeed turn to their advantage, not least because they benefited directly from the abolition of the imperial administration in Iraq. Ending the long and well-developed tradition of secretarial government at Baghdad, this deprived the secretaries themselves of their employment. The Fatimids, on the other hand, were in need of their

4 Idrīs ʿImād al-Dīn, *ʿUyūn al-akhbār*, section on Maghrib, ed. M. Yalaoui, *Taʾrīkh al-khulafāʾ al-fātimiyyīn biʾl-Maghrib* (Beirut, 1985); vol. 7, ed. and summarised A. F. Sayyid with P. E. Walker and M. A. Pomerantz, *The Fatimids and their Successors in the Yemen* (London, 2002).

ministerial expertise as they sought to build on the Ikhshīdid transformation of a provincial administration into the government of an independent state. Already the Ikhshīdids had recruited members of one of the great families of Iraq, the Banūʾl-Furāt, to head their administration in the capacity of Wazīr. The Wazīrate was one of the great institutions of the ʿAbbasid Caliphate, a prime ministerial office created to lift the burden of routine from the shoulders of the monarch. A major political appointment, it carried with it extensive powers of patronage that enabled the holder to form his own government in charge of the dynasty's affairs. Thus it was the Wazīr Jaʿfar ibn al-Furāt who had negotiated the surrender of Egypt to Jawhar, even though much of his support had evaporated with the departure of Shamūl for Syria and the defection of his fellow Iraqi and head of the financial administration, the Jewish Yaʿqūb ibn Killis, to the Fatimids. Jaʿfar was dismissed by al-Muʿizz, but Ibn Killis was restored to his position in charge of revenue together with an Ifrīqiyan colleague, and in 979 was elevated by al-Muʿizz's successor al-ʿAzīz to the Wazīrate. It was a momentous appointment that on the one hand announced the arrival of the Fatimids as successors to the ʿAbbasids in the institution of the Caliphate, but on the other hand marked the beginning of the transition from what Max Weber called the patriarchal to the patrimonial phase of government in the history of Islamic empire.[5] It was a transition from the personal rule of the founders of the dynasty at the head of their household to a regime conducted on the monarch's behalf by a minister at the head of an army of functionaries. In this capacity the role of the Wazīr was that of *wāṣita*, or middleman, between the sovereign and his servants; and while Ibn Killis and his successors remained the creatures of the Caliph, liable to instant dismissal and possible execution, their dignity was such that at the beginning of the twelfth century they were according their own histories in the *Ishāra ilā man nāla al-wizāra*, or Pointer, to those who acceded to the Wazīrate.[6]

The author of the *Ishāra* was Ibn al-Ṣayrafī, just such a functionary who headed the Dīwān al-Rasāʾil, or Chancery, the department responsible for the *rasāʾil*, or missives of the state, and one of the many Dīwān-s, or bureaux, which made up the administration of these Men of the Pen. Of these bureaux, the most numerous and important were those that dealt with revenue and expenditure, the prime concern of Ibn Killis before his elevation. Expenditure was divided between the palace, the offices of the Men

[5] Cf. B. S. Turner, *Weber and Islam* (London, Henley and Boston, MA, 1974), p. 80 *et passim*.

[6] Ibn al-Ṣayrafī, *Al-Ishāra ilā man nāla al-wizāra*, ed. A. Mukhlis (Cairo, 1924); ed. A. F. Sayyid (Cairo, 1990).

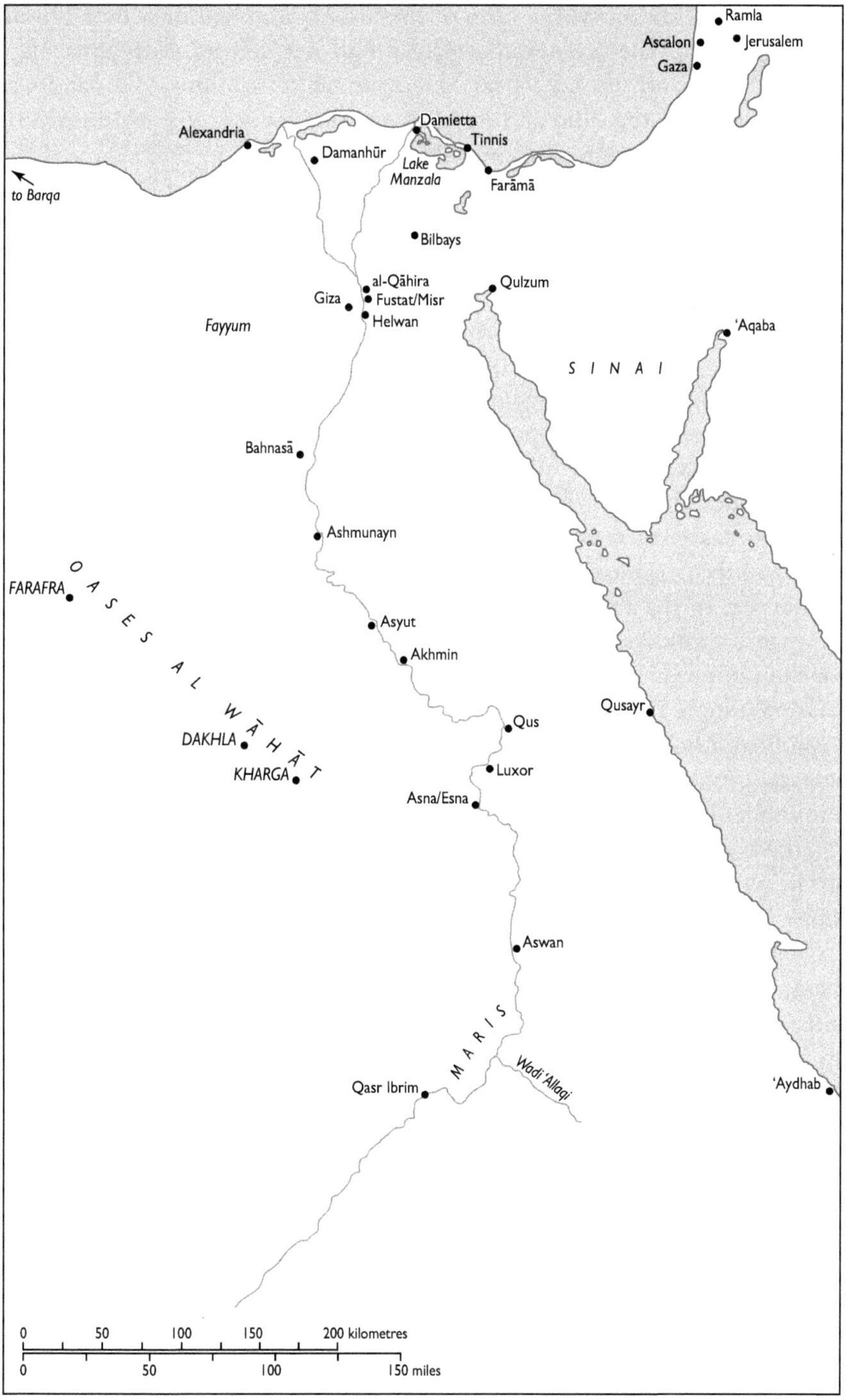

Map 4.1 Fatimid Egypt

of the Pen and the army, the Men of the Sword, who had their own Dīwān for the purpose. The revenue that paid for all was derived in the first place from the land and secondly from the commercial economy. The land was the floodplain of the Nile and its offshoot, the Fayyum depression, whose irrigation had been controlled since Pharaonic times by the ditches and dykes maintained and operated by the peasant villagers, who sowed in the autumn after the flood and reaped in the spring. From Pharaonic times they had equally been taxed with greater or lesser severity by a range of collectors, from state officials to landlords, with the tax farmer somewhere in between as a concessionary working on his own account on behalf of the government. From the time of the Arab conquest, the officials who assessed the size of the harvest and collected the revenue for the Treasury had continued to be Copts belonging to the Christian population, whose familiarity with the financial system had ensured their quasi-monopoly of its operation. But after a long period of peasant revolt from the beginning of the eighth century onwards, it was the tax farmer who had reappeared as the person responsible for the upkeep of the irrigation system in his village, and the payment of the taxes on the harvest. In the aftermath of the conflicts and risings that had continued down to the middle of the ninth century, however, much of the land had gone out of production, a situation aggravated in the 960s by low Niles. The solution adopted by Ibn Killis and his Ifrīqiyan colleague in the 970s was a complete recall and reissue of the tax farms to the highest bidder,[7] in the beginning of what Goitein in *A Mediterranean Society* called 'the Fatimid (economic) miracle'.[8]

It was a miracle, or at least an access of prosperity, based upon agriculture but heightened by the trading and manufacturing of agricultural produce to supply an export as well as an internal market. The corresponding market for imports ranged from necessities like timber and metals, from iron to the gold that maintained the purity of the Fatimid dīnār, through a whole variety of foreign produce to the luxuries of precious materials to be worked up by Egyptian craftsmanship. In all of this, Fatimid Egypt was once again the beneficiary of the collapse of Iraq, economically as well as politically; the route of the trade of the Indian Ocean through the Gulf was now diverted into the Red Sea to pass through Egypt into the Mediterranean, whose trade

[7] Cf. Brett, *Rise of the Fatimids*, pp. 331–3, and 'The way of the peasant', *Bulletin of SOAS*, 47 (1984), 44–56, at 49–51.

[8] S. D. F. Goitein, *A Mediterranean Society. The Jewish Communities of the Arab World as Portrayed in the Documents of the Cairo Geniza*, 6 vols (Berkeley and Los Angeles, CA, 1967–88), vol. 1, *Economic Foundations*, p. 33. For a fuller discussion, cf. Brett, *Rise of the Fatimids*, pp. 333–9.

converged with that of the Sahara upon Alexandria.[9] That trade now involved the Italians, headed by the merchants of Amalfi, who took back the flax of Egypt for linen made at Naples. Flax was an old Egyptian staple that fed the important linen industry at Tinnīs and elsewhere. But, grown like grain over the winter, it was now joined by the summer crops of cotton and sugarcane, grown with water drawn from the river in the low season by mechanical means. The introduction of these commercial crops from India, together with a range of vegetables such as aubergines, had revolutionised the agriculture of the Arab world and Egypt in particular, where there were now two growing seasons instead of one. The economy correspondingly grew in size to take full advantage of the country's position at the crossroads of intercontinental trade. Both cotton and sugarcane gave rise to major new industries and exports, as well as employment for a growing population. For the dynasty, that economy was the source of the wealth required to sustain its power and prestige. Its exploitation began with the tax farm, not simply an instrument of the fisc, but an investment on the part of the contractors that drew in a large section of society.

Not everyone benefited. While the peasants may have gained from the expansion of cultivation, workers elsewhere may have seen the value of their wages fall. But those who were able to make the investment as tax farmers were well rewarded, to judge by the popularity of the system. Tax farms were ubiquitous, not only on the land, where some of the takers may have been rich peasants of sufficient wealth and status, but in the towns, where all kinds of tolls and the taxes on commercial activities and properties such as bathhouses were contracted out in this way. Such investments ran the risk of extortion on the one hand, failure and forfeiture on the other, but in combination with other occupations created a vested interest in the regime on the part of a large class of middle-ranking Egyptians. A picture of their prosperity emerges from Goitein's account of the community of North African Jews attracted to Egypt by the opportunities it offered. Above them, however, tax farming blended into the far greater rewards of those in power: the Fatimids themselves and their servants, the officers of the palace, the ministries and the army, who came into the possession of estates on which, as previously in Ifrīqiya, the taxes became rents. Not only did these deliver vast wealth into the hands of the holders to be spent on the conspicuous consumption that drove the economy of the metropolis, but again as in Ifrīqiya, to be invested in commercial enterprise. Beyond the grain trade, such enterprise extended

9 Cf. A. L. Udovitch, 'Fatimid Cairo: Crossroads of world trade – from Spain to India', in M. Barrucand (ed.), *L'Égypte fatimide: son art et son histoire* (Paris, 1999), pp. 681–91.

to the industrial crops and their manufactures, and to foreign trade. Thus at his death in 991, Ibn Killis left linen and perhaps other cloth to the reported value of 500,000 dīnārs, with more in the hands of the merchants charged to trade with it. Such merchants, like the Fatimid agent Ahmad ibn Nasr, who had the expertise to handle such commissions for their clients, shared in their wealth as close associates of the regime. Investment on this scale was a major factor in Goitein's economic miracle, but one that qualifies his explanation that the Fatimid state interfered very little in the trade of its subjects; the Fatimids themselves were the traders.

The Battle for Syria

While the regime in Egypt successfully constituted itself on the basis of economic growth, it was thirteen years before al-ᶜAzīz was finally able to regain Damascus and incorporate Ikhshīdid Syria into the regular administration of the state. It was an achievement that required a major restructuring of the Fatimid army; a narrow focus of the drive for further conquest upon the reduction of Aleppo; and a corresponding confrontation with the Christian empire of Byzantium rather than an attempt upon Baghdad. Iraq under the Būyids was not only beyond the possibility of invasion, but was both a contributor to the problem and a source of the solution. In 975 before the death of al-Muᶜizz, the reoccupation of Syria following the defeat of the Carmathians in the previous year had been annulled on the one hand by the invasion of the Byzantine Emperor John Tzimisces in a campaign that reached down into Palestine, leaving only Tripoli in Fatimid hands. On the other, Damascus had welcomed as its protector a refugee from the Būyids at Baghdad, the Turkish *ghulām* Aftakīn at the head of a force of Turkish cavalry. The aim of the Emperor seems to have been the recovery of Jerusalem, and it was fortunate for the Fatimids that the threat was lifted by his death on the return journey to Constantinople in January 976. Aftakīn, however, with the backing of Damascus under its *raʾīs*, or headman, Qassām, the head of the city's militia, allied with the Carmathians and the Syrian bedouin for yet another advance into Palestine in the spring. The horde was driven away by Jawhar, recalled for his proven ability to conduct a campaign designed to settle the matter once and for all. Advancing on Damascus, he invested the city methodically with wall and ditch. But Damascus under Aftakīn and Qassām held out for five months, until winter and the return of the Carmathians forced a retreat that became a rout. Jawhar was besieged for over a year in Ascalon on the southern coast of Palestine by Aftakīn and Ḥasan ibn al-Jarrāḥ, the chief of the bedouin Arab Ṭayy of Transjordan, until in April 978 his Kutāma warriors mutinied, and he capitulated before al-ᶜAzīz was finally ready to come to his aid in person. By then Aftakīn had been reinforced by further refugees from Iraq; but deserted by Ibn al-Jarrāḥ, he was outnumbered by the Caliphal host and surrendered, only to be welcomed with his men into the Fatimid army.

The enlistment of these Turks, the heavy cavalry of the eastern Islamic world, alongside the light cavalry of the Kutāma, made good a serious deficiency in the Fatimid forces confronted by the armies of the Mashriq. The part played by the fugitive Ikhshīdid *ghilmān* in the defeat of Jaᶜfar ibn Falāḥ outside Damascus, and the success of Aftakīn himself, demonstrated the need for such warriors if the Fatimids were to match their opponents with anything other than superior numbers. So necessary were they that their recruitment continued in the ᶜAbbasid manner, with the training up of young slaves from Central Asia imported for the purpose. But their incorporation into the Fatimid ranks recreated a previous opposition within the armies of Egypt between the Maghāriba, or Westerners, and the Mashāriqa, or Easterners. At some point in the near future, the Turks were joined by the Daylamī-s, the infantrymen of the Būyids from their mountain homeland, while the Kutāma were associated with the Black infantry recruited as slaves from the Nilotic and Central Sudan. For the moment the Kutāma retained their primacy as Friends of the Imām; but the intrusion of this Turkish elite provoked a resentment that hardened over time into latent and indeed overt hostility.[10] Meanwhile, however, the adoption of Aftakīn into the following of the Caliph had turned a major obstacle to the reoccupation of Syria into an advantage that the new Wazīr Ibn Killis exploited immediately upon his appointment in 979. The despatch of his own man, al-Faḍl al-Wazīrī, to bring about a settlement finally brought the business down to the kind of politics with which, as a former servant of the Ikhshīdids, he had long been familiar.

Thus the Carmathians were bought off with the annual tribute they had enjoyed under the Ikhshīdids, while the tribal confederations of Kilāb to the east of Aleppo and Kalb to the east of Damascus were offered the chance of an alliance, and the Jarrāḥid chiefs of the Ṭayy to the south in Transjordan became lords of Palestine. At Damascus, the *raʾīs* Qassām was left in effective control under a titular governor, while the Jewish Manashshā ibn Ibrāhīm was installed as *ᶜāmil*, or financial controller, of the province, with responsibility for the payment of the troops. Beyond the limits of Ikhshīdid Syria, the quarrels of the Ḥamdānids at Aleppo presented the Fatimids with an opportunity to resume the expansion of the empire, for which the capture of the city was a necessary step. The taking of Aleppo by the Hamdānid heir Saᶜd al-Dawla in 977 had displaced the Turkish *ghilmān* of his predecessor,

[10] Cf. Y. Lev, *State and Society in Fatimid Egypt* (Leiden, 1991), ch. 5.

who had ruled the city by themselves for the past ten years. Many of these now came over to the Fatimids, to be employed and enlisted to retake the city on behalf of the Imām-Caliph. The effectiveness of Aftakīn's Turks for the Fatimid hold upon the old Ikhshīdid dominion was demonstrated in 983, when the *ghulām* Bultakīn succeeded after the Kutāma commander Salmān had failed, like his father Ja^c far ibn Falāh before him, to reoccupy a still rebellious Damascus. The *rā'is* Qassām was finally ousted from the city, and the Jarrāhids evicted from the Palestinian capital Ramla, to bring the whole of the province under the control of al-Qāhira. This was exercised in the first place by the Ḥamdānid *ghulām* Bakjūr, who, after the failure of an attack upon Aleppo, was appointed to the Syrian capital. From there, presumably with the approval of al-Qāhira, he proceeded to take Raqqa and Raḥba on the Euphrates away to the north-east. These two cities were the gateway to Iraq, while their possession by Bakjūr threatened Aleppo from the east as well as the south. But he proved unpopular at Damascus itself, and perhaps because he was becoming too independent, in 988 he was obliged by the arrival of a Fatimid force under the command of the eunuch Munīr to move off to his frontier domain at Raqqa. Munīr, like Jawdhar before him, belonged to the elite of the monarch's household, and his installation at Damascus finally brought Ikhshīdid Syria under direct Fatimid administration.

The Theatre State

In Egypt itself, the dynasty was growing into the shell of its palace city both socially and politically. Under al-^c Azīz, the smaller western palace was constructed across the square from the great eastern palace, the residence of the monarch and the site of his daily audience in the Golden Hall, which opened off the square through the Golden Door. There were nine such doors in the wall of what was in effect a fortress within a fortress, an L-shaped enclosure with courts and gardens and fountains, which contained the tombs and treasures of the dynasty, and lodged the multifarious household of the Caliph. Over the Golden Door was a balcony at which he appeared to the populace, while in the angle of the L was a place of assembly for the regular processions out of al-Qāhira.[11]

The reach of the palace city extended down the hill, past the Mosque of Ibn Tūlūn on the site of the previous city of the Tūlūnids, to embrace the old city of Fusṭāṭ in a conurbation which was the architectural setting for

[11] Cf. J. M. Bloom, *Arts of the City Victorious. Islamic Art and Architecture in Fatimid North Africa and Egypt* (New Haven, CT and London, 2007), pp. 65–9; A. F. Sayyid, 'Le grand palais fatimide au Caire', in Barrucand (ed.), *L'Égypte fatimide, Son art et son histoire*, pp. 117–25.

the ceremonial routine that gave theatrical expression to the dynasty and its claims.[12] The model of power and authority thus enacted as a demonstration of the dynasty's divine right was a mixture of piety and pomp. Headed by the Imām-Caliph, the actors were his officers, the audience his public and the occasions a weekly to yearly round of audiences, prayers and festivals, not all those of the Muslim calendar. The ᶜĪd al-Fitr and the ᶜĪd al-Aḍḥā were joined by Christian festivals, including New Year and Epiphany, which were enjoyed by the populace at large, while the Cutting of the Canal was the traditional celebration of the beginning of the flood, when the river rose to the point at which it overflowed into the irrigation system. The canal in question led from the Nile at Fusṭāṭ the length of the western wall of al-Qāhira, and the ceremony was attended from the very beginning by the Caliph in person. An occasion for him to go down to the old city itself, it was an opportunity to identify himself with his subjects of all faiths, and with the fertility of the land on which all depended. With its clearly political purpose of ordering and regulating the life of the community in accordance with the divine mission of the dynasty, whose truth it served to manifest to the outside as well as the inside world, the ceremonial round and its performance grew increasingly elaborate. But, as Paula Sanders comments in her description of the routine under the revealing title of *Ritual, Politics and the City in Fatimid Cairo*,[13] at the same time it framed a political process, the jostling for position within the swollen ranks of the regime. As a result of the character of the Egyptian sources, these politics become visible for the first time in the dynasty's history.

At their heart was not only the Imām Caliph, but the female members of his family. While the males of the family, whoever they were, remained in the limbo to which al-Manṣūr and al-Muᶜizz had consigned them, al-ᶜAzīz brought forward the ladies: his mother Durzān, his consort al-Sayyida al-ᶜAzīziyya and her daughter Sitt al-Mulk. His second consort, the mother of his successor al-Ḥākim, remains obscure, perhaps because she was a Melkite or Orthodox Christian. But of his sisters or half-sisters, Rāshida and ᶜAbda are known for their immense wealth at the time of their death in their nineties in 1050. In return for such favour, these daughters remained unwed, preserving the patrilineal succession of the dynasty while upholding the purity of its matrilineal ancestress Fāṭima al-Batūl, literally the Virgin. It was in her honour that the Great Mosque of al-Qāhira, al-Azhar,

12 For a relevant model for such display, cf. C. Geertz, *Islam Observed. Religious Development in Morocco and Indonesia* (Chicago, IL and London, 1968), pp. 35–8: 'the Doctrine of the Exemplary Center', 'the Doctrine of Graded Spirituality' and 'the Doctrine of the Theater State'.

13 P. Sanders, *Ritual, Politics and the City in Fatimid Cairo* (Albany, NY, 1994).

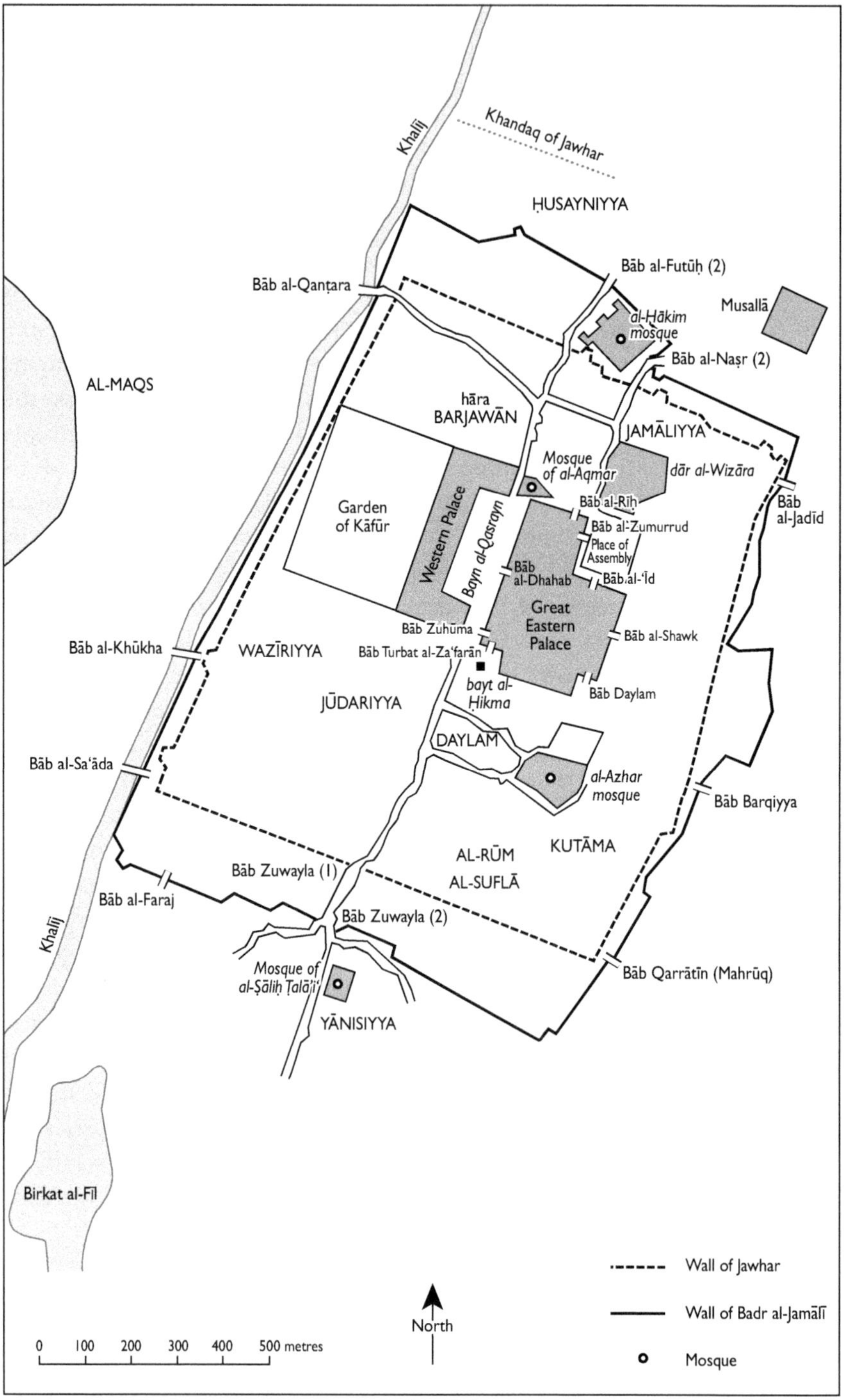

Map 4.2 al-Qāhira

was named from her other soubriquet, al-Zahrāʾ, the Luminous, and it was to exemplify her feminine ideal as the epitome of the dynasty that Jawhar had had two prostitutes flogged and paraded bareback as an earnest of the new regime. This exaltation of the mother of the line was a polemical retort to the contemptuous use of the term *fāṭimī* by the ᶜAbbasids to deride the claims of the Shīᶜites to the Caliphate as the claims of a woman,[14] and a proud identification with the name by which the dynasty is now known. Meanwhile, in her own capacity as wife and mother, Durzān stepped forward to add to the list of al-ᶜAzīz's multiple new foundations with the building for herself of a mosque and mausoleum in the Qarāfa cemetery outside Fusṭāṭ. While the Imāms themselves were buried in a prominent mausoleum, the Turbat al-Zaʾfarān, within the walls of the Eastern Palace in al-Qāhira, Durzān's foundation made the cemetery the burial ground for the other members of the family, a place of female visitation and worship, and the focus of a large and fashionable suburb. Exemplifying the prolific building activity of the dynasty, which ranged from palaces and mosques to bridges and baths, the Qarāfa mosque is likewise the first instance of the wealth which came into the possession of these royal women. The wealth in question derived from their estates and properties; spent in this way, it benefited the economy. But at the same time it turned them into important employers and patrons, increasingly influential within the ranks of the dynasty's army of servants, secretaries and soldiers, and thus in government.[15]

The City of the Caliph

As the *miṣr*, or 'garrison city' of the original Arab conquerors turned from an army camp into a civilian city on Roman lines, with the mosque in place of the forum as the centre of civic life, and the original governor turned into a monarch, so the seat of government was displaced from the centre of the city to a location outside. By the end of the ninth century, the Aghlabid Amīrs had built for themselves the palace city of Raqqāda to the south of the capital Qayrawān, complete with household, secretaries

[14] Cf. M. I. Fierro, 'On *al-fāṭimī* and *al-fāṭimiyyūn*', *Jerusalem Studies in Arabic and Islam*, XX (1996), 130–61.

[15] The whole subject is treated in D. Cortese and S. Calderini, *Women and the Fatimids in the World of Islam* (Edinburgh, 2006); see also H. Halm, 'Le destin de la princesse Sitt al-Mulk', in Barrucand (ed.), *L'Égypte fatimide, son art et son histoire*, pp. 69–72, and Y. Lev, 'Aspects of the Egyptian society in the Fatimid period', in U. Vermeulen and J. Van Steenbergen (eds), *Egypt and Syria in the Fatimid, Ayyubid and Mamluk Eras*, III (Leuven, 2001), pp. 1–31.

Figure 4.2 Ivory plaques. © Museum für Islamische Kunst – Staatliche Museen zu Berlin.

The lively little figures in the ivory carving of this frame depict the array of characters and costumes of the Fatimids at sport and leisure.

and soldiers, in a tradition stretching back to Hadrian's villa at Tivoli and Diocletian's palace city at Split (Spalato – the Palace). Raqqāda promptly became the residence of the Mahdī on his coming to power, only to be replaced by al-Mahdiyya, a fortress city well away from Qayrawān, a naval and army base on the coast looking eastwards to the conquest of Egypt and beyond. After the defeat of Abū Yazīd, it was replaced as the seat of government by the new palace city of al-Ṣabra al-Manṣūriyya, Victorious Endurance, outside Qayrawān, in a move that restored the symbiotic relationship between the city of the monarch and that of the citizens. It created the physical environment for the *rapprochement* between the dynasty and its subjects after its deliberate isolation in al-Mahdiyya. Signalled by the appointment of a Mālikite as Qāḍī of Qayrawān, this looked forward to the Amān of Jawhār in Egypt and the benevolent protection it offered to the entire population.

Al-Manṣūriyya went on to become the residence of the Zirids, for whom the relationship with Qayrawān ended in their siding with the citizens against the Fatimids. In al-Andalus, the symbiosis was repeated at al-Madīna al-Zahrā᾽, the Radiant City of the rival Umayyad Caliphate, which looked back towards Cordoba and the magnificent mosque where the Caliph worshipped, while the space between the two filled up with mansions and gardens. Meanwhile in Egypt, the construction of the palace city of al-Qāhira al-Muᶜizziyya, the Victorious City of al-Muᶜizz, continued the development of the Egyptian capital that had begun with the growth of Fusṭāṭ, out of the original army camp of that name into the city centred on the Mosque of ᶜAmr. But from there, in a steady progression rising away from the river to the north-north-east, the seat of government was moved away, first by the ᶜAbbasids to their own army camp, al-ᶜAskar, and then to al-Qaṭā᾽iᶜ, 'the Quarters' of the army of Aḥmad ibn Ṭūlūn, a palace city whose fortress mosque has survived together with the *maydān*, the parade ground. The palatial residence of the Ikhshidid Kāfūr to the west of al-Qaṭā᾽iᶜ has not survived, but on the higher ground beyond al-Qaṭā᾽iᶜ the area called the Garden of Kāfūr, bordering the Khalīj, or canal, running north-eastwards from the river, was incorporated into the site selected by Jawhār for the third palace city of the Caliphate.

He built it in the first instance as a fortress, and its walls enclosed an area of some 1,200 x 900 metres. This was bisected south to north by a high street that ran through a central piazza, the Bayn al-Qaṣrayn, 'Between the Two Palaces', the great Eastern and the lesser Western, on the pattern of the palaces at al-Mahdiyya; the Mosque of al-Azhar, 'the Luminous', was situated in the south-eastern quarter. Initially the site was three-quarters empty, but it rapidly filled up with the necessities of urban life – baths, caravanserais and markets, together with offices, residences and quarters for the troops. Continuously built and rebuilt over the next 200 years, it was enlarged and refortified towards the end of the eleventh century with the massive new walls and new gates – the Bāb Zuwayla in the south, the Bāb al-Futūḥ and the Bāb Naṣr in the north – which were built by Badr al-Jamālī to surround and replace the original walls. Meanwhile the Bāb Zuwayla at the southern end of the high street gave on to the highway running out through the suburbs that grew up beyond the walls, back to the old city of Fusṭāṭ, forming the artery that connected the two cities. The symbiotic relationship that developed between them, both economic and social, was strengthened by the administrative ties that bound the one to the other, and more theatrically by the processional descents upon the old city by the Imām-Caliph in celebration of the annual round of festivals – Muslim, Christian and specifically Egyptian in the case of the cutting or opening of the Khalīj, the Canal, as the Nile rose to fill it. The spectacle thus offered to the world was a necessary demonstration of the power and authority of the dynasty on behalf of God, one which at the same time translated the Amān of Jawhār into a series of events in which the monarch and the people could happily join.

Cf. J. M. Bloom, *Arts of the City Victorious*, pp. 37–41 for al-Manṣūriyya and al-Madīna al-Zahrā᾿ and pp. 54–70 for al-Qāhira, al-Azhar and the Palace; and P. Sanders, *Ritual, Politics and the City in Fatimid Cairo*.

The Politics of the New Regime

Under al-ᶜAzīz, the ranks in question were headed by the new generation of those who had taken the place of his father's old stalwarts, men such as ᶜAlī and Muḥammad, the sons of the Qāḍī al-Nuᶜmān,[16] Ḥusayn son of Jawhar and Salmān son of Jaᶜfar ibn Falāḥ. Together with veterans like the Kalbid Ḥasan ibn ᶜAmmār, they constituted a hereditary aristocracy, informal in the sense that they depended on the favour of the monarch, but real in the sense that they and their families continued to be favoured as the creatures of the dynasty. From 978 the soldiers among them were nevertheless confronted by Aftakīn and his Turks; and while Alī ibn al-Nuᶜmān and Muḥammad after him headed the judiciary in succession to their father in the position of Chief Qāḍī, they found themselves opposed in their office by the new man elevated over all of them, the Wazīr Ibn Killis. With his appointment in 979 the kind of rivalry for power which had undoubtedly existed in Ifrīqiya gave rise to open conflict as the minister set out to restrict the brothers' jurisdiction. At the lower level Ibn Killis removed the police from their control, depriving them of the oversight of criminal cases which the Chief Qāḍī had exercised in Ifrīqiya through the appointment of the *ḥākim*. At the higher level he brought from Ifrīqiya their father's successor as Chief Qāḍī at al-Manṣūriyya, Aḥmad ibn Abī ᵓl-Minhāl, to deal with the *maẓālim*, that is, with the appeals against injustice traditionally heard by the monarch or his deputy. Only after 991, when the Wazīr died and was not replaced, did Muḥammad, assisted by his son ᶜAbd al-ᶜAzīz, recover the full authority of his office as holder of the chief magistrature of Islam. As the one who judged by the law on behalf of God, and thus preserved the community from dissolution, he held a divine commission far superior to that of any Wazīr acting on behalf of the Caliph. The

[16] The descendants of the Qāḍī al-Nuᶜmān who held his office, with intermissions, down to the middle of the next century, are the subject of R. Gottheil, 'A distinguished family of Fatimide Cadis (al-Nuᶜman) in the tenth century', *Journal of the American Oriental Society*, 27 (1906), 217–96.

law was nevertheless the law as authenticated by the Imām, in whose service Muḥammad removed his court from the Great Mosque of ᶜAmr in Fusṭāṭ to his residence in al-Qāhira, and in whose name he preached the *khutba*, the Friday prayer in his capacity as chief *imām*, or prayer leader. Meanwhile, he oversaw not only the judiciary of the country, but the minting of the dynasty's coinage and the accuracy of its weights and measures, and acted as custodian of the estates of the deceased. But the conflict between the two sons of the author of the *Daᶜāʾim al-Islām* and this intruder into their realm had consequences for both the Dawla and the Daᶜwa, for the state as it was now constituted in Egypt and Syria, and for the doctrine which governed it.

Ibn Killis, a Jew converted to Islam and latterly to that of the Imāmate, had in his capacity as Wazīr presided over them both. Surrounding himself with scholars, he had invited Muslims, Christians and Jews to debate their faith in his presence. Their meeting under the auspices of the state was indicative of a tolerance that flowed from the Dhimma, or Protection, which the Amān offered by Jawhar and accepted by the Egyptians had extended to all who entered into obedience to the Imām Caliph. Predicated on the distinction between Muʾminūn and Muslimūn, the truly faithful and those who had yet to accept the Imām as the true authority for the faith, the terms of the Amān had reduced the bulk of the Muslim community to subjects almost on a par with the Christians and the Jews, the specifically *dhimmī* communities of non-Muslims protected by the Muslim state in exchange for their submission. And just as these communities were allowed to live under their own laws, so the jurists of the Sunnī schools were of necessity incorporated into the Fatimid judiciary, provided their judgements conformed to any specific rulings in the dynasty's own jurisprudence. This ideological tolerance of religious diversity was not simply political. It conformed to the make-up of Egyptian society, with its Jewish communities and its large and important Christian population, and which in the context of Durzān's foundation of the Mosque of the Qarāfa, featured the unusual prominence of women, whose tombstones surviving from early Islamic Egypt amount to almost 50 percent of the total.[17] It was this society which the Jewish convert and adoptive Egyptian Ibn Killis exemplified and represented at the highest level of government, making him a crucial figure in the adaptation of the incoming dynasty to its new environment.

As an Iraqi, moreover, he brought with him the intellectual breadth of the ᶜAbbasid East. That breadth was notably represented in the encyclopaedia of contemporary knowledge called the *Rasāʾil*, or Letters of the Ikhwān al-Ṣafāʾ, the Brethren of Purity, a compilation of tracts of uncertain date and

[17] Cf. J. M. Bloom, 'The Mosque of the Qarāfa in Cairo', *Muqarnas*, IV (1987), 7–20.

authorship covering mathematics, the natural sciences, philosophy and theology. The compilation appears to date from the mid-tenth century, though references to the coming of an Imām in *satr* point back to an element in their composition from the late ninth century. They cannot be Fatimid, since there is no doctrine of the Imāmate as such, but they evidently belong in the world of the Iranian Neoplatonists whom al-Muᶜizz had recruited for the Daᶜwa.[18] In the case of Ibn Killis, that doctrine was central to his ambition to displace the sons of Ibn al-Nuᶜmān from their father's position as the spokesman of the Imām, and al-Nuᶜmān himself from his position as author of the last word on the law of the Imāmate. To institutionalise the teaching of that law, he installed a group of jurists to lecture on it in the Mosque of al-Azhar. More significantly, he wrote a *risāla*, or treatise, on the law on the authority of al-ᶜAzīz, designed to supersede or at least to enlarge on the *Daᶜāʾim al-Islām*, which had been given on the authority of al-Muᶜizz. Equally significantly, however, it has not survived even in abridgement, nor has a collection of the sayings of al-ᶜAzīz comparable to al-Nuᶜmān's *Majālis waʾl- musāyarāt.*[19] To what extent al-ᶜAzīz himself aspired to emulate his father in this respect, with the Wazīr in place of the Qāḍī, is not clear, although Ibn Killis cannot have acted without permission. What is clear is that Ibn Killis' initiative died with him. After his death in 991, when Muḥammad ibn al-Nuᶜmān came into his own as Chief Qāḍī, it was he who lectured *ex cathedra* on the doctrine of the Imāmate to an audience so packed on one occasion in 995 that eleven of those present died. But since no works are ascribed either to him or to his elder brother, it must be supposed that he was lecturing from the works of his father, on which his own claim to authority was based. His triumph must be seen as a triumph of conservatism which halted the further elaboration of the faith undertaken by the Wazīr. Explaining, it may be, the noteworthy absence of legal literature from the Fatimid canon after the composition of the *Daᶜāʾim*, the hiatus it imposed left any future development uncertain.

Meanwhile, apart from the judiciary, the death of Ibn Killis in 991 left the government of the country in the hands of the Men of the Pen, the heads of the *dawāwīn*, or bureaux, whose continuous development over the past fifteen years had endowed the Fatimid state with an elaborate secretarial and fiscal administration. Over the next five years, these *kuttāb* escaped from the supervision of the palace aristocracy in the course of ministerial reshuffles, in which they figured collectively in groups of four or five. The details are minor

[18] Cf. Brett, *Rise of the Fatimids*, pp. 209–10, with reference to I. R. Netton, *Muslim Neoplatonists: an Introduction to the Thought of the Brethren of Purity* (Edinburgh, 1991).

[19] Ibid., pp. 372–3; H. Halm, *The Fatimids and their Traditions of Learning* (London, 1997), pp. 43–5.

in themselves, but illustrate the character of the regime by the end of the tenth century, and portend its future in the eleventh. Thus it was one of al-Muᶜizz's old guard, the Maghribī Jābir ibn al-Qāsim, who had deputised for al-ᶜAzīz during his Syrian campaign and acted in place of Ibn Killis during the latter's brief imprisonment in 984, who initially oversaw the financial administration; but it was one of his three associates, al-ᶜAddās, who was effectively in charge, sitting in state on a brocaded bench in a separate room of the palace, until he was found to have lost revenue in the disposal of certain tax farms dependent on the Caliph. Like Ibn Killis he was then dismissed and disgraced, stripped of his properties, paraded round the town and imprisoned for fifty-seven days, until reinstated as head of the bureaux and the affairs of Egypt and Syria. But the old Ikhshidid Wazīr, Jaᶜfar ibn al-Faḍl ibn al-Furāt, was then briefly recalled to head the financial administration, before this was given over to a consortium of four, including the Christian ᶜĪsā ibn Naṣṭūrus and the Jewish Isḥāq ibn Manashshā, with Ibn Killis' old stalwart, the Qāᵓid Faḍl ibn Ṣāliḥ al-Wazīrī, acting as accountant. In 993 Jaᶜfar, clearly an old man, was brought back again in some supervisory capacity, until after six months the consortium was finally left in charge under the direction of Ibn Naṣṭūrus.

What is revealed in this tale of ministerial appointments is an administration which ran itself through established procedures followed by experienced personnel without any necessary direction from above. They were, on the other hand, in the absence of a Wazīr such as Ibn Killis, middlemen with the confidence of the Caliph to act as the intermediary between himself and his servants, subject to a desultory supervision exercised directly through ritual dismissal and public humiliation, or entrusted to the great and good of the aristocracy. Their intrusion into the administration was not merely to hold the *kuttāb* to account. It was significant of a political process, a manoeuvring for position and influence on the part of the personnel of this patrimonial regime, success in which depended upon the coveted power of patronage. Thus the appointment of Faḍl ibn Ṣāliḥ al-Wazīrī as accountant was on the recommendation of Muḥammad ibn al-Nuᶜmān, now supreme after the death of Ibn Killis. To him al-Wazīrī had evidently turned for support, and presumably brought with him into the Chief Qāḍī's fold some or all of Ibn Killis' former clientele. All these various elements entered into the future of the regime in Egypt, but their seemingly low-key operation in these years was cut short by the unexpected death of al-ᶜAzīz in 996, just as the affairs of the empire were coming to a head.

5

The Formation of the Empire

The Prospect of Empire

Al-Muᶜizz's pursuit of the twin ideals of a universal Imāmate and a universal Caliphate had achieved two remarkable successes – the recruitment to his cause of the Sevener followers of Muḥammad ibn Ismāᶜīl in Iran, and his establishment of the dynasty in Egypt, in the heartlands of Islam. The challenge of bringing these achievements together in the universal empire to which he aspired was left at his early death to his successors. He himself had successfully delegated the rule of his Maghribi dominions to his chosen lieutenants in Ifrīqiya and Sicily. Faced with the political realities of the Middle East following the final break-up of the ᶜAbbasid empire, his son and successor al-ᶜAzīz had gone on to bring old Ikhshīdid Syria gradually under his control. By 985, therefore, the Fatimid empire had established itself as a large and aggressive polity within the Muslim commonwealth, one with which its other members were obliged to reckon. While the loyal lieutenants of the Caliph were actively campaigning in Morocco and southern Italy, the annexation of northern Syria, from Aleppo to the Euphrates, was steadily pursued with an eye to the eventual goal, the elimination of the ᶜAbbasids from Baghdad. Beyond these borders to east and west, the claim of the Imām-Caliph to rule over the whole of Islam was advanced by diplomacy, aimed in the first place at the overlordship of the Holy Places of Mecca and Medina, indispensable if that claim were to be made good. Less vital to its success but equally significant of its appeal was the summons to the Christian ruler of Muqurra on the Nile in Nubia to the south of Aswan, to resume his tributary status as a monarch whose allegiance to the Coptic Patriarch in Egypt brought his kingdom within the scope of the dynasty's Amān. A more general call was extended to the princes of the Iraqi and Iranian world, inviting them to change their allegiance from Baghdad to al-Qāhira. In that world, the followers of Muḥammad ibn Ismāᶜīl whom al-Muᶜizz had recruited as the agents of his new Daᶜwa continued their proselytisation in the attempt to win those princes to the Imāmate as well as the Caliphate of the dynasty. But after 985, even as direct rule was finally imposed upon Damascus, al-ᶜAzīz failed to bring the government of Ifrīqiya more closely under his control. With that failure, the empire created by the conquest of Egypt changed shape if not direction.

The Initial Achievement

Communication by whatever means, as John Wansbrough described it in his *Lingua Franca in the Mediterranean*,[1] is of the essence of government, and the empire centred on al-Qāhira was no exception. Prior to the conquest of Egypt, the practice of making judgements and giving directions in response to requests for guidance had not only positioned the Imām at the centre of the worldwide community of his followers, but achieved a notable political success at Multan in India, where the revolutionaries who had appealed to al-Muᶜizz had created a state in his name, the first to appear within the Fatimid fold. That practice, in which communication was a two-way process initiated from below, remained fundamental to the government of the empire. It was reversed when the initiative was that of the monarch, and messages, messengers and agents were sent out to establish and maintain the imperial connection, in the expectation of a reply. No sooner, then, had Jawhar taken possession of Egypt than he despatched Ibn Sulaym al-Aswānī to Old Dongola, the capital of Muqurra, to summon its Christian king to acknowledge his subservience to the new master of Egypt, to resume payment of the Baqṭ, to embrace Islam and otherwise enter into the Dhimma accorded to the Egyptians under the terms of the Amān. The Baqṭ, or Pact, was the agreement concluded in 652 at the time of the Arab conquests, whereby the Muqurrans bought peace and a supply of corn in exchange for slaves, which had regularly lapsed and sporadically been revived as a token of Muqurra's submission to Muslim authority. The text we have dates from the beginning of the twelfth century, but the preamble and conclusion so closely resemble those of Jawhar's Amān that it may well repeat the letter presented by Ibn Sulaym to King George. The call to embrace Islam was predictably rejected; but the momentum of the advance into Egypt had been maintained, the claim to overlordship asserted and the Nubians given notice of the new era in which they would be incorporated into the empire of the Imām Caliph. Having invaded Egypt in the past ten years, and witnessing the subsequent difficulties of Jawhar in Syria and Egypt, the Nubians may have been in no hurry to oblige; but by the 990s, the prestige of the dynasty was such that

[1] J. Wansbrough, *Lingua Franca in the Mediterranean* (Richmond, 1996).

payment of the Baqṭ had been resumed, and the aim of Ibn Sulaym's mission accomplished.[2]

Whether or not the Baqṭ was in force or in abeyance, the relationship with Nubia was not only of long standing, but close,[3] not least because its two kingdoms, Muqurra and the more distant ᶜAlwa, were not only Christian, but provinces of the Coptic Patriarchate of Alexandria, and, as such, dependencies of a Church belonging to the Caliphate, and closely associated with it.[4] It was at the same time very much in the interest of Nubia to maintain friendly relations with a strong Egyptian state for economic reasons, not least because of the strong Fatimid commitment to the desert route south-east from Aswan to the port of ᶜAydhāb on the Red Sea opposite Jedda, the port of Mecca. This was certainly commercial, as the trade of the Indian Ocean began to flow up the Red Sea and the Valley of the Nile to the Egyptian capital and on to Alexandria. But as a pilgrimage route, it was still more important to the establishment of a Fatimid protectorate of the Holy Places. Such a protectorate, with the obligation to safeguard the Ḥajj, the annual pilgrimage, had been granted to the Ikhshidids in the last days of the ᶜAbbasid empire, but rendered precarious and finally undermined by the Carmathians of Baḥrayn. To re-establish it for the benefit of the Fatimids, it was necessary on the one hand to eliminate the Carmathian threat to the pilgrimage route down the east coast of the Red Sea, and on the other to secure the alliance of the Meccans and Medinans. So central to Islam, but so remote from the seats of its empire, whether at Damascus, Baghdad or al-Qāhira, the government of the twin cities had long fallen into the hands of their inhabitants, a quarrelsome assortment of Ḥasanids and Ḥusaynids. ᶜAlids belonging to the two main lines of descent from the Prophet, these were members of the extended family to which the Fatimids themselves belonged, and connected to the Ashrāf who had given a cautious welcome to the dynasty in Egypt. This Egyptian connection was important in creating a presumption in favour of its claims. More to the point was the rise to power of the Mūsawī dynasty at Mecca. Coinciding with their conquest of Egypt, this created a single lordship with which the Fatimids could deal. The defeat of the Carmathians in 974 prompted Jaᶜfar,

2 For Ibn Sulaym and his mission, see al-Maqrīzī, *Khiṭāṭ*, ed. Wiet, III, pp. 290–2, and *Muqaffā*, pp. 252–4. Cf. Brett, *Rise of the Fatimids*, pp. 382–5.

3 The literature is considerable: cf. Y. F. Ḥasan, *The Arabs and the Sudan, From the Seventh to the Sixteenth Century* (Edinburgh, 1967); G. Vantini, *Christianity in the Sudan* (Bologna, 1981); and W. Y. Adams, *Nubia. Corridor to Africa* (London and Princeton, NJ, 1977, repr. 1984).

4 Cf. Brett, *Rise of the Fatimids*, pp. 385–90, and 'Al-Karāza al-Marqusīya. The Coptic Church in the Fatimid empire', in U. Vermeulen and J. Van Steenbergen (eds), *Egypt and Syria in the Fatimid, Ayyubid and Mamluk Eras*, IV (Leuven, 2005), pp. 33–60.

the founder of the dynasty, to recognise the Imām Caliph by offering the Friday prayer in his name. But it required a military expedition sent by al-ᶜAzīz in 976 to compel him to make a permanent submission. Thereafter the Pilgrimage proceeded each year under military escort, bearing with it the *kiswa*, or cloth, to cover the Kaaba. This recurrent demonstration of the power and authority of the Caliphate in this crucial matter was made all the more effective by the Fatimid fleet stationed at ᶜAydhāb. Still more importantly, the relationship was subsidised by the export of Egyptian grain through the port of Qulzum to feed the annual influx into the deserts of Arabia. That influx in turn created a huge annual, intercontinental fair, an occasion which tied the Meccans and their Sharifian rulers into a mutually beneficial partnership with the Fatimids in a commercial as well as political enterprise.[5]

Life and Art

Al-Qāhira was home to a style of life extending from the palace to the mansions of the great, down to the domiciles of the wealthy and the citizenry, both there and in Fusṭāṭ, one that is recorded *en passant* in the chronicles, and illustrated in what survives of Fatimid art – carvings in marble, wood and ivory; painted ceramics; and utensils, from the precious to the everyday. It was a lifestyle which for the Caliph and his ministers was both formal and informal, divided between the ceremonial round of public appearances and a more social life of entertainment and hospitality. Both were sustained by a host of officials, slaves, servants and artistes, male and female, and supported by the equally large numbers of artists, craftsmen and women who set the stage and provided the accoutrements, from the buildings to the clothes to the furniture, jewellery, metalwork, ceramics, ivories and glass, not to speak of the confectionery. The two lives intersected on the occasion of the Feasts of Sacrifice and the Breaking of the Fast, when, as described by Nāṣir-i Khusraw, the Caliph entertained high and low to a grand public banquet in his presence and elsewhere, in and around the palace. Invited to observe, he was struck by the sheer luxury and cost, not least by the sugar creations – trees, images and statuettes. The other great intersection was between the lives of men and women, the one public, the other private, but nevertheless meeting in public on the occasion of weddings and funerals, and on the more intimate occasions when guests were invited to each other's houses. The great ladies of he dynasty had their own apartments, ran their own affairs and exercised their own patronage through

[5] Cf. Brett, *Rise of the Fatimids*, pp. 390–5.

male agents, most notably al-Ḥākim's sister, Sitt al-Mulk, in residence in the Western Palace, and Raṣad, mother of al-Mustanṣir. A few of these were publicly married, like the unnamed wife of al-ᶜAzīz; many other women were married, in extravagant style, to high-ranking officers. But still other consorts, like Raṣad, had risen as concubines from the many such slave girls whose accomplishments as musicians, singers and dancers brought them into the company of men on ceremonial occasions, most famously when al-Mustanṣir was so delighted with the performance of a female drummer at the celebrations to mark the fall of Baghdad to al-Basāsirī that he gave her an estate outside the city known thereafter as Arḍ al-Ṭabbāla, the Field of the Drummer Girl. Otherwise there were the banquets at which the elite of the dynasty entertained each other, or simply through the invitation of privileged friends into the harem, as the poet Ibn Sharaf was invited by the Zirid monarch Muᶜizz. Of the servants who supported this lifestyle, the palace had its majordomo, while of the women, the ladies had personal attendants who would represent their mistresses at religious festivals within the palace.

Both life and art coincided in the doings of the Wazīr al-Yāzūrī. Gourmand as well as gourmet, extravagantly ostentatious and patron of the arts, his table was that of kings at their banquets, with everything of the best. For a banquet offered to the Caliph, the seatings, each of three carpeted mattresses, were entirely covered in white silk brocade, under canopies within a tented pavilion, all costing 5,000 dinars. He also had a liking for illustrated books and pictures, and commissioned a competition between two artists who painted, in two niches opposite each other, a dancing girl in a white dress on a black background, looking as if she were going into the wall, and another in a red dress on a yellow background, looking as if she were coming out. The reference to silk manufactures, which included the *tirāz*, or embroidered bands on hems and on the upper sleeve, extends by implication to the manufacture of linen and wool, and to the garments – robes, tunics, trousers and turbans – that were made from them. All of these survive in fragments, but especially in the paintings on ceramics, the carvings in wood and ivory, and the drawings on paper which show the wearers – warriors, huntsmen on horse or on foot, princesses, dancers, musicians playing the lute and the flute, a Coptic priest or monk and, in tilework, a head of Christ – as well as animals and birds (see Fig. 4.2). This figural art extends to glass, to the six surviving rock crystal ewers (see Fig. 5.1) and to the metalware, which apart from utensils includes statuettes of animals serving as fountainheads, perfume-burners and finials on handles and lids, all of a kind that will have featured in the service at al-Yāzūrī's feast. Rock crystal chessmen point to the popularity of the game. But the most striking image comes from the ruins of al-Manṣūriyya in Ifrīqiya, a marble relief of the

Caliph himself attended by a flute player. The seated Caliph wears the three-peaked bonnet that was his crown; on each sleeve is the band of *tirāẓ*, and in his right hand he holds a cup, another symbol of majesty; his attendant matches the images of such musicians in the Egyptian material. The faces, however, have been destroyed, the victim of an iconoclasm symbolic of the way in which the dynasty itself was eventually effaced by its opponents and successors (see Fig. 3.1). Ironically, the image has survived in a Christian context, the painting of the Norman king Roger II on the ceiling of the Cappella Palatina in Palermo. Executed, along with the ceiling itself, by Fatimid craftsmen and artists from Egypt, it depicts the King, in effect, as the Caliph, in the identical pose and costume of the figure in the relief, with only a beard to mark his difference (see Figs 11.1 and 8.1).

Cf. Nāṣir-i Khusraw, *Book of Travels*, pp. 56–7; D. Cortese and S. Calderini, *Women and the Fatimids in the World of Islam*, ch. 3; al-Maqrīzī, *Itti ͨāẓ*, II, pp. 238–9; J. Bloom, *Arts of the City Victorious*, section IV; *Trésors fatimides du Caire*, Exhibition catalogue, Institut du Monde Arabe, 1998; J. Johns, 'Muslim artists and Christian models in the painted ceilings of the Cappella Palatina', in R. Bacile and J. McNeil (eds), *Romanesque and the Mediterranean: Points of Contact across the Latin, Greek and Islamic Worlds c. 1000 to c. 1250* (Leeds, 2016)

Across the desert from Mecca and Medina, the Carmathian challenge to the dynasty faded away after the victorious expedition of al-ͨAzīz into Palestine in 978, and came to an end with the sack of their capital al-Ḥasāʾ by Bedouin tribesmen in 988. Their disappearance from the scene left the Fatimids free to contemplate Iraq, the home of their arch-rival the ͨAbbasid Caliph, but ruled by the Buyids since 945. Founded by commanders of Daylamite mercenaries from the mountains south of the Caspian, theirs was a family dominion in northern and southern Iran as well as Iraq, partitioned between three or four branches. Of these, the line in Iraq during the decade of the Fatimid conquest of Egypt, from 967 to 978, was insecure, having inherited all the problems that had undermined the ͨAbbasid regime, first and foremost the inadequacy of the country's revenue to pay the troops. Out of the troubles at Baghdad had come Aftakīn's squadron of Turks, whose surrender to al-ͨAzīz in 978 had enabled the Imām Caliph to gain control of his Syrian provinces. In that year, however, Iraq was annexed by the Buyid ruler of Fars in southern Iran, Abū Shujāʾ ͨAḍud al-Dawla Fanā Khusraw, who for the next five years headed the Buyid confederation. With an Arabic forename, an old Persian name and two titles, ͨAḍud al-Dawla, or Power of the (ͨAbbasid) State, and Shāhanshāh, King of Kings, he laid claim to both the Arab empire and its predecessor, the ancient Iranian empire of the Sassanids. Meanwhile, as a Muslim, he patronised the Twelver Shīͨites as these were coming to terms with the permanent absence of their Imām, and moving towards the formation of their own school of law in his name. Given the still nebulous authority of their Hidden Imām, this was a policy that not only distanced him from the ᶜAbbasids on the one hand and the Fatimids on the other, but gave him the religious independence to pursue his imperial ambition. In that pursuit, he followed his takeover of Baghdad by driving out the Ḥamdānid prince of Mosul, extending his dominions to the border of Syria and raising the spectre of a much more serious invasion of Fatimid territory. The threat he posed to the dynasty, both ideologically and militarily, did not however materialise. While patronising the Shīᶜites, he exiled various ᶜAlids to Shiraz in Iran, but otherwise employed them to lead the pilgrimage from Iraq. At the same time he recognised the Fatimids as ᶜAlids, and while he arrested and brought to trial the Fatimid *dāᶜī* at Basra for some unspecified offence, he seems generally to have tolerated the activities of the *duᶜāt* in the land where the *Letters of the Brethren of Purity* attest to a history of engagement with the Ismāᶜīlist tradition. That toleration continued after his death in 983, when any challenge he may have represented to the Fatimid disappeared in the family quarrels over the succession. The old problem of government in Iraq was resurrected and exacerbated by the Shīᶜite leanings of the three sons and successors of ᶜAḍūd al-Dawla at Baghdad and Shiraz, which divided the population of Baghdad into warring factions of Shīᶜites versus Sunnites. The ground was propitious for the propagation of the Daᶜwa; but the weight of al-Qāhira was not behind the kind of orchestrated campaign that had undermined the Ikhshīdids in readiness for their overthrow. Iraq was not, or at least not yet, a second Egypt.[6]

The Zirid Coup d'État

As the conquest of Egypt had demonstrated, after the failure of the Qāᵓim's initial attempts to carry the revolution in North Africa eastwards, the dynasty was prepared to bide its time. The resistance of Syria had similarly put an end to al-Muᶜizz's enthusiasm for a march to Baghdad, but not necessarily to the long-term ambition to eradicate the ᶜAbbasids, however that might be achieved. Al-ᶜAzīz was certainly not content to let matters slide, even if the immediate objectives were closer to home. In seeking to build on his success in securing Damascus, he was nevertheless doubly frustrated, in the first place by his failure to take direct control of Ifrīqiya after the death of al-Muᶜizz's viceroy Buluggīn in 984 on yet another victorious campaign in the west. Buluggīn had quickly asserted his prerogative as lieutenant of the Imām Caliph in replacing

6 For the Būyids, cf. H. Kennedy, *The Prophet and the Age of the Caliphates*, pp. 212–49; for ᶜAḍud al-Dawla, see pp. 232–6. Brett, *Rise of the Fatimids*, pp. 409–12.

Ziyādat Allāh ibn al-Qadīm, al-Muᶜizz's nominee as head of the administration at Qayrawān, with his own appointee, ᶜAbd Allāh ibn Muḥammad al-Kātib. In the manner of Ibn Killis in Egypt, ᶜAbd Allāh had then come to function as a Wazīr, a powerful figure with his own Black slave regiment, while still ultimately responsible to al-Qāhira. At the death of Buluggīn, he left his son Yūsuf in charge at Qayrawān while he himself led his troops westwards to assist Buluggīn's son al-Mansūr, fighting to secure the western frontier after his father's death. In their absence, al-ᶜAzīz moved to bring Ifrīqiya more closely into his imperial design. Communication over the distance from Egypt was crucial but slow over the three years before al-Manṣūr finally arrived at Qayrawān. The *sijill*, or official confirmation, of al-Manṣūr's succession to his father with the title of ᶜUddat al-ᶜAzīz biᵓllah, 'The Instrument of al-ᶜAzīz', did not arrive until early 985, and after the despatch by the new deputy of the requisite present to al-Qāhira, the official present of regalia sent in return by the Imām Caliph did not arrive until the summer of 986. It may have been brought, significantly, by the Dāᶜī Abūᵓl-Fahm Ḥasan al-Khurāsānī. As an Iranian from the homeland of so much Ismāᶜīlism, he may well have been a missionary for the faith. He was certainly an envoy of the Imām Caliph, welcomed by Yūsuf on behalf of his father and sent on into Kabylia to rally the Kutāma as of old, raising flags and striking coins. Equally important is the report, consistent with later practice, that on his return to Qayrawān in 987, ᶜAbd Allāh, al-Kātib, found himself appointed Dāᶜī to take the oath of allegiance from al-Manṣūr on behalf of al-ᶜAzīz. It would appear that the intention was on the one hand to recreate the Kutāma in their homeland as an army of the faithful for service presumably in the east, and on the other to return the western marches of Ifrīqiya to their old position of a frontier ruled by al-Manṣūr from Ashīr, rebuilt by Buluggīn as his capital. Neither corresponded with the intentions of al-Manṣūr. As his father's overmighty subject, ᶜAbd Allāh al-Kātib was probably doomed quite apart from his role as representative of al-ᶜAzīz; within months of al-Manṣūr's arrival at Qayrawān, both he and his son had been slain. Next year, in 988, it was the turn of Abūᵓl-Fahm, hunted down and killed, while two envoys from Egypt with letters to both of them were taken on campaign and obliged to witness his fate, allegedly roasted and eaten by the soldiery. Al-Manṣūr himself moved permanently down from Ashīr to take up residence in the Fatimid palace city of al-Ṣabra al-Manṣūriyya to establish the Zirid dynasty finally in place of the Fatimids in their Ifrīqiyan empire.[7]

Faced with this *fait accompli*, al-ᶜAzīz could only accept the result, and resume relations on a ceremonial and ritual basis. For his part, al-Mansūr

[7] Cf. Brett, *Rise of the Fatimids*, pp. 353–8.

needed his recognition by the Imām Caliph as hereditary monarch of Ifrīqiya to legitimate the rule of his Berber dynasty; al-ᶜAzīz likewise needed al-Manṣūr's allegiance to sustain his claim to universal empire. With the Friday prayer ceremonially pronounced in his name, and Zirid coins attesting to his sway, the relationship was cemented on special occasions, of which the first was in 991, when al-Mansūr's infant son Bādīs was recognised as heir apparent, Walī al-ᵓAhd, and the second two or three years later, when an exchange of presents included an elephant sent from Egypt, on which the infant Bādīs rode out to prayer. In 997, a year after the death of al-Manṣūr, Bādīs himself took the oath of allegiance to the Imām Caliph, administered by the Dāᶜī al-ᵓAlawī, sent from al-Qāhira for the occasion. Such embassies, reciprocating the presents of choice Ifrīqiyan products sent as a token of loyalty by the Zirid Amīrs, continued at intervals for the next thirty or forty years, bringing costly exotica but, more importantly, the instruments of their investiture as creatures of the Caliph.

These were, first and foremost, *sijillāt*, literally, from the Latin, 'seals', masterpieces of calligraphy authenticated with the signature of the Caliph in the form of his *ᶜalāma*, the phrase peculiar to him whose letters were intertwined to form a distinctive roundel: that of the eleventh-century Caliph al-Mustanṣir read 'Praise be to God, Lord of the Two Worlds'. Such documents were accompanied by insignia such as banners, swords and robes, which were ceremonially received and then carried or worn in procession by the Zirid monarch on the public holidays given to celebrate their arrival. The occasions were typically births, deaths and accessions, but in 1020 the *sijill* which bestowed the title of Sharaf al-Dawla on the Zirid Muᶜizz ibn Bādīs was accompanied by a second congratulating him on his news of the demise of the Umayyad Caliphate at Cordoba. Letters that celebrated such triumphs of the Fatimid cause, sent out across the world, may have been fairly frequent, a means of maintaining contact with the faithful and sustaining their morale. A more grisly token of victory came to Qayrawān in 995 in the form of the heads of Byzantines killed in battle at Aleppo. Communication was indeed all.[8]

Similar exchanges took place with the Kalbid Amīrs of Sicily, although in their case there was no comparable assertion of substantial independence, perhaps because they belonged to a clan well represented in the aristocracy of the Caliphate in al-Qāhira. Thus while Abūᵓl-Qāsim ᶜAlī, the lieutenant appointed by al-Muᶜizz, had rivalled Buluggīn in his exploits in southern Italy, dying victorious in battle against the German Emperor Otto II in 982,

[8] Cf. M. Brett, 'The diplomacy of empire: Fatimids and Zirids, 990–1062', *Bulletin of SOAS*, 78 (2015), 149–59.

his son and successor was deposed by al-ᶜAzīz at the request of his subjects, and replaced by a member of the clan in Egypt, who came accompanied by a Turkish envoy Subuktakīn. Subuktakīn stayed for at least ten years, perhaps as a go-between. In the Egyptian record, the Kalbid ruler was simply the Mutawallī, or governor, of the island, with no coinage struck in his name or any chronicler of his dynasty to match the Zirid historian al-Raqīq. Rather than pursue the invasion of southern Italy, Abū᾿l-Qāsim's successors became progressively involved in internal conflicts of the kind that had plagued the island in the mid-tenth century, aggravated by their own family quarrels.[9] What continued to bind both Ifrīqiya and Sicily to Egypt was the physical communication by sea which had been secured by the Fatimid fleets since the time of al-Muᶜizz; but from the beginning of the eleventh century even this was threatened by the rise of the maritime city states of Italy and their increasingly aggressive intrusion into the central Mediterranean. The fact remains that with the conversion of Ifrīqiya into a hereditary monarchy, the consequences for the Fatimid empire of the removal of the dynasty to Egypt became clear. What might be called the Dawla Proper, where the Caliph ruled as well as reigned, was confined to Egypt and Syria. Beyond was what might be called the Outer Dawla, a periphery of states over which he did not rule, but reigned with a varying degree of influence over rulers who acknowledged his suzerainty in the Friday prayer. If Multan had been the prototype, and the establishment of a form of protectorate over Mecca led the way, it was the withdrawal of Ifrīqiya under the Zirids which confirmed this satellite structure as the model for the expansion of the empire into what might be called the Dawla Irredenta, or Unredeemed, the regions of Islam where the Caliph neither ruled nor reigned, but which had, in God's good time, to be brought under his sway if the mission of the dynasty were to be fulfilled. Briefly, at the end of the century, such a region was the Yemen, where Ibn Ḥawshab's residual community had passed the intervening years in seclusion in the mountains. But in the 990s the Yuᶜfirid prince ᶜAbd Allāh ibn Qaḥṭān, a descendant of the renegade Ibn al-Faḍl, recognised al-Qāhira in the course of a brief career as a conqueror in the highlands and lowlands. Much more important at the time was Iran, extending north-eastwards into Khurasan and Transoxania, the scene of the Sevener activity captured by al-Muᶜizz for the Daᶜwa in the run-up to the conquest of Egypt.

[9] Ibid., 149–59. Cf. Brett, *Rise of the Fatimids*, pp. 361–3.

Figure 5.1 Rock crystal ewer with carved decoration, Egypt (probably Cairo), 1000–1050. Museum number 7904-1862 [Jameel Gallery]. © V&A.

Ewers like this were skilfully carved from rock crystal from the islands of the Indian Ocean for the greatest in the land, from the Caliph al-Azīz to the Qāʾid Ḥusayn, son of Jawhar, the conqueror of Egypt. Chessmen were also made from the same material.

The Mission in the East

In these lands, the practice of instruction in the form of replies to questions submitted by the faithful, which had structured the Book of the Teacher and the Pupil 100 years before, dictated the Mahdi's letter to the Yemen and governed the revolution at Multan, underlay the relationship of al-Qāhira to the faithful in the field. Their conversion to the Fatimid cause is apparent in the career and the writings, early in the following century, of al-Naysabūrī, the man from Nishapur in Khurasan. Coming to al-Qāhira in the reign of al-ᶜAzīz, the works he wrote in the following reign of al-Ḥākim included the *Istitār al-imām*, or Unveiling of the Imām, the first to make public a full version of the genealogy of the dynasty. At the same time, for the general instruction of the leaders of the flock, especially perhaps those of his homeland in the north-east of the Iranian world, he composed his *Risāla al-mūjaza* *al-kāfiya fī ādāb al-du*ᶜ*āt*, a Brief but Sufficient Account of the Rules of Guidance for the Duᶜāt, in which the duties of the *dā*ᶜ*ī* are set out.[10] These include the instruction of the novice in the mysteries of the Imāmate, much as in the Book of the Teacher and the Pupil. But since that was written, the Imām has appeared, requiring absolute obedience to his direction. He is nevertheless far away, so that the *dā*ᶜ*ī* must take his place at the head of the local community. The indoctrination of the believer then becomes a function of his pastoral responsibilities as one who governs in place of the Imām in a land where the Caliph neither rules nor reigns, where the state is illegitimate and its justice invalid. Forbidden to turn to the *sulṭān*, or ruler, and to the *qāḍī* he has appointed, the community he leads must submit in every way to his magistrature. Logically derived as it was from the principle of the Imāmate, such a dictatorship was only an extreme example of a principle of jurisprudence enunciated by a contemporary of al-Naysabūrī, the Mālikite jurist al-Qābisī at Qayrawān, that in the pagan Sudan beyond the borders of Islam, Muslims were required to select and obey a *nāẓir*, or supervisor, to judge in accordance with the law, lest they fall into sin and perish.[11] From that it was a short step to the *hisba*, the duty to 'command the right and forbid the wrong', which had transformed the Dāᶜī ᶜAbū ᶜAbd Allāh from a teacher into a statesman and a conqueror. That had not been the step taken by al-Naysabūrī's precursors, who had endeavoured to win over the princes of the region to their beliefs, with some success and ultimately disastrous results. On the evidence of his writings, al-Naysabūrī's own strategy was rather to win recruits against the time when the lords of the land would be either converted or overthrown. Its effect was to determine the fate of both the community and the cause in the following century.

Al-Naysabūrī had been brought up in the realm of the Sāmānids at Bukhara in Transoxania, in the third generation after al-Nasafī and al-Sijistānī, in whose time yet another attempt appears to have been made by highly-placed Ismāᶜīlīs in the service of the dynasty to seize power at Bukhara in 961. It would have occurred around the time of the recognition of the Fatimid Imāmate by al-Sijistānī, who seems to have cherished the expectation that al-Muᶜizz, as the Second Seventh in the sequence, was to be followed by the Second Coming of Muḥammad ibn Ismāᶜīl himself. Al-Sijistānī, however, vanished around 970, allegedly executed by the ruler of his native Sijistān in

[10] Al-Naysabūrī, *al-Risāla al-mūjaza al-kāfiya fī ādāab al-du*ᶜ*āt*, ed. and trans. V. Klemm and P. E. Walker, *A Code of Conduct. A Treatise on the Etiquette of the Fatimid Ismaili Mission* (London, 2011).

[11] Cf. M. Brett, 'Islam and trade in the *Bilad al-Sudan*', in Brett, *Ibn Khaldun and the Medieval Maghrib*, V.

southern Afghanistan, while his followers of the generation of al-Naysabūrī were evidently content with the Fatimid succession. They seem moreover to have been generally tolerated by the Sāmānids, if the autobiography of Avicenna may be relied upon. This major figure in the history of Islamic philosophy was the son of an Ismāᶜīlī convert, brought up in a household in which the doctrines of the new Ismāᶜīlism were discussed, and going on to study in the royal library at Bukhara. In what was evidently a cultivated and scholarly milieu, he nevertheless chose not to subscribe to this 'Egyptian' faith, to submit to the kind of discipline prescribed by al-Naysabūrī and commit himself to the sectarian antagonisms which divided the population of al-Naysabūrī's native city of Nishapur, the capital of Khurāsān to the south of the Oxus. There, the Ismāᶜīlīs were confronted by the Karamiyya, puritan revivalists and demagogues with an enthusiastic following, and by the rival factions of the Sayyids, ᶜAlids not to be won over to the Fatimid cause, but allying themselves instead with the Hanafites and Shāfiᶜites, mutually hostile followers of these two Sunnī schools of law. The decisive moment came after a major rebellion against the Sāmānids in 994 was crushed by Sebuktigīn, the Turkish ruler of Ghazna in Afghanistan, at the invitation of the Sāmānid monarch Nūḥ ibn al-Manṣūr. A nominal vassal of Bukhara, Sebuktigīn then annexed the eastern region of Khurāsān, while his son Mahmūd installed himself at Nishapur in the west. Following the deaths of both Sebuktigīn and Nūḥ in 997, Maḥmūd became the ruler of a new empire stretching from Khurāsān to the Punjab. He followed his father in adopting the militant evangelism of the Karamiyya, and posing as the champion of Islam in war upon the infidels of India and the heretics of Iran, the Ismāᶜīlīs in particular. Far from a prescription for the growing influence of the Daᶜwa in these lands, al-Naysabūrī's insistence on the authority of the *dāᶜī* then became the key to its survival.[12]

Avicenna chose to migrate westwards into the dominions of the Buyids, where his contemporary al-Kirmānī was set to become the successor to al-Sijistānī as the theologian who invested the esoteric doctrine of the Imāmate with its philosophical rationale. He or his family came from Kirmān, a region of southern Iran annexed by ᶜAḍud al-Dawla, but he settled in Iraq during the first twenty years of the eleventh century, earning the soubriquet of Ḥujjat al-ᵓIraqayn, the Proof or Witness to the Imām in the two Iraqs, Mesopotamia and western Iran. That he could flourish in this way as a *dāᶜī* working on behalf of the Fatimid Daᶜwa is a testimony to the breadth of culture which

[12] Cf. Brett, *Rise of the Fatimids*, pp. 404–7. For the sectarianism at Nishapur, see R. Bulliet, *Patricians of Nishapur* (Cambridge, MA, 1972), and C. E. Bosworth, *The Ghaznavids. Their Empire in Afghanistan and Eastern Iran, 994–1040* (Edinburgh, 1963), pp. 163–202, and ibid. for the coming of Maḥmūd and his militant Sunnism, pp. 27–54.

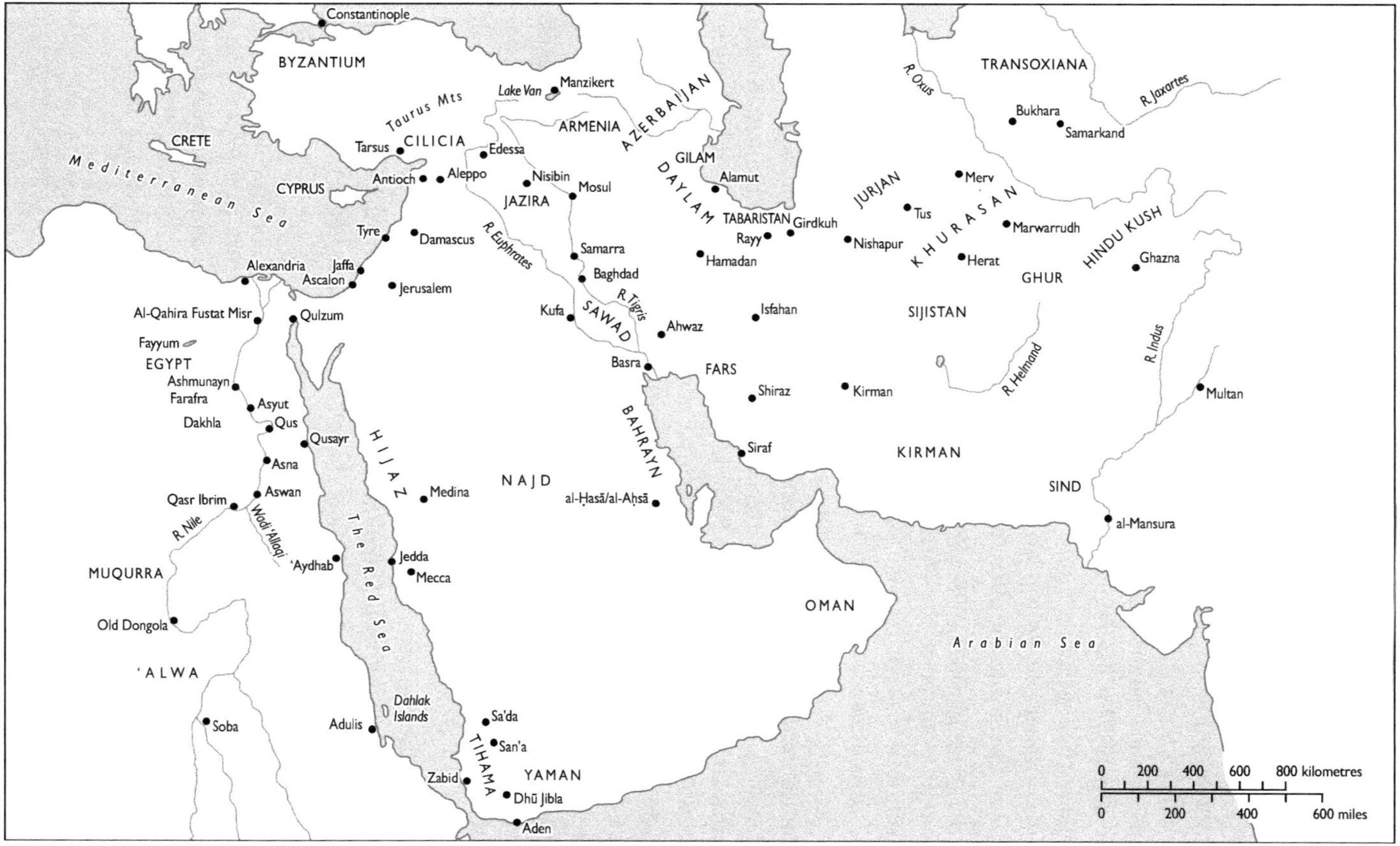

Map 5.1 The Middle Eastern World

had survived the demise of the ᶜAbbasid empire, and to a familiarity with his message and his teachings that opened the prospect of winning over the Buyids themselves. Meanwhile, however, there was the small problem of the ᶜAbbasid Caliph, still resident in his palace at Baghdad, still the nominal suzerain of the rulers to the east of the Fatimid domain, and a political figurehead for the Sunnī schools of law. As the Buyids quarrelled over the inheritance of ᶜAḍud al-Dawla, and their Shīᶜite leanings divided Baghdad into hostile factions, so the Caliphs began to reassert themselves. In 991 the Caliph al-Ṭāʾī was deposed by the reigning Buyid, but his replacement, al-Qādir, found scope to envisage a new future for himself and his office. If the reconstitution of his original empire was no longer possible, his Fatimid rival had shown the way forward to the alternative. Pursuit of the recognition of his headship of the Muslim community by the princes who ruled it in his name would not only counteract the Fatimid challenge to his historic supremacy, but substitute a majestic prestige for the power his ancestors had enjoyed. In 993, two years after his accession, he held audience for the pilgrims of Khurāsān as they passed through Baghdad on their return from Mecca. Explaining the significance of the Friday prayer in his name, he sent them on their way with a treatise on the subject, and letters to the ruler of Khurāsān. He was, in other words, attempting to beat the Fatimids at their own game. The ruler in question was nominally the Sāmānid Nūḥ ibn al-Manṣūr, although the province was in revolt; but by the end of the century it had been incorporated into the Ghaznawid empire of Maḥmūd. By origin a Turkish *ghulām*, Maḥmūd's only claim to legitimacy was the war waged in the name of Islam against the infidel in India, and the persecution of deviants from Sunnī orthodoxy in his own dominions. In recognising Baghdad, he was putting himself forward as the champion of the ᶜAbbasid Caliph in this holy war, fulfilling on his behalf one of the Caliph's prime duties as leader of the Muslim community. In targeting the Ismāᶜīlīs, he was setting himself in particular against al-Qādir's prime enemy, the rival Caliphate of the Fatimids. On the far horizon of al-Qāhira had appeared a cloud no bigger than a man's hand.[13]

Aleppo and Byzantium

If waging, and indeed leading the community in person in holy war was a prime duty of the Caliph since the time of the Arab conquests, then it was fulfilled by al-ᶜAzīz in the last years of his reign as he prepared for the final conquest of Aleppo.[14] Its possession was essential if the Fatimids were ever

[13] Cf. Brett, *Rise of the Fatimids*, pp. 411–15.

[14] Ibid., pp. 348–53, 417–18. In addition to the annalistic account by al-Maqrīzī in the

going to invade Iraq; it was on the other hand a formidable fortress under the rule of the Ḥamdānid prince Saᶜd al-Dawla, a determined opponent of the Fatimids who did not only enjoy the backing of the majority of his citizens. As an opponent of the Fatimids, he was an ally of the Byzantines, whose advance into Muslim territory in the 960s had culminated in the capture of Antioch in 969, and turned Aleppo itself from an enemy into a client of Constantinople. The defence of Islam against this unprecedented loss of ground had been a major theme of al-Muᶜizz's propaganda for the conquest of Egypt, and had entered into the Amān granted by Jawhar as a pledge to its people. The commitment had been honoured by the call to arms for the advance upon Antioch in 970–1, but promptly frustrated by the revolt of Damascus against Jaᶜfar ibn Falāh. It had then been severely tested by the invasion of Palestine by the Emperor John Tzimisces in 975. But while the death of the Emperor in 976 had lifted the threat to Jerusalem, it had done nothing to alter the position of Aleppo as a ward of Byzantium, a buffer against the empire to the south. In 983, as Damascus was finally brought under Fatimid control, the rebellious Ḥamdānid *ghulām* Bakjūr had been supplied with troops for an attack upon Aleppo, only to be thwarted by the arrival of a Byzantine army. In 991, from the base he had acquired at Raqqa on the Euphrates, he made a second attempt.

This was the fateful year in which Ibn Killis died; Munīr, the governor of Damascus, allegedly entered into treasonable correspondence with Baghdad; Bakjūr was captured and crucified by Saᶜd al-Dawla; and al-ᶜAzīz himself finally undertook the conquest of northern Syria. As far as Aleppo was concerned, insult was added to injury when Saᶜd al-Dawla forced the Fatimid envoy to eat al-ᶜAzīz's letter of protest at his treatment of Bakjūr's family. This final failure to take the city by proxy, by a warlord in Fatimid employ, brought an immediate response. State and empire came together in the form of a major expedition to bring the whole of Syria firmly into the Fatimid fold, the climax of the years spent patiently securing first Palestine and then Damascus for the Caliphate; its preparation may well have dated back to the disastrous mission of the Dāᶜī Abūʾl-Fahm to raise a fresh army from the Kutāma in their Ifrīqiyan homeland in 986–8. Its Turkish commander Manjūtakīn set out from al-Qāhira with all the pomp of Jawhar's departure from al-Manṣūriyya. At Damascus Munīr was arrested as a traitor and paraded round the city before being sent back for his ritual humiliation in the Egyptian capital. The nature of his offence is obscure; in the year

Ittiᶜāẓ, see Th. Bianquis, *Damas et la Syrie sous la domination fatimide (969–1076)*, 2 vols (Damascus, 1986, 1989), vol. 1, pp. 178–208.

when the ᶜAbbasid al-Ṭāᵓī was deposed at Baghdad, he may have been tempted to intervene in Buyid affairs. Whatever he had done cannot have been wholly criminal, since although the heads of his followers were paraded with him on pikes, he himself, in Fatimid fashion, was then invested with a robe of honour, and pardoned. His dismissal was incidental to the conduct of the methodical operation whose aim was the acquisition of Aleppo, and with it the whole of northern Syria. This was more than an end in itself, important as that was. Aleppo was, in the words attributed to Bakjūr, the entrance hall of Iraq, the key to any future invasion of the ᶜAbbasid realm. More immediately, its capture would be a blow to Byzantium, a glorious victory in the holy war which would set the seal on the conquest of Egypt and demonstrate yet again that the Caliphate of all believers had come into the hands of its true possessors. In the language of the Fatimid Imāmate, it would be a further proof of its divine mission, crowning the Caliphate of al-ᶜAzīz as the conquest of Egypt had been the culmination of his father's.

The moment was propitious, for the warrior Emperor Basil II was away in the Balkans at war with the Bulgars, leaving only the garrison of the frontier at Antioch to meet the Fatimid attack. At the end of 991, moreover, Saᶜd al-Dawla died, leaving Aleppo in the hands of the *ghulām* Luᵓluᵓ as regent for his young son Saᶜīd. With ᶜĪsā ibn Nastūrus directing the operation in Egypt, and the governor of Ramla, Ḥasan ibn Ṣālih al-Rūdhbārī, deputed to act as Manjūtakīn's secretary and paymaster-general, Manjūtakīn himself then had all the resources for a long campaign. In 992 he advanced down the valley of the Orontes, taking Homs and Hama, and routing the combined forces of Aleppo and Antioch; the heads of the dead Byzantines were sent as a trophy to al-Manṣūr in Ifrīqiya. In 993 he took Shayzar, next in line down the Orontes, and, in 994, advanced on Aleppo itself. With the Egyptian fleet preventing a Byzantine attack by sea, supplies were landed at Tripoli for a year-long siege over the winter. But, in May 995, it failed at the unexpected approach of the Byzantine Emperor himself after a forced march across Anatolia. Obeying the rule of war that a besieger should not be caught between the besieged and a relieving force, Manjūtakīn withdrew to Damascus. In a grand theatrical gesture, al-ᶜAzīz moved out of al-Qāhira to install himself to the north of the city in the great tent erected for the Imām Caliph on campaign. There he announced his departure to defend the land of Islam against the infidel, and summoned the townsfolk of al-Fusṭāṭ to join the host in fulfilment of their Muslim duty. Alarmed, they begged to be excused, in a nice comment on the way in which Muslim society had developed over the years. But before any expedition could set out, the envoys of Basil II arrived to announce his departure and arrange a truce.

The truce was a recognition on both sides that hostilities were effectively

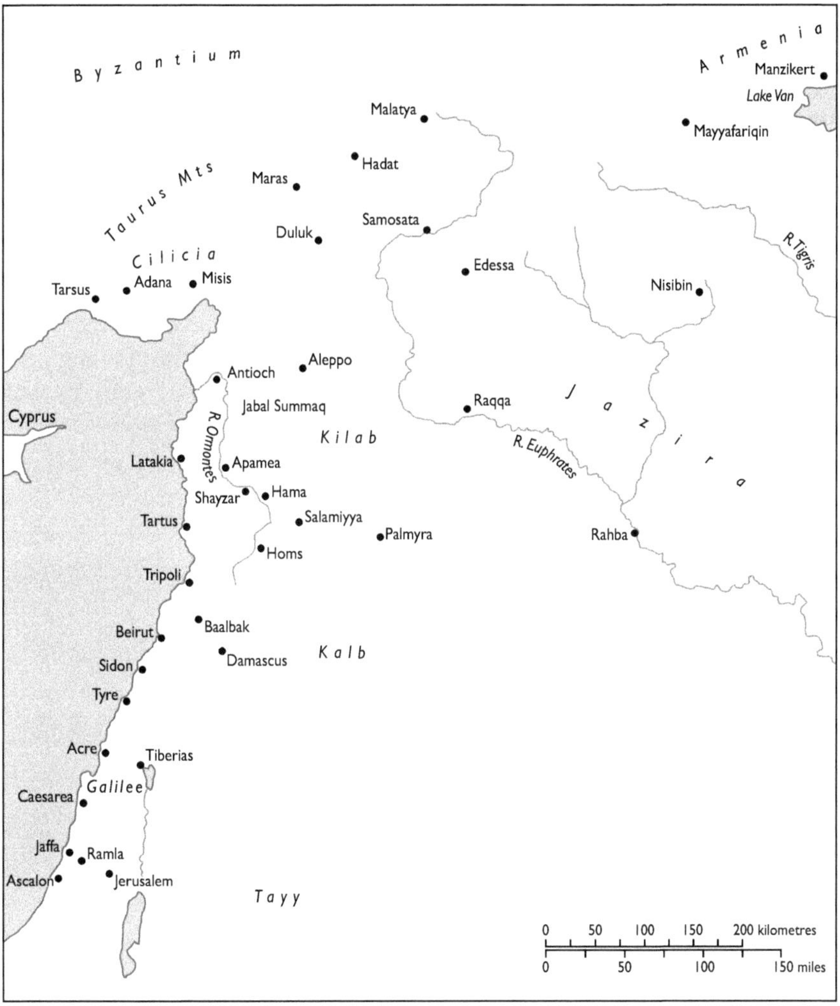

Map 5.2 Fatimid Syria

at an end for the rest of the year. For al-ᶜAzīz it was a necessary pause to gather his forces for a further expedition. He apparently remained encamped throughout the winter, while their mobilisation continued. In April 996, new warships built at al-Maqs, the port of his capital on the Nile, were manned with marines and an appeal made for volunteers for the fleet. But a fire destroyed many of the vessels. Incensed against the Christian foe, the mob attacked and plundered the Amalfitans in their yard nearby, to be severely punished by the Christian minister ᶜĪsā ibn Nasṭūrus, who set about rebuilding the fleet. The presence of the Amalfitans is evidence of the entrance of the Italians into the trade of the Mediterranean, and equally of the failure of the Sicilians to compete; it may be that the Amalfitans had brought the timber of Sicily to construct the ships. The affair is a comment on the openness of Fatimid Egypt to such trade. The refusal of the regime to identify the Amalfitans with the Byzantines, and the firm action of its Coptic minister to restore their stolen goods, are meanwhile evidence of the very specific character of the holy war upon which the Caliph was engaged. But while Egyptian corsairs brought in Byzantine prisoners to be paraded around the town, the destruction of the fleet inevitably delayed his preparations. In August, al-ᶜAzīz moved off to camp at Bilbays some twenty miles down the road to Palestine, presumably with an eye to a spring campaign in the following year. But there, two months later, he fell ill and died; and the whole enterprise took second place to the question of the succession.

6

A Failure of Direction: The Reign of al-Ḥākim bi Amr Allāh

The Regency for an Infant

The unexpected death of al-ᶜAzīz in camp at Bilbays precipitated quite a different problem of succession from those of the past. Al-Manṣūr, the son of al-ᶜAzīz, was a boy of eleven. His elder brother Muḥammad had died. The problem in the first place was that of a minor: Sitt al-Mulk, the adult elder sister of the lad, appears to have put forward in his place the adult son of ᶜAbd Allāh, the designated heir of al-Muᶜizz before his death just before his father's. But Barjawān, the Slavonic eunuch who was the boy's tutor, had set the *tāj*, or turban crown, on his head the moment al-ᶜAzīz died, and had him proclaimed as al-Ḥākim bi Amr Allāh, Ruler by the Command of God. The problem then was that of a minority, of who should govern on his behalf. As kingmaker, Barjawān was not in the position of Jawdhar, a steward in undisputed control of the household, enjoying the trust of an adult sovereign who took undisputed command of the state. The politics of the palace and the aristocracy promptly surfaced in a competition for power which rapidly came to blows as the rivalry within the army between the Maghāriba and the Mashāriqa came into play. On his deathbed al-ᶜAzīz appears to have mandated his Qāḍī, Muḥammad ibn al-Nuᶜmān, together with the doyen of the old Ifrīqiyan aristocracy Ḥasan ibn ᶜAmmār, to ensure a smooth succession. Victor over the Byzantines in Sicily and in battle with the Carmathians at Fusṭāṭ, head of the Kalbid clan in Egypt and last of al-Muᶜizz's old guard, Ḥasan was an obvious candidate for the regency. At the *bayᶜa*, the ceremony of homage to the new Caliph, he made his bid for power when the chiefs of the Kutāma, the Friends of the Imām, demanded his appointment as Wāsiṭa in place of the Kātib ᶜĪsā ibn Nasṭūrus. ᶜĪsā, the secretary who had taken charge of al-ᶜAzīz's war effort, was thus superseded in charge of the government by one of the great men of the dynasty with the title of Amīn al-Dawla, Custodian of the State. The title was the beginning of a trend to ever more elaborate honorifics which earned the Fatimids the epithet of 'this pompous dynasty' from Stanley

Lane-Poole.[1] More sinister was the execution of ᶜĪsā ibn Nasṭūrus, accused by the Kutāma of paying them less than their due in his management of the finances for the war. Elder statesman as he was, Ḥasan was not in fact independent of his supporters. He was certainly their man as he set out to restore the Men of the West to the position they claimed by right as the first and foremost of the folk of the Imām Caliph.

Not only therefore did they receive a donative of cash to celebrate the accession of the new sovereign, and more besides in the way of gifts, they were privileged with access to the presence of the monarch to the exclusion of their Eastern rivals, who were removed from their positions at al-Qāhira. The reliance of al-ᶜAzīz upon the Mashāriqa, the Turks, to conduct the Syrian campaign was similarly reversed, as command of both government and army went to those who had procured Ibn ᶜAmmār's appointment. Unlike Ibn ᶜAmmār himself, these belonged to the generation that had come of age in Egypt, men like Ḥusayn ibn Jawhar and Salmān (or Sulaymān) ibn Jaᶜfar ibn Falāḥ, sons of the conquerors of Egypt in 969. While Ḥusayn took charge of the Chancery and the Post, the departments responsible for the official utterances of the regime and its intelligence services, Salmān was given command of the army in Syria in place of Manjūtakīn. Within a year, however, these had paid the price of their coup. Manjūtakīn was defeated at Ascalon as he advanced upon Egypt, and Salmān took possession of Damascus. But in dismissing the Kutāma governor of Tripoli, Jaysh ibn al-Ṣamṣāma, in favour of his own brother ᶜAlī, Salmān alienated his natural allies among the Maghāriba established in Syria, while in the absence of his forces from Egypt, the tables were turned at al-Qāhira. Fighting in the streets of the capital between Berbers and Turks who had been supplied with arms by Barjawān ended with the flight of Ibn ᶜAmmār and Barjawān's assumption of power in September 997. In December, Salmān was evicted from Damascus by the Turkish soldiery in alliance with the citizen militia, and replaced by Jaysh as a long-standing pillar of the Fatimid regime in Syria.

The appointment of Jaysh as a governor acceptable to the Syrians was consonant with the policy of Barjawān in Egypt, where Ibn ᶜAmmār was brought back to al-Qāhira and retired with all the living allowances he had previously enjoyed. As one identified with the palace household rather than either of the main factions, Barjawān then took over control of the government as Wazīr in all but name, illustrating in the process one of its prime functions, the hearing of petitions by the monarch. Regularised since the days

[1] S. Lane-Poole, *A History of Egypt in the Middle Ages*, 4th edn (London, 1925, repr. 1968), p. 124, n. 1.

when Caesar had allegedly been murdered by conspirators pretending to be petitioners, such a hearing had continued to be a central feature of the weekly routine of the head of state from Roman times onward. It was undertaken by Barjawān with the assistance of his Christian secretary Fahd ibn Ibrāhīm, who received the petitions in the first place, passing those of importance on to Barjawān for his decision before they were taken in to al-Ḥākim for signature and returned to the petitioner for appropriate action. Young as al-Ḥākim was, the procedure inducted him into the business of government while maintaining his authority as the monarch with final responsibility for the affairs of his subjects. Otherwise, however, apart from parading in state on the great ceremonial occasions of the year, he was excluded from the management of affairs. Barjawān secured his position by placing his fellows from the palace corps of Ṣaqāliba in the critical posts of chiefs of police in al-Qāhira and Fusṭāṭ, and likewise in strategic command of the navy, of the naval port of Tripoli and of the entrance to Egypt at Gaza and Ascalon, where his brother Yamīn was installed. With these appointments he secured the approaches to and from Syria by sea and by land, a precaution against the troubles of the province. Renewed since the death of al-ᶜAzīz by the conflict of the Maghāriba and the Mashāriqa, these troubles were compounded by Byzantine aggression, by popular uprisings at Damascus and Tyre, and by fresh incursions by the nomad Arab Ṭāyy under their Jarrāḥid chief. Supported by the Byzantine fleet, the port of Tyre declared its independence; Damascus was once again in the hands of the *aḥdāth* while the Byzantines besieged Apamea on the Orontes below Shayzar and Hama. With the Fatimid forces in Syria now reunited under his command, however, Jaysh took Tyre with the aid of the Fatimid fleet and obliged Ibn al-Jarrāḥ to submit, before driving the Byzantines away from Apamea and back to Antioch. Pacification was completed in 999 with the capture and execution of perhaps 1,200 of the *aḥdāth* of Damascus, and the deportation to Egypt of the Ashrāf, the notables of the city whose suspicion of the Fatimids had been vitriolically expressed in the black legend of their origins perpetrated by the Sharīf Akhū Muḥsin. This reassertion of Fatimid control survived the sudden return of Basil II to conduct an autumn campaign almost as far to the south as Baalbek in Lebanon. After this rude interruption, the negotiations that were already in hand for a ten-year truce were promptly resumed with the despatch of a high-level delegation to Constantinople, and eventually concluded with the arrival of a Byzantine ambassador at al-Qāhira in May 1001. With that, the affairs of Syria were settled for the duration.

In thus securing Fatimid Syria both internally and externally, Barjawān was returning the Fatimid state to order while consolidating his personal position as regent, at the expense of al-ᶜAzīz's ambition to resume the conquest of empire with the capture of Aleppo. It was the policy of a caretaker, the success of which in Egypt and Syria was qualified by his handling of affairs in the west. In Ifrīqiya the new Zirid sultan Bādīs, little older than al-Ḥākim, was in the midst of his own succession crisis, challenged by his great-uncles, attacked in the west by the Zanāta allies of Cordoba, and nearer home by the Zanāta chief Fulful, whom his father had appointed governor of Ṭubna in the Zāb. By 999, he and his uncle Ḥammād had gained the upper hand, only to be challenged in the east by Barjawān in his capacity as head of government on behalf of the Imām Caliph. Formal relations between the two new sovereigns, al-Ḥākim and Bādīs, had been concluded in 997 with the arrival at al-Manṣūriyya of a Dāᶜī from al-Qāhira, the Sharīf al-ᵓAlawī, to take the oath of loyalty on a grand ceremonial occasion to celebrate their alliance.[2] But when Barjawān was approached in 999 by Tamṣūlat, the long-standing Zirid governor of Tripoli, with an offer to hand the city over to al-Qāhira in return for permission to emigrate to Egypt, he accepted. One of the Ṣaqāliba, Yānis, whom Barjawān had nominated as governor of Barqa on the western frontier of Egypt, was despatched with a considerable army to take over at Tripoli in 1000. Challenged by Bādīs to prove his appointment by the Caliph, Yānis refused, and fell in battle with a Zirid force in 1001. Tripoli, however, remained independent. Whatever the cause of the Zirid governor's flight from Bādīs's displeasure – allegedly corruption, more probably an excessive show of independence, the citizens welcomed back Yānis's men and closed the gates against the Zirid army which laid siege to the city. The siege was broken by the arrival of the rebel governor of Ṭubna, Fulful ibn Saᶜīd, at the head of his Zanāta warriors. Taking over the city with the evident support of the townsfolk, he ruled there until his death in 1010 in the name of al-Ḥākim, making only a final abortive attempt to change his allegiance to Cordoba. With a marked resemblance to the admittedly brief career of Aftakīn at Damascus, Fulful's achievement was the first step towards the creation of a new city-state, part of the proliferation of such states across the western Islamic world in the eleventh century. Its significance was more than local. This further failure of al-Qāhira to impose its control over the government of its western provinces, coming as it did in the wake of the abandonment of the Syrian campaign, was a further step towards the constitution of an outer Dawla where the Caliph reigned but did not rule. It was all the more important since the breakaway of Tripoli from Ifrīqiya was a first indication that the tensions which had surfaced within the Zirid dominions at the death of al-Manṣūr threatened the continued existence of

[2] For the history of the diplomatic relationship between the Fatimids and the Zirids in this period, and the instruments employed, see M. Brett, 'The diplomacy of empire', and Idris, *La Berbérie orientale sous les Zīrīdes*, I, pp. 86–90.

the state that the Arabs had taken over from the Byzantines, and which had been turned by the Fatimids into the foundation of their empire. After the triumphs of the tenth century, the affair of Tripoli stood at the beginning of a different story in the eleventh.[3]

A History of Controversy

That was all the more so since by the time that peace was concluded with Byzantium and Fulful had taken possession of Tripoli, Barjawān was dead, assassinated in March 1000 in the palace gardens by the young Caliph and his henchman, the parasol-bearer Raydān. It was a moment like the assassination of that other overmighty subject, the Dā^cī Abū ^cAbd Allāh, by the Mahdī at the outset of his reign, announcing as it did the determination of the new monarch to take control of his inheritance. It differed in that the inheritance was no longer the revolutionary army which had brought the Mahdī to power at the outset of the dynasty's career, but the regular armies of domestics, secretaries, soldiers and lawyers that now composed the regime at the height of its efflorescence in Egypt. It differed likewise in that the new monarch was no veteran revolutionary or determined adult devotedly served by a Jawdhar and a Qāḍī al-Nu^cmān, but brought up as a minor by a majordomo in the very different mould of the Ikhshīdid regent Kāfūr. His authority as Imām and Caliph was unchallenged, such was the discipline of the dynasty that maintained the principle of designation as sole title to the throne. But with the elimination of his mentor, it fell to him to exercise that authority in government for the purpose of the mission which had driven the creation of the empire, and which he was now called upon to advance (see Fig. 6.1). How he did so provoked a crisis of the Dawla and the Da^cwa, and a controversy in the literature that has grown with the growth of Fatimid studies over the past century.

The sources at the root of the controversy belong in the first place to the Egyptian tradition begun by al-Kindī and continued into the Fatimid period by Ibn Zūlāq, after whom it builds up from the *Akhbār Miṣr*, the largely lost chronicle of al-Musabbiḥī at the court of al-Ḥākim into the *Itti^cāẓ al-ḥunafā^ɔ*, the dynastic history compiled by al-Maqrīzī in the fifteenth century. Only the fortieth volume of the *Akhbār Miṣr* survives, covering a short period after al-Ḥākim's death, from 1023 to 1024,[4] but enough to reveal the extraordinary

[3] For the details of this history, see Idris, *La Berbérie orientale sous les Zīrīdes*, I, pp. 99–106, and Brett, 'The city-state in mediaeval Ifrīqiya: the case of Tripoli', in Brett, *Ibn Khaldun and the Medieval Maghrib*, no. XIV.

[4] (Al-Musabbiḥī) *Tome quarantième de la* Chronique d'Égypte *de Musabbiḥī*, ed. A. F. Sayyid in conjunction with Th. Bianquis, 2 parts (Cairo, 1978).

detail of this contemporary account by an Amīr closely involved in the affairs of state, whose copious information underlies the annals of later chroniclers. Thus formed, this Egyptian tradition is paralleled by a Christian tradition in the Coptic *History of the Patriarchs*, and notably supplemented by the *Ta*ʾ*rīkh* of the contemporary Melkite author Yaḥyā ibn Saᶜīd al-Anṭākī, who lived in Egypt until 1014, and knew a court physician.[5] The Ismāᶜīlī tradition continues to be represented by the ᶜ*Uyūn al-akhbar* of al-Maqrīzī's contemporary, the Dāᶜī Idrīs ᶜImād al-Dīn in the Yemen. Meanwhile, the Egyptian tradition is incorporated into, as well as supplemented by, an assorted literature of Syrian and Iraqi origin, including Ibn al-Qalānisī's chronicle of Damascus written in the mid-twelfth century; the universal chronicle of Ibn al-Athīr at Mosul in the thirteenth; and the Baghdad chronicle composed by successive members of a Sabian, that is, a Judaeo-Christian family, most notably Hilāl al-Ṣābiʾ, writing in the mid-eleventh century. Certainly as reported by the twelfth-century Ibn al-Jawzī and others, this chronicle was not only pro-ʾAbbasid but anti-Fatimid, a contribution to the propaganda war waged by the rival Caliphates. The story all these sources have variously yielded in the case of al-Ḥākim is of a string of executions of the personnel of the regime; a swinging to and fro between condemnation and approval of Sunnī Islam and toleration and persecution of Christians; an increasing number of prescriptions and proscriptions regarding the dress and comportment of Christians and Jews, the freedom of women and the eating of various foods; and the opening, closing and reopening of the Majlis al-Ḥikma, where the faithful were lectured on the doctrine of the dynasty; all of which led up to the designation of an heir to the Caliphate, but not to the Imāmate, of one who was not his son; to his acclamation as God by extremist believers; and to his retreat into asceticism, culminating in his final disappearance, supposedly murdered, in the desert. All this goes with the stories of his accessibility to the people as he rode out among them in the streets of the capital, and has been variously explained as eccentricity amounting to madness – the verdict of Yaḥyā al-Anṭākī, who had it from al-Ḥākim's physician. Such a diagnosis, at such a distance in time and in the absence of any agreed definition of insanity, is unacceptable except as a confession of bafflement, a bafflement which al-Anṭākī observed in the faithful when they explained his actions as the product of the inscrutable inspiration of the Imām. But it has contributed to the black legend of a murderous maniac which was recounted at the beginning of the twentieth century by Stanley Lane-Poole in his *History of Egypt in*

[5] Cf. J. Forsyth, *The Byzantine-Arab Chronicle (938–1034) of Yaḥyā b. Saʿīd al-Anṭākī*, 2 vols (Ann Arbor, MI, and London, 1977).

Figure 6.1 Porch of the Mosque of al-Ḥākim in al-Qāhira. Photo: Bernard O'Kane.

In the manner of the porch of the Great Mosque of al-Mahdiyya, it is aligned on the Mihrab of the prayer hall to give entrance to the Imam-Caliph.

the Middle Ages.[6] Since then the effort has gone into finding more plausible explanations in the political and religious circumstances in which al-Ḥākim took charge of the dynasty's fortunes.

All explanations envisage a crisis, but otherwise differ widely. Shaban saw al-Ḥākim as a good, ordinary Muslim, who refused to be treated as Imām; at the same time he was an economic rationalist, who imposed all his seemingly strange restrictions on food in an effort to conserve food supplies, since agriculture had been ruined by Fatimid tax-farming.[7] Vatikiotis proposed that enemies within and without had brought the state to the point of collapse, requiring not only ruthless measures, but a return to the messianism of the

[6] Lane-Poole, *A History of Egypt in the Middle Ages*, pp. 125–34.
[7] M. A. Shaban, *Islamic History*, 2 vols (Cambridge, 1976), vol. 2.

Mahdī/Qāʾim, the idea of the God-king.[8] Makarem thought that his solution was to dispense with the Imāmate and leave the state to return to pedestrian normality.[9] For Bianquis, the crisis was that of the patrimonial state, the takeover of government by the servants of the monarch, which al-Ḥākim struggled to prevent.[10] Assaad considered him to be a conscientious Imām in the tradition of the hereditary Imāmate, whose promotion of Ismāʿīlī teaching and constitution of the Daʿwa as a separate ministry resulted in the resurrection of *ghuluww*, the belief in the Imām's divinity that the Mahdī had repressed, but which now threatened to destabilise the dynasty.[11] Halm rather saw in the edicts of al-Ḥākim a belief that he was the Waṣī, the Trustee, not simply of the Prophet, like his predecessors in the line of ʿAlī, but of God Himself.[12] Harking back to Vatikiotis, Van Ess went further in seeing al-Ḥākim drawn into renewed expectations of the millennium and what he called the temptation of divinity.[13] Most recently, Walker has concentrated on the signs of crisis: a growing unpredictability leading up to a withdrawal from the affairs of both Dawla and Daʿwa following the designation of an heir to the Caliphate and the appointment of a Chief Dāʿī alongside a Chief Qāḍī who was no longer an Ismāʿīlī.[14] And certainly, behind all these attempts to find some 'method in his madness', there lurks the sense of a progression from the youth who initially revelled in his freedom to enter into the life of his capital city to the middle-aged ascetic who may have enjoyed his freedom to wander away from society, behaviour that in both cases did not conform to the expectations of the faithful, and which they struggled to understand. Instead of the clear lead given by his predecessors, there was a failure of direction in which the previous purposefulness of the dynasty was

[8] P. J. Vatikiotis, 'al-Ḥākim bi-Amrillah: the God-King idea realised', *Islamic Culture*, XXIX (1955), 1–18.

[9] S. N. Makarem, 'Al-Ḥākim bi-amrillāh's appointment of his successors', *Al-Abhath*, XXIII (1970), 319–24.

[10] Th. Bianquis, 'Al-H'akim bi amr Allah', in Ch.-A. Julien et al. (eds), *Les Africains*, 12 vols (Paris, 1978), vol. 11.

[11] S. A. Assaad, *The Reign of al-Hakim bi Amr Allah (386/996–411/1021): a Political Study* (Beirut, 1974).

[12] H. Halm, 'Der Treuhänder Gottes: die Edikte des Kalifen al-Ḥākim', *Der Islam*, 63 (1986), 11–72.

[13] J. Van Ess, *Chiliastiche Erwartungen und die Versuchung der Göttlichkeit: der Kalif al-Ḥākim (386–411H)* (Heidelberg, 1977).

[14] P. E. Walker, *Caliph of Cairo: al-Ḥākim bi-Amr Allah, 996–1021* (Cairo, 2009), a complete study of the reign which discusses the previous literature. See also Walker, 'The Ismaili daʿwa in the reign of the Fatimid caliph al-Ḥākim', in *Fatimid History and Ismaili Doctrine*, no. III.

lost. In terms of events, the progression may be traced through three successive stages of the reign.

Doctrinal Assertiveness and Messianic Revolt

The regime that al-Ḥākim inherited had evolved out of the Amān of Jawhar, the proclamation that had laid down the terms on which the Imām Caliph would govern the population under his protection as the representative of God on earth. Its equation of the entire population as his subjects in return for their obedience had been taken by al-ᶜAzīz to include the toleration of religious differences in a plural society, not least as regards the personnel of the Dawla, the burgeoning patrimonial state, who were recruited from all communities. Such toleration had been matched with a broad interest in the sciences, witness the invitation to the Coptic bishop Severus to debate in matters of faith. In such a climate, the Daᶜwa had evidently flourished, with crowds attending the lectures of the Chief Qāḍī. If then the number of the Muᵓminūn had increased, the multiplication of the faithful who believed in the Imām was the result of attraction and persuasion rather than compulsion. Obligation was generally limited to acceptance of such public symbols as the Shīᶜite call to prayer, and to an uncertain extent the application in the courts of the law as specified in the *Daᶜāᵓim al-Islām*. Following the death of al-ᶜAzīz, the conflict over the regency which had brought Barjawān to power had revealed the competition for preferment within the ranks of the household, the army and the secretariat, but this had been settled without further violence by the defeat and retirement of Ibn ᶜAmmār. With the murder of Barjawān, however, matters took a different turn as the young Caliph showed his hand.

What may appear as delight in his new-found freedom, his descent into Fusṭāṭ to mingle with the crowd in the *sūq*-s, which he ordered to be lit up all night, was equally a sign of his determination to rule in person as a sovereign should, without intermediaries. Anecdotes of these perambulations that are reminiscent of the Arabian Nights dwell on his approachability, a willingness to hear complaints in person that remained a feature of his reign. But this in turn went with a commitment to the *ḥisba*, the duty to command the right and forbid the wrong, which was rapidly illustrated after his excursions into the city had seemingly led to licentiousness, and provoked an edict which forbade women, and subsequently men, to go out after dark. When this determination was applied to his officers, the outcome was drastic. Barjawān was replaced at the head of the administration by Ḥusayn ibn Jawhar, the son of al-Muᶜizz's deputy as conqueror of Egypt, who continued to be assisted by Barjawān's Christian secretary Fahd ibn Ibrāhīm; but these were now instructed not to stand in the way of petitioners, and soon discovered how limited was their authority. In 1003, the jealousies within the regime surfaced in the denunciation of Fahd by Ibn al-ᶜAddās, the head of the Dīwān al-Kharāj, or Revenue, for the misappropriation of money. Fahd and his brother, the head of the Dīwān al-Nafaqāt, or Expenditure, were promptly executed, an execution that was only to be followed by that of Ibn al-ᶜAddās and a colleague when the falseness of the accusation was exposed. Such haste might be put down to al-Ḥākim's inexperience; but the executions were a new and significant departure from the previous practice of dismissal, disgrace and reinstatement, one which was dramatically confirmed in the following year, when no less a person than Ḥusayn ibn ᶜAlī ibn al-Nuᶜmān, Chief Qāḍī and Chief Dāᶜī, was likewise executed for the misappropriation of funds which he held in trust. What these executions reveal is that along with the moral imperative to command the right and forbid the wrong went a permanent distrust of the ministers al-Ḥākim was obliged to select from the army of secretaries, soldiers and lawyers who staffed this patrimonial state. It was a distrust that doubtless dated from his experience of Barjawān, but one that placed the conduct of government on a very different footing from the confidence in their servants of al-Ḥākim's father and grandfather. A big man, we are told, with bright blue eyes, he inspired fear; but whatever his sense of purpose as Imām and Caliph, he was an interventionist in the administration of his state rather than its director towards the goal of universal empire.

As became clear, the purpose was doctrinal, but equally at variance from the past. Continuity was maintained with the completion of the large mosque begun under al-ᶜAzīz to the north of the palace city of al-Qāhira; known today as the Mosque of al-Ḥākim, it stands now between the Bāb al-Futūḥ and the Bāb al-Naṣr, against the fortress wall built to enclose the city at the end of the century (see Fig. 6.2).

In the same way, the Majālis al-Ḥikma, the Sessions of Wisdom, at which the Chief Qāḍī delivered a weekly lecture from the works of the Qāḍī al-Nuᶜmān, continued to be held by al-Nuᶜmān's descendants in the office. In 1005, such continuity was furthered with the opening of the Dār al-Ḥikma/Dār al-ᶜIlm, the House of Wisdom or Knowledge; a library for the study of the sciences, it promoted the broad learning which had been cultivated under al-ᶜAzīz.[15] But the exercise of the *ḥisba* to guarantee weights and measures and to keep the streets clean came to include not only the Islamic prohibition of wine but the requirement that Jews and Christians should wear black as a mark of their status under Islam. Much more problematic was the Judaic

[15] Cf. H. Halm, *The Fatimids and their Traditions of Learning* (London, 1997), ch. 6, and P. E. Walker, 'Fatimid institutions of learning', in Walker, *Fatimid History and Ismaili Doctrine*, no. I.

prohibition of fish without scales, and that of three vegetables – mustard and cress, *mulūkhiyya*, or mallow, and the otherwise unidentified *mutawwakiliyya*, allegedly eaten by the Umayyad Muᶜāwiya and other enemies of ᶜAlī. Such measures might be construed as specifically Shīᶜite and correspondingly anti-Sunnī, but may betray an element of deviance in al-Ḥākim's concept of the doctrine of the dynasty from what was by now its orthodox form, an admission of elements firmly excluded by the Mahdī from the canon of the faith. They may not point to the notion of his divinity, but are more certainly reminiscent of the beliefs attributed to the Carmathians, and suggest that al-Ḥākim had begun to think over the teachings of his forebears in ways that pointed towards his future behaviour.[16] Matters came to a head towards the end of 1004, when al-Ḥākim openly abandoned the tolerance of religious diversity practised since the defeat of Abū Yazīd and envisaged by the Amān, and ordered the public cursing of all those, including the first three Caliphs, who had not recognised the original appointment of ᶜAlī as successor to the Prophet; such curses were to be written up in gilt on the walls of mosques. The edict provoked a rush of adherence to the Daᶜwa, a sign of the extent to which the Fatimids had established themselves at the heart of Egyptian society; but the challenge it threw down to a Sunnī population which had generally acquiesced in the rule of a Shīᶜite dynasty was a provocation that threatened the consensus on which that establishment was based. Such an aggressive assertion of the doctrine at the root of the Fatimid claim to the empire of Islam invited trouble at a time when popular support was most in need in the face of a major revolt.

The failure, a year into al-Ḥākim's personal rule, of Barjawān's attempt to take control of Tripoli with the defeat and death of his appointee Yānis at the hands of Bādīs, the Zirid viceroy of Ifrīqiya, prompted a yet more ill-advised expedition for the purpose. This was the despatch of Yaḥyā ibn ᶜAlī ibn Ḥamdūn, the brother of Buluggīn's old rival for the government of Ifrīqiya and clearly no friend to Bādīs, to take up the post at Tripoli at the head of a force to be drawn largely from the Banū Qurra, the Arab Bedouin of Cyrenaica. But with no money in the treasury at Barqa to pay them, these for the most part deserted him, and in 1002 he arrived with few men at Tripoli to find it under the protection of the Zanāta warlord Fulful ibn Saᶜīd. Nevertheless, in alliance with Fulful, Yaḥyā advanced in 1003 to the siege of Gabes, the city at the entrance to Bādīs's domain, with the possible ambition of taking his place as the Fatimid viceroy. But this came to nothing, and

[16] Cf. D. De Smet, 'Les interdictions alimentaires du Calife Fatimide al-Ḥākim: Marques de folie ou annonce d'un règne messianique?', in U. Vermeulen and D. De Smet (eds), *Egypt and Syria in the Fatimid, Ayyubid and Mamluk Eras*, I (Leuven, 1995), pp. 53–69.

Figure 6.2 Overview of the Mosque of al-Ḥākim in al-Qāhira. Photo: Bernard O'Kane.

Originally called al-Anwar, 'the Bright', it was begun by al-ᶜAzīz and completed by al-Ḥākim. Two-and-a-half times larger than al-Azhar, the original mosque of al-Qāhira, it was built outside the original wall of the palace city to host a much larger congregation and a more splendid monarch. Having fallen into ruin, it has been completely restored by the Ṭayyibī Ismāᶜīlī community.

Fulful retired to Tripoli while Yaḥyā returned to Egypt to face al-Ḥākim's wrath. He was in fact pardoned, but in 1004 the chiefs of the Banū Qurra were executed after a promise of safe-conduct. The upshot was a revolt not quite on the scale of the rising of Abū Yazīd, but one similarly messianic and equally menacing, which likewise threatened the dynasty itself.

Like Abū Yazīd, the Man on a Donkey, Abū Rakwa, the Man with the Goatskin Water Bag, took a similarly loaded soubriquet, in this case that of a wandering ascetic with his water bottle, to proclaim his mission. Unlike the Ibāḍī sectarian Abū Yazīd, however, his name and origin is obscure, in that he arose as al-Walīd ibn Hishām, a prince of the Umayyad dynasty in Spain, and may in fact have been one of its clients. He was at least an Andalusī, an itinerant scholar who like Abū Yazīd and Abū ᶜAbd Allāh before him, settled among the Banū Qurra as a teacher before declaring himself in 1005 to be the Commander of the Faithful with the throne name of al-Nāṣir li-Dīn Allāh, Defender of the Faith, in this case the champion of Sunnism against the Shīᶜite Fatimids. Whether or not this was a pointed reply to al-Ḥākim's edict, his declaration rallied the Banū Qurra and elements of the Berber Zanāta, Mazāta and Lawāta to lay siege to Barqa, defeating and killing the Turk Yināl sent to relieve the city, and capturing it after its governor, the eunuch Ṣandal, fled away by sea. As the nomad horde spread out towards Alexandria, in December it defeated and killed the Armenian Fātik as he advanced out of the city. But it was famine at Barqa that in the spring of 1006 drove Abū Rakwa himself to lead a veritable tribal migration to the siege of Alexandria, at the start of a campaign which for good geographical reasons replicated those of the Fatimid al-Qāʾim in 914–15 and 919–21, and, indeed, the triumphal march of Jawhar in 969. Alexandria could not be taken, and Abū Rakwa moved down the western edge of the Delta to the Fayyum, where his folk could be fed and marshalled for the assault on the Egyptian capital, whose palaces he had promised to his tribal chiefs. But he failed to take the bridge across the Nile, and in the Fayyum he was confronted by al-Faḍl ibn Ṣāliḥ, the former commander of Ibn Killis's regiment of guards and a veteran of al-ʿAzīz's Syrian campaigns, with the main Fatimid army reinforced by contingents of the Ṭayy Arabs from Transjordan under the sons of their Jarrāḥid prince al-Mufarrij ibn Daghfal. Routed, he fled south beyond Aswan to take refuge in the Nubian kingdom of Muqurra, while his horde was slaughtered and their heads taken as trophies. But on payment of an appropriate sum, the Nubians returned him in the first instance to the chief of the Bedouin Arab Rabīʿa at Aswan, who handed him over to his pursuer Faḍl. Taken back to al-Qāhira, he was duly paraded in mock finery before being done to death. Al-Ḥākim's triumph was signalled by proclamations sent throughout the land and celebrated by delegations streaming in to congratulate the Caliph on his victory.

Toleration, Persecution and Execution

The rising of Abū Rakwa had never matched that of Abū Yazīd in the scale of its threat to the dynasty. An Umayyad *mahdī* was unheard-of, and Abū Rakwa never came close enough to victory to win acceptance in Egypt; he was defeated with relative ease once the forces of the Caliphate were fully mobilised. But the rising and its success in penetrating to within striking distance of the Fatimid capital had certainly come as a shock, a blow to the prestige of a dynasty that prided itself on its victorious arrival at the summit of Islam, particularly since it came in reply to al-Ḥākim's provocative attack upon the historic opponents of his line. The response was immediate. Just as the rising of Abū Yazīd had been followed by concessions to the Mālikite majority with the appointment of a Mālikite Qāḍī of Qayrawān, so now the cursing of ʿAlī's opponents was not only prohibited but punished. At the same time the Majālis al-Ḥikma, at which ʿAbd al-ʿAzīz ibn Muḥammad ibn al-Nuʿmān, Chief Qāḍī in succession to his cousin Ḥusayn, was accustomed to deliver his weekly lecture, were suspended, and the crowds that had flocked to hear him driven away. Two or three years later the outcome as far as the Muslim population was concerned was a return to the old order. A *sijill*, or edict, of 1009 went beyond the Amān of Jawhar in placing Sunnī law and observances on a par with those of the dynasty, quoting 'there is no compulsion in religion' from the Qurʾān, and conceding that every Muslim might find his own way in his faith. But this was followed in 1010 by a reassertion of the Shīʿite call to prayer, and the restoration of the Majālis al-Ḥikma for the benefit of the faithful.

For Christians and Jews, on the other hand, there was no such return to normality. This second period of al-Ḥākim's reign did not only see the intensification of the rules regarding their dress and comportment, and the prohibition of Christian festivals. In a fiscal measure to pay the army, church property was confiscated along with the assets of the royal family. More seriously, in a complete reversal of past tolerance, and indeed patronage, of both Coptic and Melkite Churches, various churches and monasteries of both communities in and around al-Qāhira/Fusṭāṭ and Alexandria were ordered or permitted to be destroyed, along with a synagogue. This was especially shocking for the Melkites, given that the brothers Orestes and Arsenius, respectively Patriarchs of Jerusalem and Alexandria, were almost certainly al-Ḥākim's uncles on his mother's side. Orestes had died in Constantinople in 1000 in the course of the peace settlement with Byzantium, leaving Arsenius in Egypt as a wealthy and influential member of the establishment. But in 1010 Arsenius was executed and his monastery outside al-Qāhira destroyed, after the order had gone out in 1009 for the destruction of that centre of the worldwide Christian faith, the Church of the Holy Sepulchre in Jerusalem. The reason for such destruction, as well as the extent of the damage to the building, is unclear. It went beyond the determination to put non-Muslims in their place, unless as a punishment for getting above themselves; it certainly catered to the long-standing resentment of the Muslim populace at their prominence in government, and might be seen as a demonstration of the leadership expected of the Commander of the Faithful. But it took place amid rumours of a Christian messiah from the West who was predicted to appear at Jerusalem at Easter 1010, rumours which were perhaps given credence by Easter celebrations of the Resurrection at the Holy Sepulchre in defiance of al-Ḥākim's edicts. In the aftermath of Abū Rakwa's rising, determination to prevent the recurrence of such an event, Muslim or Christian, may explain so exceptional a measure.[17]

Meanwhile, the regime itself was purged of its old guard, in the shape

[17] Cf. J. M. F. Van Reeth, '*Al-Qumāma* et le *Qāʾim* de 400H.: le trucage de la lampe sur le tombeau du Christ', in U. Vermeulen and D. De Smet (eds), *Egypt and Syria in the Fatimid, Ayyubid and Mamluk Eras*, II (Leuven, 1998), pp. 171–90.

of Ḥusayn ibn Jawhar, ʿAbd al-ʿAzīz ibn Muḥammad ibn al-Nuʿmān and al-Faḍl ibn Ṣāliḥ, the head of the administration, the Chief Qāḍī and the senior general. With the title of Qāʾid al-Quwwād, or commander-in-chief, rather than that of Wazīr, Ḥusayn may have been something of a figurehead, especially after the execution of Fahd ibn Ibrāhīm in 1003. ʿAbd al-ʿAzīz, on the other hand, had risen to the task he considered rightfully his, while al-Faḍl had proved his worth in the battle with Abū Rakwa. But Ḥusayn and ʿAbd al-ʿAzīz were both dismissed in 1008, and put to death in 1011; al-Faḍl was executed in 1009. ʿAbd al-ʿAzīz was succeeded by his deputy Mālik ibn Saʿīd al-Fāriqī, Qāḍī of al-Qāhira, who was or became increasingly close to al-Ḥākim as his confidante in the Daʿwa.[18] Ḥusayn, on the other hand, was replaced by a much less prominent person, Ṣāliḥ ibn ʿAlī al-Rūdhbārī, a man from the Treasury, cast in the role of Wāsiṭa, or 'Middleman', rather than Wazīr, an intermediary between the Caliph and the administration. As such, his head and those of his successors were forfeits for whatever mistakes they may have made. Thus Ṣāliḥ was dismissed and then executed in 1009; his Christian successor Manṣūr ibn ʿAbdūn, likewise from the Treasury, was immediately made responsible for the destruction of the Church of the Holy Sepulchre, but went the same way in 1010. After him, one al-Quṣūrī lasted a mere ten days before his execution; thereafter, Zurʿa ibn Īsā ibn Nasṭūrus, son of the minister executed by Ḥasan ibn ʿAmmār, died before he too could be put to death in 1012. For the moment his successor Ḥusayn ibn Ṭāhir al-Wazzān (He of the Weigh-scales, another Treasury man) was left in charge. But in 1014 he was dismissed, to be followed in rapid succession by the execution of the Ibnā Abī ʾl-Sayyid, two brothers who held the office jointly, and by that of al-Faḍl, son of Jaʿfar ibn al-Furāt, the Wazīr who had delivered Egypt into the hands of Jawhar.

All these victims came from the predominantly financial administration – the Ibnā Abī ʾl-Sayyid had been tax-farmers of the estates of the crown – and their comings and goings over these years can be seen as an attempt to place the government of Egypt and Syria on a new footing by the promotion of such men to head the administration, an attempt undermined on the one hand by the Caliph's distrust, and on the other by the endemic corruption of his ministers. These certainly enriched themselves, and their considerable wealth was duly confiscated and held in a separate fund. And, as in the case of Fahd ibn Ibrāhīm, the rivalries within the administration played their part. Thus in 1013 the Black eunuch general Ghayn, Chief of Police and

[18] Cf. P. E. Walker, 'Another family of Fatimid Chief Qāḍīs: the al-Fāriqīs', in Walker, *Fatimid History and Ismaili Doctrine*, IV.

Muḥtasib, or Market Inspector, in the capital, fell victim to a denunciation which cost his secretary al-Jarjarāʾī both his hands, cut off at the elbow. But the revolution which terminated the dominance of the old aristocracy was much more broadly political, revealing the weakness as well as the strength of the Caliph. In the three years following the dismissal of Ḥusayn and ᶜAbd al-ᶜAzīz in 1008, Ḥusayn's prestige and popularity had been such as to challenge al-Ḥākim's authority. In fear of his life, Ḥusayn had twice fled the capital, the second time to take refuge with the Banū Qurra, a mere two or three years after the defeat of Abū Rakwa. On both occasions he had been pardoned and returned, the second time at the head of a procession of the *ahl al-Dawla*, or personnel of the state, having demanded and obtained the dismissal of the man he considered his enemy, the Wāsiṭa Ibn ᶜAbdūn. Only then did al-Ḥākim feel able to strike, removing his ally al-Quṣūrī and doing away with Ḥusayn himself as well as with ᶜAbd al-ᶜAzīz. The evident need to dismantle their clientèles and prevent their re-formation under other patrons was a major political problem, which may account for the attempt to Islamise the administration, first with an impracticable proposal in 1012 to replace its Christian personnel with Muslims and second with a decree in 1013 requiring such Christians either to convert or otherwise leave the country with all their possessions. Many did indeed leave for Antioch and Laodicea in Byzantine Syria, but the majority remained as nominal Muslims. The relative mildness of the measure nevertheless serves to bring the ongoing tale of executions into focus. There were no systematic purges of whole families, or followings, or confessions. The wealth of fallen ministers was indeed confiscated, but the heirs of Ḥusayn were allowed to inherit his fortune, while the three brothers of the Christian Zurᶜa were maintained in office. Most important for the future, al-Jarjarāʾī al-Aqṭāʾ, 'the Amputated', went on to take charge of the expenses of the palace and, still more important, to manage the estate of al-Ḥākim's influential elder sister, the princess Sitt al-Mulk. And whatever their fate, they were honoured at their promotion with personal titles that were destined to grow ever more magnificent in Lane-Poole's 'pompous dynasty'. Below the surface of events, the army of the patrimonial state marched on much as Weber supposed.

The Horizon of Empire

In the meantime, the various prohibitions regarding food, alcohol, women, baths, dogs and much else were intensified and multiplied. But in the aftermath of the rising of Abū Rakwa, what was lacking was any renewal of the imperial mission to compare with the resurrection of the dynasty following the defeat of Abū Yazīd, which had culminated in the conquest of Egypt and ended only with the untimely death of al-ᶜAzīz. In Syria the truce with Byzantium held

Figure 6.3 Fragment of a linen scarf with tapestry woven bands of silk. Egyptian, Manshiya, Fatimid, c. 1000–1200. Tiraz. Museum number 246&A-1890. © V&A.

These bands of expensive embroidery, worn especially on the sleeve, were one of the luxurious products of the Fatimid weaving industry, and an important status symbol.

fast despite the destruction of the Church of the Holy Sepulchre; Aleppo, the bone of contention under al-ᶜAzīz, remained poised between the two empires under the *ghulām* Luʾluʾ, regent for the last of the Ḥamdānids, then ruler in his own right until his death in 1009, when he was succeeded by his son al-Manṣūr. No Fatimid initiative led in 1010 to the brief pronunciation of the Friday prayer in the name of al-Ḥākim in the Iraqi cities of Mosul, Anbar and al-Madāʾin close to Baghdad; while testifying to Fatimid prestige, it was an unsuccessful attempt by the ᶜUqaylid chief Qirwāsh, head of a Bedouin Arab dynasty in control of much of the country, to bolster his position against his tribal enemies in the desert and the Buyids and their ᶜAbbasid protégés in Baghdad. To the south of Egypt, the Arab chief Abūʾl-Makārim was awarded the title of Kanz al-Dawla, or Treasure of the State, for his role in the capture and return of Abū Rakwa; as the Banūʾl-Kanz, his dynasty was left in control of the Nubian frontier at Aswan. Away to the west, the shock of Abū Rakwa produced no new initiative; despite their defeat, the Banū Qurra remained in possession of Cyrenaica, capable of giving refuge to Ḥusayn. Meanwhile, after the rout and retreat of Yaḥyā ibn ᶜAlī ibn Ḥamdūn to Egypt, relations with the Zirids of Ifrīqiya remained in abeyance. In Ifrīqiya itself the empire was in retreat, as the century-old war with the Zanāta allies of Cordoba took a new turn, and the Zirids were forced onto the defensive. Where Jawhar followed by Buluggīn at Ashīr had campaigned into northern Morocco, the western frontier had been overrun in the years following the accession of Buluggīn's grandson Bādīs by a formidable alliance of Buluggīn's rebellious brothers with the Maghrāwa chieftain Zīrī ibn ᶜAtiyya and his son al-Muᶜizz in the name of the Umayyad Caliphate at Cordoba. Not until 1004 were these finally defeated by Bādīs and his uncle Ḥammād, who in 1005 was rewarded with the government of the highland west. In 1008 he built for himself a new capital, the Qalᶜa of the Banū Ḥammād, in the mountains to the north of Msila, the former Fatimid capital of the region, but far short of the old Zirid stronghold of Ashīr. At the cost of retrenchment in the west, he thus became the effective ruler of a new dominion in the central Maghrib as he and Bādīs partitioned the Fatimid inheritance between them. Only in the east was there some compensation. The death in 1009 of the Zanāta warlord at Tripoli, Fulful ibn Saᶜīd, opened the way to the recovery of the city by the Zirids in the following year. Menaced by Bādīs, Fulful had vainly switched his allegiance from al-Qāhira to Cordoba in the hope of aid; but in 1008 the death at Cordoba of al-Muẓaffar, son and successor of the great Almanzor as Ḥājib, or Chamberlain, of the Caliph Hishām II, had plunged the Umayyad Caliphate into a crisis from which it never recovered. The fire had effectively gone out of the conflict between Fatimids and Umayyads for mastery of the Islamic West.[19]

Instead, in the absence of any fresh imperial initiative, al-Ḥākim had to contend with another and potentially more serious challenge to his title, as the politics of al-Qāhira spilled over into a rebellion which produced a fresh claimant to the Caliphate at Mecca. In the Palestinian hinterland, the Bedouin Arab Ṭayy under their Jarrāḥid chiefs had been prominent as enemies and allies of the Fatimids since their arrival in Egypt. In the revolt of Abū Rakwa, they had come to the aid of al-Ḥākim, but in the aftermath returned to their old ambition to rule over southern Palestine at Ramla, its Fatimid capital. Any incitement they required was supplied by Abūʾl-Qāsim Ḥusayn ibn al-Maghribī, a fugitive from al-Qāhira escaping the execution

[19] Idris, *La Berbérie orientale sous les Zīrīdes*, I, pp. 90–9.

visited on his brothers, perhaps as a partisan of Ḥusayn ibn Jawhar in opposition to the Wāsiṭa Ibn ᶜAbdūn. In 1010 the caravan of the Turk Yārūkh, travelling without escort to take up his appointment by Ibn ᶜAbdūn as governor of Damascus, was plundered by the Bedouin, and Yārūkh himself captured. Led by Mufarrij ibn Daghfal, grandson of the Ḥassān, the head of the Jarrāḥids, the Ṭayy went on to occupy Ramla, where at the instigation of Abūᵓl-Qāsim, Yārūkh was executed before Mufarrij could accept al-Ḥākim's offer of a ransom. In 1011 ᶜAlī ibn Jaᶜfar ibn Falāḥ, son of the Kutāma commander who had first won then lost Damascus in 970–1, failed to retake the city. With Mufarrij and the Ṭayy now committed to rebellion, Ibn al-Maghribī travelled to Mecca to invite the Ḥasanid Sharifs of Mecca to claim the Caliphate for Abūᵓl-Futūḥ al-Ḥasan ibn Jaᶜfar, son of the founder of the Mūsawī dynasty in the days of al-Muᶜizz. His chosen title of al-Rāshid liᵓl-Dīn Allāh, Rightly-guided for the Religion of God, not only evoked the authority of the Rāshidūn, the first four Caliphs, but claimed for the Ḥasanids the succession to ᶜAlī, the last of the Rāshidūn, instead of the Ḥusaynid Fatimids. The appearance of such a pretender was a double blow to the Fatimids, who had cultivated the Ḥasanids as their cousins in the holy family of the Prophet, and needed their alliance at Mecca to secure their recognition in the Holy Places. It was the more galling in that al-Ḥākim was obliged to cancel the pilgrimage in 1011 and 1012, that centrepiece of the ritual year whose orchestration by the dynasty was a necessary proof of its claim to rule over Islam.

In the event, the challenge came to nothing, along with Ibn al-Maghribī's scheme of revenge. In 1012 Abūᵓl-Futūḥ came to Ramla for his proclamation as Caliph; but in the face of al-Ḥākim's diplomatic offensive, offering money to the Ṭayy and stirring up a rival at Mecca, he rapidly returned home to beg al-Ḥākim's forgiveness, before travelling to al-Qāhira to make his submission. Ibn al-Maghribī left for Baghdad, and in 1013 the affair was over when the Ṭayy submitted to ᶜAlī ibn Jaᶜfar ibn Falāḥ at the head of a major army. Mufarrij died at Ramla in 1014, while Ḥassān sent his mother to al-Qāhira to win his pardon. Not only was it granted; he was honoured in Fatimid style with robes and a turban worn by the Caliph himself, with a seal and a white mule, on which he rode into the palace to be confirmed as chief of the Ṭayy. The tactic was a success; keeping his possessions in Palestine, Ḥassān remained a loyal as well as an essential ally of the dynasty. As a tactic, moreover, it was not employed in isolation. For the first time since taking power, al-Ḥākim had in 1012–13 sent embassies to Ifrīqiya and Sicily with diplomas and sumptuous presents, recognising the son of the Zirid viceroy Bādīs as his heir, and conferring a title on the Kalbid Amīr Jaᶜfar at Palermo. Bādīs, moreover, had been granted the government of Barqa in what was clearly an attempt to rebuild the land bridge as well as relations between the two centres of the Fatimid empire after the failed expedition of Ibn Ḥamdūn and the rising of Abū Rakwa. But at al-Qāhira, such moves were overshadowed by a far more radical revolution.

The Crisis of Daᶜwa and Dawla

The appointment of Mālik ibn Saᶜīd al-Fāriqī in 1008 to head both the judiciary and the Daᶜwa put an end to the reign of the family of the Qāḍī al-Nuᶜmān over the two offices which were the pillars of the Caliphate and Imāmate. It was at the same time central to the return towards past practice over the next two or three years: the toleration of Sunnism under the outward signs of Shīᶜite supremacy, and the resumption of the sessions of the Majālis al-Ḥikma. Much favoured by al-Ḥākim, who kept him by his side, Mālik in his capacity as Qāḍī was a foil for his master, his reputation for kindness in contrast to the severity of the Caliph. As Dāᶜī, meanwhile, he lectured assiduously to different audiences of the faithful, some officials, some women, from whom he collected the dues which the believers owed to the Imām. At the same time it fell to him to direct the worldwide community, inside and outside the empire, through correspondence with the *duᶜāt* in the field. In Egypt itself, the existence of *duᶜāt* in the provincial cities may be assumed on the analogy of Syria, where they are mentioned at Ascalon, Ramla, Acre, Tyre, Damascus and in the mountains north of Hama, and where they had won for the Imāmate a following which survives to the present day. In Ifrīqiya, where the Zirids ruled on behalf of the Caliph, it is probable that the Qāḍī of the palace city of al-Manṣūriyya served, like Mālik at al-Qāhira, as Dāᶜī of an Ismāᶜīlī community associated with the regime. In Sicily, however, where the Kalbids maintained their Fatimid connection, an Ismāᶜīlī presence can only be presumed. Outside these dominions of the empire, recognition of the Fatimids in Yemen had ended with the death of the Yuᶜfirid prince ᶜAbd Allāh ibn Qaḥṭān in 997, but the community that had revived towards the end of the tenth century went on under its Dāᶜī Hārūn ibn Muḥammad ibn Ruḥaym and his successors to form a new principality in the region of Shibam to the north of Sanaa. Hārūn's correspondence with al-Qāhira is attested by al-Ḥākim's stipulation that he should refer himself to the *Daᶜāᵓim al-Islām* in all matters of law. Passing most probably through Mecca via the pilgrimage, the correspondence is an indication of the outreach of the dynasty down the western flank of Arabia to the Indian Ocean. Important as this development in the Yemen may have been to the Fatimid cause, however, of much greater concern to the Daᶜwa were its affairs in Iraq and Iran.

Iraq was not only the seat of the ᶜAbbasid rival and Iran the home of the most lively of the Ismāᶜīlī faithful, both politically and intellectually, since their capture for the Fatimid cause in the time of al-Muᶜizz. The Carmathians may have faded away, but the memory lived on as an element in the opposition between Sunnites and Shīᶜites and the factions into which they both were split, an opposition which was polarised by the call of the Fatimids and the retort of the ᶜAbbasids. At Baghdad in 1008, Shīᶜites had shouted for al-Ḥākim in factional fighting with Sunnīs, while in 1010 both Qirwāsh at Mosul and the Bedouin chief al-Asadī at Hilla to the south of Baghdad briefly declared for al-Qāhira. The response of the ᶜAbbasid Caliph al-Qādir in 1011 was a denunciation of the Fatimids as impostors. A declaration which reiterated Akhū Muḥsin's black legend of Fatimid origins was promulgated on the authority of a council which included ᶜAlid opponents of the dynasty.[20] It may have been this manifesto which prompted al-Naysabūrī at al-Qāhira to compose his *Istitār al-Imām*, the Unveiling or Disclosure of the Imām, the work which for the first time spelled out a Fatimid list of the Mahdī's ancestors. Meanwhile, at Rayy near modern Tehran, its Qāḍī ᶜAbd al-Jabbār had written polemically against Ismāᶜīlīs and Shīᶜites in general, as well as giving the names and locations of Fatimid *duᶜāt*. Despite hostility, these had gained considerable ground in the lands of the Buyids – Iraq, Fars and Kirman in southern Iran, and in north-western Iran with its capitals at Rayy, Isfahan and Hamadhan. At Baghdad and Basra, the Dāᶜī al-Kirmānī led the philosophical development of Ismāᶜīlism in the land of the Brethren of Purity, while under the title of Ḥujjat al-Irāqayn he may have headed the province of the two Iraqs, sc. Iraq itself and Iran, exercising a wider authority over his fellows. He was clearly well established in Buyid Baghdad, lecturing to a following both there and in Basra, and following the issue of al-Qādir's manifesto, setting out with uncertain success to win over to the cause the Buyid Wazīr and governor of Baghdad, the Shīᶜite Fakhr al-Mulk.[21] At Shiraz, the Buyid capital of Fars, the Dāᶜī Mūsā ibn Dāwūd was patronised by its pro-Shīᶜite dynasty and Daylamī army from the Shīᶜite highlands south of the Caspian; a colleague was based at Kirman. At Rayy, where in the 920s and 30s al-Rāzī had finally failed to win its rulers for the cause of Muḥammad ibn Ismāᶜīl, this was upheld in the name of the Fatimids by the Dāᶜī al-Mīmadhī until he was ousted from the city, perhaps by the Qāḍī ᶜAbd al-Jabbār. Further to the east, however, from Sijistan through Khurasan to Transoxania, the story from 998 onwards was very different, as these lands with their mutually hostile

[20] Recorded by the late-twelfth-century anti-Shīᶜite historian Ibn al-Jawzī, *Al-Muntaẓam fīʾl-taʾrīkh* (Hyderabad, 1939), VII, p. 255. Cf. P. H. Mamour, *Polemics on the Origin of the Fatimi Caliphs* (London, 1934), pp. 137–9, and P. E. Walker, *Ḥamid al-Dīn al-Kirmānī. Ismaili Thought in the Age of al-Ḥākim* (London, 1999), pp. 14–15.

[21] Cf. Walker, ibid., pp. 10–16.

sects came under the rule of the warrior Turkish Sultan Maḥmūd of Ghazna. His intervention in their quarrels in the name of Sunnī Islam, and persecution of the Ismāᶜīlīs in the name of the ᶜAbbasids, coupled him with al-Qādir as one of the two great enemies of al-Ḥākim in the writings of al-Kirmānī. In 1010–11, in the course of his raids into India, Maḥmūd destroyed the little Ismāᶜīlī principality of Multan with which al-Muᶜizz had been so delighted. More ominously still, in 1012–13 he had the Dāᶜī al-Tāhartī, sent from al-Qāhira in the hope of winning him for the Fatimid cause, tried and executed on the authority of a Ḥusaynid who, as in the Baghdad manifesto, argued the falsity of the dynasty's pretentions. Reported to Baghdad, the execution was an occasion for ᶜAbbasid celebration.[22]

As a native of Khurasan, al-Naysabūrī presumably had its tribulations in mind when he wrote his prescription for the absolute obedience of the community to the *dāᶜī* in the lands where the Caliph did not rule and the Imām was far away. But by the time he composed his *Risāla*, some time between 1013 and 1015, the reverse was true at al-Qāhira, where in his postscript to the work al-Naysabūrī lamented the *fasād*, or corruption, of the body politic in the absence of firm direction by the *dāᶜī* whose duty it was to ensure the obedience of the faithful. Out of ignorance or incompetence or untrustworthiness, this unnamed person has failed to maintain their belief in the wisdom of the Imām in everything he does, whether or not they understand his acts. As a result, the people have gone astray, the Imām is angry and has locked the door against them. Repentance is called for, that the Imām may have mercy upon his people. The Daᶜwa, in other words, was in crisis, caught up in a major restructuring of the Dawla which began in 1013 with the unheard-of appointment of a cousin rather than a son as Walī ᶜAhd al-Muslimīn, al-Ḥākim's designated heir, all the more radical in view of the rigorous exclusion from government of the males of the family since the time of al-Manṣūr and al-Muᶜizz. With coins minted in his name, ᶜAbd al-Raḥmān ibn Ilyās, the cousin in question, took over the ceremony of the Caliphate together with the hearing of petitions. This recruitment of a prince from the extended family of the dynasty was followed by yet another remodelling of the government. The regime of the Wāsiṭa came to an end in 1014–15 with the dismissal of al-Wazzān, the execution of the Ibnā Abī ʾl-Sayyid, then that of al-Faḍl ibn Jaᶜfar ibn al-Furāt. At the same time Mālik al-Fāriqī, the hitherto trusted Chief Qāḍī and Chief Dāᶜī, was executed shortly after the Majālis al-Ḥikma were closed down for the third time in the reign. In their place came three permanent appointments of a very

[22] Cf. Bosworth, *The Ghaznavids*, pp. 51–4, and Walker, *Ḥamid al-Dīn al-Kirmānī*, pp. 10–16.

different kind. ^{c}Alī ibn Ja^{c}far ibn Falāḥ, the commander who had recovered Palestine from the Jarrāḥids, was made Wazīr, while the Sunnī jurist of the minority Ḥanbalī school, Ibn Abī$^{\circ}$l-$^{\circ}$Awwām, became Chief Qāḍī with a *sijill* of appointment to the jurisdiction of al-Qāhira and Miṣr (Fusṭāṭ), of Alexandria, of the Holy Places of Mecca and Medina, and of Barqa, the Maghrib and Sicily – a recital of the components of the empire and its claims which nevertheless excluded Syria. Meanwhile, the post of Chief Dā^{c}ī went to Khatkīn al-Ḍayf. This man was a Turk, a member of the *aḍyāf*, a small but evidently important corps hitherto under the command of the Chief Qāḍī. Its members seem to have undertaken important commissions; thus one of them had been deputed to oversee the destruction of the Church of the Holy Sepulchre. Khatkīn himself was a veteran who had served the Buyid ^{c}Aḍud al-Dawla as ink-bearer or secretary, the Fatimids as governor at Damascus and al-Ḥākim as a trusted agent. It was in this capacity that he took over the functions of Chief Dā^{c}ī, including the resumption of the Majālis al-Ḥikma, as an administrator rather than a jurist or theologian.

From these two appointments, the conclusion might be that al-Ḥākim had taken to extremes the promise of the Amān to rule equitably over all communities on the basis of the dictum that there is no compulsion in religion. But if so, it had been accomplished by a radical departure from the principle of the succession so ruthlessly enforced by Jawhar and his protégé al-Manṣūr at the death of the Qā$^{\circ}$im, one which is signalled in the sources by the thinness of al-Maqrīzī's narrative of al-Ḥākim's final years in the *Itti^{c}āẓ*. For these his principal source, the chronicle of al-Musabbiḥī, was evidently lacking, presumably abandoned until taken up again by the author in the next reign. For him to continue would have been to chronicle a crisis within the family, of which the alteration of the succession is likely to have been a consequence as much as a cause. The danger of doing so is apparent in the fate of Mālik al-Fāriqī, who would seem by implication to have been the *dā^{c}ī* reproached by al-Naysabūrī for the lapse of the faithful into *fasād* – demoralisation in the original sense. Of all the faults of which this person is accused – ignorance, incompetence and negligence – that of untrustworthiness seems best to fit the story that al-Fāriqī was executed for his closeness to al-Ḥākim's older sister, Sitt al-Mulk, his lady Imām, as al-Ḥākim is alleged to have called her to her face. Sitt al-Mulk, the Lady of the Kingdom, had been the favourite daughter of al-^{c}Azīz, and while she may have failed to exclude her brother from the succession in 996, was immensely wealthy and correspondingly influential. In this case, as eventually became clear, she supported the claim of al-Ḥākim's surviving son ^{c}Alī, another minor, aged eight or nine at the time, and hence that of the boy's mother to her privileged position in the family. Any suspicion on al-Ḥākim's part that the one man on whom he had evidently relied had sided with her over the succession would explain his sudden end.

Divinity and Disappearance

The population at large may have cared very little for the change in the succession. Sunnites may have welcomed the appointment of a Sunnī jurist as Chief Qāḍī, and in the capital itself people presumably grew accustomed to the increased informality of a monarch who rode abroad on his donkey, dressed as an ascetic, accompanied by a mere handful of attendants. But the shock to the faithful is apparent in al-Naysabūrī's despairing postscript to his *Risāla*. The return to a semblance of normality under Khatkīn was accompanied by the arrival of al-Kirmānī from Baghdad, coming perhaps at Khatkīn's request to mount a compelling defence of al-Ḥākim, reassert the authority of the Dāᶜī and restore the faith of the Muᵓminūn in the Daᶜwa. In a series of works beginning with his *Mabāsim al-bishārāt*, al-Kirmānī reiterated the lament of al-Naysabūrī for their loss of direction, but insisted that everything pointed towards the year 411, four centuries after the Prophet's death, when the mission of the dynasty would finally be accomplished, and the Imām Caliph and his successors would reign over the whole of Islam. However, 411H, 1020–1, was a mere five years away, and the prophecy smacks of desperation. For the moment, however, Khatkīn as Chief Dāᶜī was the Bāb, the door between the Imām and the believers, in whom they should trust.[23] Meanwhile, his colleagues in the Daᶜwa had either been invited or simply undertaken a defence of al-Ḥākim and his actions with treatises on the Imāmate: Abūᵓl-Fawāris, Dāᶜī in Syria, wrote his *Risāla fīᵓl-imāma* about this time, while al-Naysabūrī weighed in with a second work, his *Ithbāt al-imāma*, or 'Demonstration of the Imāmate'.[24] The result was a body of literature that reaffirmed the necessity of belief in the Imām as the source of knowledge and the authority for the law, which at the same time elaborated on the philosophical tradition going back to al-Sijistānī and beyond, and in effect, rescued the Imāmate from the Imām. The task for these leading lights of the Daᶜwa, who all naturally claimed their wisdom as well as their appointment from the Imām, was all the more difficult, since in the meantime al-Ḥākim

[23] Cf. Walker, *Ḥamid al-Dīn al-Kirmānī*, pp. 16–20, 38–9, 47–8.

[24] Abūᵓl-Fawāris, Aḥmad ibn Yaᵓqūb, *Al-Risāla fīᵓl-imāma*, ed. and trans. S. N. Makarem, *The Political Doctrine of the Ismāᶜīlīs* (Delmar, NY, 1977); al-Naysabūrī, *Kitāb ithbāt al-imāma*, ed. and trans. A. R. Lalani, *Degrees of Excellence. A Fatimid Treatise on Leadership in Islam* (London, 2010); cf. A. R. Lalani, 'A philosophical response from Fatimid Egypt on leadership in Islam', in U. Verrmeulen, K. D'Hulster and J. Van Steenbergen (eds), *Egypt and Syria in the Fatimid, Ayyubid and Mamluk Eras*, VII (Leuven, 2013), pp. 115–30.

had added to the novelty with the designation of a great-great-grandson of the Mahdī, al-ᶜAbbās ibn Shuᶜayb, as Walī ᶜAhd al-Muᵓminīn, or heir to the Imāmate as distinct from the Caliphate. Such a separation of the two offices was comparable to the acceptance by the Twelver Shīᶜites of an Imām who had not only been deprived of the Caliphate, but was no longer of this world; and it was the exact opposite of the Mahdī's mission to recombine the two in the final reign of God's representatives on earth. Any apparent abandonment of that mission clearly called for al-Kirmānī's assurance that it was in fact about to be fulfilled. His recourse to the kind of messianism which had anticipated the coming of the Mahdī was all the more vital, since it was aimed not only at those whom he found tempted to abandon their faith, but also at those who had turned in the opposite direction to *ghuluww*, the range of antinomian beliefs and expectations attributed to the Carmathians which had focused on the Mahdī after his appearance. Disclaimed in and denounced by the Mahdī himself as he set his dynasty on its imperial course, these beliefs had nevertheless run on, not least in the polemic of his enemies, and dramatically resurfaced at this juncture with the public proclamation of al-Ḥākim's divinity.

Fatimid Cosmology

Philosophy entered into Islam through the translation of Greek texts in the ninth century, on the one hand Platonic, on the other Aristotelian. The problem then for Muslims, as for Christians and Jews, was to reconcile their rational conclusions on the subject of a first cause for the universe with the God of prophetic and scriptural revelation. Neoplatonism, the cosmology originally propounded by the third-century Greek philosopher Plotinus, envisaged creation as the product of two emanations from a single source, Intellect and Soul, on the one hand the eternal mathematics that are the laws of nature, and on the other, the active principle that works them into the multiplicity of beings. The scheme was taken up by the tenth-century Iranians al-Nasafī and al-Sijistānī, Seveners looking and working for the coming of the second Muḥammad, who transposed the two creative emanations of the earlier eschatology, Kūnī, Essence, and Qadar, Form, into Plotinus's Intellect and Soul as the products of God's creative purpose. In the following cycle of Seven Prophets and their Seven Imāms, the Nāṭiq, or Speaking Prophet, was then deemed to have enunciated the law of his age as an instruction to humanity of the basis of a perfect knowledge of Intellect, whose deputy he is. But the understanding of that law became the task of his successor, the Asās, or Founder, without whose guidance the law in question will have been misunderstood and perverted. Only the Imām, therefore, on the basis of similar knowledge, was humanity's true guide. When al-Sijistānī was finally won over to the Fatimid cause, it was the Fatimid Imām who inherited this cosmic knowledge and responsibility on behalf of God.

Belief in that guidance was sorely tested by al-Ḥākim, and it required the advocacy of al-Kirmānī to reassure the faithful. Some thirty to forty years after al-Sijistānī, al-Kirmānī was the most sophisticated of the Fatimid philosophers, whose cosmology revised the scheme of his predecessor without entirely displacing it from the canon. Drawing on Aristotle rather than Plotinus, it envisaged ten successive emanations of Intellects or Intelligences, of which the First was the equivalent of Aristotle's First Cause, the one that moves but does not itself move. Each Intellect thereafter generated the next in a downward progression through the heavenly spheres, until they ended with the Active Intelligence in the sphere of the Moon, the one that has generated the multiplicity of the material, sublunary world of the earth. In that world, the human soul in its human body has a mind or intellect that aspires to the perfection of the heavenly prototype. But for that aspiration to be realised, however imperfectly, a Prophet is required to receive by Revelation the perfect knowledge of the heavenly Intellects, and convert it into law for the direction of mankind towards its proper goal of perception of God's creation and acceptance of His purpose. That task must be carried on by the Prophet's successors, who in this age of the Prophet Muḥammad are the Imāms of the Fatimid line, equally possessed of his understanding of God's universe and design.

Visited upon the Fatimid Imām, this tremendous persona may have preyed upon the mind of al-Ḥākim, and certainly induced the adoration of the Imām evinced in the writings of al-Shīrāzī, al-Kirmānī's successor as philosopher of the Imāmate. But after al-Shīrāzī's death in 1076, the mismatch between the ideal and the political reality led to the retreat of this omniscient Imām into *satr*, or concealment (not *ghayba*, or occultation, supernatural absence, as in the case of the Twelver Shīᶜites) in the creeds of the Iranian Nizārīs followed by the Yemeni Ṭayyibīs, leaving the Imāmate of the dynasty to disappear with the Caliphate in 1071.

Cf. P.E. Walker, *Early Philosophical Shiism. The Ismaili Neoplatonism of Abū Yaᶜqūb al-Sijistānī* (Cambridge, 1993), and *Ḥamīd al-Dīn al-Kirmānī. Ismaili Thought in the Age of al-Ḥākim* (London and New York, 1999).

Those who made the proclamation were Iranians like al-Naysabūrī who had been drawn to the capital in search of an Imām whose claim to the succession to Muḥammad ibn Ismāᶜīl had been accepted relatively recently in their homeland. In the time of al-Sijistānī, the Fatimids had been accepted as the line of Imāms leading up to the second coming of this second Muḥammad, a millenarian expectation which had not necessarily given way to the dynasty's vision of a line of sovereigns ruling by the law of the Prophet. But it says much for the formation over the intervening years of an Ismāᶜīlī creed centred upon the Fatimid Imām, that when such millenarianism came once again to the fore, it focused on al-Ḥākim, the Imām of the time. While the doubters returned to their old faith under the leadership of Khatkīn and the guidance of al-Kirmānī, others came out in 1017 with a messianic message of a kind going back 100 years, to the time preceding the advent of the Fatimids and their Mahdī. In the preaching of Ḥamza and his associates, al-Akhram and al-Darzī, al-Ḥākim was declared to be divine, while one or the other claimed to be his appointed Imām and Caliph for a new, post-Fatimid age. The problem is that while the outcome was the formation of the sect known from the name of al-Darzī as the Druzes, only the chronicle of the Christian al-Anṭākī, writing in Syria, is contemporary with the original events. The gap in the chronicle of al-Musabbiḥī leaves the Egyptian tradition thin, while those of non-Egyptian authors are generally hostile. The Druzes themselves preserved over 100 epistles or letters rightly or wrongly attributed to Ḥamza; but as a statement of their faith, these were certainly edited if not actually written in retrospect. The letters, *risālāt*, were so many tracts, the common way to state a position and refute an adversary, and they undoubtedly circulated at the time, prompting al-Kirmānī to reply to one from al-Akhram with a refutation of his associates' claims in *al-Risāla al-wāᶜiẓa*, his Admonishing Letter.[25] In their final form as scripture, not only was al-Ḥākim divine and Ḥamza his prophet, the Master of Time, but he and his four fellows were ranked in cosmic order as Intellect, Soul and Word, the Preceder and the Follower, in the manner of the original Bāṭin, or Hidden Doctrine of the Fatimids. Al-Darzī, meanwhile, seems to have struck out on his own as Muḥammad ibn Ismāᶜīl, to be denounced by Ḥamza as the Devil – ironically, since his name now attaches to Ḥamza's followers. What seems clear is that the movement had originated within the Daᶜwa. Al-Akhram, 'Slit-nosed', had probably been a *dāᶜī* himself; the names of Darzī and Ḥamza, 'Tailor' and 'Felt-maker' respectively, may or may not indicate tradesmen in the literal sense. It certainly divided the faithful into hostile factions. In his letter to al-Akhram, al-Kirmānī judged him deserving

[25] Walker, *Ḥamid al-Dīn al-Kirmānī*, pp. 21–3, 42, 50.

of the sword, while Ḥamza in his letters identified five enemies to match the five constituted by himself and his aides: Ibn Ilyās and Ibn Shuᶜayb, the designated heirs; the Dāᶜī Khatkīn; Jaᶜfar, the senior Sunnī jurist; and the Sunnī Qāḍī, Ibn Abīʾl-ᶜAwwām. The factions themselves are reported to have cursed each other publicly.[26]

The question is the attitude of al-Ḥākim himself. He may have rejected the attribution of divinity, as al-Kirmānī said in his letter to al-Akhram that he had, but nevertheless he held aloof from the controversy down to its denouement in 1019. He may have been respectful of his ruling on the freedom of religion, while content with his delegation of responsibility to the five 'enemies'. But beyond that, he was prepared to talk to the leaders in a way that suggests his familiarity with the growth of the movement within the Daᶜwa, and certainly in a way that gave the impression that he was behind it. Its followers must have been encouraged to think so, to bring matters to a head in the way that they did. The statements of the chroniclers are contradictory, and their dates at variance, but the crisis can probably be attributed to the first six months of 1019. In January al-Akhram was allowed to ride in al-Ḥākim's retinue, only to be pulled from his horse by an assailant and killed; the man himself was promptly executed. In February the Wazīr ᶜAlī ibn Jaᶜfar ibn Falāḥ was assassinated by persons unknown; with the rapid succession of Saᶜīd ibn ᶜĪsā ibn Nasṭūrus and then in April that of Masᶜūd ibn Ṭāhir al-Wazzān, a son and a brother of the former ministers, the Wazirate returned to the situation prior to 1015, with no very strong hand to cope with what happened in June. Then, uproar was provoked when devotees entered the Mosque of ᶜAmr, the Great Mosque of Fusṭāṭ, to shout, clap hands and present the Qāḍī Ibn Abīʾl-ᶜAwwām with a script proclaiming the divinity of al-Ḥākim; in the riot that followed, they were set upon, killed and burnt. Al-Darzī, perhaps the instigator, was chased by the Turkish soldiery into al-Qāhira, to take refuge with al-Ḥākim; there, he may or may not have been executed to appease his pursuers. The Turks then turned against Ḥamza himself, barricaded in the Raydān mosque outside the north gate of al-Qāhira, allegedly with al-Ḥākim's permission. Its door was burnt down, but Ḥamza escaped into hiding, and eventual execution in Mecca.

It was not the end of the affair. Al-Ḥākim moved to placate the Turks

[26] Cf. Walker, 'Ismaili daᶜwa', 35–8; D. R. W. Bryer, 'The origins of the Druze religion', *Der Islam*, 52 (1975), 47–84, 239–62; 53 (1976), 5–27; M. G. S. Hodgson, 'Al-Darazī and Ḥamza in the origin of the Druze religion', *Journmal of the American Oriental Society*, 82 (1962), 5–20; H. Halm, 'Der Tod Ḥamzas, des Begründers des Drusisches Religion', in U. Vermeulen and D. De Smet (eds), *Egypt and Syria in the Fatimid, Ayyubid and Mamluk Eras*, II (Leuven, 1998), pp. 105–13.

while punishing the ringleaders; but indiscipline in the army spread to the Black infantry, who plundered the *sūq*-s of Fusṭāṭ. Since al-Ḥākim made no move to stop them, he was promptly alleged to have ordered the sack as a punishment for the massacre at the Great Mosque; and it was left to the Turks and the Berbers to restore order. Ḥamza's letter-writing meanwhile continued, even if some of his *risālāt* were evidently written or expanded by others after the event. One such declared that al-Ḥākim had turned on his followers, persecuting them and driving them from the country. The reference may be to what happened after al-Ḥākim's death, but confirms the fact that those followers were both numerous and under their own name of *muwaḥḥidūn*, or unitarians, firmly committed to their beliefs under the instruction of the leadership. They conformed, in other words, to al-Naysabūrī's description of the ideal community under the ideal *dāᶜī*, with this difference, that they had hived off from the Daᶜwa of the dynasty in the conviction that Ḥamza was no mere *dāᶜī*, but the Imām himself on behalf of God in the person of al-Ḥākim. It was a curious variation on the alternative Shīᶜite theme of an Imām in occultation, fully realised after al-Ḥākim's mysterious end, when the Druze Imāmate was established in perpetuity. That end was not long in coming. In the fateful year 411H, 1020–1, 400 years after the death of the Prophet, al-Ḥākim vanished on a nightly excursion on his donkey into the Muqaṭṭam hills above al-Qāhira; only the donkey and a bloodstained rag were ever found. There was no fulfilment of al-Kirmānī's promise of a universal empire, only a disappearance into a kingdom not of this world.

The Repercussions in the Maghrib

After the determined construction of the Fatimid Daᶜwa over the previous 100 years as a creed which combined the messianisms of the late ninth century with the legalism of the various schools into a prescription for the rule of the Prophet's heirs over the universal empire of Islam, the Druze schism demonstrated its fragility in the absence of consistent direction by the current heir. The schism itself was all the more dangerous since it came at a time when opposition to the dynasty was passing over to the offensive with the resurrection of the ᶜAbbasids as champions of a specifically Sunnite Islam, and the championship of both by the upstart Maḥmūd of Ghazna in the east. Containment of the damage by the efforts of the three Dāᶜī-s, al-Naysabūrī, Abūᵓl-Fawāris and especially al-Kirmānī, to reaffirm the doctrine of the Imāmate was essential for the future of the Daᶜwa. Meanwhile, as far as the Dawla was concerned, the crisis contributed to the evolution of the empire in the west. The rapprochement with the Zirids after the misguided interventions of Barjawan and al-Ḥākim in the affairs of Tripoli, which had been signalled by the assignment of Barqa to Bādīs in the *sijill* of 1012–13, had been maintained with the further exchange of embassies. Thus in the following year a *sijill* announced the appointment of Ibn Ilyās, while in the following year, 1014–15, a major Zirid embassy to al-Qāhira, bearing rich presents and a letter to al-Ḥākim's sister Sitt al-Mulk from Umm Mallāl, the sister of the Zirid sultan Bādīs. It sailed to Barqa under the command of Yaᶜlā ibn Faraj, most probably the governor appointed in accordance with the *sijill* of 1012–13. But on arrival it was set upon and plundered by the Banū Qurra; the appointment came to nothing, and the death of Bādīs in the following year meant that the attempt to restore the land bridge between the two centres of the empire permanently failed.[27] Bādīs's death, meanwhile, had occurred in the midst of a dynastic crisis, the rebellion in 1015 of Bādīs's uncle and erstwhile ally Ḥammād. Virtually independent as ruler of the western highlands of Ifrīqiya from his Qalᶜa, the fortress city founded in 1008, Ḥammād was not prepared to cede his possession of Constantine to Bādīs's son and heir al-Manṣūr, after this eastern portion of his dominion had been assigned to the young man by his father as a first step towards his inheritance. Since Ḥammād was joined by his brother Ibrāhīm, Bādīs was faced with a second family rebellion after the one that followed his accession in 996. Then, the rebels had turned to Cordoba; but this time, after the collapse of the Umayyad Caliphate in 1009, Ḥammād declared for the ᶜAbbasids. Bādīs nevertheless commanded a formidable army of infantry and cavalry, with which he drove his uncles to take refuge in the Qalᶜa. There they were besieged throughout the winter of 1015–16, saved only by Bādīs's sudden death in May. It says much for the strength of the Zirid sultanate that his second son Muᶜizz, a boy of about nine, was promptly proclaimed after the equally sudden death of his elder brother, and, moreover, that the army under the nominal command of Muᶜizz took the field again in the following year, forcing Ḥammād to submit. The outcome was nevertheless the partition of Ifrīqiya in a family settlement that recognised Ḥammād and his son al-Qāʾid as the independent rulers of their territories. It was the end result of the Fatimids' promotion of the tribal chieftains of the central Maghrib, on the one hand to keep the western frontier of their North African empire, and on the other to take their place in that empire as viceroys of the Caliphate in Egypt. But it was a historic step in the *longue durée* of North African history, as the former Byzantine province of Africa, which the Arabs had made a cornerstone of their empire, broke apart in the transition from Late Antiquity to the High Middle Ages.[28]

[27] See above, n. 2.
[28] Idris, *Berbérie orientale*, I, pp. 106–19.

Al-Qāhira had no hand in the matter, except insofar as it congratulated Muᶜizz on his accession with a *sijill* which conferred on him the title of Sharaf al-Dawla, and with it the legitimation of his power and authority. It was for Muᶜizz, then, or rather for those who acted in his name, to combat on behalf of the Caliphate the wave of anti-Ismāᶜīlism that began with Ḥammād's recognition of Baghdad in 1015. In that same year, Ismāᶜīlīs were massacred at Tunis at the instigation of the Mālikite jurist Muḥriz ibn Khalaf. The massacre stemmed from the old animosity between the Mālikites and those, notably Ḥanafites, who had gone over to the Fatimids, which had revived in the context of the gathering strength of an ideological Sunnism in the east. At Tunis it roused the populace of a city which was beginning its rise to prominence in opposition to the dominance of the old capitals Qayrawān and al-Mahdiyya. The animosity caught on: following the accession of Muᶜizz in 1016, similar massacres took place at Qayrawān and elsewhere, notably Tripoli. Again they were associated with jurists, Ibn Khaldūn al-Balawī at Qayrawān and Ibn al-Munammar at Tripoli; at Qayrawān and the palace city of al-Manṣūriyya they were accompanied by rioting and plundering of the *sūq*-s. Al-Balawī was killed by the authorities, extensive reprisals followed and there was no recurrence. With the excitement over, the regime settled down under the regency of Muᶜizz's aunt, Umm Mallāl, and her minister, the senior officer Muḥammad ibn Ḥasan, recalled from Tripoli to take over the administration. Like the regency of Barjawān, it offered scope for the overmighty subject; but, equally, it was not adventurous, as the amicable settlement with Ḥammād clearly showed. That was presumably on the initiative of Umm Mallāl, who preferred to compose rather than pursue the family's quarrels in the broader interest of dynastic stability. It was an arrangement that proved successful over the years, matched as far as the Fatimid empire was concerned by close relations with al-Qāhira. Two embassies arriving in 1021, but despatched before al-Ḥākim's disappearance, brought confirmation of Muᶜizz's title together with appropriate insignia, and congratulations on the news of the demise of the Caliphate at Cordoba, evidently in reply to a communication from al-Manṣūriyya. What is not clear is the extent to which the killings of Ismāᶜīlīs, running into many thousands in the sources, but certainly into notional rather than real figures, left the Zirids to rule in the name of the Fatimid Caliph over a population with little or no following for the Fatimid Imām.[29]

However that may be, the wave of anti-Ismāᶜīlism only emphasised the fact that the Zirid monarchy, since its inception under al-Manṣūr, had

[29] Idris, *Berbérie orientale*, I, pp. 119–20, 143–9.

governed in practice if not in principle in accordance with the Fatimid Amān. More than ever, it was a model for a universal Fatimid empire, ruled with justice by monarchs holding their title from the Imām Caliph. The constitution of that empire, on the other hand, depended upon the recognition of the Caliphate by rulers yet to be won for the cause. And here the Da^cwa in the last years of al-Ḥākim's reign enjoyed an adventitious success at Aleppo, whose annexation had been a goal of Fatimid policy down to the death of al-^cAzīz, but which since the truce with Byzantium had remained balanced between the two empires under the Ḥamdānid *ghulām* Lu^ɔlu^ɔ and his son al-Manṣūr. Lu^ɔlu^ɔ had dispossessed the last of the Ḥamdānids in 1004 to rule as a client of Byzantium; at his accession in 1010, al-Manṣūr had declared for the Fatimids. But in 1016 al-Manṣūr was expelled by his commandant Fatḥ, and turned for help to the Byzantines in Antioch. Ensconced in the citadel, Fatḥ consequently invited the Fatimid governor of Afamiya on the northern frontier of Fatimid Syria to occupy the town. Meanwhile, Bedouins of the Kilāb, the northernmost of the tribal confederations on the eastern borders of Syria, camped outside the city under the leadership of Ṣāliḥ ibn Mirdās to demand the territory treacherously denied them by al-Manṣūr in payment for their military service. But the city preferred the Fatimids; the Arabs were driven away by a Fatimid host of regular troops and Bedouin from the other two confederations, the Kalb and the Ṭayy; Fatḥ was installed with his men as governor at Tyre; and an Armenian commander, Fātak, took charge of Aleppo. At long last, therefore, the city had fallen into Fatimid hands, and the start of raiding across the Byzantine frontier suggested a return to aggression. But the initiative was local; and far from being an instrument of empire, within a year or two Fātak had made himself independent. As an Armenian like his namesake killed in the rising of Abū Rakwa, he signalled the arrival of yet another ethnicity in the make-up of the Fatimid army, of great importance for the future. Much of that importance lay in the fact that these were men of Christian background at home in the northerly world of Anatolia and the Syrian marches, whose introduction into Fatimid service in Syria and Egypt was destined to change the fortunes of the dynasty. Meanwhile, however, in the absence of any particular commitment to the Fatimid cause, Fātak simply demonstrated the fact that in Syria, allegiance to the Caliphate was more often a matter of convenience rather than conviction; and that while the acquisition of Aleppo continued to be a Fatimid ambition, for the moment under al-Ḥākim it was not an opportunity to be exploited, least of all against Baghdad.

7

The Regime of the Pen

The Return to Dynastic Orthodoxy

The Imāmate may have been rescued by al-Kirmānī and his colleagues in the Da^{c}wa, but the Caliphate was a different matter. The outcome of the succession crisis precipitated by the disappearance of al-Ḥākim on one of his habitual nocturnal expeditions was a regime in which the Caliph took little or no part in the affairs of state, leaving his ministers to rule in his name. It began with the ruthless elimination of his designated heirs – the conclusive repudiation of a dangerous folly, in the course of a brief but decisive struggle for power. The search that discovered al-Ḥākim's mule and a blood-stained garment failed to find the body, but pointed to his murder by persons unknown. Seven Bedouin who were known to have accosted him earlier in the night were promptly executed, but the matter did not end there. His disappearance in February was not made public until the Feast of Sacrifice in March; in the meantime it was announced that he had withdrawn from his people in anger at their ingratitude for his benefits. But after the prayer on the day of the ^{c}Īd had been said in his name, his fifteen-year-old son ^{c}Alī was crowned as Imām Caliph under the title of al-Ẓāhir li-i$^{\circ}$zāz Dīn Allāh. With this return of the succession to the son of the previous Imām, al-Ḥākim's designated heirs were set aside, the one imprisoned, the other, Ibn Ilyās, fetched from Damascus to take his own life. At the same time the title chosen for the new prince, He Who Appears Openly to Strengthen the Religion of God, was a clear statement of a return to dynastic orthodoxy. The politics behind this reaffirmation of dynastic principle, however, came into the open shortly afterwards with the execution of Ibn Dawwās, the commander of the Kutāma who had put an end to the sack of Fusṭāṭ by the Black infantry, and with al-Ḥākim's disappearance had taken charge of the government. The execution was on the orders of Sitt al-Mulk, al-Ḥākim's elder sister, who seemingly denounced him to al-Ḥākim's bodyguard of Ṣaqāliba as the murderer of their master. Having failed at the death of her father al-^{c}Azīz to install an adult on the throne in place of her brother, the Lady of the Kingdom, resident in the Western Palace, thus took undisputed control of the state on behalf of her nephew.[1] The story itself has the familiar air of a kingmaker despatched the moment his work was done. Ibn Dawwās comes out of it as a principal ally of the princess, one who may indeed have disposed of al-Ḥākim on her behalf. But as commander of the Kutāma, especially after the murder of the Wazīr ᶜAlī ibn Jaᶜfar ibn Falāḥ, he had not only the power to secure the succession but the independence to pose a threat to her authority. That authority rested on a much wider circle of clients forming around her and her protégé, al-Ḥākim's son, perhaps since the designation of Ibn Ilyās and the abrupt execution of the Qāḍī al-Fāriqī in 1014; these now provided her with the personnel to rule until her death in 1023. That left only the disappearance of al-Ḥākim to be explained away. Not until 1024 was he officially declared to have been murdered, when a rebel in Upper Egypt was caught and confessed to the deed. For the Druzes, on the other hand, it was the final proof of his divinity, of his absence against the time when he should come again. As the dynasty returned to its open doctrine under a new Imām, their belief in his return completed their formation as a sect, and turned their *ghuluww* from a movement within the Daᶜwa into a schism that put an end to the internal threat they had posed to the Daᶜwa and by extension to the Fatimid cause.

It did not put an end to the pursuit of Ḥamza's mission by his lieutenants and followers. Vigorously denounced and persecuted by al-Qāhira, these took refuge in Upper Egypt and more especially in the mountains of Syria, where a significant number of the dynasty's *duᶜāt* had been won for the cause. Ḥamza himself disappeared, perhaps executed in Mecca, but his successor al-Muqtanā continued to proselytise, sending out letters to all and sundry, including the Byzantines, until 1043. The last was symptomatic of a quarrel with the leading Syrian Dāᶜī Sukayn, and with it the propagation of the creed came to an end, while its followers retreated into the closed community that has survived to the present day. That they could survive in this way in Fatimid Syria says much for the heterogeneous character of the country and the nature of Fatimid rule from its base in the cities. Equally it says something for the faith of the majority who remained within the Fatimid fold. The poetry of al-Muᵓayyad fīᵓl-Dīn al-Shīrazī, appointed Dāᶜī of Fars in succession to his father at Shiraz in 1025, apostrophises al-Ẓāhir not only as the son of al-Ḥākim who has indeed strengthened the religion of God. He is the master of

[1] For Sitt al-Mulk and her ability to take charge of the succession, see H. Halm, 'Le destin de la princesse Sitt al-Mulk', in M. Barrucand (ed.), *L'Égypte fatimide: son art et son histoire*, pp. 69–72, and D. Cortese and S. Calderini, *Women and the Fatimids in the World of Islam*, pp. 117–27, et passim. Her residence is described by A. F. Sayyid in Barrucand, *L'Égypte fatimide: son art et son histoire*, p. 122.

all creatures, seen and unseen, omniscient, radiant, pure and righteous, the light for whom the poet is consumed by love and longing. Hyperbolic as they are, the terms of these and all the other odes in al-Shīrazī's *Dīwān* betray an emotional devotion to the Imām of the time, al-Ẓāhir and his successor al-Mustanṣir. They suggest that while al-Ḥākim may have slipped back uncontroversially into the dynastic scheme, the legacy of the *ghuluww* of his last few years may have been a heightened spirituality on the part of the remaining faithful. Together with al-Naysabūrī's communal discipline, such spirituality prepared them to survive the vicissitudes and eventual disappearance of the dynasty which had formed them to be the elite of the Muslim community, turning like the Druzes into a sectarian minority.[2]

The Political Settlement

Meanwhile, al-Shīrazī's devotion betokened a fresh but paradoxical enthusiasm for the dynasty and its cause. The paradox was in the object of that devotion, the Imām himself. This was no longer a monarch in the mould of either the Mahdī or al-Ḥākim, actively pursuing a purpose, but a figurehead invested by the faithful with all of al-Shīrazī's attributes of holiness, and by his servants with the charisma by which they ruled in his name.

There was no question of al-Ẓāhir's taking power as his father had done; as head of state he functioned in a ceremonial capacity, holding audience and riding out in sumptuous processions, all described in detail by al-Musabbiḥī in the only fragment of his original to have survived, the fortieth volume, for the years 1024–5 (see Fig. 7.1). It was indeed the theatrical performance of a theatre state, in which the degree of closeness to the monarch was a sign of rank and status, but in which the positioning was determined not by the monarch but by the jockeying of his underlings for power. Among these the Ṣaqāliba, who in the days of Jawdhar and Barjawān had been the intimates and deputies of the Caliph in control of the state, remained as a palace guard under the Swordbearer who kept the curtain before the throne, and served as executioner. Their predominance as agents of the dynasty, however, had ended with the murder of Barjawān and the disgrace of al-Ḥākim's accomplice Raydān following the abortive expedition of Yaḥyā ibn ᶜAlī to Tripoli. In that capacity a corps of Black eunuchs, *khuddām* (sing. *khādim*), had appeared, beginning with Ghayn, chief of police in 1013. Much closer to the throne was Miᶜḍād , who had presented al-Ẓāhir to the assembly as the successor to his father on the occasion of the ᶜĪd, and in the role of Barjawān

[2] Al-Muʾayyad fīʾl-Dīn al-Shīrāzī, *Dīwān al-Mu,ayyad fīʾl-Dīn al-Shīrāzī dāᶜī al-duʾāt*, ed. M. K. Husayn (Cairo, 1949), trans. M. Adra as *Mount of Knowledge, Sword of Eloquence* (London, 2011).

played a major part in the formation of the government that came to power following the death of Sitt al-Mulk. A military figure, he and his fellows were all the more powerful since under al-Ḥākim the recruitment of Black infantry into the army had been greatly expanded. Purchased as slaves from Nubia and via the trans-Saharan trade through Zawīla in the Fezzan, these now formed a major component of the army, between the Maghāriba, the Berbers, on the one hand, and the Mashāriqa, the Turks and Daylamīs, on the other. As such, they provided the palace with a force to offset the other ethnic groups with their long-standing rivalry.[3]

On the other hand, Miᶜḍād was no Barjawān, in that he shared power in a cabal of eight with its other chief member, al-Jarjarāʾī, al-Aqṭā, 'the Amputated'. Named for his native place outside Baghdad, al-Jarjarāʾī was the latest of the Iraqi secretaries drawn to Egypt by the prospect of employment. Having survived his involvement in the downfall of Ghayn in 1013, which cost him the loss of his hands, by the end of al-Ḥākim's reign he was jointly in charge of the Treasury, and acting for Sitt al-Mulk as the steward of her estates. Retaining control of her vast wealth, he emerged at her death as the politician with the means and the ability to create his own party of government before his formal appointment as Wazīr in 1028. In the interim, the post of Wāsiṭa or Wazīr was filled by nominees. During the reign of Sitt al-Mulk, al-Ḥākim's last Wāsiṭa, ᶜAmmār ibn Muḥammad, Khaṭīr al-Mulk, survived for a mere seven months before his execution; his successor Mūsā ibn al-Ḥasan went the same way after nine. This man had held the important positions of chief of police in Fusṭāṭ and governor of Upper Egypt; his temporary appointment as head of the Chancery in place of the secretary Ibn Khayrān, followed by his elevation to the Wisāṭa, suggests a plot on the part of his rivals to eliminate him. Thereafter the appointments were largely titular. Al-Wazzān, dismissed by al-Ḥākim in 1013, was reappointed in tandem with al-Jarjarāʾī, who kept for himself the lucrative dīwāns, or boards of revenue, of the port of Damietta and the textile town of Tinnis, as well as the dīwān, the estate, of Sitt al-Mulk. Al-Wazzān was followed in 1024 by al-Rūdhbārī, a veteran from the reign of al-ᶜAzīz, when he had provided the logistical support for Manjūtakīn's advance on Aleppo in 991; he was finally dismissed in 1027 to make way for al-Jarjarāʾī. The real struggle for power took place within the cabal at a time in 1024 when Egypt was gripped by one of its periodic famines, the troops were unpaid and mutinous, and the Arab tribes of Syria were in revolt.

No sooner had the cabal constituted itself after the death of Sitt al-Mulk

[3] Cf. Lev, *State and Society in Fatimid Egypt*, pp. 88–9.

Figure 7.1 Mounted Cavalier. Ceramic plate. © Freer Gallery of Art, Smithsonian Institution, Washington, DC; Purchase – Charles Lang Freer, Endorsement, F1941.12.

Lustreware, made by firing the piece with oxides of copper and silver, and painted with representations of people, animals, birds and vegetation, was a major product of Fatimid industry. This example shows an aristocratic horseman out hawking.

than it descended into a fatal quarrel. With the dismissal of al-Wazzān in March 1024, the offices of state were reallocated to its members. In May Mi^{c}ḍād was invested with general authority, and in August he and his principal colleagues – al-Jarjarā$^{\circ}$ī himself, the Ḥasanid shaykh al-Qazwīnī and the treasurer Ibn Badūs – gained exclusive entry to daily private audiences with the Caliph. But in October, as the famine developed and revenues fell, while the Jarrāḥids once again advanced into Palestine and the troops sent against them mutinied, Mi^{c}ḍād dismissed his powerful fellow eunuch Rifq from his command in the Delta. Within the cabal, Ibn Badūs was challenged to find the wherewithal to pay the army. Ibn Badūs was the odd man out, as a Christian convert to Islam who had not taken advantage of the opportunity to return to the Church. His real fault, however, was to side with Rifq against

Mi^cḍād , and for this he now paid the price. He was arrested and executed on a trumped-up charge of treasonable correspondence with Ḥassān ibn Jarrāḥ, on suspicion of a Christian conspiracy. Rifq himself promptly seized the Treasury as well as Ibn Badūs's house, and only gave it up after two weeks on the order of the Caliph. By January 1025, he was nevertheless assisting with the arrangements for al-Ẓāhir to watch the celebrations for the Feast of the Epiphany, and was subsequently honoured by the Caliph along with Miᶜḍād and a fellow eunuch Nabā in what may have been a ceremony of reconciliation. But with the end of the surviving fragment of al-Musabbiḥī's chronicle, the sequel is not clear. Both Miᶜḍād and Rifq disappear from the record, to resurface twenty years later; Ibn Khayrān, the long-serving head of the Chancery, survived until his death in 1039, in a post which, however important for the written instruments of government, posed no threat to those in power. From their ranks, however, al-Jarjarāʾī finally emerged in January 1028 with the title of Wazīr, granted in a *sijill* of appointment which entrusted him in practice as well as principle with the duty of *wizāra*, to 'lift the burden' of government from the shoulders of the Caliph in the manner of ᶜAlī, Joseph and Aaron vis-à-vis Muḥammad, Pharaoh and Moses. In that capacity he ruled on behalf of the Caliph until his death in 1045. With him, as a politician as well as an administrator, the takeover of government by the servants of the dynasty, which al-Ḥākim had so brutally forestalled, was finally achieved.[4]

Egypt and Syria under al-Jarjarāʾī

Coming after the turbulence of the past quarter-century, this long period of stable government by the minister rather than the Caliph was a remarkable achievement, attributable in the first place to the minister himself. Handless as he was, obliged to rely upon his secretary al-Quḍāᶜī to write and sign for him, al-Jarjarāʾī was a statesman whose administrative ability was coupled with the political skills to acquire the allies and clients he needed to form his government. He was, on the other hand, no reformer, but a successful operator of the system that had evolved over the past sixty years, and whose workings and problems had been exposed in the critical years following the death of Sitt al-Mulk. Of these, Syria had once again demonstrated its difference from Egypt in the renewed threat to the province of the Bedouin Arabs on its eastern borders, the Kilāb, Kalb and Ṭayy. The advance of Ḥassān ibn Jarrāḥ upon Ramla was coupled with the advance of the Kalb upon Damascus and,

[4] For the history of this episode and its implications, cf. M. Brett, 'The execution of Ibn Badūs', in U. Vermeulen, K. D'Hulster and J. Van Steenbergen (eds), *Egypt and Syria in the Fatimid, Ayyubid and Mamluk Eras*, VII (Leuven, 2013), pp. 21–9.

most important of all, the taking of Aleppo from its Fatimid governor by Ṣāliḥ ibn Mirdās, the Kilābī Arab chief who had attempted to take over the city in 1016. Fātik, the Armenian then installed by the Fatimids, had been murdered and replaced in 1022 after his bid for independence; but the city fell under the control of Ṣāliḥ in 1024. The coalition that then developed between Ṣāliḥ, the Kalbid chief Sinān and the Jarrāḥid Ḥassān came close to imposing upon the cities and the sedentary populations of the province a government by protection, *ḥimāya*, in place of the centralised administration of the Fatimids at Ramla and Damascus. All would have been happy to rule on behalf of al-Qāhira; but as Wazīr, al-Jarjarāʾī was not prepared to treat. The Turk Anūshtakīn al-Dizbīrī, previously in command of the Egyptian frontier at Ascalon, was sent to restore the Fatimid position. Al-Dizbīrī was the outstanding soldier of his generation; in 1029 he routed the Arab coalition at the battle of Uqḥuwāna near Lake Tiberias, in which Ṣāliḥ was killed, and went on to rule at Damascus for the next decade as the Syrian prop of al-Jarjarāʾī's regime. The Mirdāsids accepted Fatimid suzerainty; but Aleppo remained in their hands, and from the point of view of the empire, the situation remained much as it had been since the death of al-ʿAzīz. Al-Jarjarāʾī was as conservative in the matter as Barjawān had been.

In Egypt itself, the crisis had revealed the manoeuvring for preferment at the heart of government, against a background of famine which similarly exposed the flaws in the financial system on which the whole edifice rested. The system itself was heavily dependent on the tax farm to produce the revenue for the tax collector – not a simple process, since as far as the agricultural economy was concerned, it involved the annual calculation of the size of the harvest. The calculations and accountancy were largely in the hands of Copts, now free to return to their Christianity, who benefited from what was a largely reserved occupation. The other beneficiaries were the tax farmers, particularly the great and good, who might be granted estates and other properties with or without a tax liability. Among these were certainly the members of the royal family, not least the princesses, who were, like Sitt al-Mulk, immensely wealthy. In normal years the income thus accumulated by the state and its servants was sufficiently distributed, or redistributed, to ensure a general prosperity; and a low Nile was not necessarily a problem. The problem as reported by al-Musabbiḥī in 1024 stemmed in the first place from the claim of Ibn Badūs, as Treasurer, that nothing was left over to pay the troops after the expenses of the palace had been met. A proposal to draw on the hoarded wealth of the palace was rejected together with a levy on the merchants of the city. Those merchants, in fact, will have borne some of the responsibility for the famine itself, in that they traded in the grain which, in addition to the amount collected in kind in the form of *kharāj*, of land tax, was either speculatively bought for resale by the state or sold by the estate holders. Low Niles predictably led to hoarding, high prices and shortages, particularly in the capital, which depended upon imports of food in the way that the countryside did not – a classic phenomenon common to London and Paris in the early modern period. The cabal, too weak to take the necessary decisions, had evidently been paralysed; Miᶜḍād could only use the regimental guard of Ṣaqāliba to put down mutineers and plunderers in the capital until the good harvest in the spring of 1025. The vested interests involved, those of the palace, the members of the imperial family and all those to whom al-Jarjarāᵓī looked for support in the army of secretaries and soldiers, remained as a constant to be exploited by the Wazīr, who was himself in charge of the lucrative *dīwān*-s he had reserved for himself. They were, on the other hand, ignored at his peril. The power of life and instant death that al-Ḥākim had chosen to exercise had entered into the practice of the regime. As the loss of his hands had shown, quite apart from the experience of his predecessors, al-Jarjarāᵓī could not take for granted the favour of a Caliph like al-Ẓāhir who was generally content to leave the government in his charge.

That said, as an administrator he presided efficiently over the workings of government through the Dīwān al-Majlis, a council formed by the heads of the main departments which had evolved out of the Dīwān al-Zimām, the Board of Control, a name that speaks for itself.[5] The Dīwān had its own head and permanent secretary, and was generally responsible for the round of ceremonies that were the routine of this theatrical state; for the grant of the benefices with which the servants of the state were rewarded, and that of the robes that went with high office; for the similarly important registration of gifts received from and sent out to other princes and heads of state; and for the audit of the most important expenditures of the state, to keep track of any discrepancies between one year and another; all to be recorded in the registry of the Dīwān. The audit was covered by the Dīwān al-Naẓar, or Supervisory Board, whose head drew up all the paperwork required for submission to the Wazir at specified times in his capacity as head of the Dawāwīn al-Amwāl, the boards of revenue which collected the kharaj or land tax together with the taxes on other sources of income. His counterpart in charge of expenditure was head of the Dīwān al-Rawātib, or Tartīb, who kept the list of all those entitled to pay, military and civilian. This had originally come under the

[5] The various Dawāwīn are listed by A. F. Sayyid, in *A-Dawla al-fāṭimiyya fī Miṣr: tafsīr jadīd/ Les Fatimides en Égypte: nouvelle interprétation* (Cairo, 1992), ʻal-Dawāwīn al-fāṭimiyyaʼ, pp. 257–67, et passim. While some of these came and went, and others changed their names, the basic structure remained constant.

Dīwān al-Jaysh, or Army Board, which kept the records of the personnel of the armed forces, high and low. Their provision with arms and equipment, barracks and supplies, fell to other departments. The Dīwān al-Khāṣṣ, or Board of the Elite, meanwhile, dealt with the income destined for the upkeep of the palace, the vast expenses of the Caliphal household, while the Dīwān al-Rasāʾil or al-Inshāʾ waʾl-Mukātaba, the Chancery, issued the sijillāt, the edicts and correspondence of the dynasty. And in particular there was the Bayt al-Māl, or Treasury, of which the unfortunate Ibn Badūs had been head before he was hauled away for execution. His story is significant of its function as a recipient of funds and as a channel for expenditure. He was taken at his desk, on which his papers and accounts were spread out; these he was required to stamp and seal, likewise the Bayt al-Māl itself and the Khizānat al-Khāṣṣ, the Treasury, for the expenses of the palace. That these were two separate treasuries is confirmed by the subsequent appointment of two separate heads, Ṭayyib and Masarra, both Treasury men with the soubriquet al-Khāzin, and both certainly Copts. But the flow of cash between the two emerges from the previous story that Ibn Badūs had been unable to pay the troops sent out against Ibn Jarrāḥ because the expenses of the palace came first.

The story of Ibn Badūs is important as an illustration of the financial administration actually at work. The problem is that the sources that describe its structure and operation are at best late Fatimid, and for the most part post-Fatimid, running from al-Makhzūmī and Ibn Mammāṭī at the end of the twelfth century to al-Maqrīzī and al-Qalqashandī in the fifteenth. Al-Makhzūmī[6] and Ibn Mammāṭī[7] were both Fatimid officials who described the system for the benefit of Saladin and his Ayyubid successors; al-Maqrīzī and al-Qalqashandī were primarily concerned with the Mamlūk system, and insofar as they refer to the Fatimid administration, do not give a systematic account of its evolution. The term *dīwān* is itself a loose term for office, covering the major boards and their subsidiaries as well as, in the case of al-Jarjarāʾī, his stewardship of the estate of Sitt al-Mulk. The information as to the sources of revenue; the taxes levied; their assessment and collection; the allocation and expenditure of the income, together with the commercial transactions involved in the process, is not easy to match up. Syria had its

6 Al-Makhzūmī, *Al-Muntaqā min Kitāb al-minhāj fī ʿilm kharāj Miṣr*, ed. C. Cahen and Y. Raghib (Cairo, 1986); cf. C. Cahen, *Makhzūmiyyāt. Études sur l'histoire économique et financière de l'Égypte médiévale* (Leiden, 1977).

7 Ibn Mammātī, *Kitāb qawānīn al-dawāwīn*, ed. A. S. Atiya (Cairo, 1943); English trans. R. S. Cooper, *Ibn Mammātī's Rules for the Ministries*, microfilm reprint of PhD dissertation, University of California, Berkeley, CA, 1973 (Ann Arbor, MI and London, 1979).

own fiscal regime, its Dīwān al-Shām, with another for Damascus. Within Egypt, the distinction between private property and that of the state, which in principle owned the land and the right to its taxation, was blurred by the urban and rural estates of the Caliph and members of the dynasty, the princesses in particular, and likewise by the benefices conferred on its servants, all carefully registered, and held precariously by their recipients. These might or might not be reclaimed; the Dīwān al-Mufraḍ set up by al-Ḥākim for the estates of his victims eventually became the Dīwān al-Murāja^c^a, the Office of Reversals. As previously in the different circumstances of Ifrīqiya, the income from such estates created an immensely wealthy elite, albeit one that was never able to convert its holdings into the hereditary possessions of a landed aristocracy. As far as the state itself was concerned, the sources of revenue were first and foremost the land and its produce, followed by the non-Muslim communities, Christians and Jews; the taxation of both of these categories was recognised as legitimate in the law of Islam. Apart from these were trade in the form of imports and exports as well as internal marketing; commercial properties; manufactures and manufacturing; and tolls. Their taxation went back to pre-Islamic times, but came into the category of *maks* (pl. *mukūs*), illegal impositions in the eyes of the law, but condoned by the doctrine of *siyasa shar^c^iya*, or lawful policy-making. Additionally there was mining, of alum, natron, salt and emeralds, of which alum, used in textile manufacture and tanning, was a highly profitable state monopoly, sold for export by the Matjar.[8] This commercial arm of the state was principally a buyer and seller of grain at a profit for the Treasury, but served a strategic purpose in the procurement for the state of essential materials such as imported iron and timber for weapons and ships.

As to the taxes themselves, the long and detailed tally from the post-Fatimid period had certainly grown out of the Fatimid list, and is indicative of its variety.[9] The *kharāj*, or land tax, was levied in kind on the winter crop of grain that was harvested in spring, but in cash on the winter crop of flax, and more generally on the array of vegetables and crops such as sugarcane and cotton which were grown throughout the year but particularly by irrigation in summer. So too were the taxes on orchards, vineyards and olive groves, as well as those on pastureland and livestock, and on fisheries. The whole repertoire reflected the agricultural revolution of the previous century and the prosperity it had generated, all the more so for the processing and manufacturing industries to which these crops gave rise. These in turn were

8 Cf. Y. Lev, *State and Society in Fatimid Egypt*, p. 164.

9 Described by H. Rabie, *The Financial System of Egypt,* A.H. *564–741*/A.D. *1169–1341* (London, 1972), pp. 73–132.

taxed, both the goods themselves, such as sugar and linen cloth, and the workshops, oil presses, tanneries and so on that produced them, not to speak of beer and wine after the rescinding of al-Ḥākim's edicts. Businesses in general, shops, workshops, baths, *funduq*-s or hostelries, required licences to operate. Taxes on trade extended from market dues to harbour dues and taxes, to taxes on imports and exports, which varied according to the kind of goods, and taxes on the merchants themselves. As with the agricultural revolution, the revenues from such taxes benefited from the growth in intercontinental trade between Europe, Asia and Africa that passed up and down the Nile and the Red Sea to and from the Mediterranean and the Indian Ocean. Syria, at the terminus of landward trade out of Asia, will likewise have enjoyed a healthy tax return. It is equally likely that the general prosperity was reflected in the poll tax on non-Muslims, which was imposed at a variable rate on rich and poor alike. The Jewish population had been augmented by the immigration of Jews from North Africa who had followed the Fatimid flag to Egypt. The Copts were still a large proportion of the population of Egypt, both urban and rural. The long-term shrinkage of their numbers will to some extent have been offset by the overall growth of that population in Fatimid times up towards its maximum pre-modern level of four to five million. Meanwhile, in the Church and the blossoming fiscal administration the Copts, together with the Melkite minority, benefited from reserved or effectively reserved occupations, sufficiently rewarding to create a well-to-do section of their community largely unaffected by the persecutions of al-Ḥākim's reign.

Tax assessment and collection was another matter.[10] Valuation was essential, and had been long before Ibn Killis and ᶜUslūj ibn al-Ḥasan revalued and reissued the tax farms at the outset of the Fatimid regime. The procedure was most elaborate in the case of the harvest, particularly the harvest of grain cultivated on the floodplain of the Nile. According to al-Makhzumi, writing immediately after the end of the Fatimid period, the extent of the flooded land in any one year was measured and its plots assigned to the peasants. When the crops had grown, the yield was estimated and the tax payable by each peasant was calculated. In the case of orchards and vineyards, the survey took place every three years, allowing for newly planted trees and consequent variations in yield. Those responsible were officials of the fisc who worked with the village head to ensure cultivation for the benefit of the state. There is no doubt that the procedure was of long standing; the problem is that in al-Makhzūmī's time, the land was parcelled out in *iqtaᶜat*, or portions, among

[10] Ibid., pp. 133–61.

the troops of Saladin's army, as it had been among the soldiery of the Fatimids for the past 100 years. These *iqta*ᶜ*at* were basically tax farms, of a kind that went back before their militarisation to the practice of al-Jarjarāʾī's day. Then it would appear that the farms were let for a period of four years on the basis of an estimate of the average yield over that time. Tax farms of this kind were ubiquitous, blending into the kind of control that al-Jarjarāʾī exercised over the revenues of Tinnis and Damietta. In the case of the land, however, the tax farmer had an obligation, in conjunction with the village head (who may at times have been one and the same person), to maintain and operate the canals and dykes of the irrigation system. There is no necessary conflict between such a tax farm and an annual inspection and estimate of the harvest; there is nevertheless an area of uncertainty, which extends to the collection of the grain that was owed in tax and its despatch by river, perhaps four times a year. The third party here was the governor of the *kūra*, the administrative district, of which there were between fifty and seventy. For 100 years after the Arab conquest, he had been in charge of the whole system, but by this time policed an operation apparently conducted by the clerks of the state. What force he had at his disposal for this and other purposes is unclear. But throughout the countryside there were reservations for companies of Blacks, who formed a self-supporting militia, and whose purpose can only have been to maintain order as and when required.[11]

The New Queen Mother

The Dīwān al-Kharāj thus found itself in possession of a large quantity of grain distinct from the grain that was bought from the producers for sale by the Matjar, and again it is not clear how much of it was used to pay salaries, especially those of soldiers, in kind. A large quantity went to the Hijaz to feed the annual pilgrimage and ensure that the Ashrāf who controlled the Holy Places continued to acknowledge the Fatimid Caliph as the heir to the Prophet. Much of it will have found its way onto the market. What is clear from the structure of the administration is that, as income and expenditure, it was all accounted for, all the more because of the jealousies which could turn discrepancies into accusations of corruption. In the case of the conspiracy of Ibn al-ᶜAddās to oust Fahd ibn Ibrāhīm from control of the finances at the outset of al-Ḥākim's reign, the consequences for both were fatal; al-Jarjarāʾī himself had lost his hands in similar circumstances. But after the turbulence of al-Ḥākim's reign and the years following his death, his undisputed control of the government kept such rivalries in check. That may well have been

[11] Cf. Lev, *State and Society*, pp. 94–5, quoting al-Maqrīzī.

because he paid the price for quiescence in the opportunities there surely were for making money out of an official position, not least in his own case as head of the dīwāns of Tinnīs and Damietta. Concern for continuity was apparent in the retention of Ibn Khayrān as head of the Chancery. Standing apart from the financial administration, although not beyond the scope of its accountants, this was a department which will have made money out of the fees for its services. The office and its holder evidently posed no threat to the authority of the Wazīr, though its functions were vital to the operation of government. Its head was the Man of the Pen *par excellence*, the master of the dynasty's diplomas, deeds, decrees and correspondence, all written to standard formulae in a calligraphic hand. Among them for the present purposes were the *sijillāt* of appointment to the highest posts, replete with the evermore grandiose titles bestowed on its servants by what Stanley Lane-Poole called 'this pompous dynasty'. As utterances of the Imām Caliph, these documents rewarded those promoted with a share in his glory, incorporating them into the hierarchy of the Caliphate, ostentatiously on display in its ceremonial round.

Appointments to those other great offices of the Caliphate and Imāmate, those of Chief Qāḍī and Chief Dāʿī, were still more conservative. The restoration of the old order was completed with the appointment of al-Qāsim ibn ʿAbd al-ʿAzīz ibn Muḥammad ibn al-Nuʿmān in the first place as Chief Dāʿī in succession to Khatkīn in 1023, and as Chief Qāḍī at the death of Ibn Abīʾl-ʿAwwām in 1027. This reunion of the law and the mission of the dynasty in the person of the great-grandson of the Qāḍī al-Nuʿmān was uncontested. Al-Jarjarāʾī was no Ibn Killis, nor Qāsim his grandfather Muḥammad, at loggerheads over the judiciary and the doctrine of the dynasty. Instead, both returned as of right to the custody of the family most entitled to act and speak in these matters on behalf of the Imām Caliph. With al-Qāsim's appointment, the doctrine which his ancestor had defined was reaffirmed, not only symbolically but in practice with the resumption of the Majālis al-Ḥikma. These sessions at which the doctrine was expounded and explicated, and which had been so abruptly suspended by al-Ḥākim, served their various congregations in the manner of church services, bringing the faithful together in regular assemblies. They were presumably attended by the faithful who made the pilgrimage from abroad to the seat of the Imām whose sacred figure was so ecstatically celebrated by al-Shirāzī. From his poems it is clear that the Daʿwa continued to flourish in the Iranian world, and that al-Qāhira was an almost mystical pole of attraction for the members of its communities. But for these, its existence in the mind may have been in inverse proportion to its activity on the ground. Initiative in the service of the cause remained with al-Shirāzī and his fellow *duʿāt*.

That was all the more so since the Imām Caliph himself, the figure on whom both Dawla and Da^c^wa turned, remained in the background. Al-Ẓāhir's involvement in the business of government was limited to his participation in the routine of audience and ceremony, his interest to the maintenance of his state. At his death in 1036 he was succeeded by his seven-year-old son with the title al-Mustanṣir biʾllah, He Who Asks for Victory by God. This accession of yet another minor nevertheless changed the political scene, in that al-Jarjarāʾī could no longer rely on the complacency of the palace. Ruqiyya, the queen mother of al-Ẓāhir, may have been his ally. But she was now replaced by Raṣad, the Black concubine of al-Ẓāhir, who as regent for her son set out to bring her own people forward into government, first and foremost the merchant who had introduced her into the palace.[12] This was the Jewish Iranian al-Tustarī, who seems to have been a surrogate father on whom she relied, not least to manage her estate as al-Jarjarāʾī had managed that of Sitt al-Mulk. Together with his brother, he thus emerged as an ambitious and influential political figure with whom the Wazīr had to reckon for the second half of his term of office, down to his death in 1045. He remained unchallenged in control of his subordinates in the administration, but these now began to take on the aspect of a party of government faced with an opposition in waiting. The opposition in question was all the more significant because it involved not only the Men of the Pen but the Men of the Sword, the army. Rivalry within its ranks had come into the open in the conflict between the Maghāriba and the Mashāriqa, the Kutāma and the Turks, following the death of al-ᶜAzīz. In 1030 Berbers and Turks had clashed again, before al-Ẓāhir's appearance above the Golden Gate of the palace calmed them down. But at the accession of al-Mustanṣir they combined to demand and obtain with menaces a rise in salary. With Raṣad, however, the Black Queen Mother, a third factor entered into play as she looked to the Blacks, the *ᶜabīd al-shirāʾ* or 'purchased slaves', as a base for her authority. Coming from Nubia or the Central Sudan via Zawīla in the Fezzan, their numbers had greatly increased under al-Ḥākim, and although for the most part they constituted a low-paid infantry, quartered in the capital as well as distributed up and down the Valley and Delta, they outnumbered the Turks; and following the death of al-Jarjarāʾī, the effect of Raṣad's favour in the political battle that ensued was to provoke a mutual hostility with ultimately disastrous consequences.[13]

[12] Cf. Cortese and Calderini, *Women and the Fatimids in the World of Islam*, pp. 110–14, et passim, and Calderini, 'Sayyida Raṣad: a royal woman as "Gateway to Power" during the Fatimid era', in U. Vermeulen and K. D'Hulster (eds), *Egypt and Syria in the Fatimid, Ayyubid and Mamluk Eras*, V (Leuven, 2007), pp. 27–36.

[13] Cf. Lev, *State and Society*, pp. 94–5; see Chapter 8 below.

The Army in the Mid-Eleventh Century

On the first day of Ramaḍān, 415/1024–5, our lord (al-Ẓāhir) rode out in golden robe and turban with his slaves and troops and the men of his Dawla. Over his head a golden parasol was carried by Bahā᾽ al-Dawla Muẓaffar al-Ṣiqlabī, and behind him Ibn Futūḥ al-Kutāmī bore the lance after the custom of his father. Before him went the Turks, the Kutāma, the Qayṣariyya, the ᶜAbīd, the Bāṭiliyya, the Daylam and the other contingents of the army, and behind him came the other men of his Dawla with Nasīm al- Ṣiqlabī (the Ṣāḥib al-Sitr or Master of the Curtain at the daily audience).

Al-Musabbiḥī, *Chronique d'Égypte*, p. 61

In 439/1047–8, at the ceremony of the Opening of the Canal by al-Mustanṣir, the contingents were the Kutāma, the Bāṭiliyya, the Maṣāmida, the Turks and Persians, collectively called the Mashāriqa, the ᶜAbīd al-Shirā᾽, the Bedouin, the Ustādhs, Black and White, the Sarā᾽ī-s and the Zanj. Each man was paid monthly by the treasury at fixed times at a fixed rate according to his rank, out of the money paid into the treasury by the tax collectors. There was thus no question of the troops collecting their salaries themselves from the taxpayers.

Nāṣir-i Khusraw, *Safarnāma/Book of Travels*, pp. 48–9

These two quotations describe a Fatimid army in the mid-eleventh century which had been formed in the reign of al-ᶜAzīz by the recruitment of the Turks and Daylamī-s into its ranks. Its heterogeneous character is spelt out in these somewhat different lists of its contingents. The first, from the detailed annals of the courtier al-Musabbiḥī, is the most reliable, but lacks the explanations of the visitor Nāṣir-i Khusraw. The palace corps of Ṣaqāliba in the first list has turned into the Black and White Ustādhs or eunuchs in the second, where the Sarā᾽ī-s, or men of the palace, may be the other, unspecified, men of the Dawla in the first. The Maṣāmida, or Berbers, of the High Atlas who appear in the second can be grouped with the Kutāma under the head of Maghāriba, 'Westerners'; so might the Bāṭiliyya, or Champions, an obscure contingent who are said to have come from North Africa before the Fatimids, and perhaps the Qayṣariyya of the first list, 'Caesar's men', who are to be equated with the Rūm, or 'Romans', sc. Byzantines of whatever provenance. The Turks and the Daylam, the Persians, of the second list are the Mashāriqa, or 'Easterners'. The ᶜAbīd al-Shirā᾽, or Bought Slaves, are Blacks, Sūdān, from the Nubian and Trans-Saharan slave trade. The Bedouin of the second list played an important part as tribal auxiliaries. Nāṣir-i Khusraw's statement that those on parade came from the Ḥijāz is puzzling but not impossible, given the ties of the dynasty with Mecca. So too is the mention of the Zanj from the East African coast, a source of slaves going back at least as far as the ninth century, but in this unique reference coming without explanation. None are drawn from the peasant population, and all apart from the Bedouin of the Egyptian desert are of foreign origin. But Nāṣir-i Khusraw's statement that the Turks and Persians were mostly born in Egypt will hold good for the Kutāma, and will probably have applied to a greater or lesser extent to some of the others. *Ḥujra*-s, or barracks, existed for the military training of the Turkish *ghilmān* (sing. *ghulām*), the mounted cavalry elite, and possibly for others. Apart from the Turks, the Kutāma were cavalrymen and so too were the Bāṭiliyya, and according to Nāṣir-i Khusraw, the Ustādhs were mounted. Each contingent, he says, fought with the weapons of its country of origin, whether swords or spears; there is no mention of archery. Despite the prestige of the Turks and the Kutāma, the infantry formed the majority of the regular army and its centre on the battlefield, with the cavalry on the wings. Pitched battles, however, were the exception. In 1027 the army of Egypt went out under the Turkish *ghulām* al-Dizbirī, in conjunction with the Bedouin Kalb of Syria, to rout the Mirdāsid ruler of Aleppo and his ally, the Jarrāḥid chief of the Bedouin Ṭāyy, at the battle of Uqḥuwāna; conversely, the same army under the Black eunuch Rifq was routed by the Aleppans in 1049. In Egypt the problem was with the nomads, the Berber Lawāta and the Arab Bedouin, whose invasions under Abū Rakwa in 1005 and by the Banū Qurra in 1051 bracketed a period when they were more a nuisance than a threat. For most of the time the army in Egypt formed garrisons in the capital and the main cities, while outside the capital the Blacks were given land in the villages to support themselves and provide a military presence in the countryside. Like these Blacks, the Egyptian Bedouin were self-sufficient on the fringes of the Valley and Delta.

Meanwhile their pay was crucial, a demand upon the state that had to be met to ensure its survival. In the famine in 1024–5, the troops mutinied and rioted. At the accession of al-Mustanṣir they demanded a rise in salary with menaces. In 1047 the attempt of al-Ṭustarī to adjust the pay of the Maghāriba and Mashāriqa resulted in his murder by the Turks. Such rivalries within the army led to the warfare of the 1060s and 1070s, when the army disintegrated, its various troops taking over the country and beggaring the state, before it was effectively abolished and rebuilt along different lines by Badr al-Jamālī.

Syria, meanwhile, was once again a problem. The long-standing peace with Byzantium had been renewed in 1027, with on the one hand the maintenance of the mosque in Constantinople with its prayer for the Fatimid Caliph, and on the other permission for the Emperor to rebuild the Church of the Holy Sepulchre. It was nevertheless broken in 1030 with the arrival at Antioch of the new Byzantine Emperor Romanos III at the beginning of a fresh campaign to extend the empire in northern Syria. Aleppo under the Mirdāsid prince Naṣr ibn Ṣāliḥ ibn Mirdās once again accepted Byzantine suzerainty; the Ṭayy under Ḥassān ibn al-Jarrāḥ were again seduced into an alliance; the catepan or governor of Antioch captured the series of fortresses along the mountains between the Orontes and the Byzantine cities of the coast; while the strategos or general George Maniakes captured Edessa, annexing the plain to the north of Aleppo. By 1034 Romanos was dictating his terms for a renewal of the peace with al-Qāhira; but his death in that year brought a softening which encouraged Naṣr in Aleppo to revert to his Fatimid allegiance. When peace was finally concluded in 1036 following the accession of al-Mustanṣir, Byzantium was left in possession of its territorial gains, but otherwise the relationship was as before, with Byzantium once again committed to the rebuilding of the Church of the Holy Sepulchre. Events, however, took a new turn when al-Dizbirī at Damascus, who had been unable to halt the Byzantine advance, now marched upon Aleppo. Naṣr, its Mirdāsid prince, newly honoured by al-Qāhira and awarded the government of Homs, had emerged as a rival whom the old Turkish warrior was not prepared to tolerate. Given that Naṣr had betrayed the empire, Constantinople merely demanded that al-Dizbirī replace him as a tribute-paying vassal. Naṣr was duly killed in battle, and in 1038 Aleppo was for the first time annexed to the Dawla proper, where the Caliph ruled as well as reigned. But as the ruler of this new Syrian domain, al-Dizbirī himself had become an overmighty subject, who now took it upon himself to attack the Byzantines in Antioch. It says much for the conservatism of the regime in al-Qāhira that far from seizing the opportunity for holy war upon the infidel, or turning to the invasion of Iraq, al-Jarjarāʾī now disowned his man in Damascus. Denounced as a traitor, with his troops turned against him, al-Dizbirī fled from Damascus in 1041 to die at Aleppo in January 1042. The Mirdāsids in the person of Naṣr's brother Thimāl promptly returned, and Aleppo reverted to its dual allegiance to Constantinople and al-Qāhira.

The Beginnings of Secession in the West

Beyond the borders of Syria, however, and outside the self-contained relationship between the two empires, the Christian and the Caliphal, the prospect for that empire and its imperial mission continued to deteriorate. Out to the west, the Zirids had finally lost control of Tripoli in 1022 to the Banū Khazrūn; its petty dynasty had initially recognised the Fatimids, but by 1034 coins had been struck in the city with a Sunnī inscription. In Ifrīqiya itself, the Zirid sultan Mu^{c}izz ibn Bādīs continued to be faced with incursions of the Zanāta, whose warriors were still in occupation of his southern borders. More importantly, in 1036 he intervened in Sicily at the invitation of opponents of the Kalbid amīr Aḥmad al-Akḥal. Headed by his son ^{c}Abd Allāh, the Zirid invasion brought to a head a crisis which over the next few years put an end to the Kalbid dynasty, its Sicilian state and its relationship to al-Qāhira. The origins of the crisis were internal; al-Akḥal ruled over an island deeply but obscurely divided between the 'people of Sicily' and the 'people of Ifrīqiya', as previously between Arabs and Berbers. The original division between Muslims and Christians was blurred in a population marked by varying degrees of Islamisation, but persisted in regional differences between west, east and north. All such elements were variously in opposition to each other, but equally to the demands of central government. It was a revolt against taxation which had brought al-Akḥal to power in 1019 in place of his unpopular brother Ja^{c}far; and in 1036 it was 'the people of Sicily' who turned against him, perhaps for the same reason, perhaps in support of Ḥasan, the brother who succeeded him, but certainly provoked by his dealings abroad.

In the absence of a Sicilian chronicle, the passing references in the external Arabic sources must be compared with the Byzantine version for a complete although still sketchy account which turns on the triangular relationship of the Kalbids with the Fatimids, the Byzantines and the Zirids. At his accession, al-Akḥal had duly recognised the Imām Caliph, and in 1024 had received a mission which conferred on him the title of Ta$^{\circ}$yīd al-Dawla, or Support of the State. Despite the truce between the Fatimids and Byzantines, however, al-Akḥal had resumed the old war upon the Byzantines in southern Italy, incidentally attacking Christian fortified villages that had presumably lapsed in some way from their obligations. As a way of rallying support on the island, this nevertheless came up against a Byzantine determination to reconquer Sicily. A Byzantine invasion in 1025 was only halted by the death of the Emperor Basil II, and for the next ten years the Sicilians continued their aggression, so much so that when Romanos III laid down his conditions for a renewal of peace with the Caliphate, they included a demand that no support be given to its Sicilian vassals. But in 1035, perhaps because of the rebellion of his brother, al-Akḥal abruptly turned to Constantinople, sending his son to the Emperor and receiving the title of Magister. In 1036 the 'people of Sicily' promptly appealed against him to the Zirid Mu^{c}izz, who was thus presented with the opportunity to take the island for himself. Al-Akḥal was besieged and killed at the capital Palermo, but in 1038 the island was invaded by George Maniakes, the conqueror of Edessa. Either because of a defeat by the Byzantines or a rebellion against him by the Sicilians, ᶜAbd Allāh was driven out; on the other hand, in 1040 Maniakes himself became a rebel, leaving Sicily to claim the imperial throne before his death in battle in 1043. At Palermo Ḥasan took the title of Ṣamṣām al-Dawla, or Battleaxe of the State, which argues for his recognition by al-Qāhira, but by the time of al-Jarjarāᵓī's death in 1045, Palermo seems to have been in the hands of a *shūra*, or council of notables, while the regions fell to local lords. A whole province of the Fatimid empire had slipped away.[14]

For the moment, the imperial ambitions of the Zirid sultan had been dashed, but were beginning to take shape in a different direction, one which, as in the case of Sicily, would lead within the next twenty years to a similar disintegration of his state. Throughout the 1020s, relations with al-Qāhira had been close. The death of al-Ḥākim and the accession of al-Ẓāhir had been followed, as in Sicily, by embassies which in 1023–4 conferred on Muᶜizz the title of Sharaf al-Dawla wa ᶜAḍuduhā, Glory and Strength of the State; and it may be the fault of the sources that no more is heard of such visitations and the celebrations that accompanied them, after an exchange of embassies in 1029. The Fatimid coinage continued to be minted at Qayrawān, and it cannot be a coincidence that in 1035, the year of al-Akḥal's approach to Constantinople, Muᶜizz received presents from Byzantium. Coming at a time when Constantinople and al-Qāhira were negotiating the renewal of the peace between them, it is possible that for one brief moment the aim of Byzantium was to include both Sicily and Ifrīqiya in a comprehensive pact between the two empires. By the 1030s the relationship with the Fatimid suzerain may nevertheless have cooled. After the suppression of the anti-Ismāᶜīlī riots at the beginning of his reign, Muᶜizz was now faced with a more serious growth of opposition to his Fatimid loyalties among the Mālikite scholars of Qayrawān. Their biographies tell of his debates with them, naturally to their advantage. But their increasing assertiveness meant that by the 1040s, following the expulsion from Sicily, a break with al-Qāhira was becoming attractive as a measure to recover the political initiative at home and abroad. In the west, Muᶜizz was on the defensive: his Ḥammādid cousin al-Qāᵓid, ruling since the death of Ḥammād in 1028, had gone to war with him in 1040, the first sign of a fresh ambition on the part of the Ḥammādids to extend their territory at Zirid expense. Like his father Bādīs before him,

[14] Cf. Idris, *La Berbérie orientale*, I, pp. 159–70, 175; A. Metcalfe, *The Muslims of Medieval Italy* (Edinburgh, 2009), pp. 70–87; L. C. Chiarelli, *A History of Muslim Sicily* (Santa Venera, 2010), pp. 119–32.

Mu^{c}izz was forced to undertake a two-year siege of the Qal^{c}a before he capitulated. To the east, however, a new situation was developing along the road to Egypt. Barqa had remained in the hands of the Banū Qurra under their Amīrs Mukhtār ibn al-Qāsim and his son Jabbāra since the ignominious failure to install a Zirid governor in 1014. At Tripoli, the Banū Khazrūn had likewise remained in control under Khalīfa ibn Warrū and his successor Sa^{c}īd ibn Khazrūn since the revolt of its Zirid governor in 1022. It was a control that most probably rested on an alliance with Ibn al-Munammar, the jurist who had stirred up the anti-Ismā^{c}īlī riots in the city in 1017, and as a leading citizen may have been responsible for the breach with al-Qāhira attested by the coinage in the 1030s. But in 1038 Sa^{c}īd had been killed by the Zughba, a branch of the Banū Hilāl, Arab nomads who in the late tenth century had lived on the western fringes of the Wāhāt, the oases of Bahariya, Farafra, Dakhla and Kharga to the west of the Egyptian Nile. Fifty years later, however, their appearance at Tripoli was not merely incidental. It signalled the intrusion of a new people on to the Libyan and Ifrīqiyan scene, warrior Arab tribesmen in search of fresh pasture on the Mediterranean coast, a new factor in the social and political equation that rapidly came into play. At Tripoli, Sa^{c}īd had been succeeded by his brother Muntaṣir, who promptly expelled Ibn al-Munammar as a troublemaker from the city. But for Mu^{c}izz, as he returned from his victory in the west, the whole episode had altered the position in the east in ways he sought to turn to his advantage.[15]

The Threat from the East

This fading of the empire in the West, where the Caliph reigned but did not rule, was matched in the East, in the lands where the Caliph neither ruled nor reigned, by the steady growth of an active opposition to his pretentions. This formed in the first place around the ^{c}Abbasids in Baghdad, al-Qādir and al-Qā$^{\supset}$im, and second around the Ghaznawids in eastern Iran, Maḥmūd and his son Mas^{c}ūd. Both gained strength as the Buyids of western Iran, with their Shī^{c}ite leanings and inclination to the Fatimids, lost control of Baghdad to its factions and Turkish garrison, and struggled to manage their family disputes and Daylamite, Turkish and Kurdish militias. After his denunciation of the Fatimids as impostors in 1010, al-Qādir went on to claim a religious authority for himself as the champion of Sunnism, condemning Shī^{c}ism, requiring the veneration of the Rāshidūn, the first four Caliphs, and affirming the

15 Cf. Idris, *La Berbérie orientale*, I, pp. 153–67, 172–87; M. Brett, 'The central lands of North Africa and Sicily, until the beginning of the Almohad period', *The New Cambridge History of Islam*, vol. 2, pp. 52–3, and 'The Zughba at Tripoli, 429H (1037–8 AD)', Society for Libyan Studies, *Sixth Annual Report*, 1974–5, pp. 41–7.

uncreated nature of the Qurʾān in decrees of 1018 and 1029. It was a major step towards the rigidification of sectarian divisions in Islam, symptomatic of the way in which Sunnī jurists were beginning to assert the doctrines of their schools as a creed of its own. In 1031 al-Qādir was succeeded by his son with the messianic title of al-Qāʾim, a clear response to the Fatimids and an equally clear affirmation of his dynasty's new mission. In Baghdad itself he was sufficiently independent to appoint a Wazīr, Ibn al-Muslima, to manage his politics; meanwhile, he took office a year after Maḥmūd at Ghazna had been succeeded by his son Masᶜūd, and the alliance with these champions of the holy war upon the infidel and the heretic became still closer and more purposeful.[16]

In the manner of the Fatimids and their lieutenants in Ifrīqiya and Sicily, al-Qādir had bestowed on Maḥmūd at the outset of his reign in 999 the titles of Walī Amīr al-Muʾminīn and Yamīn al-Dawla wa Amīn al-Milla, Right Hand of the State and Guarantor of the Community of the Faithful, titles which from the very first envisaged a Sultan, a man of power, who would rule the empire of Islam on the political and religious authority of the Caliph. Honorific as they may have been, Maḥmūd had acted upon them as the champion of the Caliph in the course of his endless wars, which in 1029 culminated in the annexation of Rayy from its Buyid prince. Not only was the northern half of the Buyid domain thus swept away, but the conquest was announced to the Caliph as a victory for the Sunnī cause, one that had wiped from the region the Ismāᶜīlīs and other deviants from the true faith along with the regime that had encouraged them. When Masᶜūd succeeded his father in 1030, the declarations became still more explicit along with the titles awarded by Baghdad. Responding to the arrival of the *manshūr* or *sijill* of al-Qāʾim in 1033 investing him with the government of lands conquered and yet to be won, he put on the turban and drew the sword that came with the embassy, declaring that with it all heresy would be exterminated, and lands that were ruled by enemies would be subdued. Baghdad would be freed from the Buyids, the Fatimids overthrown and the Byzantines attacked.[17] As a declaration of intent, it raised the ambition of the Ghaznawids to the level of universal empire, in the manner of the Fatimids in the previous century as they set out to take Egypt en route to Baghdad. For the moment it remained hollow. Masᶜūd was obliged to contend with the invasion of nomads from a different quarter from the Banū Hilāl, the Turkmen or Turcomans of Central Asia, specifically the Oghuz or Ghuzz from the vicinity of the Aral Sea. Part

[16] Cf. Kennedy, *The Prophet and the Age of the Caliphates*, pp. 241–3.

[17] Cf. Bosworth, *The Ghaznavids*, pp. 53–4.

pagan, part Muslim, displaced by clan conflict and the need for pasture, they came south in disparate bands, but more importantly under the leadership of the Seljuq chieftains, Ṭughril and his brothers Chaghrī, Mūsā and Ibrāhīm Īnal. Climbing up out of the Qara Qum desert into Khurasan on the Iranian plateau, they compelled the formidable but ponderous Ghaznawid army to lumber after their light horse archers, until in 1040 Masᶜūd was brought to battle at Dandānqān in the desert south of Merv. The rout of his thirsty and demoralised soldiery was complete; many of his *ghilmān* deserted to the victors; and from the battlefield Ṭughril announced his triumph to Baghdad. With that announcement in the manner of Maḥmūd, the Seljuqs took over from the Ghaznawids as holy warriors for the faith; and the declared intention of Masᶜūd to win an empire for the ᶜAbbasids in the west was set to become a reality.[18]

Meanwhile, the Ismāᶜīlīs in the Ghaznawid empire had continued to be persecuted; at the fall of Rayy to Maḥmūd in 1029, they had been massacred and their books burnt. Despite Ghaznawid boasts to the contrary, the Daᶜwa nevertheless survived, partly because of its hold in the Būyid homeland of Daylam in the mountains to the south of the Caspian, beyond the reach of Maḥmūd's armies. Equally importantly, it continued to exert its old intellectual attraction in an Iranian society and civilisation still flourishing beneath the zealous militarism of its rulers. But in the remaining Būyid dominions in Fars and Kirmān, in the homeland of al-Kirmānī and his congregation, it suffered a major setback after years in which the Dāᶜī al-Muᵓayyad fīᵓl-Dīn al-Shīrāzī had enjoyed the support of the prince Abū Kālījār and his Daylamite regiments in spite of the hostility of his Turkish soldiery and predominantly Sunnī subjects. Beginning in 1038, the anger generated by the openness of al-Muᵓayyad's Fatimid observances culminated in 1043 in an appeal to al-Qāᵓim which brought his minister Ibn al-Muslima to Shiraz with the authority to overrule Abū Kālījār and drive al-Muᵓayyad permanently from the city. For the next two years he made his way around the Fertile Crescent, up through the territories of the Mazyadids and ᶜUqaylids, the Bedouin dynasties which between them controlled Iraq to the south and north of Baghdad itself, before arriving at al-Qāhira in 1045. In the year of al-Jarjarāᵓīs death, his arrival marked the entry of a major new actor onto the Fatimid stage in the crisis that developed at home and abroad in the years following the exit of the great Wazīr, as well as a major new author, whose

[18] Ibid., pp. 267–8, and Bosworth, 'The political and dynastic history of the Iranian world (A.D. 1000–1217)', in *The Cambridge History of Iran*, vol. 5, *The Saljuq and Mongol Periods*, pp. 1–202, at p. 23; A. C. S. Peacock, *The Great Seljuk Empire* (Edinburgh, 2015), pp. 20–48.

autobiography and poetry are an invaluable contemporary supplement to the chronicle tradition.[19]

His journey, indeed, had already touched on yet another element of the crisis to come, one that did not only illustrated the situation in Iraq in the years following the end of effective Būyid rule at the beginning of the century. In 1044 the Mazyadids and ᶜUqaylids under their chieftains Dubays and Qirwāsh were obliged to sink their differences in an alliance against a new foe. Independently of the Seljuqs, the Turkmen were migrating westwards around the Caspian into Azerbaijan and across the highlands of northern Iran into northern Iraq and Byzantine Anatolia. They were both drawn and driven, on the one hand by the need for pasture and on the other by the desire to escape from Seljuq control. After Dandānqān they had expanded over all the Iranian portion of the Ghaznawid empire. Leaving the eastern provinces to Chaghrī and Mūsā, Ṭughril as their leader had turned west with Ibrāhīm Īnal to take over Rayy and its old Būyid dominions, while claiming for himself the overlordship of all the Ghuzz. Those who had reached as far as Iraq had become competitors of the Arab Bedouin for both pastureland and power, briefly taking Mosul from the ᶜUqaylids before being driven away by the coalition. But their migration continued, introducing into the lands of the old Arab empire a new people who radically altered its ethnic mix as well as its politics. In both respects it was an epoch-making event. Where the Fatimids, and indeed the Būyids, had made their conquests with tribesmen from within that empire, drawn into battle by the appeal of Islam and its claims to rule, for the first time tribesmen from without had entered into its internal rivalries, brought to a head over the past century by the Fatimid challenge for the Caliphate. With their response to that challenge, the world that had given it birth was about to change.

[19] Al-Muᵓayyad fīᵓl-Dīn al-Shīrāzī, *Sīrat al-Muᵓayyad fīᵓl-Dīn al-Shīrāzī dāᶜī al-duᵓāt*, ed. M. K. Husayn (Cairo, 1949), summarised by A. H. al-Ḥamdānī, 'The Sīra of al-Muᵓayyad fīᵓl-Dīn ash-Shīrāzī', PhD thesis (London, 1950), and by M. Adra in *Mount of Knowledge, Sword of Eloquence*, Introduction.

8

The Crisis of the Empire

In the thirty years that followed the death of al-Jarjarāʾī in 1045, the Fatimid empire, at home in Egypt and Syria, and abroad in the lands that recognised the Caliphate as well as in those that did not, was overwhelmed and almost destroyed in a crisis of its own making. The grand mission of the Mahdī and his successors in the Maghrib to recreate a universal empire of Islam, which after the conquest of Egypt had become a drive to win universal recognition for their Caliphate, may have faltered after the death of al-ʿAzīz. Now, however, it was reinvigorated in response to a Sunnī imperialism that threatened the existence of both Caliphate and Imāmate, only to be decisively checked as the regime of the Pen imploded at al-Qāhira, and the dynasty itself came close to extinction at the hands of its Men of the Sword. That both Dawla and Daʿwa survived was down to the strength of the dynasty's charisma in Egypt and its faith abroad; but the crisis for both was part of the crisis of the Islamic world as a whole, transformed by the forces that had been mobilised to meet the Fatimid challenge for the headship of the community. In the new world that came into existence, it was the turn of the Fatimids to meet the challenge of their opponents, in ways that saw both the empire and its mission evolve over the next 100 years in distinctly different ways.

From al-Jarjarāʾī to al-Yāzūrī

In Egypt itself, the sources continue to be the writers in the Egyptian tradition, extant in the *Akhbār Miṣr* of Ibn Muyassar and the *Ittiʿāẓ* of al-Maqrīzī, together with the *Ishāra ilā man nāla al-wizāra*, Ibn al-Ṣayrafī's biographies of the Fatimid Wazīrs.[1] With the death of al-Jarjarāʾī, the competition for control of the government resumed over the next five years. The outcome was a transition from one government to another, from that of al-Jarjarāʾī to one eventually formed by a newcomer with the favour of the Queen

[1] Ibn al-Ṣayrafī, *Al-Ishāra ilā man nāla al-wizāra*, ed. A. Mukhlis, *Bulletin de l'Institut français d'archéologie orientale du Caire*, XXV (1924).

Mother. Eventually, because the appointment of al-Yāzūrī in 1050 had been the climax of a protracted and indeed murderous conflict between the Wazīrs who succeeded al-Jarjarāʾī at the head of his government and Raṣad, the Queen Mother, in her attempt to secure effective control of the government for her own nominees. Of these the first was al-Tustarī, the agent of her fortune and then of her wealth as the steward of her estates. It was as steward of the estates of Sitt al-Mulk that al-Jarjarāʾī had risen to the Wazīrate, a position for which the Jewish al-Tustarī was not necessarily disqualified, but for which he lacked the kind of career in the ranks of the administration that the Christian ʿĪsā ibn Nasṭūrus had enjoyed. Such a career had been followed under al-Jarjarāʾī by his successor as Wazīr, the converted Jew al-Fallāḥī. But while he was nominally in charge of the administration, he was obliged to accept the appointment of al-Tustarī to the Treasury, the central office which had been the downfall of Ibn Badūs. Where Ibn Badūs had lacked the stature to use its control over income and expenditure to his advantage, however, with the favour of the Queen Mother al-Tustarī used it to establish himself at the heart of al-Fallāḥī's government, at the expense of the Wazīr's authority. At the Treasury, he set out to build an alternative patronage party on behalf of the Queen Mother, with fatal results. The latent hostility between the corps of the army once again erupted into fighting in 1047 between the Berber Maghāriba and the Turkish Mashāriqa, when al-Tustarī raised the pay of the one to the detriment of the other. For this he was murdered by the Turks with the possible connivance of the Wazīr; in revenge, the Queen Mother had al-Fallāḥī executed in 1048. According to Ibn Muyassar, this was the moment when Raṣad turned to the Blacks, the ʿAbīd al-Shirāʾ, as a third and more reliable force, increasing their numbers with further purchases apparently on her own account. With government still in the hands of al-Jarjarāʾī's people, al-Fallāḥī was succeeded as Wazīr by al-Jarjarāʾī's nephew Abūʾl-Barakāt, while a successor to al-Tustarī was found for Raṣad by the Black eunuch Rifq, the erstwhile rival of al-Jarjarāʾī's old ally Miʿḍād. With his patronage of al-Yāzūrī, a minor *qāḍī* from Yāzūr in Palestine who had come to al-Qāhira to seek his favour, and for whom he now procured the stewardship of the Queen Mother's estates, Rifq thus reappears as a dominant figure in the politics of the regime, one who may well have remained an opponent of al-Jarjarāʾī, and encouraged the Queen Mother in her determination to replace his clientele with people of her own. At all events, the next two years saw a struggle for power in which Abūʾl-Barakāt vainly attempted to prevent his eclipse by his rival.

With the support of the Queen Mother, al-Yāzūrī had become the intermediary between the Caliph and the Wazīr, a testimony to the prerogative of a monarch who no longer governed in person, but whose approval was given in audience for the minister's course of action. Where this requirement had no doubt been a formality for al-Jarjarā'ī, it was now given only after consultation with the Queen Mother, concealed behind a screen, and her new favourite. The government, on the other hand, remained with the personnel put in place by al-Jarjarā'ī, for whom Abū'l-Barakāt was a guarantor of continuity. As head of this government, Abū'l-Barakāt's effort to recover the authority of his uncle turned in the first place on the old problem of Aleppo, where the Mirdāsid Thimāl had refused the annual tribute of 20,000 dīnārs agreed in 1042. The matter was complicated by al-Jarjarā'ī's previous choice of Nāṣir al-Dawla al-Ḥasan ibn Ḥamdān as governor at Damascus in succession to al-Dizbirī; a scion of the former ruling dynasty of Aleppo, he had an interest in the recovery of the city which was doubtless a factor in his appointment. In 1048 he made an unsuccessful attack on the city; but on the orders of Abū'l-Barakāt, executed the brother of al-Tustarī on the familiar charge of treasonable correspondence with the enemy, a deed for which he was duly dismissed and imprisoned. Instead, in 1049 a grand expedition was sent out against Aleppo under the command of Rifq; but the intended triumph came to nothing when the army was once again defeated and Rifq himself mortally wounded, dying in the citadel of Aleppo. In the meantime Abū'l-Barakāt had made an attempt to remove al-Yāzūrī from the scene by appointing him Chief Qāḍī, and thereby Chief Dāʿī, in succession to the aged al-Qāsim ibn ʿAbd al-ʿAzīz, the last of the descendants of the Qāḍī al-Nuʿmān. The move was malicious as well as expeditious, since al-Yāzūrī had begun his career as a Sunnī jurist of no great distinction, with no qualification for the role of Chief Dāʿī. It nevertheless failed in its purpose, since al-Yāzūrī's son deputised for him in the palace while he attended to his new duties. Disgraced by the Aleppan fiasco, Abū'l-Barakāt himself was dismissed and imprisoned in March 1050. The gap thus left between al-Yāzūrī and al-Jarjarā'ī's placemen in the government was briefly filled by the appointment of a Wāsiṭa rather than a Wazīr, a middleman to go between them and al-Yāzūrī, who was now unrivalled as the representative of the Caliph. But the efforts of this person, Ṣāʿid ibn Masʿūd, to rouse their hostility to the man who was now the effective head of government rapidly led to his dismissal, and to the final appointment of al-Yāzūrī as Wazīr in June 1050. In his further capacity as Chief Qāḍī and Chief Dāʿī, he now enjoyed an unprecedented combination of power and authority on behalf of the palace. In Rifq he had lost a powerful patron, while politically he lacked a base in the administration, whose incumbents feared that they would now be set aside for his appointees. One such was al-Mu'ayyad al-Dīn al-Shīrāzī, who had helped him with his duties as Chief Dāʿī, and now became head of the Chancery; an ally was Nāṣir al-Dawla al-Ḥasan ibn Ḥamdān, now restored to favour. Al-Yāzūrī was nevertheless in a strong position to confront the worsening situation abroad with an aggressive response to the mounting threat to east and west, a response that briefly if belatedly resurrected the aim of conquering Baghdad.[2]

The End of Empire in the West

Encouragement came from an unexpected quarter. The Daᶜwa in the Yemen, which had revived at the end of the tenth century and entrenched itself in fortresses to the north of Sanᶜa, had found itself a Dāᶜī in one Sulaymān al-Zawāḥī from the mountains of Ḥarāz to the west of Sanᶜa. There al-Zawāḥī had chosen as his successor one ᶜAlī ibn Muḥammad al-Ṣulayḥī, son of a local *qāḍī* and chief of the Ḥamdānid clan. Designated as the new Dāᶜī, al-Ṣulayḥī had set out like Abū ᶜAbd Allāh before him to create a tribal following for the conquest of the Yemen in the Fatimid name. In 1047 he had built the mountain fortress of Masār, from which in 1048 he had taken Sanᶜa together with Shibam and its Ismāᶜīlī territory to the north, creating a wholly new dominion to add to the Fatimid empire and resume its imperial progress.[3] It was a cause for celebration at al-Qāhira, as al-Yāzūrī's propaganda for his own imperial mission made clear. For the moment, however, the Wazīr was required to wait upon events that were still in the future. Over the past ten years, the imperial purpose of the Seljuq chieftain Ṭughril had been slow to develop in the aftermath of Dandānqān. His half-brother Ibrāhīm Īnāl at Hamadan in western Iran had sided against him with the Turcomans who were opposed to his control, while the death of Abū Kālījār at Shiraz in 1048 had only recently removed the only Būyid capable of holding up his advance. The Daᶜwa in Iran had survived and even flourished, making a convert of the poet, philosopher and future Dāᶜī of Khurāsān, Nāṣir-i Khusraw, who spent the three years from 1047 to 1050 in the Egyptian capital; as a contemporary witness, his Safar-nāma, or account, of his journey to and from his native Badakhshan, is a major contribution to the literature of the dynasty.[4] In

[2] Al-Yāzūrī is the subject of a long biography by Ibn al-Ṣayrafī, and his career extensively followed by al-Maqrīzī.

[3] The sources for this and the history of the Ṣulayḥids down to the mid-twelfth century are the '*Uyūn al-akhbar* of the fifteenth-century Dā'ī Idrīs 'Imād al-Dīn, vol. 7, ed. A. F. Sayyid with summary by P. E. Walker and A. Pomerantz under the title *The Fatimids and their Successors in Yaman: the History of an Islamic Community* (London, 2002), and the mid-twelfth-century 'Umāra al-Yamanī, *Ta'rīkh al-Yaman*, ed. and trans. H. C. Kay, *Yaman, its Early Mediaeval History* (London, 1892).

[4] *Nāsir-I Khusraw, Safar-nāma*, ed. and French trans. C. Schefer, *Sefer Nameh* (Paris, 1881); Eng. trans. W. M. Thackston, Jr, *Naser-e Khosraw's Book of Travels (Safarnama)* (Albany, NY, 1986); biography by A. C. Hunsberger, *Nasir Khusraw, the Ruby of Badakhshan* (London, 2000).

the year that al-Yāzūrī took office, however, Ṭughril took Isfahan from its Kākūyid prince, a Daylamī whose father had taken it from the Būyids. As Ṭughril Beg, the title by which he is commonly known, he proceeded to make the city his capital, finally transforming himself from a warrior nomad into a statesman whose arrival in Baghdad was only a matter of time. But at this particular time, al-Yāzūrī's immediate concern was with the West, where the Zirid viceroy Muᶜizz ibn Bādīs had formally repudiated his Fatimid allegiance in favour of the ᶜAbbasids in 1048–9.[5]

He had done so ceremoniously, changing his colours from Fatimid white to ᶜAbbasid black, having the *khuṭba*, or Friday prayer, pronounced in the name of al-Qāᵓim, and minting a coinage with the Qurᵓānic legend 'Whosoever seeks a religion other than Islām, it shall not be accepted from him' – a pointed denunciation of the Fatimids as non-believers. According to al-Muᵓayyad fiᵓl-Dīn, the change of allegiance had been negotiated by al-Qāᵓim's Wazīr Ibn al-Muslima; the emissary would have been the poet al-Dārimī, arriving in the previous year to summon the sultan to declare for Baghdad. But the decision to do so had certainly been taken for Muᶜizz's own political purposes. The biographical tradition of the Mālikite scholars and jurists of Qayrawān and Ifrīqiya tells a long story of their confrontation with their ruler, directly or indirectly, over his Fatimid allegiance, notably in 1045–6 in the case of their colleague al-Tūnisī, who was forced to recant his opinion that in certain circumstances it was permissible for man to marry a Shīᶜite. In their hostility to Shīᶜism the jurists had popular support, at least at Qayrawān; the change of allegiance not only enabled Muᶜizz to claim that support for himself, but gave him the authority to dispose of a fanatical preacher such as Ibn ᶜAbd al-Ṣamad. In 1051 Ibn ᶜAbd al-Ṣamad was deported, with orders to the governor of Gabes to see that he joined the pilgrim caravan to Egypt; out from Gabes he was then killed by an Arab, a murder of which Muᶜizz was accused. The reference to an Arab is doubly significant, since it points to the Banū Hilāl, to the Zughba who had killed Saᶜīd ibn Khazrūn at Tripoli some twelve years previously, and their relatives the Riyāḥ, and to the second element in the story. It was with the Riyāḥ in particular that Muᶜizz had entered into an unspecified agreement on terms that evidently involved land, in particular the Jaffāra plain between Gabes and Tripoli where Ibn ᶜAbd al-Ṣamad had been murdered. The plain, lying

5 Cf. Idris, *La Berbérie orientale sous les Zīrīdes*, I, pp. 175–203, for detailed references to the breach with the Fatimids. For the following account, see in the first instance, M. Brett, 'ᶜAbbasids, Fatimids and Seljuqs', in *The New Cambridge Medieval History*, vol. 4, part 2, pp. 675–720, at pp. 695–8, and M. Brett, 'The central lands of North Africa and Sicily', in *The New Cambridge History of Islam*, vol. 2, pp. 48–65, at pp. 52–6.

Figure 8.1 Palermo, Palazzo dei Normanni, Cappella Palatina: the three painted wooden ceilings of the side aisles and the central nave from below. After Johns,'Pitture', *Atlante 2*, frontispiece (photo: Gigi Roli © Cosimo Franco Panini Editore Spa), where 'Johns, "Pitture", *Atlante 2*, frontispiece' = JJ, 'Le pitture del soffitto della Cappella Palatina', in B. Brenk (ed.), *La Cappella Palatina a Palermo* (Mirabilia Italiae 17), 4 vols (Modena, 2010), vol. I, *Atlante I*, frontispiece.

The ceiling, with its paintings of King Roger of Sicily and other figures, was constructed by Fatimid craftsmen in the twelfth century, and is a splendid example of Fatimid woodwork, which has largely disappeared in Egypt itself.

between the scarp of the Jabal Nafūsa to the south and the sea with the island of Djerba to the north, was the main route into Ifrīqiya from the east and by the same token the way out to Egypt. Persistently under threat from the sectarian Berber Ibāḍīs of the Jabal and Djerba, not to speak of the Zanāta and most recently the Lawāta, nomadic Berbers from the east who may have been displaced by the Hilālīs, it had over the years called for punitive expeditions to pacify the whole region. And it may have been after his victory over the Lawāta in 1045–6 that Muʿizz turned to the Hilālīs as warlike newcomers to be recruited as policemen of the plain and its surroundings.

Muʿizz had in fact a grander design on the Libyan coast, one that would take his new allegiance as the starting point of an offensive directed at Egypt itself. At Tripoli, where the ʿAbbasids had been recognised for the past twenty years, Muntaṣir ibn Khazrūn received a present of 100,000 dīnārs, an earnest of an alliance which extended to Barqa, where in 1051 Jabbāra ibn Mukhtār denounced the Fatimids from the pulpit, proclaimed his allegiance to Muʿizz and advanced to the siege of Alexandria in conjunction with his fellow tribesmen of the region, the Banū Qurra. In such an imperial scheme, the recruitment of the Arabs to secure the route as far as Tripoli would have played an essential part. As a scheme, however, it came to nothing. Al-Yāzūrī won a symbolic as well as a military victory when not only did his forces repel the attack on Alexandria, but they captured the envoy sent from Baghdad with insignia and presents for Muʿizz. Seized by the Byzantine allies of the Caliphate as he travelled through their territory, he was sent on to al-Qāhira, where he was paraded on a camel hung with bells, while the black robe and banner were burnt in a pit together with the diploma of investiture. Much more important was the defeat in the spring of 1052 of Muʿizz himself in a battle like that of Dandānqān, where the well-equipped army of a powerful monarch had been routed by a nomad horde. At Ḥaydarān, not far to the south of Qayrawān, he and his troops were ambushed by the Arabs as they straggled through broken country. Most fled, apart from the bodyguard with which Muʿizz made his way back to his capital. His baggage train was plundered, while the Arabs spread out over the countryside, their chiefs planting their headgear here and there as a sign of possession.[6] It would appear that the Arabs, specifically the Riyāḥ under their chief Muʾnis ibn Yaḥyā, had advanced past Gabes into central Ifrīqiya in breach of their previous agreements, while Muʿizz had retaliated with a major expedition of a kind not simply to defeat them but to tour the south with a show of force. For Muʿizz

[6] Cf. M. Brett, 'The military interest of the battle of Ḥaydarān', in V. J. Parry and M. E. Yapp (eds), *War, Technology and Society in the Middle East* (London, 1975), pp. 78–88.

the outcome was disaster. The loyalty of the Ṣanhāja, the tribal elite of the dynasty who provided his cavalry and his military governors, was in doubt. Meanwhile, the Arabs had quarrelled over the booty of the battle, presenting al-Yāzūrī with the opportunity to intervene. The Amīr Makīn al-Dawla ibn Mulhim was sent to settle the dispute and urge the Arabs to besiege Qayrawān. By 1053 Muᶜizz was confined to his capital, lending a hand to its citizens in the building of an improvised wall, while Ibn Mulhim took possession of Gabes. There he received the submission of the Ḥammādid al-Qāʾid in the person of Ibn Buluggīn (ᶜAbd Allāh ibn Ḥammād), husband of Muᶜizz's sister, and another of his brothers, together with that of the Ṣanhāja notable ibn Yalmū or Walmīya. Described as the head of his clan, this person is otherwise unknown, but is of sufficient importance to have been made governor of Gabes in alliance with the Riyāḥī chief Muʾnis ibn Yaḥyā, who was now lord of the hinterland, and sufficiently established to employ a secretary for his correspondence. Having thus reclaimed Ifrīqiya for the Fatimids, in 1054 Ibn Mulhim returned to al-Qāhira with a delegation of Ifrīqiyan notables and the Caliph's share of the booty of Ḥaydarān, there to be received with due pomp and ceremony.

Imperial Propaganda

The *sijill*, Latin *sigillum*, or seal, was the document produced by the Fatimid chancery and signed rather than sealed by the Caliph with his monogram, to confer appointments, register decisions, make proclamations and conduct official correspondence. It was composed according to a formula common across the Mediterranean world of the Middle Ages, with a preamble authenticating its origin with the Caliph, a statement or recapitulation of the context, the message itself and the final instruction to the recipient. A major instrument of Fatimid diplomacy, it served to maintain and strengthen the ties which bound the empire together. For this purpose, not only did it state the entitlement of the monarch to the Caliphate, but presented his actions as the working of God's will. The *sijill* of al-Mustanṣir, sent to the Yemen in 445H/1053–4 is a case in point, a piece of imperial propaganda contributing to the dynasty's own self-serving version of events. Addressed to al-Ṣulayḥī in the course of his conquest of the Yemen, and preserved in the Yemenī collection of such *sijillāt*, it recounts the success of the mission of the Amīr Amīn al-Dawla to Ifrīqiya in the wake of the defeat of the rebel Zīrid Muᶜizz ibn Bādīs by the Banū Hilāl at the battle of Ḥaydarān in 1052. Its success in persuading them to besiege Muᶜizz in Qayrawān resulted in the return of much of

Ifrīqiya to Fatimid allegiance, but led to the abandonment of Qayrawān by Muᶜizz for al-Mahdiyya, and the disintegration of the Ifrīqiyan state. As a contribution to the history of the subject, it is at the root of the entirely false claim that the tribes of the Banū Hilāl were sent from Egypt by the Wazīr al-Yāzūrī to punish Muᶜizz for his recognition of Baghdad. Stripped of much of its florid phraseology, it can be abbreviated as follows:

In the name of God, the Compassionate, the Merciful.

PRAISE
BE TO GOD
LORD OF THE
TWO WORLDS

(the *ᶜalāma* of al-Mustanṣir, written by his Noble Hand, as it would have appeared in the original document to the right of the text, not, as in the copy, in the text itself)

From the Slave and Friend of God, Maᶜadd Abū Tamīm, the Imām al-Mustanṣir bi'llāh, Amīr al-Mu'minīn, to the Amīr Sayf al-Imām al-Muẓaffar fī'l-Dīn Niẓām al-Mu'minīn ᶜAlī ibn Muḥammad al-Ṣulayḥī, greetings.

The Amīr al-Mu'minīn praises to you the God than whom there is no other god, and beseeches His mercy upon his ancestor Muḥammad, Seal of The Prophets and the greatest of those sent by God, and upon his pure family, the Ṭāhirūn, and His salvation, that the work of God may be accomplished.

As to the subject, praise be to God Who has dispatched His angels to visit the realm of misfortune on the one who has entered the house of iniquity through his falsity, stripping him of all blessing. The Amīr al-Mu'minīn praises Him as the one and only Conqueror, and beseeches His mercy upon his ancestor Muḥammad the Caller to the Truth, and upon his designated successor at the head of the community, the towering beacon and sharp sword of his Prophethood, ᶜAlī ibn Abī Ṭālib, and upon the Imāms of his line, the appointed guardians, unblemished in lineage, to whom God has entrusted the fullness of His places of worship, and in the fineness of their zeal has set them on the way to the kingdom of heaven.

There has reached you from the seat of the Amīr al-Mu'minīn news of the accursed Ibn Bādīs in the confusion of his affairs when his allegiance to the Dawla was muddied. Its strong thread was snapped when the Amīr al-Mu'minīn shot from the quiver of his judgement arrows that pierced his vitals, and struck him with blades that severed his joints, and loosed upon him the tribes of Riyāḥ and Zughba who threw him into the prison of a siege from which there was no deliverance, taking possession of all the domains of which he had been so proud, until he stood upon the brink of ruin, by the manifest grace of God.

For he sent the Amīr Amīn al-Dawla wa Makīnuhā Ḥasan ibn ᶜAlī ibn Mulhim to the lands of Ifrīqiya to unite the aforementioned Arabs and prevent them from quarrelling, so that through him they should come to agreement upon the extirpation of the unbeliever.

Now a letter has reached the Amīr al-Muᵓminīn congratulating him on his good fortune. For the Arab tribes have submitted to him, and according to the decrees of his absolute power the mill has turned upon its pole. For the Amīn al-Dawla went with them in an army that crowded over the earth until they encircled the citadel of the traitor, left helpless by the might of God.

Many then came to submit to the Amīn al-Dawla, so that no fortress of the sea or shore was not given by God to the Amīr al-Muᵓminīn. He is now returning, a stage away, accompanied by a crowd of pilgrims making their *hijra* to his throne, having left the accursed Ibn Bādīs cut off from the earth and poised on the edge of the abyss. Destruction has opened its mouth for him, and by God's grace it will not be long before its swallows him.

The Amīr al-Muᵓminīn acquaints you with this fresh information that you may publish it from the pulpits and spread it abroad in town and country, God willing.

Written in the month of Ramadān in the year 445.

Praise be to God alone, and the blessing of God upon His Chosen One, Muḥammad, the Seal of the Prophets and the greatest of those sent from God, and upon his family.

God is sufficient for us: how excellent the Deputy, the Friend and the Companion.

The full translation is given in Brett, 'The Ifrīqiyan *sijill* of al-Mustanṣir, 445/1053–4', in U. Vermeulen and K. D'Hulster (eds), *Egypt and Syria in the Fatimid, Ayyubid and Mamluk Eras*, VI, pp. 9–16. For its place in a series of such *sijillāt*, see 'Fatimid historiography: a case study – the quarrel with the Zirids, 1048–58', in M. Brett, *Ibn Khaldūn and the Medieval Maghrib*, no. VIII. For the formulaic structure of such documents, see J. Wansbrough, *Lingua Franca in the Mediterranean*, ch. 2.

The source for this account of the mission of Ibn Mulhim is a *sijill*, or letter, sent to the similarly victorious al-Ṣulayḥī in the Yemen, which in spite of its boastfulness establishes the nature and date of the Egyptian intervention in the wake of Ḥaydarān, and conclusively disproves the traditional story that al-Yāzūrī had sent the Banū Hilāl from Egypt to punish the rebel viceroy. The story in question has its roots in the Egyptian tradition, where it took shape from the accusations levied at the Wazīr at the time of his downfall, accusations which in this case sprang from the hollowness of the triumph which was celebrated in the *sijill* and in the verse of al-Yāzūrī's poet Ibn Ḥayyūs.[7] Mu^cizz himself was not overthrown, but his position at Qayrawān in the midst of a countryside overrun by the Arabs had been rendered untenable. As he prepared to leave the palace of al-Ṣabra in 1055, the exodus from the great capital began; when he finally departed in 1057 for the original Fatimid stronghold of al-Mahdiyya, the Arabs entered Qayrawān and sacked it. One of the great cities of the Islamic world was left a shadow of its former self, still a place of scholarship but little more than an outpost of the dynasty on the coast.[8] There at al-Mahdiyya, Mu^cizz returned to his Fatimid allegiance, issuing a Fatimid dīnār in 1058 and sending a present to al-Qāhira in 1060, but to little purpose. Ifrīqiya, the old Byzantine province of Africa which had survived the Arab conquest to become the foundation of the Fatimid empire, had finally ceased to exist as a state. By the time Mu^cizz died in 1062, most of its cities were independent, and the Hilālīs dominated the interior; his son and successor Tamīm was obliged to enlist them in 1065 against the invasion of the new Ḥammādid ruler al-Nāṣir ibn ^cAlannās. Having defeated al-Nāṣir's attempt to take advantage of his predicament and replace him in the lands he had lost, Tamīm began the long but only partially successful attempt over the forty-seven years of his reign to recover the coastal cities and some influence in the interior.

As with Ifrīqiya, so with Sicily. Ḥasan, the last of the Kalbids, honoured by al-Qāhira with the title of Ṣamṣām al-Dawla, survived to about 1053, but as suzerain of three rivals for the succession – Ibn al-Thumna at Syracuse in the east, Ibn al-Ḥawwās at Enna and Agrigento in the centre, and Ibn Mankūd at Mazara in the west, with a *jamā^ca*, or council, in readiness at Palermo. After his demise, it was Ibn al-Thumna who made a bid for succession, turning for assistance in 1060 to the Normans who had replaced the Byzantines as rulers of southern Italy. But the arrival of Roger, brother of Robert Guiscard, Duke of Apulia and Calabria, with sixty knights, turned instead into a thirty-year-long campaign of conquest to create a Norman state on the island, and eventually the Norman Kingdom of Sicily and southern Italy. For the next ten years or so, however, this campaign was set back by

7 Cf. M. Brett, 'The Zughba at Tripoli, 429H (1037–8 A.D.)', Society for Libyan Studies, *Sixth Annual Report*, 1974–5, pp. 41–7, and 'Fatimid historiography: a case study – the quarrel with the Zirids, 1048–58', in Brett, *Ibn Khaldun and the Medieval Maghrib*, no. VIII.

8 Cf. M. Brett, 'The poetry of disaster. The tragedy of Qayrawān, 1052–1057CE', in K. D'Hulster and J. Van Steenbergen (eds), *Continuity and Change in the Realms of Islam. Studies in Honour of Professor Urbain Vermeulen* (Leuven, 2008), pp. 77–89.

what may have been the last fling of the Fatimid empire in the west. After the death of Muᶜizz, no more is heard of any Fatimid allegiance, and by the death of Tamīm in 1108 it had surely lapsed. Immediately upon his accession, however, Tamīm set out to repeat the invasion of Sicily which his father had undertaken in similar circumstances in the 1030s. Clearly ambitious to restore the fortunes of his dynasty with a major coup, he despatched his sons Ayyūb and ᶜAlī to establish themselves on the island. Over the next seven years, they were unable to defeat the Normans, securely based at Troina in the north-east. After the death in battle of both Ibn al-Thumna and Ibn al-Ḥawwās, Ayyūb nevertheless established himself at Palermo as ruler of the west and centre, and nominally king of the whole. If Tamīm had indeed begun his reign in the Fatimid name, the conquest of Sicily would indeed have been a triumph of the Dawla to compare with that of al-Ṣulayḥī in the Yemen. As it is, however, the sources are meagre; and in 1069 the whole enterprise failed when the brothers were driven out by the Sicilians themselves. Palermo itself fell to the Normans in 1072, leaving Roger with the tedious task of reducing the island's many fortresses over the next eighteen years. But with the Zīrid withdrawal, Muslim Sicily was effectively doomed, and the island lost not only to Tamīm but to the Fatimids.[9]

For their part, the Banū Hilāl passed into legend as a locust-like horde who had laid the country waste.[10] In this sense, the legend was not true; but, like the Turcomans, the Hilālīs had introduced a new and important element into the population, changing its constitution and its ways of life. Without a Ṭughril Beg to turn them into empire builders in the name of the Fatimids who had enlisted them, they nevertheless established themselves as an estate of whatever realm there was, serving as warriors under the lesser and greater dynasties that succeeded each other in the Maghrib. In that respect they differed from the third race of nomads to be drawn from outside the original Arab empire into the ideological struggle of the Fatimids and ᶜAbbasids that came to a head in the middle of the eleventh century. Worked on by the preaching of Ibn Yāsīn, a missionary who derived his inspiration from the Mālikite scholars of Qayrawān, the Ṣanhāja nomads of the western Sahara banded together under his dictatorship in the manner of Abū ᶜAbd Allāh's

[9] Cf. M. Brett, 'The central lands of North Africa and Sicily', pp. 56–7; Idris, *La Berbérie orientale*, I, pp. 283–5.

[10] Cf. M. Brett, 'The flood of the dam and the sons of the new moon', in *Mélanges offerts à Mohamed Talbi à l'occasion de son 70e anniversaire* (Tunis, 1993), pp. 55–67, and in Brett, *Ibn Khaldun and the Medieval Maghrib* (Aldershot, 1999), IX; Brett, 'The way of the nomad', *Bulletin of SOAS*, 58 (1995), 251–69, and in *Ibn Khaldun and the Medieval Maghrib*, X.

Kutāma. Under the name of al-Murābiṭūn or Almoravids, 'bound together' as holy warriors upon the heretic and the infidel, they came out of the desert to conquer Morocco between 1055 and 1085, and then Muslim Spain. By 1058, the year when Muᶜizz reverted to a Fatimid coinage, they had taken up the cause he had abandoned, minting their coins at Sijilmāsa with the Qurᵓānic legend he had previously employed: 'whosoever seeks a religion other than Islam, it shall not be accepted from him'. Unlike the Turcomans and Hilālīs, the Almoravids and their clansmen did not enter into the population of the lands they conquered, but while Ifrīqiya disintegrated, they created in the Muslim West a great new Sunnī empire to match that of the Seljuqs in the East. As this empire expanded under their successors the Almohads to cover the whole of the Maghrib, it added yet another twist to the Fatimid tale, yet another outcome of the Fatimid Mahdī's bid to rule over Islam and the Islamic world.

The Failure in Iraq

Meanwhile, al-Qāhira celebrated its triumph. Signed by the Caliph himself, the *sijill* which announced the triumph in the West was appointed to be read from the pulpits of the Yemen, where al-Ṣulayḥī was repeating the exploits of Ibn Ḥawshab and Ibn al-Faḍl at the outset of the Fatimid career 150 years earlier.[11] Echoed in praise of al-Yāzūrī in the poetry of Ibn Ḥayyūs, its declaration that the Commander of the Faithful had, in his supreme power, cleared away the clouds for the good of the people, expressed a confidence in the future that in 1054 may have been genuine. It was certainly followed over the next three years by a further initiative, astonishing given the absence of such adventurism over the past half-century, one which envisaged the taking of Baghdad and the final extirpation of the ᶜAbbasids. As in Ifrīqiya, it was a response to the ᶜAbbasid challenge, represented in this case by the far more formidable threat of the Seljuqs, and, as in Ifrīqiya, it took advantage of the opportunity offered by events outside al-Qāhira's control.

These began inauspiciously with a setback in the wake of a low Nile, which in 1054–5 led to a serious shortage of grain. Whereas in 1024–5 the ruling cabal had done nothing to alleviate the famine, al-Yāzūrī now released grain onto the market and forced the price down. But that left nothing with which to supply the Holy Places for the pilgrimage, and when in 1055 a request for grain was made to Constantinople, it was refused by the new Empress Theodora. Al-Yāzūrī's response was war, sending Ibn Mulhim after

[11] Cf. M. Brett, 'The Ifrīqiyan *sijill* of al-Mustanṣir, 445/1053–4', in U. Vermeulen and K. D'Hulster (eds), *Egypt and Syria in the Fatimid, Ayyubid and Mamluk Eras*, VI (Leuven, 2010), pp. 9–16.

his return from Ifrīqiya to invade the coastal strip of Byzantine territory in the direction of Antioch, only for him to be taken prisoner following the landing of a Byzantine armada. To make matters worse, by the end of the year Theodora had rejected the Fatimid alliance symbolically as well as politically, when in response to Seljuq overtures she ordered the prayer in the mosque at Constantinople to be said in the name of the ʿAbbasids. With the Turcomans already in Byzantine Anatolia and the Seljuq Sultanate on the march, her response was evidently calculated. The Seljuq overtures, in fact, were part of a much grander campaign on the part of the Sultan. In December 1055 Ṭughril Beg finally arrived at Baghdad with the declared intention, twenty-five years after the original promise of the Ghaznawid Masʿūd, to make both the pilgrimage and war upon the Fatimids. For the moment, he did neither, remaining at Baghdad throughout 1056, putting an end to the ineffectual rule of the Būyids in the person of Abū Kālījār's son and successor, and coming to an understanding with al-Qāʾim in the course of negotiations conducted with the Caliph's Wazīr Ibn al-Muslima. The settlement, however, was not complete. Al-Basāsirī, the commander of the Turkish forces of the Būyids, and the bitter enemy of Ibn al-Muslima in the battles between Sunnīs and Shīʿites that racked the city, was driven out with his men. In a country which outside Baghdad was under the control of its Bedouin Arab dynasties, all of whom were likewise threatened by the Seljuq advance, his first refuge was with the Mazyādid prince Dubays at Ḥilla. But the obvious recourse in a conflict governed by political and religious ideology was to the Fatimids; and moving up the Euphrates to Raḥba, al-Basāsirī appealed to al-Qāhira for aid.

The appeal was immediately answered. With Fatimid forces, now under the command of al-Yāzūrī's son, already engaged in northern Syria, the Wazīr turned to his head of chancery, the erstwhile Dāʿī al-Muʾayyad fīʾl-Dīn al-Shīrāzī, for his experience in the affairs of Iraq, and commissioned him to respond.[12] Early in 1056, al-Muʾayyad departed with a huge amount of gold coin and military equipment – horses and weapons – with which to pay and arm a coalition made up in the first instance of troops from Damascus and Arabs of the Banū Kalb and Banū Kilāb, in alliance with the Mirdāsid Thimāl at Aleppo. Joining al-Basāsirī at Raḥba, with great difficulty al-Muʾayyad then created a highly unstable alliance with the Iraqi Arabs, sufficient for an advance upon Mosul on the Tigris under the command of al-Basāsirī. In January 1057 the largely Bedouin army defeated a Seljuq force sent up from

[12] The episode is recounted at first hand by al-Muʾayyad himself in his autobiography, *Sīrat al-Muʾayyad fīʾl-Dīn, daʿī al-duʿāt*, ed. M. K. Husayn (Cairo, 1949). Cf. Peacock, *The Great Seljuq Empire*, pp. 48–51, and Bosworth, 'The Iranian World (A.D. 1000–1217)', in *The Cambridge History of Iran*, vol. 5, pp. 45–8.

Baghdad at Sinjār halfway beyond Raḥba, and proceeded to besiege and take Mosul, while as far south as the Arab-controlled cities of Kufa and Wāsiṭ the prayer was said for the Fatimids.

Such a success coincided with the final abandonment of Qayrawān by the Zirid al-Muᶜizz, his removal to al-Mahdiyya and his return to Fatimid allegiance. At the same time the death of the Empress Theodora six months earlier had brought about a renewal of the alliance with al-Qāhira, the release of Ibn Mulhim, and his return to the command of an army undistracted by the previous war. The euphoria, however, did not last. Later in the year Ṭughril himself came up from Baghdad to recapture Mosul; al-Muᵓayyad's coalition disintegrated and al-Basāsirī fell back beyond Raḥba to Bālis further west on the Euphrates, while al-Muᵓayyad retreated to Aleppo. There he continued his efforts, working on al-Yāzūrī's behalf to persuade Thimāl to exchange the city for the lordship of Beirut and Acre on the coast. In January 1058 the transaction was completed, and Ibn Mulhim took over the citadel, not without a fight with the *aḥdāth*, the city militia. This securing of the fortress which had seemed to hold the key to the Fatimid bid for Baghdad certainly strengthened the Fatimid position in Syria vis-à-vis the Seljuqs, but was more than offset by the triumphant return of Ṭughril to Baghdad, finally to be received by al-Qāᵓim in person and to be invested with the title of King of the East and the West. He was, in other words, to be the universal ruler of a universal empire on behalf of the Caliph, a Sultan, or Man of Power, who for the first time since the Fatimid failure to carry their conquests eastwards appeared able to turn the imperial aspiration into reality.

Marking, as it seemed, the failure of al-Yāzūrī's great gamble, the investiture of Ṭughril Beg as champion of the ᶜAbbasid Caliphate proved to be the death of the Wazīr. At the end of February al-Yāzūrī was dismissed and subsequently executed. The sources tell different stories of different accusations, the most substantial of which is that he had sent all the wealth of the state for the conquest of Baghdad, thus provoking the Seljuq conquest of Syria and the ruin of Egypt. The judgment is a judgment of hindsight, to be matched with the similar allegation that in sending the Banū Hilāl to Ifrīqiya, he had brought about its destruction. But there is of course no question that the money had been sent, and the accusation points to a political opposition to the Wazīr strong enough to secure his overthrow on the grounds of financial recklessness and exposure of the state to invasion and conquest. Reflecting the innate caution and conservatism of the Fatimid establishment, that opposition may have dated back to the circumstances of al-Yāzūrī's appointment over the heads of al-Jarjarāᵓī's successors, and may have been compounded by his actions in forcing down the price of grain to the detriment of those who stood to gain from the shortage. But as in the case of Ibn Badūs, his death as distinct from his dismissal is put down to an evidently trumped-up charge of treasonable correspondence with Ṭughril Beg, and making preparations to flee to Baghdad with all his treasure. More plausible, though no less enigmatic, are the stories that implicate al-Mustanṣir, the Caliph himself, whose assent to both dismissal and execution had undoubtedly been required. Thus al-Yāzūrī's right-hand man al-Bābilī, promptly appointed as his successor, would either have secured and acted on the Caliph's permission for the execution, or proceeded against those who had carried it out without orders. But al-Mustanṣir himself is alleged to have grown resentful of al-Yāzūrī's ostentatious wealthiness, so that in the account of the execution itself, the fallen minister was visited in prison at Tinnīs by the Caliph's *Kātib al-Sirr*, or confidential secretary, with a demand for his riches and the warrant for his execution. There he was duly beheaded by Ḥaydara al-Sayyāf, the Swordsman, after telling where the accounts of his property were to be found, in answer to the Caliph's peremptory question 'Where is my wealth?' The body was flung on a dunghill for three days, but then recovered, embalmed and properly buried with the head.[13]

The story is by no means clear; al-Bābilī in particular appears as both treacherous villain and loyal follower who was indignant at the execution. Whatever the truth of the matter, he was made a scapegoat, dismissed, though not executed, after a mere two months in office. What is suggested by this complicated tale of intrigue is a determination on the part of al-Mustanṣir, more than twenty years after his accession, finally to assert his authority at the expense of his mother and her protégé. It would certainly have been the first time since the death of al-Ḥākim that the Caliph had intervened in person in the government of his state and, equally certainly, it was fraught with consequence. Al-Yāzūrī's downfall was no ordinary affair, as its echo in the literature makes clear; and its outcome went far beyond the controversy it provoked. The regime that had been put in place after the death of al-Ḥākim, resting as it did on the ability of the Wazīr of the Pen to construct a party of clients and allies within the administration, was shaken beyond recovery by the inability of al-Yāzūrī's successors to form such a government, or indeed any government at all. For the next two years al-Bābilī's successor Ibn al-Maghribī, again appointed from the entourage of al-Yāzūrī, managed to maintain the continuity of his patron's administration. His authority was nevertheless significantly curtailed. On his return from Aleppo later in the year, al-Muʾayyad was at last appointed to the position he craved as Chief

[13] Cf. M. Brett, 'The execution of al-Yāzūrī', in U. Vermeulen and D. De Smet (eds), *Egypt and Syria in the Fatimid, Ayyubid and Mamluk Eras*, II (Leuven, 1998), pp. 15–27. The article deals with the circumstances and the consequences of the event.

Dāᶜī, not by the Wazīr but by al-Mustanṣir, the Imām Caliph himself, with a *sijill* of investiture which hailed him as the ideal candidate, the one to fill the long vacancy in the Daᶜwa, and to be the door through which the believers came to their faith. The document does not only suggest a further cause for the Caliph's dissatisfaction with the Wazīr who had, however notionally, held the posts of Chief Qāḍī and Chief Dāᶜī. For the first time since the death of al-Ḥākim, it reveals a personal commitment on the part of the Imām to the propagation of the faith. It is of a piece with the long didactic correspondence subsequently conducted by al-Mustanṣir with the leadership of the community in the Yemen, in which he resumed the letter-writing of his predecessors in the Maghrib a century earlier. There was no resumption, however, of al-Ḥākim's damaging reinventions of his role. Al-Mustanṣir did nothing to gainsay the devotional image of the Imām as the way to God's salvation, which was cherished and preached by the Chief Dāᶜī he had chosen for the part.

In the administration, the influence of the Queen Mother was by no means at an end. The new Wazīr Ibn al-Maghribī, who had been imprisoned by al-Bābilī, enjoyed her favour, and with the release of others similarly imprisoned, his appointment meant a return to government as before. On the other hand, he lacked the stature of his predecessor, and in the government he was appointed to direct, the support he could command from his colleagues was yet to be established. In dealing with the problems he had inherited, however, it was his good fortune to enjoy for as long as it lasted the unexpected success of the enterprise which had cost al-Yāzūrī his life. The Wazīr's execution was closely followed by the departure from Mosul of Ṭughril Beg's half-brother Ibrāhīm Īnāl. Returning to Iran, he left the city to be besieged and recaptured by al-Basāsirī and Quraysh, its ᶜUqaylid prince who had been expelled by the Seljuqs. In response. Ṭughril once again came up from Baghdad, only to be called away to Iran as Ibrāhīm Ināl finally entered into open rebellion. In Ḍecember 1058 al-Basāsirī with his ally Quraysh took possession of Baghdad together with revenge upon his enemy, the ᶜAbbasid Wazīr Ibn al-Muslima, who was wrapped in a raw bull's hide and crushed to death. Prayer was finally said for the Fatimids in the city which had been their goal for 150 years; but the ᶜAbbasid Caliph himself was retired to the protection of Muhārish, the Bedouin cousin of Quraysh, at Ḥadītha on the Euphrates, who refused to send him to Egypt despite a substantial bribe. Only the insignia of the Caliphate was despatched to al-Qāhira, where their arrival was greeted with great festivity. The Western Palace prepared for al-Qāʾim remained unoccupied; but such was the euphoria that the *ṭabbāla*, the female drummer who sang the praises of the event, was rewarded with an estate by the Nile. The euphoria, however, could not and did not last. Ibn al-Maghribī, mindful of the charge brought against al-Yāzūrī, refused any further financial or military assistance to al-Basāsirī; he may have reckoned that the money was better spent on what would have been the major coup, the unsuccessful attempt to buy the person of al-Qā᾿im himself. Instead, the return of Ṭughril in December 1059 drove Quraysh back to Mosul and al-Basāsirī to flee towards Syria, only to be overtaken and killed in January 1060.

The Breakdown of the Regime

Ṭughril did not follow up his victory with an advance into Syria; the consolidation of the family empire of which he was the head was of more immediate importance than the ᶜAbbasid cause of which he was the champion. Essential as that championship was to his Sultanate, further conquest was to be undertaken only when practicable. That was not before his death in 1063, or before his son and successor Alp Arslan had asserted his authority over the older princes of the clan. The empire itself was evolving along the familiar lines of the *ghulām* state into a series of dominions under monarchs with all the trappings of professional armies and tax-collecting bureaucracies, while the Turcomans whose chiefs they had been turned into unruly subjects or went their own way. Beyond the reach of the Great Seljuq Sultan, they were pushing out westwards like the Banū Hilāl, nomads in search of pasture and warriors ready to fight. Entering Syria, they were already upsetting the balance of power, helping once again to shake the Fatimid hold on the country. The two years that followed the end of the Iraq adventure saw the return of Aleppo into Mirdāsid hands, an all-too-familiar setback which this time was aggravated by the involvement of the Turcomans. Against the loss of Aleppo could be set the spectacular conquest of the Yemen by ᶜAlī al-Ṣulayḥī, which promised a fresh start for the Fatimid enterprise. But that did not reckon with the situation in Egypt itself.

The conquest of the Yemen by ᶜAlī al-Ṣulayḥī was indeed a triumph. Having established himself at Sanᶜa over the previous decade, in 1060 he opened a campaign across the highlands to the south as far as Aden, before turning on the principality of Zabīd in the lowlands of the Tihama bordering the Red Sea. Its elderly ruler Najāḥ had died in 1060; his sons were now driven away to the Dahlak islands off the Eritrean coast. With most of the Yemen now in his power, in 1062 ᶜAlī turned northwards towards Mecca, where the long-established reign of the Ḥasanid Sharīf-s Abū᾿l-Futūḥ and his son Shukr had ended with Shukr's death in 1061, and, with it, the equally long-standing pact with al-Qāhira that ensured the pilgrimage and its provision in return for recognition of the Imām Caliph. Before his death, Shukr had been tempted to renounce that allegiance, giving al-Ṣulayḥī the excuse to invade in the name of al-Mustanṣir. With Shukr dead, in 1062 he marched north, obliging the Zaydī Imām of Saᶜda to submit, and arrived at Mecca to put an end to the quarrels of the Ḥasanids over the succession. Having imposed the Hāshimite Muḥammad ibn Jaᶜfar upon the warring clans as prefect of the Holy Places, he returned to Sanᶜa to build himself a palace city and establish a family dominion. His brother founded the city of Taᶜizz as the capital of the south, his sons ruled the Tihāma, while Aden was the hub of the intercontinental trade between the Indies and the Mediterranean which accounted for much of the wealth of Egypt. Meanwhile, he sent his Qāḍī, Lamak ibn Mālik, on to al-Qāhira to prepare for his own visit. That never materialised; but Lamak stayed there for five years with al-Muᵓayyad fīᵓl-Dīn, becoming an adept of the Daᶜwa with the learning required to make his homeland a new centre of its teaching and its mission to the world. Such a centre was all the more firmly established as the relationship with al-Qāhira went from strength to strength; the *sijillāt*, signed by the Caliph, were not only preserved by the recipients as the scripture of the Imām, but became part of a correspondence with the Ṣulayḥids in which al-Mustanṣir took an increasingly personal interest on behalf of the Daᶜwa and its future.

ᶜAlī's success was certainly compensation for the trouble that began at Aleppo and spread to Egypt itself. In 1060 Maḥmūd, the nephew of Thimāl, the Mirdāsid prince who two years previously had accepted the government of Jubayl, Beirut and Acre in exchange for ceding Aleppo to the Fatimids, succeeded in ousting its Fatimid governor and recovering possession of the city. Sent to regain it, the governor of Damascus, Nāṣir al-Dawla Ḥusayn ibn Ḥamdān, son of the governor who had made the unsuccessful attack on the city in 1048, was himself disastrously defeated at the battle of Funaydiq, when he was deserted by the contingents of the Kalb and the Ṭayy.[14] In 1061 Thimāl was paid by al-Qāhira to retake the city on his previous terms, that is, as a vassal of the Fatimids; Nāṣir al-Dawla, ransomed from captivity, briefly returned to Damascus before his recall to Egypt. But there, in October 1060, the Wazīr Ibn al-Maghribī had been dismissed, perhaps like his predecessor Abūᵓl-Barakāt after the disaster of 1049, as a result of the Aleppan fiasco. There was no replacement until March 1061; thereafter, however, for the next six years, Wazīrs came and went, with many, like al-Bābilī, serving several times over, for months, weeks or even days at a time, to a total of well over thirty. In the aftermath of the execution of al-Yāzūrī, Max Weber's description of the patrimonial state as 'characterized by rapid turnover and instability of personnel, but great stability of social struc-

[14] Cf. J. Den Heijer, 'La révolte de l'émir Nāṣir al-Dawla b. Ḥamdān contre le Calife fatimide al-Mustanṣir biᵓllāh (première partie), in U. Vermeulen and K. D'Hulster (eds), *Egypt and Syria in the Fatimid,Ayyubid and Mamluk Eras*, V (Leuven, 2007), pp. 109–19.

tures', was taken to extremes. The personal rivalries of the secretaries of state ensured that not one of them appointed to the Wazīrate enjoyed the support required to form a government, but instead fell victim to their intrigues. Al-Mustanṣir himself contributed to the crisis when in the course of 1061 he intervened to reinstate al-Muʾayyad fīʾl Dīn as Chief Dā ᶜī, and dismiss the Wazīr Ibn al-Mudabbir who had banished him to Jerusalem. With this failure on the part of Ibn al-Mudabbir to resume the role of al-Yāzūrī at the head of both Dawla and Daᶜwa, the regime of the Men of the Pen lost all of its *raison d'être*.

The breakdown of the political system they had conspired to create after the deaths of al-Ḥākim and his sister was matched by the inability of the Caliph to take back control of the administration after the forty years in which his direction had been in abeyance. Both were exposed by a failure to fulfil the monarch's essential obligation to dispense justice through the hearing of petitions, the ultimate recourse of his subjects which affirmed the bond between ruler and ruled, and which in the case of the Fatimids was implicit in the Amān of 969. As Wazīrs came and went and procedures broke down, petitions were presented to al-Mustanṣir himself, who undertook to hear them in person. But he was promptly deluged with up to 800 a day, of every kind, and was obliged to desist. In this limbo, with or without the Wazīr, the administration nevertheless continued on its round. And, ominous as it was, the simmering conflict within the army that in 1062 erupted into fighting on parade between the Turkish Mashāriqa and the Blacks in the presence of al-Mustanṣir was for the moment brought under control. The Turks remained in the capital, while the Blacks were relocated to Damanhūr downstream in the direction of Alexandria. In Syria, however, the regime was in fresh trouble. It was not only Aleppo that slipped away. Following the return of the city to the Mirdāsids, in 1062–3 Makīn al-Dawla ibn Mulhim had been appointed governor of the Syrian coast at Acre, and Nāṣir al-Dawla replaced at Damascus by the Armenian *ghulām* Badr al-Jamālī. But in 1063 the Twelver Shīᶜite Qāḍī of Tyre, Ibn Abī ᶜAqīl, declared his independence of the Fatimids as ruler of the city. No immediate action was taken against him, since in 1064 Badr al-Jamālī was driven out of Damascus by a revolt of the garrison led by the Kutāma Ḥaydara ibn Manzū, and more importantly that of the citizens under the head of the important ᶜAlid families in the city, Abū Ṭāhir Ḥaydara. By 1066 Badr had returned, but Abū Ṭāhir Ḥaydara remained at the head of an opposition not simply to Badr but to the Fatimids themselves. The situation was reminiscent of the resistance to the Fatimid conquest in the 970s and 80s, a reassertion of the political character of the city under the headship of a leading citizen. As such it chimed with a wider phenomenon exemplified by the independence of Tyre: the growth of municipal autonomy and the rise of the city state from end to end of the Mediterranean, taking place at the expense of the empires of the past.

In Ifrīqiya, Tripoli had escaped the Zirids in the first half of the century; out of the mid-century débâcle, Tunis emerged as a city state under its own dynasty, beginning its long career as the principal port and eventual capital of the country. In Syria the process had already been under way at the time of the Fatimid arrival, a major factor in the dynasty's long and only partially successful struggle to win the country for their empire and their cause. Its hard-won success at Damascus had been followed by failure at Aleppo, where the townsfolk were headed by a Raʾīs, or Shaykh al-Balad, a Head of the City drawn from one of the leading families. With their own militia, the Aḥdāth, the inhabitants had played a major part in maintaining the independence of the city over the years that the Fatimids had attempted to conquer it, keeping it as a city state under the protection rather than the rule of the various occupants of its majestic citadel – Ḥamdānid, Mirdāsid and, intermittently, Fatimid. In the thirteenth century, civic pride found expression in the biographical dictionary of Ibn al-ʿAdīm, as it already had at Damascus in the twelfth-century chronicle of Ibn al-Qalānisī. Tyre, however, was different in that its new ruler was himself a citizen, one whose judicial authority as Qāḍī was now translated into *siyāsa*, sway over the city. In this he was not alone: at Tripoli on the coast to the north, Ibn Abī ʿAqīl's fellow Shīʿite Qāḍī Ibn ʿAmmār had similarly taken charge of the city, the founder of a dynasty that ruled for the next fifty years. For the moment he may have ruled in the Fatimid name; but the appearance of these two new city states on the Syrian littoral was a sign of the times, the growth of trade which over the past 100 years had enriched the economy as well as the state in Egypt. The Fatimid regime, with the elaborate bureaucracy that governed the economy, was equipped to take full advantage of its opportunities, not only trading abroad for the materials required by the state, but immensely enriching the dynasty and its servants with the wealth not only to buy, but to invest in trade. Much of that Egyptian trade was with Syria, by land and by sea: for fruit, and cereals when necessary; for iron from Beirut; and for manufactures, especially paper, glass, silk and probably soap. The country meanwhile was an entrepôt for the intercontinental trade between Byzantium and the Mediterranean and Iraq and Iran. For the Fatimids, participation in that trade was sufficiently important for the Caliphate to maintain ships at Tripoli in the first half of the eleventh century; but for Tripoli itself, and for the other cities of the coast, the prosperity it generated was an incitement to independence from an imperial regime in crisis at home and challenged abroad.

The Implosion of the State

The crisis came to a head in 1067. Away in the Yemen, the promise of a great Arabian empire ended abruptly with the ambush and killing of ᶜAlī al-Ṣulayḥī on his way to Mecca by the sons of al-Najāḥ, the ruler of Zabīd whose death in 1060 had been the opportunity for al-Ṣulayḥī's conquest of the Tihāma. ᶜAlī was succeeded by his son al-Mukarram; and it is a tribute to his achievement that his state survived under the direction, first of al-Mukarram's mother Asmaᵓ and second of his remarkable consort, al-Sayyida Arwā. But the Zaydī Imāms in the north regained their independence, and Sanᶜa was abandoned as a capital for a new palace city well to the south at Dhū Jibla near Ibb on the road to Taᶜizz. There, following the return of Lamak from Egypt as Dāᶜī of the Yemen, together with al-Sayyida's personal commitment to the cause, the Daᶜwa took on a new lease of life as the driving force of the state. Lamak's return, however, coincided not only with ᶜAlī's death (which may have been its prompt), but in Egypt with the final collapse of the regime of the Pen into the hands of the Men of the Sword in the course of a protracted revolution which brought both the dynasty and the country to their knees. The *fitna*, or fighting, between the elements of the army began with the outbreak of war between the Turks and the Blacks, on the occasion of a Turkish demand for an increase in salary and allowances. The response of the Blacks was to take the old invasion route down the western side of the Delta from Damanhūr to Gizeh, from where they threatened to cross the Nile into the capital. But at Gizeh they were attacked by the Turks and forced to withdraw southwards. In the absence of an effective Wazīr, the cause of the conflict was not simply the long-standing antagonism between the Mashāriqa, the Maghāriba and the Blacks, but a confrontation at a higher level between Nāṣir al-Dawla Ḥusayn ibn Ḥamdān and the palace in the person of Raṣad, the Queen Mother.[15] The former, the previous governor of Damascus, vanquished at Aleppo, was now the commander of the Turks; the latter was identified with the Blacks, whose regiments she had built up with the purchase of slaves and the supply of arms and money. Following the execution of her protégé al-Yāzūrī, she had come to exercise a more direct influence over the affairs of state. In her opposition to Nāṣir al-Dawla, however, she was confronting more than an ambitious Man of the Sword, none other than a challenge to the dynasty itself, one that extended from Egypt to Damascus, and through Damascus to Baghdad. Some three years earlier, the

[15] Cf. J. Den Heijer, 'La révolte de l'émir Nāṣir al-Dawla b. Ḥamdān contre le Calife fatimide al-Mustanṣir biᵓllāh (deuxième partie)', in U. Vermeulen and K. D'Hulster (eds), *Egypt and Syria in the Fatimid,Ayyubid and Mamluk Eras*, VI (Leuven, 2010), pp.17–25.

replacement of Nāṣir al-Dawla as governor of Damascus by Badr al-Jamālī may have been the occasion for the initial revolt of the garrison and the citizens. But Nāṣir al-Dawla's victory over the Blacks in Egypt now coincided with a fresh rebellion in the city by Abū Ṭāhir Ḥaydara. Not only was he, like Akhū Muḥsin before him, a Ḥusaynid in opposition to the claims of the Fatimids, but he may have had his own pretentions to the Caliphate. In 1068 his revolt, again in conjunction with rebellious troops of the garrison, succeeded in ousting Badr al-Jamālī for a second and last time, and driving him away to Acre. Badr al-Jamālī figures in the sources as Nāṣir al-Dawla's hated rival; but beyond the alleged animosity, and whatever Abū Ṭāhir's motives may have been, the coincidence of his uprising with events in Egypt points to a concerted bid to seize power over the Fatimid state.

In Egypt itself, Nāṣir al-Dawla's victory over the Blacks had indeed given him power but so far no position in government, and his action was destructive rather than constructive. His power was in fact precarious; lacking any great following of his own, ethnic or otherwise, he had exploited the rivalries within the army to turn them to his advantage. But the Turks had taken their own advantage of their victory to press for ever higher pay, a demand which the Wazīrs who continued to come and go were unable to resist, still less to satisfy. Just as the inability of the ᶜAbbasids to pay their troops out of the diminished revenues of Iraq had underlain the collapse of their empire in 945, so now the Fatimids faced destitution in a land where the fiscal administration had broken down as the soldiery and the Bedouin roamed the Valley and the Delta. Having emptied the Treasury, in 1067–8 the Turks plundered the immense treasure of the dynasty, the hoarded wealth of regalia, of gold, silver, jewellery, ivory, glass, ceramics and fabrics, all worked into the ceremonial objects which had been received as presents and given out as tokens of the Caliphate and Imāmate; and what had been a mere proposal to pay the troops in the famine of 1024–5 became a shocking reality. With the treasures of art and craft went the treasures of books as the libraries were stripped. The situation worsened in the course of 1068, when Nāṣir al-Dawla and his Turks were first defeated and then once again victorious over the Blacks to the south, and reached a dénouement in the capital at the end of the year, when the Turks turned on their commander with the accusation that he had kept more than his share of the loot. Their leader was one Ildakiz, in collusion with the Wazīr Khaṭīr al-Mulk in an attempt by al-Mustanṣir himself to regain some sort of control. Nāṣir al-Dawla was driven out of al-Qāhira to Gizeh, revenging himself with the assassination of the Wazīr before he was attacked by the Turks and forced to flee in the direction of Alexandria. There, however, he rallied the Bedouin, like other rebels before him, and in 1069–70 took control of the Delta, from Alexandria right across to Damietta.

The consequence of this unsuccessful attempt to take charge at al-Qāhira was not merely a breakdown of central government, but famine across the country as the land went out of production, the annual routine of cultivation interrupted year on year by the general insecurity. The capital, which relied on the countryside for food, was the first and worst to be affected, all the more because Nāṣir al-Dawla blocked any supply from the north. Those who could do so left, with merchants taking whatever they could of the Fatimid treasure, now worthless in the capital itself; those who remained starved, and died of hunger and disease. The horror of it survived in tales of ridiculous prices, every animal eaten and finally cannibalism, with vultures feeding on the dead; those of al-Qāhira tell of deserted palaces, and al-Mustanṣir himself left sitting, it was said, alone on a mat, fed only by charity. By 1070 the Turks who had expelled Nāṣir al-Dawla were equally hard pressed, joining with the Caliph in an attempt to break the blockade; but an expedition into the Delta was defeated, while skirmishes with the Blacks in the Valley to the south only made matters worse. At Alexandria, on the other hand, Nāṣir al-Dawla was not only well supplied by sea, but made a decisive move. Having sent to the Seljuq Sultan Alp Arslan for aid in return for recognition of his overlordship and that of the Caliphate at Baghdad, in 1070 he had the Friday prayer said in the name of the ᶜAbbasids as Alp Arslan himself prepared to invade Syria. Bribing the Meccans to abandon al-Qāhira for Baghdad, the Sultan seemed finally committed to the much-vaunted mission to abolish the Fatimids in the name of Sunnī Islam. For Nāṣir al-Dawla to side with him was a matter of prudence as well as ambition.

Syria, however, was in flux, not only because of the collapse of the Fatimid regime, but because of the growing intrusion of the Turcomans, a crucial factor that determined both the outcome of Alp Arslan's campaign and that of the ongoing rebellion at Damascus. At Aleppo the Mirdāsid Maḥmūd ibn Thimāl had relied upon them to take control of the city from his uncle, only to be faced with rebellion by his Bedouin kinsmen the Kilāb. More importantly, the growing Turcoman intrusion into Byzantine territory had prompted the Emperor Romanos Diogenes to return to warfare on his Syrian frontier, bringing it closer to Aleppo and further down the Euphrates with the capture of Artah and Manbij. For Alp Arslan the danger from Byzantium was a cause of concern which required the conclusion of a truce before he entered Syria in January 1071. At Aleppo the prayer had already been said for the ᶜAbbasids, to the disgust of the largely Shīᶜite townsfolk; but the Seljuq invasion was abruptly halted by news of an advance by the Emperor, not into Syria but into Armenia in an apparent threat to Alp Arslan's previous conquests and alliances in the Caucasus. Turning away to the north-east, the Sultan confronted the Byzantines at Manzikert or Malazgird north of

Lake Van in Armenia, in a battle that altered the course of history in the Byzantine as well as the Islamic world. The third such victory in the series from Dandānqān to Ḥaydarān, it opened the way into Anatolia for a Turkish conquest and eventual Turkification and Islamisation of the plateau that had been the heartland of the Byzantine empire. With this ending of the dominance of the eastern Mediterranean by the two great empires of the past, the transformation in the balance of power across the region was complete, yet another element falling into place in the transition from the Early to the Later Middle Ages, right across from Europe and North Africa to Iran. For the moment, however, with the lifting of the immediate threat to Egypt, Syria was left to an attempt by Badr al-Jamālī at Acre to recover what he could of his lost power and authority. Tripoli and Tyre were now independent; his siege of Tyre in 1070 had been broken by a Turcoman horde, while Ramla was held by a brother of Nāṣir al-Dawla. More important was Damascus, where the rebellion of Abū Ṭāhir Ḥaydara had degenerated into the rule of Muʿalla ibn Ḥaydara, the son of the Kutāma commander who had led the Fatimid troops in the city in revolt against Badr. Abū Ṭāhir Ḥaydara was now dead, betrayed to Badr and put to death after a ritual humiliation; but fighting had continued in the city, in the course of which the Great Mosque was set on fire. Badr's recourse was to the Turcoman chief Atsiz, invited to aid him in retaking both Ramla and Damascus. This Atsiz did, but quite independently of Badr, taking Ramla and Jerusalem for himself, and closing in on Damascus. Over the next four years he raided around the city, plundering the garden belt on which every spring the nomads pastured their flocks. Badr himself remained at Acre, turning away from the interior to secure his hold on the coast from Acre down to Ascalon.

In Egypt itself, the Turks at al-Qāhira/Fusṭāṭ had been driven in 1071 to settle with Nāṣir al-Dawla in Alexandria and to receive his right-hand man, ohe Shādhī, as his representative. Nāṣir al-Dawla's blockade of supplies was briefly lifted, allowing provisions to reach the city. But Shādhī, once installed, refused to send on to Alexandria the gold that was now at his disposal, so that Nāṣir al-Dawla himself came in the summer with his army of Bedouin to ravage the outskirts of the city and once again cut off provisions. The city, however, was not taken, and he withdrew to Alexandria to be rewarded with the arrival of the black robes and banners of the ʿAbbasids in Baghdad. But in the spring of 1072 he returned, to enter al-Qāhira unopposed, and take control of the state with the assistance of Ibn Abī Kudayna, one of the many previous Wazīrs now once again reappointed to the post. Desolate in his palace, al-Mustanṣir was allotted a monthly pension of 100 dīnārs; but the prayer was still said in his name. For the moment, at least, it was not politic to take the final step of terminating the Caliphate. That was not least because

Ildakiz and his Turks, who three years earlier had turned on Nāṣir al-Dawla with al-Mustanṣir's blessing and driven him from the city, remained loyal to the monarch they had reduced to destitution. Their willingness to take back their old commander was at best conditional, and despite his return to power in the capital, Nāṣir al-Dawla's position was as precarious as ever in the absence of a substantial army of his own. The blockade had certainly been lifted, and the city was now supplied with provisions brought in from al-Mahdiyya and Sicily. On the eve of the fall of Palermo to the Normans, the island was evidently still trading with Egypt, while the mention of al-Mahdiyya may have indicated the continued loyalty of the Zirid Tamīm. But whatever his intentions towards the Caliphate, and however he intended to rule in conjunction with Ibn Abī Kudayna as Wazīr, Nāṣir al-Dawla's reign lasted no more than a year, cut short by assassination in the spring of 1073. Suspicious of his intentions towards the dynasty, the Turks under Ildakiz murdered him in the palace where he had taken up residence. In the absence from Egypt of anyone of suitable stature to take his place, it was left to the Caliph himself to take the initiative. Turning to Nāṣir al-Dawla's old enemy Badr al-Jamālī at Acre, he invited him to take power.

Badr al-Jamālī was part of the Armenian influx into Syria which had begun in the tenth century with the settlement of Armenians along the newly established Syrian borders of the Byzantine empire, where they had served in the Byzantine army as cavalry and infantry. By the time of al-Ḥākim there were Armenians in the Fatimid forces confronting Abū Rakwa; Badr al-Jamālī himself had begun his military career as a *ghulām* in the service of the Banū ᶜAmmār at Tripoli. In the course of the eleventh century this Armenian diaspora had grown with the turbulence in Armenia itself, where the break-up of its kingdom had been followed by its annexation by the Byzantines between 1020 and 1050, and the disruptive invasion of the Caucasus and Anatolia by the Turcomans. As far as the Fatimids were concerned, this arrival in the lands of Islam of yet another people from outside the old Arab empire came to rank with the Banū Hilāl and the Turcomans as a crucial factor in their history. In the factional politics of al-Qāhira, the choice of Badr to take the place of Nāṣir al-Dawla as governor of Damascus proved decisive. At Damascus he had evidently been an intruder, out of place and unwelcome in the city as well as at odds with Nāṣir al-Dawla in the latter's bid for power in Egypt; but back at Acre he had secured the coast from Acre down to Ascalon, recruiting an army of fellow Armenians, infantry and cavalry archers, and taking command of the Fatimid fleet. What he had, in other words, was what Nāṣir al-Dawla had lacked, a following of his own, which in the circumstances was the only disciplined force remaining in what was left of the Fatimid dominion. The Caliph's invitation may well have been awaited. His response was certainly immediate. Taking advantage of a most unseasonable calm, at a time when navigation should have been too dangerous to attempt, he set sail in the depths of winter, to arrive in Egypt in January 1074. From Damietta he made for the capital, where with exemplary ruthlessness he swept away the remnants of the old regime. Welcomed by the Turks, he had their commanders murdered at a banquet, and proceeded to execute Ibn Abī Kudayna and the clutch of Wazīrs who had come and gone over the past ten years. Over the next two years or so he pursued the Turks who had fled up the Nile into Upper Egypt, to recover the Valley from the Blacks and from the Juhayna and Tha ʿāliba, the Arab Bedouin who had lived off it for the past ten years. At the same time he cleared the Berber Lawāta from the Delta and recaptured Alexandria, until by 1076 the whole country was firmly under his control.

In Syria it was another story. Muʿallā ibn Ḥaydara, who had governed Damascus with difficulty since 1069, fled in 1075 as Atsiz's depredations caused increasing hardship. His Berber troops elected another leader, but these quarrelled with *aḥdāth*, or city militia, at a time when shortages became still worse, and Atsiz finally attacked. In 1076 Damascus surrendered, and the Turcoman took possession of the city in the name of the ʿAbbasids, with the regnal title of al-Malik al-Muʾaẓẓam, the Mighty King. While recognising as his suzerain the new Seljuq Sultan Malik Shah, he was effectively independent as the ruler of the dominion he had won for himself in central and southern Syria at the expense of the Fatimids and their empire. The mid-century crisis of that empire, part of the wider crisis of the Islamic world for which the Fatimid challenge for its leadership bore an essential responsibility, had closed with a radical change of regime at al-Qāhira and the loss of the North African, Sicilian and Syrian provinces that had formed its extent in its heyday. The consequences, as Badr al-Jamālī strove to restore both its power and its glory, were all the more profound.

9

The Fatimid Renascence

The Deputy of God's Deputy

As a Man of the Sword rather than the Pen, with the title of Amīr al-Juyūsh, or Commander of the Armies, rather than that of Wazīr, Badr al-Jamālī has been branded a military dictator under whom the dynasty entered its final century at the beginning of a long decline towards extinction at the hands of Saladin. Halm has gone further in arguing that he was in fact a precursor of Saladin, a Sultan or Man of Power in complete charge of the state to the exclusion of the Caliph.[1] It is certainly the case that by an *ᶜaqd*, or binding agreement, of 1078, al-Mustanṣir abdicated to him his own Sultanate, the complete responsibility for government entrusted to him by God as His Caliph in His religion and His world. He made him in fact his own Khalīfa, or Caliph, in a ceremony at which, in the presence of the servants of both Dawla and Daᶜwa, he clothed his new Lieutenant in new robes of office, and sealed the pact with what amounted to a coronation. He invested him with the sword of state, perhaps no longer the original Dhū᾿l-Fiqār, the Sword of ᶜAlī which had been worn and drawn by al-Muᶜizz at his entry into al-Qāhira as proof of his Imāmate and Caliphate, but certainly its successor as the Caliph's own token of his God-given right to reign over Islam. The fullness of the power and authority which, in al-Mustanṣir's own words, he had no choice but to confer upon the champion who had come to the rescue of the state, was spelled out in the reading of the *sijill* of his appointment. In the expression of al-Māwardī, the contemporary theorist of the ᶜAbbasid Caliphate, Badr al-Jamālī had become a Wazīr al-Tafwīd, a plenipotentiary as distinct from a merely executive minister, a Wazīr al-Tanfīdh. Writing as the ᶜAbbasid al-Qā᾿im was losing whatever independence he may have regained under the Būyids to the incoming Ṭughril Beg and the Seljuqs, al-Māwardī's prescription for the government of the

[1] H. Halm, 'Badr al-Ǧamālī – Wesir oder Militärdiktator?', in U. Vermeulen and K. D'Hulster (eds), *Egypt and Syria in the Fatimid, Ayyubid and Mamluk Eras*, V (Leuven, 2007), pp. 121–7.

Muslim community by a monarch in place of the Caliph was a veiled recognition of the reality of a world in which power had passed irrevocably into the hands of the Seljuq Sultan, a king called by whatever name.

Halm has a point, but one that fails to take the measure of Badr's unique position in the Fatimid as distinct from the ᶜAbbasid Caliphate. That position is spelled out in the titles bestowed upon him by the Caliph: al-Sayyid al-Ajall, Amīr al-Juyūsh, Sayf al-Islām, Nāṣr al-Imām, Qāḍī quḍāt al-Muslimīn, Dāᶜī duᶜāt al-Muᶜminīn, Abūʾl-Najm, Badr al-Mustanṣirī. Translated, these become The Most Mighty Lord, Commander of the Armies, the Sword of Islam giving Victory to the Imām, Qāḍī of the Qāḍī-s of the Muslims, Caller of Callers to the Faithful (Abūʾl-Najm, Father of the Star, a nice conceit to match the literal meaning of Badr, the Full Moon, in the astronomical imagery of al-Mustanṣir's eulogy), Badr al-Mustanṣirī instead of al-Jamālī, the Caliph's own creature. What they mean is that Badr has inherited the title and role of the Qāʾim when designated by the Mahdī as the Sword of the Imām for the conquest of Egypt. He has, moreover, taken charge of that essential function of the head of state, the dispensation of the law to the Muslim community as well as justice in general to all subjects. Equally importantly, he has become head of the Daᶜwa, a position which, as al-Mustanṣir insisted in his letter to Aḥmad al-Mukarram, the second of the Ṣulayḥid dynasty in the Yemen, was more than nominal: all questions of the faith were to be addressed to him. In fact, Badr himself was not competent in either capacity, as the inscription of his titles in the Mosque of Ibn Ṭūlūn makes clear: he is the Kāfil Qudāt al-Muslimīn, or Leader of the Qāḍī-s of the Muslims, and Hādī, or Guide, of the Duʾāt al-Muᶜminīn, the Callers to the Faithful. Thus he appointed as Qāḍī al-quḍāt, or Chief Qāḍī, Abū Yaʾlā Ḥamza ibn al-Ḥusayn, the latest of the long line of al-Fāriqī-s, but no successor to al-Muʾayyad fīʾl-Dīn when he died in 1078. The position here remains obscure, since in the case of the Yemen, both al-Mustanṣir and Badr corresponded with Aḥmad al-Mukarram on the same subjects. The fact remains that as The Most Mighty Lord, Badr had taken power on behalf of the Fatimid Caliphate; that he had taken it over in its entirety, both Dawla and Daᶜwa, Caliphate and Imāmate; that through his efforts, again in the words of al-Mustanṣir, 'God had caused the sun of the Fatimid state, *al-Dawla al-Fāṭimiyya*, to rise to the zenith in the heaven of power, dispersing the darkness of its helplessness in the absence of a capable champion'; and that it was indeed in the capacity of champion that he was the man he was, no Sultan coming in from the outside like Ṭughril Beg and Saladin, but an insider identified with the dynasty and its cause.[2]

[2] Cf. M. Brett, 'Badr al-Ǧamālī and the Fatimid Renascence', in U. Vermeulen and J. Van Steenbergen (eds), *Egypt and Syria in the Fatimid, Ayyubid and Mamluk Eras*, IV (Leuven, 2007), pp. 61–78.

The real comparison is with Jawhar 100 years earlier. Jawhar, like Badr, had arrived in Egypt with a mandate to take over the government from those in power and impose a new order in the image of the Caliphate. The authority granted to both for this purpose was absolute; in the case of Jawhar, it stemmed from his prior designation as the Sword of the Imām, in Badr's case from the warrant of the letter which had offered him power if he would only come to the rescue. In the case of Jawhar, that authority ceased when the Caliph himself arrived; in Badr's case it was confirmed after the deed was done. By the time al-Muᶜizz took over from his deputy, however, Jawhar had handed down to the Egyptians the terms of the agreement by which they were to be governed under the incoming regime of the Imām Caliph. By the time of his formal installation in 1078, Badr had begun to restructure the government that had grown out of the original ᶜAhd al-Amān. The major changes that he brought about determined the features of the regime for the next 100 years, together with its legacy to the dynasty's successors.

The Reconstruction of the Regime

The problems that confronted him were the familiar ones of the *ghulām* state, to pay for the army on which its survival ultimately depended. The inability to pay its troops out of the shrunken revenues of Iraq had led to the collapse of the ᶜAbbasid empire in 945. On a minor scale, the Fatimids had faced the same problem in the famine of 1024–5, and on a major scale in the crisis of the *fitna* and *shidda*, the strife and famine of the previous seven or eight years that had almost served the Fatimids in the same way. If they had been saved by the murder of Nāṣir al-Dawla and the arrival of Badr al-Jamālī, the problem remained acute in a country where the fiscal administration had ceased to operate over large areas, where land had gone out of production in the continued anarchy and where the population that should have brought it back under cultivation had itself shrunk in the year-on-year famine. Badr's solution was the same as that of Ibn Killis and ᶜUslūj ibn al-Ḥasan when these had sat together on the orders of al-Muᶜizz to reallocate the tax farms to the highest bidder, setting the finances on a new footing after the disorders of the late Ikhshīdid period and the Fatimid conquest. In this case land-tax farms were created or recreated for allocation to his soldiery under the name of *iqṭāᶜāt* (sing. *iqṭāᶜ*), 'portions', on the one hand to pay them and on the other to bring the land back into production. For that to happen, however, the land itself had to be surveyed and its taxable value established, an operation that went together with a structural reform of local and provincial government. This was a reform that was probably long overdue, in that the fifty to seventy *kuwar* (sing. *kūra*), the units of local administration taken over by the Arabs from the Byzantines, had lost their original responsibility for cultivation and taxation, and thus much of their purpose. By the time of the Fatimids' arrival, the little towns that were their capitals each had their *wālī* or governor, their *ḥākim* and *shurṭa*, their magistrate and police, perhaps their *qāḍī* and detachment of troops. Some were more important than others, some the capitals of groups of such *kuwar*; in amalgamating them all into twenty-six *aʿmāl*, Badr's reform may have finalised a process already under way. Meanwhile, these *aʿmāl* were grouped still further into five major provinces: Alexandria; Sharqiyya and Gharbiyya, the eastern and western Delta; Qūṣ, the capital of Upper Egypt; and Middle Egypt south of al-Qāhira/Fusṭāṭ, at Ashmunayn and Bahnasa. To each of these provinces, then, was assigned a Mushārif, an official responsible for the assessment and collection of taxes from tax-farmers and taxpayers. For this purpose, it would seem that the old *kuwar* now functioned as tax districts administered by his agents. The taxes themselves were nevertheless much as before, assessed in the same way; and collected in a quasi-military operation backed by police and troops.[3]

Alexandria

In 1084 Badr's son al-Awḥad revolted against his father in Alexandria with the support of elements of the army and the Bedouin of the hinterland. It was a revolt that echoed the similar rebellion of the son of Aḥmad ibn Ṭūlūn 200 years earlier and the takeover of the city by Nāṣir al-Dawla in his bid for power during the *fitna* of 1066–73, and anticipated its role as the refuge from which Nizār sought to challenge the accession of his brother Aḥmad to the throne in 1094. From the other direction, Alexandria had been the point of entry into Egypt for the Fatimids, for the abortive invasions of the Qāʾim and the triumphant arrivals of Jawhar and al-Muʿizz. It was a history that pointed to Alexandria not only as the second city of Egypt, but also as one that retained something of the original isolation of the Greco-Roman city from the rest of the country, when it had been the capital, but when it was described as being *by* rather than *in* Egypt, a Mediterranean rather than a Nilotic foundation. It was not in fact on the Nile, being some thirty miles to the west of the Rosetta branch of the river, to which it was linked by a canal dating from the time of the city's foundation. In Roman times a principal function of the canal had been to extract the grain on which Rome itself depended, but with the foundation and growth of Fusṭāṭ/Cairo as the new Egyptian capital in the heart of the country, Alexandria had become the Mediterranean

[3] M. Brett, 'The way of the peasant'.

outlier of the major port of al-Maqs on the Nile beneath the walls of al-Qāhira, through which flowed the country's trade with the Maghrib and Europe. This was not limited to the imports and exports of Egypt itself, but extended to the trade with the Indian Ocean up and down the Nile and the Red Sea, for which Fatimid Egypt was the entrepôt. In this capacity Alexandria not only prospered, but as a maritime city retained something of its former cosmopolitan character, which kept it at a certain distance from the rest of the country and its rulers.

Its difference was apparent in the city itself. The canal that connected it to the river transport system required constant dredging, and if the Nile was too low, dried up, to the detriment of trade. But it also supplied water to the city through underground pipes connected to cisterns. Above ground, the city, within walls and gates of Roman and Byzantine origin, was smaller than in Antiquity, but nevertheless retained the original grid pattern of its streets, with colonnades and buildings still surviving to impress the visitor. It was not centred, like the original Arab foundations – Fusṭāṭ, Qayrawān and Cordoba – on a Great Mosque, but rather on the main east-west street running parallel to the two harbours, at the entrance to which a new lighthouse had been built to replace the Pharos of old. Along the street itself were the *sūq*-s, an original mosque and one in Maghribī style which the Fatimids took for their *Jāmi*ᶜ, or Great Mosque, complete with courtyard and garden. This, in the Sūq al-ᶜAṭṭarīn, or perfume market, was at the western end of the street by the Byzantine fortress and the administrative quarter. Courtyard houses and gardens were a notable feature of the city, the gardens themselves extending to the south beyond the walls to Lake Mareotis or Maryūt, while suburbs appeared out to the east and west. As with Cairo, the population was mixed, Muslim, Christian and Jewish, and was still in principle the seat of the Coptic Patriarch; but the removal of his residence to Cairo was indicative of the way in which Alexandria had been downgraded without losing its vitality. Following the departure of Nāṣir al-Dawla for Cairo in his bid to take power in the capital, the city had become more or less independent, necessitating its reconquest by Badr on his arrival in Egypt. But after the death of Badr, its central position on the intercontinental routes of travel brought about a revival that produced a religious and hence political challenge to Fatimid authority.

Commercially, in the era of the Crusades, it profited from the growth of the trade of the Italian city states with the eastern Mediterranean which followed the creation of the Latin states. Meanwhile, at the end of the eleventh century the arrival of the great Mālikī scholar al-Ṭurṭūshī from al-Andalus, followed early in the twelfth by that of the Shāfiᶜī scholar al-Silafī from Iran, made the city into a major centre of Sunnī teaching. While al-Ṭurṭūshī made himself unpopular by his preaching against the infidels and the vices of the city, he and al-Silafī nevertheless established Alexandria as a pole of religious opposition to the creed of the Imāmate. That in turn attracted the attention of the politicians struggling for power in the capital after the murder of al-Āmir. Thus Riḍwān al-Walakhshī, in the course of his attempt as Wazīr to strip the Caliph of his religious authority, founded a Sunnī *madrasa* in the city, to be followed with a second foundation in 1149 by the similarly ambitious Ibn Sallār before his seizure of the Wazīrate. In 1164 the Alexandrians welcomed Saladin as a champion of Sunnism in the course of Shīrkūh's unsuccessful invasion, in what was the city's last defiance of the dynasty before Saladin brought it to an end.

Cf. M. Frenkel, 'Medieval Alexandria – life in a port city', *Al-Masāq*, 26 (2014), 5–35; P. Walker, 'Fatimid Alexandria as an entrepôt in the East-West exchange of Islamic scholarship', ibid., 36–48; N. Christie, 'Cosmopolitan trade centre or bone of contention? Alexandria and the Crusades, 487–857/1095–453', ibid., 49–61.

These administrative reforms seem all to have been in place by the end of the 1070s. The five provinces were military commands, with Qūṣ in particular, on the buckle of the river just north of Thebes and Luxor, in command of the southern frontier at Aswan, the route across the desert to the east to the port of Quṣayr, and the route south-east through Aswan to ᶜAydhāb, the Fatimid naval base and port for Mecca. The problem is with the *muqṭaᶜūn*, the soldiers who held the *iqṭāʾāt*, their allocation of tax-farms of greater or lesser value according to their rank. The *iqṭāᶜāt* themselves were quite clearly tax-farms in the sense that the bulk of their yield went to the state, while the soldier/farmer took only what was due under the *ᶜibra*, the amount at which the *iqṭāᶜ* had been valued for the purpose of his remuneration. What is not clear is the extent to which at this early stage he was charged with the personal oversight of cultivation. For much of the time he must have been absent on duty or on campaign, when, in accordance with previous and subsequent practice, he was entitled to pay and expenses. As far as the taxation of his *iqṭāᶜ* was concerned, it is probable that this continued to be entirely in the hands of the Mushārif and his staff of assessors and collectors, leaving the *muqṭāᶜ* to receive his share either on the spot or away at his post. What is clear is that there had been a major shift away from a system under which the army was paid by the relevant Dīwān out of revenues allocated for its upkeep, to one in which the individual soldier had become a landholder with a personal stake in the land. Egypt was far from the system that was becoming the Seljuq norm, in which the *iqṭāᶜ* of the Seljuq warrior was a grant not only of its revenues but of powers of government in return for his military services; the mechanism of central government was far too well developed to permit any such devolution. But Badr's expedient introduced a new and important element into the composition of state and society, integrating the personnel of the army into the structure of the administration and the economy with profound consequences for the future.

As was to be expected, Badr did indeed quarter his Armenians in the capital, within al-Qāhira itself. A hundred years after its foundation, the palace city of the dynasty was evolving along with the old city of Fusṭāṭ from the exclusive residence of the Imām Caliph into the conurbation to which it has given the name of Cairo. Within its walls, al-Qāhira had already acquired a commercial character with the appearance of shops and markets to serve the large population of its substantial households, a profitable investment for the royal landlord who rented out the premises directly or indirectly through his favours to his ministers. Outside the walls, the Black regiments had been quartered to the south, and others to the north, while an overflow had developed in the direction of Fusṭāṭ some two miles away to the south. Fusṭāṭ itself had changed in the course of the eleventh century; while the eastern areas of the city had been progressively deserted, on the bank of the Nile to the west, building land had been reclaimed from the river. But these developments had been set back by the *fitna* and *shidda*, the years of warfare, famine and disease that had led to the abandonment of much of Fusṭāṭ by a depleted population, and similarly of the area in the direction of al-Qāhira occupied by the remains of al-ʾAskar, the camp of the ʿAbbasid army of occupation, and those of al-Qaṭāʾiʿ, the Ṭūlūnid quarters centred on the Mosque of Ibn Ṭūlūn. At the same time the original brick wall and gates of al-Qāhira had either crumbled away or been damaged in the course of the fighting, removing the physical barrier separating the Imām Caliph from his subjects. To begin the regeneration of the capital, Badr authorised the building by the surviving population of houses within the old enclosure of the palace city using materials from the abandoned quarters of Fusṭāṭ. This major step towards the transformation of the Caliphal precinct into the nucleus of the civilian city of Cairo was not necessarily delayed and may have been accelerated by the reconstruction of its walls and gates, which began in 1087 and lasted for some four or five years,

The new enceinte enclosed an area somewhat larger to the north and south, with a new salient to the east. While the wall itself has not survived in its entirety, the three great gates of Bāb Zuwayla to the south, and Bāb al-Futūḥ and Bāb al Naṣr to the north remain as Badr's outstanding monument (see Fig. 9.1). They were built by three architects from Edessa, the city which before the disaster of Manzikert had been a key to the Syrian frontier of Byzantium with strong Armenian connection. The architects themselves were indeed Armenians, master builders in the Armenian tradition to whom Badr turned for their expertise in constructing what were in effect Byzantine fortresses, built according to the rules and measurements of Armenian architecture. In calling upon them for such a mighty work, Badr's purpose was more than the defence of the city against the possibility of a Seljuq invasion. An Armenian fortress for Armenian troops, it entrenched as well as advertised his power and position as the master of Egypt and the empire in the service of the Fatimid cause. Thus the inscription above the entrance of the Bāb al Naṣr has at its centre the Fatimid credo: *In the name of God, there is no god but God; Muḥammad is the Prophet of God; ᶜAlī is the Walī or Trustee of God; may His blessings be upon them both, and upon the Imāms of their line for ever.* But on the curtain wall from the Bāb al-Futūḥ to the Bāb al Naṣr, which now enclosed the Mosque of al-Ḥākim within the fortification, is an inscription almost 195 feet long, similar, once again, to those previously put up on the walls of Edessa and elsewhere in the region of Diyarbekr, which celebrates the raising of the protective wall around the Victorious City of al-Muᶜizz by the servant of the Imām al-Mustanṣir, Commander of the Faithful, the Amīr al-Juyūsh. After reciting the full range of Badr's titles, however, it goes on to proclaim the wider achievement of his government in strengthening the state, and bringing about the unity of *al-khāṣṣa waʾl-ʿāmma*, the upper and the lower classes, the elite of the dynasty and the populace. All this has been piously accomplished in the hope of God's reward for his service in safeguarding the throne of the Caliph. Towards the end of his life, as an old man approaching eighty, the inscription bore witness to the fulfilment of his mission (see Fig. 9.2).

Meanwhile, it set the seal on a building programme that had included the restoration of the Mosque of Ibn Ṭūlūn, that of the Nilometer on the island of Roda, built in the ninth century to measure the height of the Nile flood, and the mausoleum of Sayyida Nafīsa, the first ᶜAlid to be buried in Egypt, and as such a monument taken over by the Fatimids. Beyond these restorations, Badr had built for himself a new residence, al-Muẓaffar, to the north of the Western Palace, in place of that built by Ibn Killis to the south-west. A new mosque had been built on the island of Roda, and most famously the so-called Mashhad al-Juyūshī, a small but exquisitely ornamented chapel built visibly but inaccessibly on the Muqattam cliff overlooking the city below. All were furnished with more or less splendid inscriptions, the Mashhad with verses from the Qurʾān that seem to point to the Amīr as the one to whom God has given victory in forgiveness of sin; but however they served as a reminder of the new power in the land, as a contribution to the reconstruction of the capital they will have provided welcome employment and morale for a population attempting to recover from the destruction of the previous years.[4]

[4] Cf. Bloom, *Arts of the City Victorious*, pp. 121–34.

Figure 9.1 Bāb al-Naṣr, al-Qāhira, or Gate of Victory. Photo: Bernard O'Kane.

One of the two northern gates of al-Qāhira in the new enceinte of the palace city, built by Badr to turn the city back into a fortress.

The Seljuqs in Syria

The converse of this ostentatious championship of the Imāmate and Caliphate is that al-Mustanṣir, the Imām Caliph himself, who had resigned his state into the care of this new Malik, or king, was secluded in the palace, with no record of the parades, processions and excursions that had previously been the routine of the sovereign at the head of his household, his ministers and commanders. The household itself, along with those of the family and its ladies in particular, had dwindled down in the course of the famine from the notional figure of 30,000 inhabitants of the palace in mid-century. The entourage of the monarch, the Whites and the Blacks who had been so important a factor in government since the foundation of the dynasty, had lost their power and influence, while the fate of the assets that had enabled the Queen Mother, and the princess Sitt al-Mulk before her, to control or manipulate the government, is unknown. Raṣad herself did indeed remain active at least until the grant of full control to Badr by the *sijill* of 1078; she is on record in that year as receiving the Coptic Patriarch and corresponding with the Queen Arwā in the Yemen in the tradition of such correspondence between the leading ladies of the dynasty and its satellites which went back at least to the time of Sitt al-Mulk. But until such time as the wealth of the family could be reconstituted, al-Mustanṣir was a pensioner dependent on a Treasury that was subject to Badr's control. In the absence of any threat from the palace, that control was challenged only briefly, from a familiar quarter in the histories of the time. In 1084 his son al-Awḥad rebelled against him, taking possession of Alexandria with the support of elements of the army and Arab Bedouin as a base from which to challenge his ageing father for the succession. The rebellion was rapidly put down; al-Awḥad was captured, and Alexandria made to pay for the building of yet another mosque. The son's fate is unknown; as summarised by the thirteenth-century annalist Ibn Muyassar, the chronicle record for Badr's reign is very sparse. But with the buildings and inscriptions, the correspondence of al-Mustanṣir, together with the Coptic *History of the Patriarchs* and the more copious Syrian material, it is possible

Figure 9.2 Foundation inscription in Bāb al-Futūḥ, or Gate of Victories. Photo: Bernard O'Kane.

Part of the calligraphic inscription commemorating the construction of the Gate by Badr al-Jamālī/al-Mustanṣirī in the name of the Caliph.

to see the ways in which Badr set about the task of reconstructing not simply Egypt, but the Fatimid empire.

An initial but essential success was in 1076, when the prayer was once again offered in Mecca and Medina for the Fatimids after Alp Arslan had procured it for the ᶜAbbasids in 1069, with the resumption of grain supplies for the pilgrimage. Syria was another matter. No sooner had he and his army left Acre for Egypt than the undefended city was besieged and taken by yet another Turcoman chieftain, variously called Shakalī and Abū Mankalī, along with Badr's sons and womenfolk. These were honourably treated and sent off to Egypt, while Shakalī moved inland to take Tiberias as his capital. Following the fall of Damascus to Atsiz in 1076, he then joined with Atsiz in 1077 to invade Egypt in the absence of Badr in the south after his victories over the Arabs in Upper Egypt and Aswan. Atsiz's invasion was partly prompted by the last of the Turks slaughtered by Badr in 1074, the son of Ildakiz who had fled to Damascus with his share of the loot from the Fatimid treasure. His crushing defeat by Badr on his rapid return to the north was thus the final act in Badr's assumption of power, which briefly promised the restoration of the Fatimid dominion in Syria. Routed and driven back to Damascus, Atsiz was besieged in the city by Badr in the following year, only for the siege to be abandoned in the face of a new threat. In 1977 Syria had been invaded by Tutush, the brother of the new Seljuq Sultan Malik Shah, commissioned to complete the conquest of Syria abandoned by Alp Arslan, and annex it as an *iqṭāᶜ* in the Seljuq sense of the term, that is as an appanage for him to rule as an addition to the family empire of the Sultanate. In 1078 Tutush, despite a formidable army, had nevertheless been halted, like the Fatimids before him, by the inability of even the best-equipped force to take Aleppo, given the strength of the city and, in this case, the coalition of Arabs and Turcomans assembled by the ᶜUqaylid prince of Mosul in support of the last Mirdāsid. But in response to an appeal by Atsiz, Tutush had no difficulty in raising Badr's siege of Damascus, going on to put Atsiz to death and taking Damascus for himself as his capital. There, faced by the complicated politics of Syria, he found himself in the same position as the Fatimids in his attempt to conquer the north, not least since the place of the Byzantines had been taken by his cousin Sulaymān ibn Kutlumish. Independently of the Sultan, this Seljuq prince had founded his own dominion at Konya in previously Byzantine Anatolia, and now came forward as a rival for Byzantine Antioch and Aleppo. In 1085 Sulaymān took Antioch and advanced on Aleppo, before falling in battle with Tutush in 1086. Aleppo then finally fell to Tutush, only for Malik Shah himself to arrive to place his own men, Yaghi Siyan and Aksunkur, as his governors in Antioch and Aleppo respectively. Tutush himself withdrew to Damascus, while his Turcoman ally Urtuq took up position as his dependent in Jerusalem. The Seljuq domination of Syria was all but complete.

For ten years after his retreat from Damascus, Badr had not attempted to intervene. He had not come to the aid of the ᶜUqaylid Arabs besieging Tutush in Damascus in 1083, and when in 1089 he finally invaded the country once again, it was with a different objective, the reconquest of the coastal cities he had abandoned fifteen years earlier. Under the command of his *ghulām*, Nāṣir al-Dawla al-Juyūshī, his armies took Acre, Tyre and Sidon, the last of these from Tutush, an occasion for celebration as the garrison and its possessions fell into Fatimid hands. Four years later, Tyre rebelled, only to capitulate the moment it was once again besieged. This repossession of the southern half of the Syrian littoral was secured not only by the army but by the Fatimid fleet, with its ability to respond relatively rapidly to any attack, and most probably by fortification: both came into play in the years following the arrival of the First Crusade some ten years later. Meanwhile, the connection with Egypt was made fast by the fortress city of Ascalon, at the head of the route from Cairo via the western Delta and the coast, and at the foot of the line of Palestinian ports. In 1091 its salient position as a lynchpin of the empire was confirmed by its elevation into a holy place with the miraculous discovery of the head of Ḥusayn, the martyred son of ᶜAlī from whom the Fatimids claimed descent. A *mashhad*, or mausoleum, that served as a congregational mosque was promptly built by Badr, and dedicated by him in the long inscription on the *minbar*, the stepped pulpit from which the preacher addressed the worshippers. The text carved into the elaborate woodwork of this splendid setting for the Friday prayer in the name of the Imām Caliph told of the revelation of the head as a divine favour to Badr, who has built the shrine for the veneration of the faithful at his own expense as his offering to God. Fortuitously or not, almost at the end of his life, the discovery came to crown his career with the grandest statement of his pre-eminence as the elect of God for the salvation of His Imāmate and Caliphate. For the purpose of the dynasty he served, not only did Ascalon gain in stature as the entrance to the domain of the Imām Caliph from the East. Possession of the head turned it into a place of pilgrimage for Shīᶜites in general, renewing the appeal of the Fatimids to the wider world of Islam at the outset of their renascence.[5]

[5] Ibid., pp. 134–6.; D. De Smet, 'La translation du *ra's al-Ḥusayn* au Caire fatimide', in U. Vermeulen and D. De Smet (eds), *Egypt and Syria in the Fatimid, Ayyubid and Mamluk Eras*, II (Leuven, 1998), pp. 29–44.

The Coptic Realm

Meanwhile, Badr had turned his attention to the south, to Nubia, Ethiopia and the Yemen. Nubia was in theory a dependent of the Caliphate in virtue of the Baqṭ, the treaty concluded with the Arabs at the time of the original conquest; and its king had been summoned to submit to the Fatimids at the time of their own conquest of Egypt. But although the mission of Ibn Sulaym al-Aswānī had procured a resumption of the Baqṭ, which appears to have been paid down to the 990s, by the beginning of the eleventh century Aswan had fallen into the hands of the Arab Rabīᶜa who were instrumental in having the pretender Abū Rakwa returned to his pursuers. The title of Kanz al-Dawla, or Treasure of the State, with which their chief was rewarded had confirmed him and his tribesmen, now known as the Banūᵓl-Kanz, in control of the southern frontier of Egypt at Aswan. From there they had come to take over the Māris, the Valley to the south as far as the clifftop fortress of Qaṣr Ibrīm, the seat of the Nubian Lord of the Mountain. But they had been crushed by Badr, who had recovered Aswan and placed it in the hands of his governor at Qūṣ. The way was then open for a fresh approach to the Nubian king at Old Dongola. Nubia, however, was Christian, as was Ethiopia, and Badr's dealings with them involved the Christians of Egypt, a population which through its various Churches played an unusually prominent part in his statesmanship. That prominence finds its expression in the *History of the Coptic Patriarchs*, biographies of the heads of the church from the time of its foundation by St Mark. Its preface is attributed to Severus ibn al-Muqaffaᵓ, the bishop of Ashmunayn who disputed with Ibn Killis on matters of religion, but was in fact written 100 years later by Mawhūb ibn Manṣūr ibn Mufarrij, who translated the series from the earlier Greek and latterly Coptic in which they had been written down to the previous generation, and began the subsequent series in Arabic (see Fig. 9.3).

The preface that he wrote describes the See of St Mark over which the Patriarch presided as beginning with Egypt followed by the Pentapolis, glossed as Barqa in Cyrenaica and the Fezzan in southern Libya. Further west are Qayrawān, Tripoli and Ifrīqiya; to the south are Nubia and Ethiopia. Historically, this can never have been the case, since Ifrīqiya, originally Byzantine Africa, had always belonged to Rome and still did. Ifrīqiya, on the other hand, with its capital of Qayrawān, was, at least in principle, a province of the Fatimid empire to which the Patriarch at Alexandria was subject. The See of St Mark, in other words, is envisaged as identical with the Fatimid dominions in the Maghrib as far as the Fezzan in the depths of the Sahara. Meanwhile, the appearance on the list of the actual ecclesiastical provinces of Nubia and Ethiopia brings these within the scope of those dominions as envisaged by the Fatimids themselves.[6]

Ibn Mufarrij himself had welcomed the arrival of Badr as the God-sent deliverer of his people from the previous anarchy, who had restored it to prosperity at what may nevertheless have been a decisive moment in its history. In the long decline of the Copts from the people of Egypt at the time of the Arab conquest into a relatively small minority of the population, the famine may well have been the tipping point at which they turned from a very substantial to a much smaller proportion of the population. Their numbers may never have recovered, as their rate of reproduction was outstripped by that of the Muslims. This long-term factor, the most plausible explanation of the decline, was no doubt partially the result of a drift into the Muslim population, but was accelerated by a loss of reproductive capacity as Christian women married Muslim men, and Christian men went into the Church as celibate monks and priests. In doing so, however, they entered an institution that was both wealthy and influential, and together with the fiscal administration provided the occupations to maintain the existence of the community in a comfortable niche. There, its solidarity had been illustrated by the return of its members to the faith after al-Ḥākim's attempt to Islamise the administration was abandoned. While Ibn Mufarrij's translation of *History of the Patriarchs* into Arabic acknowledged the passing of Coptic as a spoken and written language, his Arabic biographies of the Patriarchs Christodoulos and Cyril make clear that the Church itself flourished under Badr, who employed it not least in his dealings with the Christian kingdoms to the south.[7]

While elevated above the stars, in the words of al-Mustanṣir's eulogy, as the champion of the dynasty, Badr the Armenian was dependent on his Armenian troops, some if not all of whom were evidently Christian, along with the Armenians who followed him into Egypt. Thus in 1087 he welcomed the arrival of an Armenian patriarch for the Armenian community. His arrival was likewise agreeable to Ibn Mufarrij, who describes his subsequent welcome by the Coptic Patriarch Cyril, on the grounds that the Armenians were of the same Monophysite faith as the Copts and by extension the Nubians and Ethiopians. As far as the Coptic Church itself was concerned, Badr had turned to it as an instrument from the time of his own arrival. Thus in pursuit of the Kanz al-Dawla, the lord of Aswan who had fled into Nubia at his approach in 1076, he had the Patriarch Christodoulos send the bishop Mercurios in the

[6] M. Brett, 'The Coptic Church in the Fatimid empire', pp. 33–60.

[7] M. Brett, 'Population and conversion to Islam in Egypt in the Mediaeval period', in U. Vermeulen and J. Van Steenbergen (eds), *Egypt and Syria in the Fatimid, Ayyubid and Mamluk Eras*, IV (Leuven, 2007), pp. 1–32.

Figure 9.3 Lustre bowl with a priest, Egypt (probably Cairo), 1050–1100. Museum number C. 49-1952. © V&A.

Closely involved with the regime, the Coptic Church and its members shared in the common culture and art of the dynasty.

company of the Amīr Sayf al-Dawla with letters to the Nubian king successfully demanding his return. According to *History of the Patriarchs*, he had previously put to death one ᶜAlī al-Qifṭī, who had falsely accused the Metropolitan of Nubia, one Victor, of destroying a Nubian mosque. Christodoulos, who had consequently been arrested as the Metropolitan's superior, had accordingly been released, in an echo of a previous story that he had been arrested and then released by al-Yāzūrī on a similarly false charge of advising the King of Nubia against payment of the tribute due in accordance with the Baqṭ. As told by Ibn Mufarrij in his biography of the Patriarch, the point of the tale is distinction to be preserved between Church and State, namely the reply of Christodoulos to Badr's request for advice about al-Qifṭī's fate, that it was for Badr as the secular authority, from the Church's point of view, to decide on his punishment, not the Church. Whatever the truth of the matter, Christodoulos died shortly afterwards, and the consecration of the new Patriarch Cyril in 1078 was the occasion for his ceremonial reception by al-Mustanṣir, seated together with the Queen Mother Raṣad and his sister. Arranged by Badr, this was followed by Badr's own reception of the Patriarch in his own court, and the command to the prefect of Miṣr, that is, Fusṭāṭ, to escort him to his residence in the city. The price to be paid for this exceptional honour was that Cyril was forbidden to return to Alexandria, on the grounds, said Ibn Mufarrij, that Badr needed him in the capital especially to deal with the Nubian and Ethiopian correspondence.

In the hands of Cyril, the Patriarch for the next fourteen years, the Coptic Church indeed became Badr's instrument for binding the Christian monarchies of Nubia and Ethiopia into the empire as vassals of the Caliphate. This was most easily accomplished in the case of Nubia, in the case, that is, of the kingdom of Muqurra rather than the more distant kingdom of ᶜAlwa. Muqurra, with its royal capital at Dunqula (Old Dongola) and northern capital at Faras, was in regular contact with Egypt. Whether or not the terms of the Baqṭ were fulfilled, trade and people moved up and down the Nile between the two countries; the Kings had complied with requests to return such rebels as Abū Rakwa and the Kanz al-Dawla; while its Church was at its most magnificent in terms of cathedrals, churches and monasteries. A royal Church dependent on royal patronage, it had its own distinctive art and architecture, with Nubian as the liturgical language, in an alphabet of Greek and Coptic letters. With its bishops and metropolitan archbishops nominated by the King for consecration by the Coptic Patriarch, it nevertheless belonged very firmly to the See of St Mark. The connection was all the stronger from the relative closeness to Aswan of the ecclesiastical city of Faras, where the Metropolitan Victor most probably had his seat, while the Nile continued to serve as the pilgrimage route to Jerusalem. In 1079, in the year after Cyril's elevation, these various factors combined to provide Badr with an initial coup. The aged King Solomon of Muqurra had abdicated in favour of his sister's son George, and retired to the monastery of St Onuphrius, most probably at Faras. But from there he was seemingly abducted by a relative of the Kanz al-Dawla, the rebel whom he had previously returned to Badr, and was sent on via Aswan to Cairo. There he was royally received by Badr, and palatially housed as his guest until his death and burial in the following year. However the affair was contrived, the result was a triumphal assertion of Fatimid suzerainty over Muqurra. That Muqurra itself subscribed to the unequal relationship was apparent ten years later, when in 1089 the new King Basil sent to Cairo a handsome present, together with the son of his predecessor George to be consecrated bishop by the Patriarch. Through the Church, the Nubian monarchy was firmly tied into the Fatimid regime.

Ethiopia, Ḥabash in the Arabic of the Qurʾān, was a different matter. Ruled by its kings of the Zagwe dynasty, its Church depended like that of Muqurra upon the Coptic Patriarchate, which not only appointed but sent out a Metropolitan from Egypt to be its head. The sending was required by both Church and State; in the tenth century a long lapse in the appointment had coincided with, and allegedly had been responsible for, a protracted succession crisis. A new appointment had only been made in response to a plea from the King himself, sent via King George of Muqurra to the Patriarch Philotheus in the reign of al-ᶜAzīz. The story is evidence of a fellowship between the two kingdoms, as well as the importance of the Nile as the route from Ethiopia, not simply into Egypt but beyond to Jerusalem for the pilgrimage. But despite this geopolitical factor, and the kingdom's dependence on the apostolic succession to St Mark, the Ethiopian Church had developed quite separately from the Church in Egypt, while the monarchy, not yet perhaps claiming descent from Solomon, still saw itself as heir to the Kingdom of Israel and champion of the faith at the head of a Christian empire. In seeking to assert a Fatimid claim to overlordship, Badr could only rely upon the agency of the Metropolitan, on the one hand his subject, but on the other a foreigner to the country, a figurehead of doubtful ability to influence affairs. And though he clearly made the effort to win some kind of recognition, the story in *History of the Patriarchs* is far from clear. One Severus, the nephew of a previous Metropolitan familiar with the country, seemingly obtained the appointment as Metropolitan on the strength of a promise to bring the kingdom into a tributary relationship with the Caliphate, and once there, sought to bring about a reformation with a campaign against polygamy. In 1089, however, Rijal, the brother of Severus, arrived with a gift that Badr considered inadequate, while in Ethiopia, an unpopular Severus had been taken into custody after his life had been threatened. Badr's response, according to Ibn Mufarrij, was to order the Patriarch Cyril to send two bishops to demand the implementation of a previous agreement whereby four mosques were to be built, an annual gift of a certain value was to be supplied, the Daᶜwa established and Muslims allowed into the country. The bishops were apparently sent with letters from the Patriarch and Badr himself, but the upshot of what appears to be an attempt to draw Ethiopia formally into the Fatimid empire through the imposition of a second Baqṭ-like *ᶜahd* is unknown.[8]

The Realm of the Yemen

Across the Red Sea from Ethiopia, meanwhile, the Yemen remained as the outstanding achievement of the Daᶜwa in the eleventh century, still ruled over by the heirs of ᶜAlī al-Ṣulayḥī despite his killing in 1067 by the

[8] For these relationships with Nubia and Ethiopia, see Brett, 'The Coptic Church in the Fatimid empire', pp. 33–60.

Najāḥids. His death had put an end to his conquests, and to the prospect of an Arabian empire stretching as far as Mecca; but his gains had been more or less secured by his son and successor Aḥmad al-Mukarram. More or less, since the Najāḥids had regained Zabīd in the Tihāma, the Zaydīs remained at Saᶜda in the north and Sanᶜa was abandoned as the capital for Dhū Jibla in the mountains well to the south. Behind him, moreover, stood his mother Asmāᵓ and more particularly his queen, Arwā. When in 1074 al-Mukarram was crippled by a stroke, it was Arwā who took control of affairs. When al-Mukarram himself died in 1084, she became regent for her son al-Mukarram II, and when he too died in 1090, she became queen in her own right as al-Malika al-Sayyida and al-Sayyida al-Ḥurra, the Lady Queen and the Noble Lady, the titles by which she is known.[9] Needless to say, such a succession was not unopposed, or without the intervention of Cairo. In contrast to the Christian kingdoms of Nubia and Ethiopia, where Badr had turned to the Coptic Patriarch to exercise his ecclesiastical authority along with his own on behalf of the Caliph, the Yemen was a land not simply of Islam but of Īmān, faith in the sense of belief in the Imām as well as submission to God. For the Ṣulayḥid faithful, the authority of the Imām was paramount and his personal instructions indispensable. The result, as in the case of Nubia and Ethiopia, was a dual correspondence, conducted on the one hand by Badr, whom the Yemenis had been instructed by al-Mustanṣir, in his *sijill* of 1078, to obey in all things. On the other, it was conducted by al-Mustanṣir himself, some perhaps entirely in his own hand, but all certainly with his calligraphic signature in the form of the phrase 'Praise be to God, the lord of the two worlds'. Presumably at Badr's insistence, his letters took care to praise the Amīr al-Juyūsh, whose name, along with those of his sons, was mentioned along with that of al-Mustanṣir in the Friday prayer. But where Badr's letters have not survived, those of al-Mustanṣir, to the number of sixty-six, were preserved and copied by the Yemeni faithful as sacred texts.[10] Their number demonstrates his personal involvement with the Daᶜwa in the Yemen, and concern for its success. Quite apart from Badr's determination to resurrect the empire under his control, they reveal him in this latter part of his reign to be a scholar, one who may have been ineffective as Caliph, but as Imām took the task of guiding the faithful with the utmost seriousness.

The cooperation between the Imām and his Amīr was most in evidence

[9] For Asmāᵓ and Arwā and their critical importance, see Cortese and Calderini, *Women and the Fatimids*, pp. 127–38.

[10] *Al-Sijillāt al-Mustanṣiriyya*, ed. A. M. Mājid/Magued (Cairo, 1954), from MS, Library of the School of Oriental and African Studies, London, catalogue no. 27155. Cf. P. E. Walker, *Exploring an Islamic Empire. Fatimid History and its Sources* (London, 2002), p. 124.

over the succession to al-Mukarram followed by that of his son, in the first place the succession of a minor, in the second, that of a woman. At the death of al-Mukarram the supreme position of Dāᶜī as head of state was claimed on the one hand by Arwā's half-brother Sabaᵓ ibn Aḥmad, and on the other by ᶜĀmir al-Zawāḥī, son of the Dāᶜī who had launched ᶜAlī al-Ṣulayḥī on his career. But al-Mustanṣir ruled in favour of the son, on the grounds that a minority was no bar to the Imāmate; and the *sijill* of investiture was duly entrusted along with letters from Badr to his personal envoy, Jawhar al-Mustanṣirī. When the son died in his turn without a brother to inherit, once again it was for the Caliph and his Commander jointly to rule that Sabaᵓ ibn Aḥmad should marry the queen and thus maintain the male line. But this was a ruling that satisfied the requirement of a man for the purpose with a token marriage and a nominal appointment, while leaving Arwā herself in overall charge of both Dawla and Daᶜwa in the role of Ḥujja. The actual title she enjoys in the Yemeni literature may have been retrospectively attributed to a formal designation by al-Mustanṣir, but undoubtedly corresponded to her regency on behalf of the Imām Caliph in this new branch of the Fatimid empire, whose lively politics were matched by the liveliness of the mission. The strategic position on the route to India gained with the acquisition of Aden was an opportunity to proselytise out to the East, beginning in 1083 with the appointment by al-Mukarram of two new *duᶜāt* to Oman and India, approved by al-Mustanṣir and confirmed by letters issued by the *majlis*, or office, of Badr. The mission to Oman came to nothing, but that to Gujarat on the north-western coast of India took root under its Dāᶜī Marzubān. At his death in 1089, Arwā's nomination of his son as his successor was once again approved by Cairo, and a merchant community built on the Indian Ocean trade out of Aden went on to flourish on the distant horizon of the Fatimid empire. Such an outcome presupposed the strength of a preaching firmly grounded in the history and theology of the Imāmate as this had developed down to the time and work of al-Muᵓayyad al-Dīn al-Shīrāzī. While the Ṣulayḥids bore the title of Dāᶜī as leaders and directors of the community and Arwā herself in the capacity of Ḥujja was certainly learned in the teachings of the Daᶜwa, it was left to the Qāḍī Lamak ibn Mālik to raise those teachings in the Yemen to the level of Fatimid scholarship reached in the course of the previous 150 years. The emissary of ᶜAlī al-Ṣulayḥī to al-Qāhira as the *fitna* and *shidda* unfolded in Egypt from 1066 to 1069, Lamak had spent his time as the student of al-Muᵓayyad and had returned to found a Yemeni school of Ismāᶜīlism capable of developing as well as preserving the doctrine and literature of the Imāmate independently of the fortunes of the Dawla.

The Rising in Iran

In Badr's time, those fortunes had revived. On the other hand, the death of al-Muᵓayyad in 1078, coinciding with Badr's assumption of the direction of the Daᶜwa as well as the Dawla, had left the dynasty in Egypt without a person of comparable learning and authority to speak on behalf of the Imām to the faithful in Iraq and Iran. There, in the homeland of the Ismāᶜīlī philosophical tradition, there was no equivalent to the Ṣulayḥids with whom al-Mustanṣir could correspond, nor a Lamak ibn Mālik openly to teach the faith; instead, al-Muᵓayyad's second disciple, Nāṣir-i Khusraw, had been driven into hiding.[11] This celebrated poet and philosopher, the author of his *Safar-nāma*, or account, of his seven-year journey to and from al-Qāhira, returned to Khurāsān in 1052 as its Ḥujja, or Proof, of the Imām, its chief Dāᶜī. There, however, he was forced to take refuge from persecution with an Ismāᶜīlī chieftain in the mountains of Badakhshan at the head of the Oxus in north-eastern Afghanistan. By the time of his death in 1077, such persecution had taken its toll, and the centre of Ismāᶜīlī activity was about to shift westwards into Iran and the heart of the Seljuq empire, into the lands abandoned by al-Muᵓayyad al-Dīn al-Shīrāzī some forty years earlier. There, over a period of some thirty years covering the reigns of Alp Arslan and his son Malik Shah from 1063 to 1092, the administration was in the hands of the great Wazīr Niẓām al-Mulk, a minister brought up under the Ghaznawids who endeavoured to convert the family dominion of the Seljuqs into a centralised state on the Ghaznawid model. In his *Siyar al-mulūk*, or Rules for Kings, he set out the principles of such a state before denouncing as its enemies a historical ragbag of heretics variously called Carmathians and Bāṭinīs. These in his own time were clearly the Fatimid Ismāᶜīlīs, against whom he set himself up as a champion of Sunnism, not simply in principle but in practice.[12] In 1067 he founded the Niẓāmiyya at Baghdad, the first of a series of *madrasa*-s, or colleges, for the teaching of the Sunnī doctrines of the law. The intention was not simply to give Sunnism institutional form as the orthodoxy of Islam, but to train up the personnel of the imperial government he was endeavouring to create. That government was on the Fatimid model of a bureaucracy headed by a central Dīwān overseeing four departments dealing with taxation and accountancy, the secretariat, the army, and what the ᶜAbbasids had once called the post, an inspectorate of intelligence and

[11] For his career, see Hunsberger, *Nasir Khusraw*.

[12] Niẓām al-Mulk, *Siyāsat-nāma/Siyar al-Mulūk*, trans. H. Darke, *The Book of Government or Rules for Kings* (London, 1960). For his career, cf. Peacock, *The Great Seljuq Empire*, pp. 66–71.

matters requiring investigation. Staffed in the provinces as well as the capital by his sons, relatives and clients, it worked to control the administration of Malik Shah's dominions from Iraq to Khurāsān, including that of the *iqṭāᶜāt*, the allotment under the Seljuq system of the revenues and government of districts large and small in return for military and political service. Efficiency together with abuses, on the other hand, made for unpopularity, as the Ismāᶜīlī enemy was set to demonstrate.

The Ismāᶜīlī Daᶜwa in the former Būyid realm had remained quietly active under the leading Dāᶜī Ibn ᶜAṭṭāsh, working clandestinely out of the Seljuq capital Isfahan. Change came about when continued proselytisation resulted in the conversion of the young Ḥasan-i Ṣabbāḥ at Rayy. Taken up into the Daᶜwa by Ibn ᶜAṭṭāsh, in 1076 he set off for Cairo to meet al-Muʾayyad fīʾl-Dīn; but the journey was roundabout and long, and by the time of his arrival in 1078 al-Muʾayyad was dead. With Badr now in charge of the Daᶜwa, Ḥasan's stay of two years at Cairo and Alexandria failed to include an audience with al-Mustanṣir, and he probably received little encouragement from the newly appointed Hādī, or Guide, of the Duʾāt. In the light of his future career, it is unlikely that he was commissioned by Badr to return to Isfahan in 1081 and set out as he did on his career as a revolutionary. For the rest of the decade he travelled Iran as a preacher less of Ismāᶜīlism than hatred of the Turks, appealing in particular to the Daylamīs of the Elburz mountains south of the Caspian. The race of the Būyids and the backbone of their armies, with a long-standing history of Shīᶜite rebellion, the Daylamīs were ready listeners, and when in 1090 Ḥasan took possession of the immense mountain fortress of Alamut, his success was assured. It dominated the upper valley of the Shah Rūd, the river which, some forty miles to the west of Alamut, turns to the north at right angles to cut down through the mountains to the sea. This was the region known as Rūdbār, or Bank of the Rūd, over which he set out to gain control. At the same time, in 1091–2, he sent from Rūdbār a *dāᶜī* from Quhistān, some 600 miles away in the mountains to the south of Khurāsān, back to his homeland to stir up a rebellion in which the cities of Qāʾin, Birjand, Tabas and Dara all fell to the Ismāᶜīlīs, in what amounted to a nationalist uprising against the Turks. After the failure of the local Seljuq *amīr* to dislodge him from Alamut, in 1092 his hold was then assured by the rout of the expedition sent by Malik Shah, the Seljuq Sultan himself. The siege was broken by a convergence of the Ismāᶜīlīs of the region on the attackers, and the threat of further action was removed by the death in quick succession of Niẓām al-Mulk and Malik Shah himself. Niẓām al-Mulk was murdered, the first victim, according to legend, of the *fidāʾūn*, the self-sacrificing killers who have earned for Ḥasan-i Ṣabbāḥ's Ismāᶜīlī following the name of Assassins. Stabbed to death as he was carried in his litter, he was more certainly the victim of Malik Shah himself and his wife Terken Khatun, fearful of this overmighty and overweening subject with a personal army of several thousand *ghilmān*. With the death of Malik Shah almost immediately afterwards, his murder turned out to be the preliminary to a protracted struggle for the succession between the Sultan's sons and brother, which, as far as the Ismāᶜīlīs were concerned, meant the abandonment of the campaign to recover Quhistān as well as Rūdbār, and the opportunity to extend their holdings from end to end of the Elburz range, as well as into the Zagros mountains overlooking the plain of Khuzistān in southern Iraq.[13]

The Crisis of Succession in Egypt and Iran

It is ironic that these two enemies, the Sunnī Wazīr Niẓām al-Mulk and the Ismāᶜīlī Dāᶜī Ḥasan-i Ṣabbāḥ, should both have been champions of Iran and the Persian language, resurrected in literary form by Firdausī at the beginning of the century in his national epic, the *Shāh-nāma*, or Book of Kings, and now used by both of them instead of Arabic. The one had endeavoured to take over the Seljuq state; that he was murdered rather than dismissed and executed shows how near he came to success. The other, meanwhile, had set out to challenge the Turkish dominion. Almost 200 years after the Fatimids had burst on the scene, however, Ḥasan-i Ṣabbāḥ was no Abū ᶜAbd Allāh with a Mahdī in waiting to spring on the world. His relationship to the Imāmate derived from that seminal event was abruptly terminated when, in a curious parallel to events at Isfahan, Badr and al-Mustanṣīr died one after the other at Cairo in 1094 and, as at Isfahan, the question of the succession was thrown open. The result in this case was very different. Badr was not murdered; moreover, after the rebellion of his son al-Awḥad in 1084–5 he had designated his second son al-Afḍal as the heir to his position, using the regal term of Walī ᶜAhdihī. And furthermore, he had married his daughter, al-Afḍal's sister, to Aḥmad, the Caliph's youngest son, with the evident intention to perpetuate his power and authority in association with the hereditary monarchy. The designated successor to al-Mustanṣir, on the other hand, was presumed to be his eldest son Nizār, a grown man who looked forward to his accession and the appointment of his own man, the Berber Ibn Masāl, as Wazīr. Neither succession was straightforward. Badr's position was unassailable, but at his death al-Afḍal had to reckon with the residual power and authority of the Caliph to appoint his successor. Thus on Badr's

[13] For Ḥasan-i Ṣabbāḥ and his career, see B. Lewis, *The Assassins. A Radical Sect in Islam* (London, 1967); M. G. S. Hodgson, *The Order of Assassins* (The Hague, 1955); F. Daftary, *The Assassin Legends. Myths of the Ismāᶜīlīs* (London, 1994).

death, a show of force was required to have the Turkish Amīr Lāʾūn dismissed by al-Mustanṣir after a faction in the army had contrived his very brief appointment. On the death of al-Mustanṣīr himself, al-Afḍal was obliged swiftly to forestall the accession of Nizār by placing his own candidate, his brother-in-law Aḥmad, immediately on the throne, and presenting him to his elder brothers as the designated Imām under the title of al-Mustaᶜlī biʾllah, Elevated by God. Faced with this *fait accompli*, Nizār fled away to Alexandria with his brother ᶜAbd Allāh and his right-hand man Ibn Maṣāl, there to join its Turkish governor, the Amīr Nāṣir al-Dawla Aftakīn, and proclaim himself Caliph under the defiant title of al-Muṣṭafā li Dīn Allāh, The Chosen One. In 1095, al-Afḍal's first attempt to defeat his forces was repelled, and they advanced on Cairo; but there they were defeated, driven back to Alexandria and besieged until they surrendered. Ibn Maṣāl had already fled, but Nizār and Aftakīn were taken back to Cairo, where despite the safe-conduct they had been given, Nizār was walled up alive and Aftakīn executed. So too was Barakāt, the Amīn al-Duʾāt, or head of the Daᶜwa under Badr and his son, together with the Chief Qāḍī, who had dared to proclaim ᶜAbd Allāh Caliph under the title of al-Muwaffaq.

The whole affair is reminiscent of Jawdhar's coup at the death of the Qāʾim in 946, when Ismāᶜīl succeeded to the Imāmate and Caliphate with or without his father's *naṣṣ*, or designation, while his brothers and uncles were placed under house arrest as monkeys who had turned from the true faith. But while the two episodes each affirmed the principle of exclusive succession to the throne which was the distinctive strength of the dynasty, the difference was apparent. Nizār had come out in open opposition, while Aḥmad was a mere puppet; and al-Afḍal had succeeded where Niẓām al-Mulk had failed to establish a Wazīral dynasty intimately connected to the ruling family. As far as the Fatimids and their mission were concerned, however, the price of that success was high. While the Yemenis, now ruled by Arwā in her own right as the Sayyida al-Malika, the Royal Lady, accepted the explanation that al-Mustanṣīr had indeed designated Aḥmad before his death, his accession was the occasion, and perhaps the opportunity, for Ḥasan-i Ṣabbāḥ to break free from Cairo in the name of Nizār. The claim in the literature that he had been told by al-Mustanṣīr during his visit to Cairo that Nizār was the heir is certainly untrue, although both he and his followers may well have anticipated his accession as a relief from the rule of Badr. That may explain the speed with which he recognised the vanished Nizār, alive or dead, as the true successor, a recognition that left him as the supreme representative of this hidden Imām, the authority for the faith and the ruler of his state. The theological basis for this radical departure from the Fatimid doctrine of a Caliphate destined to last until the end of time was provided by his Daᶜwa Jadīda, his New

Calling, a doctrine of the Imāmate that may have originated with his own conversion to Ismāᶜīlism, which was said to have occurred, in what survives of his autobiography, when a serious illness convinced him of its truth. This new version of the Fatimid *taᶜlīm*, its teaching or instruction, refined the dynasty's rejection of *ikhtilāf*, the divergence between the Sunnī schools of law, on the grounds that there was only the one law for which the one Imām was the sole authority. For Ḥasan-i Ṣabbāḥ the choice of whom to believe turned the individual into his own authority for the law and for the faith, a clearly unacceptable state of affairs which applied as much to the Imām as to the schools. For his acceptance by the believer, therefore, the Imām could not depend upon external criteria such as genealogy or the word of another, but only upon his fulfilment of the need for him felt by the believer. *Taᶜlīm*, in other words, had become a devotional and spiritual experience which in the physical absence of the Imām enabled Ḥasan to realise in his own person al-Naysabūrī's description of the Dāᶜī and his responsibilities at the head of a new religion.[14]

The Daᶜwa Jadīda consummated the break with the Imāmate in Cairo. Over 100 years after the Iranians had entered the Fatimid fold they departed to resume the attempt at revolution which had been aborted in the mid-tenth century, and to take their philosophical tradition in a different direction. With their secession, the Daᶜwa began its prolonged period of separation from the Dawla which was consummated with the end of the dynasty some eighty years later. Meanwhile, however much that secession may have damaged the Fatimid cause, the moment for al-Afḍal as well as for Ḥasan was propitious. The Seljuq empire, which had dominated the scene for the past forty years, was in the throes of a succession crisis that pitted the sons of Malik Shah, Maḥmūd, Berk Yaruq and Muḥammad Tapar, against each other and their uncle Tutush, in the midst of rebellions by other Seljuq princes, Turks and Arabs.[15] In 1096 a covert Ismāᶜīlī officer of the Seljuqs gained for Ḥasan the great fortress of Girdkuh in the region of Damghan at the eastern end of the Elburz chain. Comparable in its way to Alamut, Girdkuh extended Ḥasan's empire the length of the mountains south of the Caspian, while he himself proceeded to consolidate his hold on Rūdbār with the capture of the fortress of Lamassar. One Abū Ḥamza had established himself near Arrajan in the Zagros mountains, while at Isfahan, in the Seljuq capital itself, the Ismāᶜīlīs recruited by the Dāᶜī Ibn ᶜAṭṭāsh rose in revolt. They were driven out by the populace, but Aḥmad, the son of Ibn ᶜAṭṭāsh, gained the nearby

14 Cf. Hodgson, *The Order of Assassins*, pp. 148–59.

15 Cf. Bosworth, 'The Iranian world (A.D. 1000–1217)', *The Cambridge History of Iran*, vol. 5, pp. 102–19; Peacock, *Great Seljuq Empire*, pp. 76–82.

castle of Shahdiz with its Daylamī garrison, to which was added that of Khalinjan. By 1100, a loose horseshoe of Ismāᶜīlī fortresses had sprung up in the mountains encircling Iran from the Zagros round to Quhistān, a frame for the communities in cities such as Qazvin and Rayy. And while the Seljuqs were too preoccupied with their rivalries to move against them, the Ismāᶜīlīs took to the assassination by their *fidāʾūn* of the officers of Berk Yaruq as he fought to hold on to the Sultanate against his rival Muḥammad Tapar.

All this was potentially to al-Afḍal's advantage as the new champion of the Imām Caliph. While he was securing his own succession to Badr, and that of his protégé Aḥmad to al-Mustanṣir at the expense of Nizār, Tutush had left Damascus after the death of Malik Shah to claim the Sultanate for himself. In 1093 he proclaimed himself Sultan at Baghdad and in 1094 advanced into Iran as far as Rayy. But in 1095 he was defeated and killed by the forces of Berk Yaruq. With his death the prospect of Syria's incorporation into an even greater Seljuq empire evaporated. Instead, Syria relapsed into its habitual disunity, with the Seljuq *ghulām* Yaghi Siyan in possession of Antioch, Aleppo and Damascus ruled by Tutush's two sons, Riḍwān and Duqāq respectively, and Jerusalem held by the Artuqid Ilghāzī. Over the two years following the death of Tutush, the two brothers fought each other over his inheritance. Duqāq at Damascus was relatively secure under the tutelage of his Atabeg Ṭughtakīn, the 'father' assigned to a young Seljuq prince who might, and in this case did, marry the prince's mother to become his father-in-law. Riḍwān's Atabeg, on the other hand, deserted his protégé to take Homs for himself, adding to all the problems of ruling the city that Riḍwān had inherited from his Mirdāsid predecessors. Yaghi Siyan, meanwhile, exploited their rivalry in an effort to maintain his hold over the lower valley of the Orontes. There, the picture was complicated by the presence in the Jabal Anṣāriyya, the range of mountains between the valley and the sea, of the Ismāᶜīlī survivors from the Syrian origins of the Mahdī, while the way south up the river to Hamah and Homs was blocked by the fortress of Shayzar, in the hands of the Arab Banū Munqidh. In these circumstances, al-Afḍal took the opportunity to extend the Fatimid dominion up the coast with the recovery of Tyre in 1097, and to push inland from the coastal plain of Palestine with the capture of Jerusalem from the Artuqid Ilghāzī in 1098.

In that year, however, a wholly new factor entered the Syrian equation, a completely unexpected outcome of Alp Arslan's victory at Manzikert. The consequent occupation of Byzantine Anatolia by Turcoman nomads and *ghāzī*-s, warbands of holy warriors, had been followed by the establishment of the Seljuq prince Sulaymān ibn Kutlumish at Nicaea across the Sea of Marmora from Constantinople. His attempt to extend this new dominion eastwards through Cilicia and Antioch into Syria had ended with his defeat and death at the hands of Tutush in 1086. His son Kilij Arslan, however, had returned to Nicaea after the death of Malik Shah to resume his father's empire-building, and this at a time when the Byzantine Emperor Alexius Comnenus had begun to think of a counter-attack with the help of mercenaries from the Frankish West. His appeal to Pope Urban II in 1095 to summon up a force to fight the infidel chimed with the growth of papal enthusiasm for the recovery of Jerusalem for Christianity, and led with remarkable speed to the preaching of what turned out to be the First Crusade at Clermont in France at the end of the year. The response from high and low was immediate. Preceded by a horde of commoners, the more disciplined army of noblemen and knights set out in 1096, recaptured Nicaea in 1097, then fought its way across Anatolia to arrive at Antioch in 1098. Yet another new folk from outside the old Arab empire had entered the original domain of Islam, the latest of such arrivals in the chain of events set off by that empire's revolutionary history, specifically by the challenge of the Fatimids for the Caliphate and Imāmate of the believers. Coupled with the departure of the Nizārīs from the Da^{c}wa, it was an event that set the Fatimid renascence on a new course in a new world, politically and ideologically.

10

The Reorientation of the Dynasty

The Battles of Ramla

The arrival of the Crusaders outside Antioch in 1098 heralded a new departure for the Fatimids as they came to terms with a challenge not only to their empire but to the faith for which they claimed authority. That was all the more so because the challenge was not recognised until it was too late. In sending an embassy to the Franks at Antioch, one that returned to Cairo with presents and a Frankish delegation, al-Afḍal had seen in this attempt by the Byzantine Emperor to recover his lost lands the arrival of a band of Christian warriors comparable to his own Armenians, with whom he could ally in pursuit of his Syrian ambitions. When, after beating off the attack of Kitbugha, the Seljuq Atabeg of Mosul, the Crusaders took the city and turned south, fighting their way down the coast until they took Jerusalem by storm from its Fatimid garrison in July 1099, al-Afḍal brought up his army too late to save it. What was more, at Ascalon he and his troops were routed by a surprise charge of the Frankish knights. His camp was plundered, and while he himself retreated to Cairo, Ascalon was besieged until the Crusaders retreated in their turn, having quarrelled amongst themselves over who should have the city. Like Dandānqān, Ḥaydarān and Manzikert, this was yet another victory that should not have been won, but, like them, proved irreversible. On Christmas Day, Godfrey of Bouillon was crowned King of Jerusalem; and over the next twenty-five years, the formation of the Latin states not only closed the prospect of a Fatimid Syria, but provoked a different attempt by the dynasty to take over the leadership of Islam in war upon the infidel.

The attempt began at once with a determined effort on the part of al-Afḍal to overcome the shame of Ascalon with a fresh campaign to dislodge these novel intruders into the Fatimid sphere. In the event there were three such campaigns, in 1101, 1102 and 1105, punctuated as far as al-Afḍal was concerned by the death at the end of 1101 of his protégé, the Caliph Aḥmad al-Mustaᶜlī, and the accession of his five-year-old son al-Manṣūr under the title of al-Āmir bi-aḥkām Allāh. Since al-Mustaᶜlī had been married to al-Afḍal's sister, the infant was in fact his nephew, and was promptly married to his daughter; almost as his father, then, al-Afḍal placed the child in front of him on his horse as he rode out in procession to display the new monarch to the crowds. The *sijill* which was then read out on the occasion of his presentation to the assembly was not so much an announcement of the succession as a repetition of the appointment of Badr al-Jamālī as Badr al-Mustanṣirī in 1079, the plenipotentiary deputy of the Imām Caliph, all the more strongly since it was evidently composed by the chief secretary Ibn al-Ṣayrafī to al-Afḍal's dictation. Thus the address to all servants and subjects of the dynasty, high and low, was followed by a lament for al-Mustaᶜlī as one who had faithfully followed the ways of his ancestors in government and religion, and the promise of his successor to follow equally faithfully in his path, not least in obeying his father's instruction to maintain al-Afḍal in his high place as ruler on his behalf. Safely back in the palace, then, the little boy could pose no threat to the Sayyid al-Ajall, the Most Mighty Lord, who ruled in his stead as the Sword of the Imām and the Friend of the Commander of the Faithful. What was then required was a military victory.[1]

The campaigns that had begun earlier in the year all centred on Ramla, the old Fatimid capital of Palestine on the plain to the north of Ascalon, the Egyptian bridgehead into Syro-Palestine that served as the Egyptian base. Given that these campaigns were equally part of the history of the Crusades, they were not only recorded in the Latin as well as the Egyptian and Syrian sources, all with different versions. As the battles of Ramla, they figure variously in the modern literature too, which has sought to explain the lack of Egyptian success. Crusading historiography, from Grousset to Runciman, dismissed the Egyptians, either as indolent and unwarlike, or else with a huge but untrained army; Smail considered the army old-fashioned, a stationary target for the charge of the Frankish knights. Hamblin retorted that the

[1] The history of the Crusades is narrated from the Latin and Arabic sources in the standard work of S. Runciman, *A History of the Crusades*, 3 vols. (Cambridge, 1951); see also P. M. Holt, *The Age of the Crusades, The Near East from the Eleventh Century to 1517* (Harlow, 1986). For the Egyptian involvement, beginning with the battles of Ramla, see M. Brett, 'The battles of Ramla (1099–1105)', in U. Vermeulen and D. De Smet (eds), *Egypt and Syria in the Fatimid, Ayyubid and Mamluk Eras*, I (Leuven, 1995), pp. 17–37. For the longer history of the confrontation of the Fatimids with the Crusaders, see M. Brett, 'The Fatimids and the Counter-Crusade, 1099–1171', in U. Vermeulen and K. D'Hulster (eds), *Egypt and Syria in the Fatimid, Ayyubid and Mamluk Eras*, V (Leuven, 1995), pp. 15–25, and 'The Muslim response to the First Crusade', in S. B. Edgington and L. Garcia-Guijarro (eds), *Jerusalem the Golden. The Origins and Impact of the First Crusade* (Turnhout, 2014), pp. 219–34.

Egyptian army was a balanced fighting force that suffered from poor leadership and, more importantly, the disadvantage of arriving too late in response to Crusader aggression. More recently, Lev has selectively agreed with both Runciman and Hamblin, while Köhler has argued that the Fatimids were content with the Kingdom of Jerusalem as a barrier against their enemies the Turks. That is certainly not the case. As ruler on behalf of the Imām Caliph, al-Afḍal had entered into the compact with the Muslim community set out in the Amān of Jawhar at his entry into Egypt, namely to take the community into the *dhimma*, or protection of God. But at the heart of that compact lay the much simpler obligation dating back to the Arab conquests, namely that the Commander of the Faithful would lead the community in war upon the infidel and, equally, defend it from attack. Performance of that duty was a test of fitness for the office. Accordingly, to follow up his triumphal occupation of Egypt and invasion of Syria, Jawhar had sought justification for the conquest in holy war upon Byzantium in the name of al-Mu^{c}izz. Some thirty years later, al-^{c}Azīz himself had ostentatiously entered into the commitment. For al-Afḍal, the minister who had assumed sole responsibility for the Caliphate, the undertaking was crucial to his credibility.

In 1101 the campaign had come too late to prevent the fall of Arsuf and Caesarea, further up the coast from Jaffa, to the Crusaders. It been entrusted to the Amīr Sa^{c}d al-Dawla al-Qawwāsī, the Archer, advancing from Ascalon towards Ramla, the former Fatimid capital of southern Palestine. Ascalon itself, after a year in which the city, along with Arsuf and others along the Palestinian coast, had made overtures to Jerusalem, was now firmly established as a *ribāṭ*, a frontier fortress against the infidel and the base of Fatimid operations, offensive and defensive, for the next fifty years. Ramla was a strategic target, halfway between Jerusalem and Jaffa, the port that was the Frankish kingdom's outlet to the sea and to Europe. On this occasion, the outcome had been an inconclusive battle outside Ramla in which, depending on the sources, either the first Frankish charge was broken while the second succeeded; or the first succeeded until the Muslims rallied and drove the enemy back. Whatever the truth, the Egyptians evidently fought well, although Sa^{c}d al-Dawla fell as a martyr in the holy war, and the army retreated to Ascalon. Jaffa had nevertheless been identified as the principal objective, as much because it threatened the Fatimid hold on the coast as for its value to Jerusalem. This emerged more clearly in the following year, when after the death of al-Musta^{c}lī and the accession of al-Āmir, al-Afḍal sent out a second army under the command of his son, Sharaf al-Ma^{c}ālī, to do battle at Ramla and retake Jaffa in conjunction with the fleet. The campaign almost succeeded. The Franks were slaughtered at Ramla, but King Baldwin managed to escape into Jaffa, while the Egyptian siege of the city by land

and sea was broken by the arrival of a fleet from Europe. Once again the army retreated to Ascalon; but the victory at Ramla was such that it could be celebrated in a despatch from Sharaf al-Maᶜālī, in which he hailed his father's zeal for the defence of Islam, its people, land and religion, for which no sacrifice had been too great. The humiliation of the enemy was his heart's desire. The glory thus won certainly qualified al-Afḍal to appear as the champion of the holy war despite the setbacks of the next two years.[2]

In 1103 Jaffa was again the objective, but the campaign came to nothing, since the commander to the army, Tāj al-ᶜAjam, apparently refused to leave Ascalon to join forces with Ibn Qādūs in command of the fleet off Jaffa. The fleet, essential to the maintenance and defence of the Fatimid position on the Syrian littoral, had previously raised the siege of Acre; but in 1104 the city was left to its fate, its Fatimid governor fleeing first to Damascus and thence to Cairo. With Acre, which had played such a part in the politics of state and empire over the past forty years, the Fatimids lost their capital on the coast, all the more significant since the Franks thereby acquired a major rather than a minor port like Jaffa, one that rapidly became the kingdom's second city. Designated as *thughūr* (sing. *thaghr*), frontiers against the infidel whose inhabitants were committed to the holy war, the remaining Fatimid possessions of Tyre, Sidon and Beirut were left exposed to inevitable attack as the Crusaders fought to secure control of the entire coast. For the moment they survived; and meanwhile what is important is that in 1103 al-Afḍal had written to the Seljuq Duqāq and his Atabeg Ṭughtakīn at Damascus calling upon them for aid in his holy war. On that occasion the Seljuqs excused themselves, but when the request was renewed in 1105, Ṭughtakīn, now sole ruler at Damascus, did send a contingent to the third and final battle in the series, for the good reason that those who opposed his accession at Damascus were in league with the Franks. Honours on both sides, say the Muslim sources, were even, though they admit the battle was lost, and with it, in retrospect, the hope of recovering Jerusalem. From the Fatimid point of view, what matters is the request itself. Couched in the format of the *sijillāt*, the nature of the letters to Damascus may be gauged, and their content reconstructed, from the glorification of al-Afḍal in the despatch from the battlefield in 1102. They would have extolled his achievements as a champion in the holy war as a prelude to the invitation to join with him in its pursuit. What is significant is the fact that he was summoning a previous enemy to become his ally, as the lieutenant of the Caliph of God and His Prophet, in the discharge of

[2] A fragment from the Genizah material, the despatch is published by G. Khan in *Arabic Legal and Administrative Documents in the Cambridge Genizah Collections* (Cambridge, 1993), no. 111, p. 428.

the duty of the Commander of the Faithful to lead all Muslims against the infidel. While the proclamation of al-Āmir had upheld the supremacy of the dynasty in its exclusive claim to power and authority, the overture to Damascus signified not only the abandonment of any attempt to reconquer Syria for the empire, but an ideological shift away from the confrontational approach of the past towards a more oecumenical appeal to the generality of Islam to join in the common cause. From that point of view, the Crusade had given the dynasty fresh purpose at a time when the political scope of the Dawla and the sectarian scope of the Daᶜwa had been severely curtailed by invasion and schism.

The Reform of Badr's Regime

That purpose was pursued for the next fifty years or more; the Fatimids were permanently at war with the Crusaders in a way that the Syrians on the far side of the Latin kingdom were not. Under al-Afḍal that war was vigorously conducted in raids and sorties out of Ascalon, together with naval expeditions to defend the cities of the coast; for twenty years or so, said Ibn al-Ṣayrafī, he never ceased to exert himself in *jihād* against the Franks. War, however, is costly, and the effort required was accompanied by a major military and fiscal reform, one that revealed the extent to which Egypt was still recovering from the crisis of the *fitna* and *shidda* some thirty to forty years previously. What was involved was a revision of the *iqṭāᶜāt*, Badr's allocation of lands and their revenues to his soldiery in payment for their services. That in turn went along with a rectification of the growing discrepancy between the lunar and solar years, the one used for accountancy, the other for the assessment and collection of agricultural revenues. The architect of these reforms was not al-Afḍal himself but his lieutenant, al-Baṭāʾiḥī. Son of the Amīr Nūr al-Dawla Abū Shujāʾ al-Āmirī, in other words a scion of the military elite, al-Baṭāʾiḥī may not himself have been a military man, but as al-Afḍal's indispensable adjutant, was promoted to the new rank and title of al-Qāʾid, the Commander. He was taken up by al-Afḍal in 1107 following the dismissal of his predecessor, the *ghulām* or *mamlūk* Tāj al-Maᶜālī al-Mukhtār, disgraced for abusing the trust of the great man. With the boy Caliph secluded in the palace, al-Afḍal was in fact ruling in patriarchal style through the household he had established, first in the Dār al-Wizāra, the palace he built for himself in al-Qāhira to the north of Great Eastern Palace of the Caliphs, and subsequently in the significantly named Dār al-Mulk, or Seat of the Kingdom, the palace he had built to the south of Fusṭāṭ on the bank of the Nile.[3] At the same time, to establish the

[3] Cf. Bloom, *Arts of the City Victorious*, p. 129.

essential link between this household and the administration, al-Baṭāʾiḥī's promotion was coupled with the creation of a new office to oversee the finances, the Dīwān al-Taḥqīq, or Office of Verification, placed in charge of the Christian Yuhannā ibn Abīʾl-Layth.[4] The creation of this Dīwān points to a new determination to get to grips with the problems of government, while the appointment of a Christian as its head indicates its political purpose, to separate the running of the administration from the making of policy. How the previous conflation of the two under the Wazīrs of the Pen had worked out in practice under the overrule of Badr is not clear, but this solution to the problem of government enabled al-Baṭāʾiḥī, charged by al-Afḍal with the management of his kingdom, to act with a speed that suggests that his proposals for the reorganisation of the system had led to his appointment.[5]

The information about the reforms he carried out comes from al-Maqrīzī, but derives from the narrative of al-Baṭāʾiḥī's career written at the end of the century by his son, al-Maʾmūn ibn al-Baṭāʾiḥīʾ. In principle, it had always been necessary, after thirty-three years during which the number of lunar years was one year ahead of the solar year, to operate a *taḥwīl*, a conversion, to bring the accountancy of the lunar year into line with the collection of the *kharāj*, or land tax, by the solar year, a procedure which in this case had seemingly been neglected for so long that the discrepancy ran to four years. By what devices the discrepancy had previously been accommodated is unknown; but in this case the matching of the agricultural cycle from August to August 1107–8 with the coincidental lunar year of 501 was accompanied by yet another procedure, a *rawk*, or cadastral survey of the land for the purpose of tax assessment. That in turn was a procedure that should in principle have been carried out every thirty years to bring the *kharāj* into line with the productivity of the land. That kind of assessment was supposedly carried out every year by the taxmen; but the *rawk* made in that same year of 1107–8 had an additional purpose. It went together with a reallocation of the *iqṭāʿāt*, the land grants to the military which gave to each of the recipients a specific income ffrom a specific source, while serving as so many tax farms on behalf of the fisc. But after thirty or so years, and with the army on a war footing, the *iqṭāʿāt* themselves had changed in value, some more, some less productive, making the higher ranks that much richer than before and the lesser that much poorer, while the arrears owed to the state from valuations

4 For the creation of this Dīwān, see Sayyid, *Les Fatimides en Égypte*, p. 161.

5 For the reforms of al-Baṭāʾihī, following on from those of Badr, see M. Brett, 'The way of the peasant' and 'The origins of the Mamlūk military system in the Fatimid period', in U. Vermeulen and D. De Smet (eds), *Egypt and Syria in the Fatimid, Ayyubid and Mamluk Eras*, I (Leuven, 1995), pp. 39–52, at pp. 41–4.

that were too high could only be collected by coercion, and thus at great expense. To solve the problem, which clearly affected the morale of the army at a critical juncture as well as the income of the state, the original *iqṭāᶜāt* were cancelled and the land put up for auction for what the soldiers themselves reckoned it was worth. Somewhat obscurely, then, the lesser ranks were invited to bid for the lands previously in possession of the higher ranks, up to a specified amount, and were then confirmed in its possession for thirty years. Meanwhile, the higher ranks were invited to bid for the lands formerly held by the lesser, lands that were declared to be extensively uncultivated, with few peasants and yields far below the original assessment. They nevertheless did so, acquiring such of those lands as they wanted at their own estimate of the value to them. The result, it was alleged by al-Baṭāʾiḥī's son in his account of his father's career written later in the century, was all-round satisfaction, with lands that had not been taken up by the soldiery returned to the direct administration of the state.

It is clear from this account that the underlying problem was a shortage of cultivators. One of the original purposes of the *iqṭāᶜāt* had been to provide some framework for the return of a much reduced peasant population to the cultivation of lands gone to waste in the course of the *shidda*. This had evidently been successful to the extent that the better land in the possession of the higher ranks had been recolonised, but only at the expense of the land in the possession of the lower ranks, which had been drained of its occupants. The imbalance created in this way by a population rising back to the average of four to five million which was characteristic of the mediaeval period created its own difficulty for the state in the land still left to be brought back into taxable cultivation. As far as the state was concerned, the situation was further complicated by the fact that the higher ranks had meanwhile taken the opportunity to develop their own private properties on their holdings, with gardens and presses most probably for sugarcane and olive oil. These they were allowed to keep in return for the appropriate tax. But, quite evidently, they had taken advantage of their *iqṭāᶜāt* to slip into the practices of the landholding aristocracy of the dynasty that dated back to the time of Ibn Killis, with consequences that became apparent over the next fifty years. Meanwhile, the need of the state to extend the area under cultivation led to the construction of a new canal in the Delta, branching out from the Damietta arm of the river into the Sharqiyya, the district to the east. Begun in 1113 on the initiative of al-Baṭāʾiḥī under the auspices of al-Afḍal, this was an expensive undertaking whose cost was disputed between the tax-farmer, the Jewish Ibn al-Munajjā, and the state in the person of Ibn Abīʾl-Layth; but on completion was ceremoniously opened in the presence of the Caliph. And in 1119 al-Baṭāʾiḥī returned to the problem of the calendar with an ambitious project for an observatory that would further refine the astronomical tables compiled 100 years earlier at the behest of al-Ḥākim, and supersede those compiled in Baghdad 200 years before, a feat of engineering that was never in fact completed.[6] Nevertheless, while al-Afḍal undoubtedly took the credit, in al-Baṭāʾiḥī he had a minister who set his reign over Egypt on a firm basis at a critical time in the history of both Dawla and Daʿwa.

The Conflict with Jerusalem

Faced with the relentless consolidation of the Frankish presence in Palestine/Syria, the cause of the Dawla had fused with that of the Daʿwa in the call to holy war in the defence of Islam. In Egypt itself, the army was redeveloped, not only through the revision of the *iqṭāʿāt* as the basis for an effective force of cavalry. Apart from the Armenians, the Black troops who continued to provide the infantry and the light cavalry of the tribal Arabs, al-Afḍal set out to create a cavalry elite from the sons of soldiers and other servants of the dynasty, recruiting them as boys and training them up in horsemanship and archery to match the horse archers of the Seljuqs and Turcomans. This move to bring the Fatimid army into line with the forces of these erstwhile enemies involved the establishment of seven *ḥujarāt*, or barracks, as palace schools for the boys, who after graduating continued to be called *ṣibyān* (sing. *ṣabīy*), or youths, rather than the equivalent term *ghulām/ghilmān*. Such an education compared with the traditional upbringing of the *ghulām* in the household of his master, but in its state-sponsored formality looked backwards as well as forwards to previous Fatimid practice. For the moment, however, it served to produce regiments of ceremonial guardsmen not as yet employed in the field.[7] There, the soldiery and the fleet continued to operate out of Ascalon, with the aim of preventing or, as it transpired, delaying the fall of the remaining cities of the Palestinian and Syrian coast. As far as these cities were concerned, Hamblin's contention that the Fatimid forces, reacting to aggression, typically arrived too late on the scene has a point. By land, however, Ascalon remained a thorn in the Frankish side, a *ribāṭ*, or frontier fortress, for the conduct of the holy war upon the infidel. Its purpose was not so much to win a decisive victory as to fulfil the obligation of *jihād*, one that made the city all the more important, since the danger it posed to the route from Jaffa to Jerusalem made its capture a Frankish objective. The danger was immediately demonstrated a year after the third battle of Ramla, when in 1106 a squadron out of Ascalon massacred pilgrims en route to Jerusalem, overran Ramla,

6 Cf. Halm, *The Fatimids and their Traditions of Learning*, pp. 87–90.
7 Cf. Lev, *State and Society*, pp. 100–2.

routed an expedition from Jaffa and rode up towards Jerusalem. In 1107 the target was Hebron to the south of Jerusalem, and in 1110 the Egyptians reached the walls of Jerusalem itself. Meanwhile, as the coastal cities came under attack, the fleet was equally deployed. Constructed in the arsenal at Fusṭāṭ, it was large but not excessively so by comparison with the Venetian, Genoese and other fleets that now sustained the Frankish dominions; in 1115 some seventy galleys and sailing ships were counted off Jaffa.[8] Typically doubling as warships and supply ships for the beleaguered ports, their building, maintenance and regular expeditions represented a major charge on the state, all the more because of the need to replace those lost in action. As the only Muslim navy in the eastern Mediterranean, they were evidently at a disadvantage, not simply numerically, but because of the distance over which they were required to operate, all the more because of the prevalence of the north wind down the Syrian coast. What had so opportunely blown for Badr al-Jamālī in 1074 now frequently prevented their sailing. Moreover, for a fighting force, the professionalism of this fleet is not clear. Oarsmen may have been press-ganged; the proportion of soldiers to seamen is unknown, and likewise the command structure. However it was manned, in the circumstances it turned in a creditable performance over a long period of time, arguing for considerable motivation on the part of its crew, quite apart from the persistence of al-Afḍal in sending it out year after year.

Ascalon

Ascalon, on the coast of Palestine almost due west of Jerusalem, was the first major city on the coastal route from Egypt through Jaffa, Acre, Tyre, Sidon, Beirut and Lattakia to Antioch. At the same time it controlled the route to Ramla, some twenty-five miles away on the coastal plain to the north, which served as the Fatimid capital of southern Palestine until the Turcoman invasion and conquest of Jerusalem in the 1070s. During the reign of al-ᶜAzīz it was described by the geographer al-Muqaddasī as a fine city, well fortified and strongly garrisoned, with a Great Mosque paved with marble in the cloth market, and a silk industry and a flax industry based on the import into Syria of Egyptian flax, as well as a fertile hinterland. At the same time it played an essential military role in the ongoing Fatimid struggle to secure and extend their dominion in Syria, especially in defence against, for example, the invasions of the Bedouin Ṭāyy under their Jarrāḥid chiefs in the 1010s and 20s. After

[8] Ibid., pp. 107–14.

Badr al-Jamālī took power in Egypt, and Syria apart from the coastal cities fell to the Seljuqs and Turcomans, it became the lynchpin of his efforts in the 1080s to recover Damascus, as well as the location chosen for his own glorification as the champion of the dynasty. His construction of a congregational mosque and shrine for the head of the martyred Ḥusayn was duly recorded in the long inscription on the *minbar*, or pulpit, that memorialised his deed and devotion.

Left by Badr at his death in 1094, Ascalon was thus not only the sole fortified city in southern Palestine, guarding the route in and out of Egypt to and from Syria, but a symbol of the dynasty soon to become a *thaghr*, a frontier fortress in the holy war upon the infidel. The disintegration of Seljuq Syria following the departure of its conqueror Tutush was the opportunity for Badr's son al-Afḍal to take Jerusalem from the Turcoman Artūqids in 1098, but equally for the armies of the First Crusade to take it from him in 1099 as the capital of their new Kingdom. Ascalon then immediately became the focal point of the conflict between the Fatimids and the Franks with the surprise and rout of al-Afḍal's army outside the city. The massacre that ensued was not only that of the Fatimid infantry, but also that of the citizens, both tradesmen and the *aḥdāth*, or militias. While al-Afḍal retired to Egypt, the city was besieged by the Crusaders, who settled on a ransom of 20,000 dīnārs; but having quarrelled among themselves, left without the money. The episode is instructive not only for the vulnerability of an infantry army, unsupported by the light cavalry of the Bedouin, to the charge of the mailed knights – the new factor in the warfare of Islam – but for the participation in the battle with the infidel of the townsfolk. As the Fatimids had discovered at Damascus, with their militias these citizens were politically active, and as the Crusaders were to discover at Tyre, fighters for the faith; at Ascalon in 1111 they proved it with the massacre of the governor and the Frankish knights he had brought from Jerusalem in an attempt to take the city over to the other side. Together with the Crusaders' demand for a ransom in 1099, the attempt was symptomatic of the other face of the confrontation with the Christian invaders, a willingness on both sides to deal with each other to their own advantage.

That willingness was not shared by the Fatimids themselves. Left completely isolated by the fall of the other cities of the coast to the Franks, Ascalon continued to develop as a fortress. As described by the Latin historian William of Tyre in the middle of the twelfth century, its double wall on the landward side ran in a semicircle around the city, with towers and four gates facing up and down the coast, inland towards Jerusalem and out onto the port. It was a major command for the Fatimid forces, with a large garrison regularly relieved from Egypt. Its population was initially swollen by refugees from Ramla; thereafter it served as the heavily guarded entrance to Egypt through which passed the trade with Syria, continuous despite the ongoing warfare with Jerusalem. For the Crusader kingdom, it was a prospective acquisition to round off its territory, but at the same time a menace by land and sea, an advance post for the Fatimid fleet and a base for repeated raids towards Jaffa and Jerusalem. Thus in 1126 it was granted in advance to Hugh, lord of Jaffa; from 1136 it was targeted by the building of a ring of castles ending in 1150 at Gaza to the south, until in 1153 it succumbed to an eight-month siege by the King himself and his whole army. As well as the garrison, the entire population, with all its belongings, was allowed to retire to Egypt, together with the head of Ḥusayn. From being both the symbol and the instrument of the Caliphate's stance in the holy war, Ascalon not only became a Christian city; its occupation cleared the way for the Frankish invasions of Egypt in the 1160s.

For the references to al-Muqaddasī, see M. D. Yusuf, *Economic Survey of Syria During the Tenth and Eleventh Centuries* (Berlin, 1985), pp. 65–6, 127, 131, 173; for the reference to William of Tyre, *Chronicon*, see A. V. Murray, *The Crusades: an Encyclopedia*, 4 vols (Santa Barbara, CA, Denver, CO and Oxford, 2006), vol. I, s.v. Ascalon.

Thus, after the governor of Sidon had bought off King Baldwin in 1106, when the city was eventually besieged by Baldwin in 1108, the Fatimid fleet defeated that of the Italians outside the harbour, while Ṭughtakīn advanced from Damascus. Not only was the siege of Sidon lifted, but Tripoli was occupied by the Fatimids in the absence of Fakhr al-Mulk, the last of the Banū ᶜAmmār, who in face of the threat of conquest had left the city to seek the aid of the Seljuq Sultan and ᶜAbbasid Caliph at Baghdad. Fakhr's family and treasures were shipped off to Egypt by the new governor, Sharaf al-Dawla. But when the next year, 1109, Tripoli was besieged by sea and by land by the combined forces of the Franks from Jerusalem, Antioch and Edessa, the north wind prevented the arrival of the Egyptians, and Tripoli became yet another Crusader principality. In 1110 it was the turn of Beirut and finally that of Sidon. In both cases, Fatimid squadrons sailing this time out of Tyre were driven off by fleets from Genoa and Pisa, Norway and Venice, and while Beirut was stormed, Sidon surrendered on terms at the end of the year. What may have seemed an unstoppable career of Frankish conquest nevertheless came to a halt over the next two years, in 1111 and 1112. Fearing an immediate attack after the fall of Sidon, Shams al-Khilāfa, governor of Ascalon with responsibility for the government of Tyre, attempted to buy Baldwin off with a sum to be levied from the merchants of Tyre. But faced with deposition by al-Afḍal for this truck with the enemy, he fled to Jerusalem, returning with a Frankish force of some 300 men to garrison the citadel. But the citizens revolted, killing Shams and all his Franks, leaving Ascalon to resume its strategic role in al-Afḍal's holy war. Meanwhile, as an instance of popular feeling against the Franks, its citizen uprising was matched later in the year by the resistance of the citizens of Tyre to a major assault by Baldwin. In this case the Fatimid fleet was not involved; but Baldwin himself had no help from the sea to clinch its investment, and in 1112 the siege was lifted after a heroic defence as Ṭughtakīn came once again from Damascus with his own forces and a horde of volunteers. The outcome was the replacement of the Fatimid governor ᶜIzz al-Mulk with a Damascan Turk, while the Friday prayer continued to be said in the Fatimid name. The city was resupplied by the Fatimid fleet, which came with presents for the new governor, Masᶜūd, and for Ṭughtakīn himself. The arrangement was a further step in the alliance between Cairo and Damascus, one that al-Afḍal could claim for himself as an acknowledgement of his leadership in the holy war.

Ṭughtakīn, on the other hand, had more pressing problems to deal with, as northern Syria continued to be fought over by the Franks at Jerusalem, Antioch and Edessa; by Riḍwān at Aleppo; and by successive invaders from Iraq commissioned by the Great Seljuq Sultan Muḥammad Tapar: Mawḍūd, the governor of Mosul, in 1111–13 and Bursūq ibn Bursūq, the governor of Hamadhān, in 1115. With Baldwin himself committed to the many-sided conflict, in 1113 the Egyptians raided out of Ascalon as far as Jerusalem, and in 1115 nearly captured Jaffa. In that year, however, Baldwin turned back to dealing with Egypt, setting out to reach the Gulf of ᶜAqaba and cut the route from Damascus to Egypt, together with the pilgrimage route to Mecca. Having begun the building of the castle of Montreal to the south-east of the Dead Sea, in 1116 he arrived on the Gulf at ᶜAyla (ᶜAqaba), which he garrisoned and fortified together with the offshore island of Jazīra Farᵓūn. A further castle was then constructed on the coast to the south of Tyre, before in 1118 he invaded Egypt itself with a substantial force of 200 cavalry and 400 infantry. Farama on the coast to the east of the Delta was taken and its mosques destroyed, but the expedition turned back before reaching the Nile, cut short by his illness; he died at al-ᶜArīsh on the coast on the way home. Baldwin's purpose – a demonstration, a retaliation, a reconnaissance – remains obscure. But the destruction of the mosques at Farama would indicate a recognition of the religious dimension of the conflict, of the stand taken by al-Afḍal on the holiness of a war conducted in fulfilment of the duty of the Caliph. It certainly prompted a counter-demonstration – the advance of an Egyptian army up the coast from Ascalon to Ashdod, to confront without giving battle to the forces of Jerusalem mustered by the new king, Baldwin II. Both sides were evidently reluctant to engage, the Franks not least because of the threat from Ṭughtakīn in their rear; and the stand-off which lasted throughout the summer of 1118 served primarily to bring hostilities, for the moment, to an honourable close, one that, from the Fatimid point of view, preserved the image of the Imām Caliph and his minister as the champions of Islam against the infidel.

Nubia and the Yemen

Meanwhile, to the south, up the Nile and down the Red Sea, the policies put in place by Badr to secure the empire and its interests in Nubia, Ethiopia and the Yemen were actively pursued by his son. Where Ascalon served as the forward station of empire to the north, to the south the same purpose was served by Badr's selection of Qūṣ in the vicinity of Luxor as the seat of the military government of the southern frontier. Its governor did not only command the route up the Nile through Aswan to the Nubian kingdom of Muqurra. He controlled the route through the port of ᶜAydhāb to Mecca on the one hand, Aden and the Yemen on the other. More so than the route up the Nile, this was the vital route for the lucrative trade with Mecca and the Indian Ocean, in which the dynasty and its personnel were heavily involved and which in large measure compensated for the problems of the agricultural economy. Not only, therefore, did it sustain the prosperity of Egypt beneath the ripples on the political surface, it made of Qūṣ a second capital of the country and the empire in its dealings with its southern flank. As far as Nubia and Ethiopia were concerned, those dealings continued to involve the Church, whose loyalty was only strengthened by the military and religious confrontation of the Fatimid Caliphate with the Christian Franks. In the course of that confrontation, the Coptic Christian population of Egypt sided with the dynasty for religious as well as patriotic reasons. In *History of the Coptic Patriarchs* the author adds a postscript to the biography of the Patriarch Michael, 1093–1102, to the effect that since the Franks took Jerusalem, the Jacobite Copts have been unable to make the pilgrimage, since in the eyes of the Franks they are hated infidels. The noble lord al-Afḍal has meanwhile spared no expense in fighting them in holy war, but has been left with only Ascalon and Tyre in the hands of his governors, such are the decrees of God. Al-Afḍal himself maintained his father's patronage of the Church, to the extent, we are told, of relaxing in the monastery of St Mercurius to the south of the capital, after its restoration by two Christian officials. The Church in turn was the medium of the relationship with Ethiopia, although the record is such that only one incident is known.[9] In 1101, twelve years after the affair

[9] Cf. Brett, 'The Coptic Church in the Fatimid empire', pp. 58–9.

Figure 10.1 Bāb al-Futūḥ, or Gate of Victories: archway. Photo: Bernard O'Kane.

The interior of the arch of the passage through the Gate between its two massive towers. Together with the Bāb al-Naṣr, the Bāb al-Futūḥ controlled the entrance into al-Qāhira through the northern wall.

of Severus in 1089, the King of Ethiopia sent to request a new Metropolitan. No candidate, however, presented himself, and the monk eventually sent by the Patriarch as the new Metropolitan George I proved incompetent and venal. He was sent back to Egypt with a letter of complaint from the King to al-Afḍal, who imprisoned him. It would seem that Badr's aggressive approach had given way to a more cordial relationship between the two monarchies which probably reflected their commercial interests.

In the case of the Nubian kingdom of Muqurra, a much more serious incident enabled al-Afḍal not only to reaffirm Badr's patronage of the Christian state, but to reassert the power of Egypt through a forcible renewal of the Baqṭ. The King of Muqurra, perhaps the Basil who in 1089 had sent a present to Badr together with the son of his predecessor for consecration as a bishop, had in 1107–8 prepared to invade Egypt, prompting an order to the governor of Qūṣ to invade Nubia. This dramatic development, however, was linked to a struggle for the Nubian throne, in which the King in question was killed by his brother, and an infant, probably the future George IV, put on the throne by his mother. She in turn wrote to al-Afḍal begging off the Egyptian invasion, and requesting his favour and protection. The invasion accordingly went ahead as an expedition that handed down al-Afḍal's terms in the form of a text of the Baqṭ, which although it purported to reproduce the original dictated by ᶜAbd Allāh ibn Abī Sarḥ in 652, spoke in Fatimid fashion of the Dhimma of God, requiring the annual delivery to the Imām of the Muslims of the 360 male and female slaves, all physically perfect, and stipulating that the Nubians maintain the mosque at (Old) Dongola clean and properly lit, and otherwise give every necessary assistance to Muslims in their territory. The terms recall those that Badr had endeavoured to impose upon the Ethiopians, and apart from their symbolic value as an expression of Fatimid suzerainty, could obviously serve to justify future Egyptian intervention. None such, however, appears to have been necessary; no more is heard of the matter, whether or not the tribute was paid, or the other provisions of the treaty carried out. The only record is the tombstone of King George IV, recording his birth in 1106, his accession in 1131 and his death in 1158, found in a church in the Wadi Natrun to the west of the Delta. Reminiscent as it is of the reception, death and burial of King Solomon at Cairo in 1080, the inscription and its location suggests a continuation of the relationship of the kingdom to the Caliphate which had been established under Badr. As, probably, in the case of Ethiopia, the requirement to favour the Muslims in Nubia points to the reaffirmation of the long-standing commercial relationship between the two states, while the treaty itself confirmed the inclusion of the piously Christian Nubian monarchy within the scope of the Fatimid Dawla.[10]

Beyond the Red Sea, on the other hand, in the Yemen, Iran and round again to Syria, the relationship continued to evolve in the aftermath of the death of al-Mustanṣir and the consequent schism. In the Yemen, following its acceptance of the Mustaᶜlian succession, that evolution began at the time of the Crusaders' arrival in 1098 with the deaths of Arwā's nominal husband Sabaᵓ and of the Dāᶜī Lamak ibn Mālik. The death of Sabaᵓ left her in undisputed charge of the state and the mission; that of Lamak was followed by her appointment of Lamak's son Yaḥyā as his successor. With no further guidance from the Imām himself after the death of al-Mustanṣir, and without apparent intervention on the part of al-Afḍal for the next twenty years, the standards of the Daᶜwa were then upheld by Yaḥyā, while the Dawla, on the other hand,

[10] Ibid., pp. 58–9, and H. Halm, 'Der Nubische *baqṭ*', in U. Vermeulen and D. De Smet (eds), *Egypt and Syria in the Fatimid, Ayyubid and Mamluk Eras*, II (Leuven, 1998), pp. 63–103, at pp. 94–8.

gradually separated out into its component parts. Arwā continued to preside from her palatial Dār al-ᵓIzz in the centrally situated capital of Dhū Jibla. But while they remained faithful to the Ismāᶜīlī Da ᶜwa, Ḥamdānids from ᶜAlī al-Ṣulayḥī's own clan took possession of his original capital of Sanᶜa, while two Ḥamdānid brothers installed by al-Mukarram at Aden in 1083 had founded what was fast becoming an independent, Zurayᶜid, dynasty that thrived on the intercontinental trade through the port. In 1119 al-Afḍal was sufficiently concerned with the situation to take the unprecedented step of sending one ᶜAlī ibn Najīb al-Dawla with an escort of twenty of his Ḥujarī household cavalry to take the country in hand. In place of the commands and instructions that had characterised the relationship of the Imāmate and Caliphate with its Yemeni vassals since the death of al-Ṣulayḥī, the despatch of such a legate to take charge of their affairs is evidence of the importance attached by al-Afḍal on behalf of the Fatimids to the preservation of this, the centrepiece of the empire since the mid-eleventh century crisis. From Dhū Jibla, with the support of other Ḥamdānids and their tribal cavalry, Ibn Najīb al-Dawla set out to stabilise the situation on behalf of the queen.

Iran and the Daᶜwa Jadīda

By contrast, the breakaway regime of Ḥasan-i Ṣabbāḥ at Alamut was not only holding its own in Iran, but gaining a foothold in Syria, entering Aleppo, attempting to establish itself at Damascus and taking over the Ismāᶜīlī communities in the mountainous north-west, the region of the Orontes Valley. With its recourse to assassination as its weapon in its war upon the Seljuqs, it played a lively part in their struggles over the succession to the Sultanate, while Ḥasan-i Ṣabbāḥ on behalf of his hidden Imām threw down a major challenge to the Sunnī orthodoxy promoted by Niẓām al-Mulk. Thus, following the acquisition by the Ismāᶜīlīs of the fortresses of Girdkuh at the far end of the Elburz and of Shahdiz and Khalinjan outside Isfahan, their *fidāᵓī*-s, 'self-sacrificers' or assassins, posed a serious threat to the entourage of the Seljuq Sultan Berk Yaruq, whose members went about in arms and armour in fear of murder. Berk Yaruq's response was nevertheless limited, preoccupied as he was with the challenge of his half-brother and rival Muḥammad Tapar for the Sultanate. But having for the moment defeated and driven Muḥammad away to Khurāsān in 1100, in 1101 he countenanced an alliance with Sanjar, a second half-brother who was the ruler of Khurāsān, to attack the Ismāᶜīlī strongholds in Quhistān. Two campaigns mounted by Sanjar in 1101 and 1104 succeeded in destroying the Ismāᶜīlī fortress of Tabas, but still left the Ismāᶜīlīs in possession of the region. Berk Yaruq himself had all suspected Ismāᶜīlīs massacred in Isfahan itself and in Baghdad, but not until after his death in 1105 did his successor,

Muḥammad Tapar, lay siege in 1107 to the castle of Shahdiz outside his capital Isfahan, the most obvious challenge to his Sultanate. Even then, it was a negotiated surrender, with numbers of the garrison leaving for Quhistān in the east and the fortress of Arrajān in the mountains to the west, before its commander, the Dāᶜī Ibn ᶜAṭṭāsh, finally rejected the terms and held out until the citadel was stormed and he himself was executed, flayed alive. At the same time the new Sultan turned his attention to Alamut itself. In the same year, 1107, the fortress was invested by his Wazīr, Aḥmad, son of the great Wazīr Niẓām al-Mulk, but to no avail, despite the hardship caused. Instead, every year from 1109 onwards, the valley of Rūdbār was laid waste to starve the Ismāᶜīlīs out, until in 1117 Lamasar and Alamut were systematically besieged. But the siege was lifted in 1118 on the death of Muḥammad and the accession of his son Maḥmūd; and thereafter, the quarrels of the Seljuqs over the succession, eventually resolved in favour of Sanjar, left Ḥasan-i Ṣabbāḥ securely ensconced in his citadels.[11]

Despite the difficulties of these ten years, Ḥasan's campaign had continued. He was unchallenged as the Ḥujja, or supreme representative, of the Nizārī Imām, whoever he might be – Nizār himself, who had escaped death and was in hiding, or his equally well-concealed son or grandson. His Daᶜwa Jadīda, or New Calling, had driven the assassinations which, given the difficulty of striking at men in armour, had targeted the secretaries, judiciary and scholars of the Seljuq state, among them the Qāḍī of Isfahan and the Qāḍī of Nishapur. Meanwhile, the infiltration of his faithful into Syria had begun at Aleppo, with its large Shīᶜite element, and in the Jabal Summaq and Jabal Bahra, the ranges on either side of the Orontes as far south as Homs, with their various communities of Ismāᶜīlīs and Shīᶜite Nuṣayrīs or ᶜAlawites. At Aleppo his missionaries had found a patron in the Seljuq Riḍwān, anxious for any allies in the complicated struggle for power in Syria, and who was most probably behind their assassination of his former Atabeg, Janāḥ al-Dawla, Amīr of Homs, at Friday prayer in 1103. And both Riḍwān and Ṭughtakīn at Damascus were from their point of view well rid of Mawḍūd, the Atabeg of Mosul, murdered in Damascus in 1113 at the end of his failed attempt on behalf of Muḥammad Tapar to lead a coalition against the Crusaders. But the mission of Ḥasan's envoys, the Dāᶜī al-Ḥākim al-Munajjim followed by Abū Ṭāhir, working from their base in Aleppo, failed to secure an equivalent of Alamut or Shahdiz. In 1106 Abū Ṭāhir successfully contrived the capture of Afāmiya/Apamea on the Orontes from its Fatimid Ismāᶜīlī warlord Khalaf ibn Mulāᵓib, but was driven out by Tancred, the Frankish prince of Antioch;

[11] Cf. Lewis, *The Assassins*, pp. 49–58.

again in 1114, Ismāʿīlīs who had been won for the cause only briefly captured and held the fortress of Shayzar. And after the death of Riḍwān in 1113, his son and successor Alp Arslan, seemingly in response to the demand of the Sultan, Muḥammad Tapar, acted together with the *rāʾīs* Ibn Badīʿ at the head of the city militia to execute Abū Ṭāhir and his fellows, and drive out his followers. Nevertheless, by the end of the decade, the Nizārīs were not only permanently ensconced in Syria, but back along the route to Iran, and were preparing to turn their attention to Damascus.[12]

Behind all the terrorism, subversion and empire-building, in his Daʿwa Jadīda Ḥasan-i Ṣabbāḥ had confronted not only the political establishment of Sunnism, but also its doctrine in a way that went far beyond the challenge offered by the Fatimids. In his endeavour to come to terms with the physical absence of the Imām, he had asked the question of how in that case the Imām was to be known. The Fatimids themselves had answered that question to their own satisfaction, if not to that of their opponents, by a variety of appeals, in the first place to the proposition that God would not have left His community without a successor to His Prophet to guide the faithful. That proposition was elaborated by the doctrine of the Seven Prophets, each followed by Seven Imāms, a scheme encapsulated in a Neoplatonic cosmogony and cosmology, and taught principally by analogy and scriptural reference. The identification of this scheme with the Fatimids was effected through the tradition of the designation of ʿAlī by Muḥammad as his successor, and thence its perpetuation through the designation of the son by the father in the direct line of descent from ʿAlī. As he sought to explain his rejection of the Fatimid Imāmate in Cairo, the point for Ḥasan-i Ṣabbāḥ was not that all this was necessarily wrong, but that its acceptance relied upon the decision of the believer to recognise the truth of what he was told – a decision that in effect placed the believer in the impossible position of sitting in judgment on the divine dispensation. Behind any such decision, he proposed that there had to be a recognition on the part of the believer of his own spiritual need for guidance, when in the darkness of his ignorance the Imām was self-evident as the sun to the eye. In this, Ḥasan-i Ṣabbāḥ was carrying to its conclusion the ecstatic adoration lavished upon the Imām in the person of al-Mustanṣir by al-Shirāzī in his poetry, which describes his own journey into the physical and spiritual presence of God's appointed. In the absence of the physical presence of the Imām, his spiritual presence was all the more real, and so too was the absolute authority of his direction, and the submission this required.[13]

[12] Ibid., pp. 97–104.
[13] Cf. M. G. S. Hodgson, *The Order of Assassins* (The Hague, 1955), pp. 54–61.

Ḥasan's writings have survived only in quotation from an autobiography and a theological work by his contemporary al-Shahrastānī, the Sunnī author of a list of religions and sects, but the challenge they laid down was not only to the Fatimids in Egypt, but still more so to the Sunnī establishment, centred as its teachings were upon the traditional authority of the jurists in their different schools of law. Their teaching of Sunnī doctrine in the *madrasa*-s founded by Niẓām al-Mulk had been designed to refute the similarly traditional beliefs of the Shīᶜa, Twelvers and Seveners alike; but Ḥasan's Daᶜwa Jadīda required a different answer. That was eventually provided by the celebrated theologian al-Ghazālī, author of the *Iḥyāᵓ ᶜulūm al-Dīn*, or Revival of the Sciences of Religion, and canonised as the Mujaddid, the Renewer of Islam, at the beginning of the sixth century of the Hijra. Eventually, because after teaching at the Niẓāmiyya in Baghdad from 1091 to 1095, al-Ghazālī withdrew into seclusion for many years to explore the reaches of mysticism beyond the rules of jurisprudence and the logic of theology. But when the answer finally came in works beginning with his *Munqidh min al-dalal*, or Deliverance from Error, it conceded the two main points of Ḥasan's doctrine, the necessity of an infallible instructor, whose acceptance depended upon immediate recognition. Comparing it to dreaming, that recognition he called *dhawq*, or taste; but what was to be recognised in this way was not the Imām in succession to the Prophet, but the legacy of Qurᵓān and Ḥadīth, a Scripture that constituted his infallible and self-evident instruction, accessible to everyone who sought the light in the darkness. The dialectic of claim and counter-claim that had attended the rise of the Fatimids had not only provoked the political crisis of the mid-eleventh century, but had also led to a new departure for Islam as a whole.[14]

The Restoration of the Caliph

Meanwhile, in 1121, al-Afḍal himself was assassinated, at the third attempt, but by whom is not clear. All three attacks were made in the street in the course of his routine or ceremonial rides; the first by a single person in 1115 and the second by three in 1118 both miscarried. Protected by his guards, he was unharmed. Nevertheless, they were not without consequence. Al-Afḍal was not well, obliged to delegate the writing of his calligraphic signature to his brother Jaᶜfar, and in 1115 he ceremonially appointed his son Samāᵓ al-Mulk, his commander in the battles of Ramla, as his deputy. The appointment was reminiscent of Badr's previous appointment of al-Afḍal as his heir,

[14] Cf. M. Brett, 'The Lamp of the Almohads. Illumination as a political idea in twelfth-century Morocco', in Brett, *Ibn Khaldun and the Medieval Maghrib*, VI, pp. 3–7.

and evidently had the same dynastic purpose. But the prospect of a smooth succession ended with the second attempt on al-Afḍal's life, which he suspected of being the work of his sons. These, therefore, he deprived of their horses, followers and income, with the result that when in 1121 he was indeed assassinated, he was succeeded not by Samāʾ al-Mulk or some other intended son, but by his long-standing lieutenant al-Baṭāʾiḥī in what amounted to a coup in collaboration with al-Āmir, the Caliph himself. The murder itself, as al-Afḍal was out in procession on the last day of Ramadan, was ascribed in the Egyptian tradition to the Nizārīs, some twenty of whom under the leadership of one al-Badīʿ had previously been discovered and executed by al-Afḍal; and indeed, al-Afḍal's name was on the list of victims of the Assassins discovered at Alamut after its final surrender to the Mongols in 1256. But then, so too was the name of Niẓām al-Mulk; and just as his murder is now held to be the work of the Sultan Malik Shah, so the Damascan chronicler al-Qalānisī attributed the killing of al-Afḍal to the Caliph and the man who replaced him, al-Baṭāʾiḥī. The probability is that it was indeed the work of Alamut, hostile not simply to the Fatimids in Cairo but to al-Afḍal in particular as the man responsible for the fate of Nizār. But whether or not al-Baṭāʾiḥī had a hand in the matter, or knew what was afoot, he came up instantly to have the body taken into the Dār al-Mulk, keeping secret overnight the actual death until he could fetch al-Āmir himself. On the arrival of the Caliph in the morning, he was then promptly appointed in al-Afḍal's place as al-Qāʾid al-Maʾmūn, the Trusted Commander, with all the titles of his two predecessors. Later in the morning, this supersession of Badr's dynasty at the head of state was ceremonially completed, firmly but courteously, by the Caliph at the breaking of the fast in the Dār al-Mulk, where al-Baṭāʾiḥī had carefully arranged the ritual meal the night before. While the adult sons of al-Afḍal were locked away to prevent any attempt to claim their father's inheritance, his infant son was seated to al-Āmir's right, with al-Baṭāʾiḥī to his left, and on behalf of the Caliph, al-Afḍal's brother Jaʿfar returned the greetings of the assembled company. The communal eating of the traditional dates and the food that followed, all handed out or blessed by al-Āmir, sealed the necessary pact between the monarch and the dead man's family, after which the obsequies of al-Afḍal could be performed with all honour due to this great servant of the dynasty, the uncle of the Caliph himself. But at the same time that he was laid to rest alongside his father in Badr's mausoleum, his vast treasure was carted away to replenish the hoard in the palatial store at al-Qāhira. Its removal was an earnest of a new relationship between monarch and minister after the years in which the Caliph had played little or no part in government. Exactly a century after the disappearance of al-Ḥākim, a young Caliph was poised to recover the direction of the state.

The relationship itself was one of alliance, in which the minister was entrusted as before with the responsibilities of government, in return for bringing the monarch out from his seclusion into the public eye. This calculated display of the master clearly redounded to the advantage of the servant who was thus visibly associated with the person of the Caliph. It was effected through the celebrations of the ritual year, systematically and sumptuously staged in all their theatricality by al-Baṭāʾiḥī in his new capacity as the Wazīr al-Qāʾid al-Maʾmūn. From his son and the similarly late-twelfth-century historian Ibn Ṭuwayr come the descriptions, in elaborate detail, of the processions and ceremonies of the years 1121 to 1124, those in particular that celebrated the New Year on the first of Muḥarram; the ᶜĪd al-Aḍḥā or ᶜĪd al-Ḥajj, the Feast of Sacrifice or Pilgrimage; the ᶜĪd al-Fitr, or Breaking of the Fast; the perfuming of the Nilometer followed by the cutting of the dam to fill the canal that ran from the Nile past al-Qāhira, when the river rose to the right height for irrigation; and finally the Festival of Ghādir Khumm to celebrate the designation of ᶜAlī by Muḥammad as his successor.[15] The resurrection of this festival after a lapse of some 100 years followed on from Badr's installation of the head of Ḥusayn at Ascalon, and betokened the fresh emphasis being placed by the dynasty upon ᶜAlī and the ᶜAlid saints in its efforts to renew its image as the champion of Islam.[16] The processions themselves were ordered in such a way as to link the palace city more closely with Fusṭāṭ, giving visual expression to the progressive colonisation of al-Qāhira by the population of the old city that had taken place since the *fitna* and *shidda*. That development was furthered by al-Baṭāʾiḥī, whose appetite for construction now extended beyond the observatory project to the building of new housing in the old and largely derelict Ṭūlūnid quarter of al-Qaṭāʾiᶜ beyond the Bāb Zuwayla of the palace city in the direction of Fusṭāṭ. Fusṭāṭ itself was provided with new open spaces, and the old pavilions of the dynasty along the Nile were restored. In al-Qāhira, he built the al-Aqmar mosque for the dynasty and a palace for himself, while renovating the Fatimid tombs outside the walls. Meanwhile, a caravanserai was built to attract merchants into the city, and in the interest of both prestige and trade, a new mint was opened there to maintain the purity of the coinage. The gold *dīnār* had always served the dynasty as demonstration and proof of its claims, and was put to good use for the purpose in the distribution of gold and silver coins as part of the annual ceremonies now lavishly staged by al-Maʾmūn. Its circulation was all

[15] See Sanders, *Ritual, Politics and the City in Fatimid Cairo*, pp. 87–98, 127–9.

[16] Ibid., pp. 87–98, 127–9, and C. Williams, 'The Cult of ᶜAlid saints in the Fatimid monuments of Cairo', *Al-Muqarnas* I (1983), pp. 37–52, and III (1985), pp. 39–60.

the more necessary to meet the challenge of the Nizārīs and their counter-currency, but in particular to restore confidence in the currency in the face of inferior imitations circulated by the Franks. With the mint then acting as an exchange, its foundation was equally important in turning the palace city into a commercial centre.

The festive combination of dynasty and city, which contributed to and profited from this upsurge of prosperity, promised to restore the Fatimids to their previous splendour at the outset of a new career, one in which the Caliph would return to view as the ruler of Islam on a wave of popularity. To the extent that this popularity depended upon the prosperity, al-Baṭāʾiḥī resumed his old role in charge of the fiscal system to confront once again the obstinate problem of tax-farming and the military. In 1122 he remitted all arrears of tax from the tax-farms on condition that the full quota was paid in future, and furthermore stopped the sale of tax-farms, *ḍamānāt*, to the highest bidder before the previous contract had expired. Both were comprehensive measures that applied to tax-farms in general, as the list of such farms makes clear: estates, districts, villagers, houses, shops, baths and government offices. Meanwhile, a case was brought against petty cultivators who had used water-wheels to irrigate plots of state land without permission, while a further charge was brought against landowners in general, that they had surreptitiously added state land to their own. This was a charge pointing back to the *aqwiyāʾ* or *mumayyazūn*, the higher-ranking soldiers of the Afḍalī *rawk* of 1107–8, who had protested at the reallocation of their *iqṭāʿāt* lest it include property which they claimed to own: gardens, lands and presses, presumably for sugarcane and olive oil. Taken together, the conclusion to be drawn from all these measures is that tax collection continued to be difficult, to the point at which the state was prepared to indulge a scramble for tax-farms; but on the other hand, that such farms were desirable. Under their thirty-year contracts, the *muqṭāʿūn*, or military tax-farmers, were in principle exempt from such competition; nevertheless, like others on the land as far down as the peasantry, they were surely involved in the usurpation of the state domain. The domain in question was either the uncultivated land specified in the Afḍalī *rawk* as needing to be brought under cultivation, or fields and orchards close to the river under artificial irrigation. The fact that much of the uncultivated land was still waste appears from a decree that provided that anyone who reclaimed such land as a tax-farm would be exempt from tax for the next four years; meanwhile the present occupants of such land were confirmed in its possession Whatever the land, its conversion into tax-farms or private property attests on the one hand to the expansion of the cultivated area by a population still growing back towards its former level, and on the other to the difficulty experienced by government in keeping this expansion under fiscal control. The country itself was evidently prosperous, though the state was struggling.[17]

The dark side to the regime was its concern with security in the wake of al-Afḍal's murder. Afraid for his own life as well as that of the Caliph, exposed as both of them were to assassination in their ceremonial processions, al-Baṭāʾiḥī, al-Qāʾid al-Maʾmūn, took extraordinary precautions to prevent the infiltration of *fidāʾī* murderers into Egypt. A new governor was appointed at Ascalon with orders to purge its administration of all office holders who were not known to the citizens, while a watch was set for would-be entrants into Egypt who were likewise unknown in the city as regular travellers. That meant a halt to all caravans, and the sending to Cairo of a list of all merchants and their merchandise, their camel-drivers and others travelling with them, to be verified before they were allowed to proceed. The merchants themselves were nevertheless to be treated well, without unnecessary vexation – a nice comment on al-Baṭāʾiḥī's parallel encouragement of trade, and similarly on its continuous flow through the Frankish states despite the occasional hostilities. The wealth it generated was too valuable to all concerned to be cut off for religious and political reasons. In the capital, including al-Qāhira and Fusṭāṭ, the same logic will have applied, though here the inquiry was equally thorough, and still more drastic. All inhabitants were listed by name, residence and occupation, along with their visitors, and women sent into the houses to make further inquiries. All suspects thus identified were proscribed and arrested in a swoop by the police, many incriminated by money from Alamut in their possession.[18] Comprehensive as they were, these measures were by their nature a defensive reaction to the Nizārī threat, and a more positive response to the underlying challenge of Ḥasan-i Ṣabbāḥ to the legitimacy of the dynasty was called for, some final proof of al-Āmir's right to the Imāmate and Caliphate. This was produced by a meeting of the Caliph and the Qāʾid with the family of al-Āmir and the high officers of the Daʿwa, to take the testimony of Nizār's sister, that from behind a curtain veil she had seen al-Mustanṣir on his death bed summon the young Aḥmad and bless him, and then whisper the designation into the ear of her aunt, al-Mustanṣir's sister, so that when al-Afḍal came after his death to ask the old lady on whom he had conferred the Imāmate, she declared in the hearing of Nizār's sister that it was indeed Aḥmad, al-Mustaʿlī. The outcome was a splendiferous *sijill*, the *Hidāya al-Āmiriyya*, or Divine Āmirid Guidance, which adduced the Qurʾān and its various interpretations at great length in support of the story.

[17] Brett, 'The way of the peasant', pp. 52–4.

[18] Ibn al-Jawzī, *Al-Muntaẓam*, vol. 9, pp. 120–1; Lewis, *Assassins*, pp. 60–1.

While it may have been sent to Alamut to win the Nizārīs back to the fold, it served more importantly to affirm the historic mission of the Fatimids in the person of al-Āmir, at the outset of his emergence from obscurity as the visible representative of God on earth. Whether consciously or not, it harked back to the appearance of the Mahdī and his defence of his title in his letter to the Yemen 200 years before.[19]

The Return to Personal Rule

Like the Mahdī's letter, the *Hidāya al-Āmiriyya* was certainly despatched to the faithful in the Yemen, together with a substantial force of Armenian and Black archers to serve under al-Afḍal's emissary Ibn Najīb al-Dawla. His mission to restore the power and authority of the Ṣulayḥids on behalf of the Queen al-Sayyida Arwā and bring the country directly under Fatimid control was clearly endorsed by al-Baṭāʾiḥī, whose idea it may originally have been. But the promise of new empire in the Yemen, strategically situated at the entrance and exit from the Red Sea, ended in 1124 when Ibn Najīb al-Dawla lost much of his new army in a failed attempt to reconquer Zabīd, and found himself besieged by the Yemenis in his fortress of al-Janad to the south of Arwā's capital Dhū Jibla. This was not an isolated affair; it took place in the context of a grander purpose on the part of al-Baṭāʾiḥī, al-Qāʾid al-Maʾmūn, to match the glorification of the Caliph in Egypt with triumph abroad, not only in the Yemen but in Syria and the holy war. Thus in 1122 the Egyptian navy sailed up to Tyre and took it back without difficulty from Ṭughtakīn's governor, who had ruled there in the Fatimid name since the relief of the city in 1111. This was a preliminary to a greater design in the following year. After the effort of al-Afḍal to create a force to match the Frankish knights, in 1123 the result was put to the test by his successor in a determined attack upon Jaffa by land and sea. The prospective triumph owed nothing to Damascus; the victory was to be the Caliph's alone. It was carefully, and ostentatiously, prepared, with reviews by al-Āmir of the army as well as the navy as it sailed from the capital down the Nile. Joined by the tribal Bedouin and splendidly equipped, the army was accompanied by physicians, muezzins for the call to prayer, and Qurʾān readers; the ships carried soldiers and siege engines. Jaffa was duly besieged; but the army was heavily defeated by the Franks coming to its relief: the cavalry fled, the Black infantry were massacred and the wealth of equipment lost. The ships sailed back to Ascalon, but there they were surprised by a superior Venetian fleet, with heavy losses.[20] The navy, then, was

[19] S. M. Stern, 'The Epistle of the Fatimid Caliph al-Āmir (al-Hidāya al-Āmiriyya) – its date and its purpose', *Journal of the Royal Asiatic Society* (1950), pp. 20–31.

[20] Cf. Lev, *State and Society*, pp. 102–3.

in no condition to break the siege of Tyre by the Venetians and the Franks the next year, in 1124. Without it, all Ṭughtakīn could do was negotiate the city's surrender on terms that guaranteed a peaceful takeover by the Franks of this last Muslim port on the Levantine coast.

Both in Syria and the Yemen, therefore, the imperial enterprise was a fiasco; and its failure proved fatal to its architect and to his man in the Yemen. As the Qāᵓid al-Maᵓmūn, al-Baṭāᵓiḥī's relationship to the Caliph was quite different from that of al-Afḍal. As al-Afḍal's lieutenant, he had evidently worked well with both the army and the administration, a relationship that he carried over into his own regime. On the other hand, he had not inherited the following in the army that had kept Badr and his son in power, not least since he had excluded al-Afḍal's sons from the succession, and despite the ceremony of the breaking of the fast on the morning after al-Afḍal's murder, seems to have put most of them to death. Instead, he had exchanged al-Afḍal for the Caliph as his patron. Thereby he had placed himself in the position of al-Yāzūrī, a minister with full responsibility for the government, but one who was nevertheless dependent upon the favour of a monarch to whom he had restored the powers of the Caliph after their appropriation by Badr and his son. As al-Yāzūrī had discovered, those powers were those of life and death, physically located in the great Eastern Palace, whose construction, begun by Jawhar, had made of it a city within a city. Within its walled fortress-like enclosure, the household of the sovereign, with its corps of eunuchs and guardsmen,[21] was a formidable garrison resurrected to prominence and power in the ceremonial routines redeveloped by al-Baṭāᵓiḥī. To it, towards the end of 1125, the Wazīr fell victim. Al-Baṭāᵓiḥī was arrested along with thirty of his entourage, and imprisoned along with his brother Ḥaydara. The reason may have been all too familiar, that his power and wealth had excited the sovereign's jealousy and fear. But it was his loss of Tyre to the infidel that al-Āmir is said to have reckoned as the greatest of the sins he had committed against his master. And, like al-Yāzūrī, he seems to have been slandered by his enemies, specifically al-Āmir's secretary Ibn Abī Usāma. He is said to have accused him of plotting with al-Āmir's brother Jaᶜfar to murder the Caliph and take his place, and likewise to have ordered Ibn Najīb al-Dawla in the Yemen to strike coins in the name of Muḥammad ibn Nizār. An envoy had indeed been sent to the Yemen, presumably by al-Baṭāᵓiḥī, to deal with the situation following

[21] The categories of the officers of state, including the members of the household at this period, are listed by al-Qalqashandī, *Ṣubḥ al-Aᵓshā fī ṣināᵓat al-inshāᵓ* (Cairo, 1912–38), vol. III, pp. 480–8; trans. B. Lewis in *Islam from the Prophet Muhammad to the Capture of Constantinople*, 2 vols (New York, 1974), I, pp. 201–8.

the defeat of Ibn Najīb al-Dawla in the previous year. He had, however, returned after al-Baṭā'iḥī's fall with accusations from Ibn Najīb al-Dawla's opponents, supported by ostensibly Nizārī coins, that he was a traitor who had come out for the rival Imāmate. The Caliph duly sent out a detachment to arrest him, whereupon he was captured by his tribal enemies, and against the wishes of the Queen was shipped back to Egypt to public disgrace and imprisonment. In 1128 both he and al-Baṭā'iḥī were executed, and their headless bodies crucified at the Bāb al-Futūḥ.

Al-Āmir was thus left to rule without a Wazīr, a post for which there was no longer the queue of candidates from the Men of the Pen that had lined up after the execution of al-Yāzūrī, nor for the moment a Nāṣir al-Dawla, a military man determined to fill it. To take charge of the administration, al-Āmir first called upon his Chief Qāḍī, Abū'l-Ḥajjāj to supervise the *dawāwīn* in addition to his responsibility for the judiciary and for the *maẓālim*, the hearing of petitions – an office that he had evidently discharged under al-Baṭā'iḥī. But he refused on the grounds of incompetence in such matters; and while Ibn Maysar, his successor as Chief Qāḍī in 1127, continued to hear petitions, oversight of the administration fell to the Caliph for the first time since al-Ḥākim. The result was disastrous for the image that al-Baṭā'iḥī had cultivated so assiduously. To take charge of the *zakāt* and the *maks*, the first being the tax levied on Muslims in the guise of the alms they were obliged to give to the poor, and the second the various non-religious taxes, which together accounted for much of the revenue, he appointed a Muslim, Ibn Abī Qīrāṭ, and a Samaritan Jew, Abraham, and over them a Copt, Ibn Qusā. This person had risen from tax-collecting in the Delta to serve in the central administration under Abū'l-Barakāt Yuḥannā ibn Abī'l-Layth, the head of the Dīwān al-Taḥqīq, the office created in 1107. In that capacity, Ibn Abī'l-Layth had been in charge of the financial administration under al-Afḍal, and on al-Afḍal's death had been invested with a robe of honour by al-Āmir. He continued in office until finally dismissed in 1132, but was now eclipsed by his erstwhile subordinate. Ibn Qusā had obtained his commission by alleging the misappropriation of funds by the Coptic secretariat and offering to root out such corruption for the benefit of the Treasury. Having originally come from the Church as a monk, he was grandly entitled Holy Father, Thirteenth Apostle, Lord over the heads of government and the Church, and set to work with confiscations not only from Christian officials but from an ever-widening public in the city, from Fusṭāṭ to al-Qāhira. Whether or not he acted properly in the interest of the state, he was necessarily, and increasingly, unpopular, especially as a Christian placed over Muslims. That unpopularity extended to the Caliph himself, to the point at which al-Āmir was threatened with a popular rebellion. The inevitable result was that in 1129 Ibn Qusā and his two assistants were arrested. The latter were imprisoned, but Ibn Qusā was ignominiously beaten to death with shoes; beheaded, his corpse was nailed to a plank, to float down the Nile to the sea. As for al-Āmir, he was obliged to admit to a mistake, and, exceptionally on the part of the Imām Caliph, atone for his error by freeing slaves and giving alms, and most notably by fasting for two months prior to Ramadan.

The Murder of the Caliph

In this way, over the three years since the removal of al-Baṭāʾiḥī, the attempt by the inexperienced monarch to create his own regime had demonstrated the problem faced by the Caliph in resuming the direction of the state in Egypt. Meanwhile, abroad, in the wake of the fall of Tyre and the expulsion of Ibn Najīb al-Dawla from the Yemen, the outlook for the empire was not good. In Syria, al-Āmir returned to the war with the Franks, sending a fresh fleet up the coast in 1126, but with little success. At the same time he reverted to al-Afḍal's policy of making common cause with the Seljuq princes. Thus the naval expedition coincided with the advance of al-Bursuqī, the Atabeg of Mosul who had taken possession of Aleppo in 1125, upon the fortress of Atharib in the direction of Antioch. But this too failed, and the Fatimid alliance with al-Bursuqī came to nothing when he was assassinated on his return to Mosul; al-Āmir's embassy, taking presents and a substantial aid in gold dīnārs, turned back on the news of his death. The replacement of al-Bursuqī at Mosul and Aleppo by the Atabeg Zangī in 1127–8, coupled with the death of Ṭughtakīn and the accession of his son Būrī at Damascus in 1128, created a new situation in which the Fatimids took no part. That was not true of the Nizārīs, who had continued to take over the Daᶜwa in Syria. Between them and the Fatimids, the contrast was as stark as ever. Despite the continued loyalty of the Yemen under its long-lived Queen, and the expansion of the Daᶜwa from there into India, al-Shīrāzī had not found a successor of comparable stature to develop and promote the faith. While in Egypt its followers and their tradition of learning remained centred in al-Qāhira under the continued direction of a Chief Dāᶜī, its message was diluted in the ceremonial routine of the dynasty, which, as in the case of the holy war, sought to embrace the community as a whole in a common Islam. But the attempt, such as it was, to bring the Nizārīs back into the fold with proof of the legitimacy of the Mustaᶜlian succession had not weighed with Ḥasan-i Ṣabbāḥ. He died at Alamut in 1124; having allegedly put his two sons to death on charges of drinking wine and conspiracy, his chosen successor was the commandant at Lamasar, Buzurgumid, aided by three associates equally of his choosing. With Ḥasan's death, the long and distinguished line of Ismāᶜīlī philosophical theologians came to an end. But there was no halt to the Nizārī offensive, which echoed in its own way the revolutionary origins of the Mahdī and his dynasty, not least in Syria.

After the execution of the Dāʿī Abū Ṭāhir and their expulsion from Aleppo in 1114, the Nizārīs had returned to the city in 1119 under the direction of his successor Bahrām, as allies of its new ruler, Il Ghāzī. After

Figure 10.2 The Mihrab of the Mosque of al-Azhār. Photo: Bernard O'Kane.

The focus of the mosque; the original has been replaced, first by the Caliph al-Āmir, who presented the mosque with a vast wooden minbar carved out of a single log, which is now in the Cairo Museum of Islamic Art.

Il Ghāzī's death in 1122 they were finally expelled in 1124, but not before Bahrām had transferred the seat of his operations to Damascus, where, with a recommendation from Il Ghāzī, he emerged from clandestinity to a welcome by Ṭughtakīn and his Iranian Wazīr al-Mazdaganī. Not only was he provided with a headquarters in the city, but more importantly, with the fortress of Banyas on the frontier with the Kingdom of Jerusalem, across the Jordan inland from Tyre. With this acquisition at the end of 1126 he seemed at last to have obtained his Alamut. As a warlord with a warlike following, who earlier in 1126 had joined with Ṭughtakīn in an expedition against the Franks, he rebuilt its fortifications and set out to create a local dominion, but in 1128 was killed in an attempt to conquer and win the hill people to the north, a miscellany that included both Druzes and ᶜAlawite Nuṣayrīs. His successor Ismāᶜīl endeavoured to carry on, but the death of Ṭughtakīn in the same year was followed in 1129 by a coup on the part of his successor Būrī. The execution of his father's Wazīr was the signal for a popular uprising against the Nizārīs, who were massacred and expelled, leaving Ismāᶜīl to turn over Banyas to the Franks. It was, however, by no means the end for a militant movement that played to great effect on the old divisions within Syrian society to win a similarly militant following. Its enemies had cause to fear. Thus in 1131 Būrī was assassinated.[22] Far more importantly, the affair spilled over into Egypt. Bahrām's head, hand and ring had been sent to Cairo by his killers, to be received in triumph. But in October 1130 al-Āmir himself was assassinated, six months after the birth of a son, Muḥammad, had put an end to the affair of Ibn Qusā with a grand celebration throughout the capital. For a fortnight, the city had been decorated overall for the ceremonies, the feasting and the distribution of largesse, while the good news of a presumptive heir to the Imāmate and Caliphate was announced to the world in *sijillāt*, which were sent most notably to the Yemen. There, the text was preserved to become a testament to the succession in the aftermath of what was to come.[23] From his pavilion on the island of Roda offshore from Fusṭāṭ, al-Āmir rode across the narrow bridge to witness the celebration at the height of the Nile flood. There, unprotected by his escort, strung out before and behind, he was jumped by nine assassins and stabbed to death. With the heir a baby, and no Wazīr to take control on his behalf, the return to government by the Caliph was abruptly stalled, and the dynasty left exposed to a threat to its very existence.

22 Cf. Lewis, *The Assassins*, pp. 104–7.

23 Ibn Muyassar, *Akhbār Miṣr*, pp. 109–10; Idrīs ᶜImād al-Dīn, *ᶜUyūn al-akhbār*, VII, pp. 254–6; S. M. Stern, 'The succession to the Fatimid Imām al-Āmir, the claims of the later Fatimids to the Imāmate, and the rise of Ṭayyibī Ismailism', *Oriens*, IV (1951), pp. 193–255.

11

The Final Failure

The Interruption of the Succession

For the final forty years of the dynasty, as Walker observes in *Exploring an Islamic Empire*, the sources are fuller and more numerous, as the Egyptian tradition comes closer to the time when it was recorded in the extant chronicles, and blends with the Latin and Syrian sources. A recent addition, not previously published, is the contribution of the late-fourteenth- century Egyptian historian Ibn al-Furāt, the relevant sections of whose universal history are the subject of the DPhil thesis of Fozia Bora.[1] As far as Egypt is concerned, the result is a narrative of successive and finally successful attempts to go beyond the wielding of power and authority by Badr al-Mustanṣirī and al-Afḍal in the name of the Imām Caliph, and take the place of the Fatimids in the name of another. The first was immediately provoked by the murder of al-Āmir. Dying as he did, without either an adult son or a Wazīr to assume the regency in the manner of Barjawān and al-Afḍal, it fell to the palace to rise to the occasion. This it did at once in the form of an alliance between ᶜAbd al-Majīd Muḥammad ibn al-Mustanṣir, a much older cousin of al-Āmir born at Ascalon in 1074, and one Hizār al-Mulk Hazārmard or Jawārmard. This was an intimate of al-Āmir who had held responsibility for the army, and by this time had taken charge of the *maẓālim*, the hearing of petitions. His prompt appointment as Wazīr looks to have been a seizure of power by a would-be al-Afḍal or al-Baṭāʾihī in collusion with ᶜAbd al-Majīd in the capacity of regent, or indeed as Caliph with the regnal title of al-Ḥāfiẓ li-Dīn Allāh, Keeper of the Religion of God. Tales that were probably put out in justification of the new dispensation had al-Āmir designating ᶜAbd al-Majīd as regent for the unborn child of a concubine, after dreaming of his own death. No mention was made of the actual baby Muḥammad, who disappears from the record

[1] F. Bora, 'The Mamluk historiography of the Fatimids reconsidered: Ibn al-Furāt's *Taʾrīkh al-duwal waʾl-mulūk*', DPhil thesis, University of Oxford, 2010.

and whose fate is unknown, presumed dead if not murdered by the new monarch and his Wazīr. But an arrangement which broke so radically with the dynastic principle of *naṣṣ*, the designation of the son as successor to his father in the Imāmate, was abruptly terminated by a yet more radical break with the dynasty itself.

This was accomplished by a revolt of the soldiery in favour of Aḥmad, the only surviving son of al-Afḍal, with the mysterious nickname of Kutayfāt, 'little shoulder-blades'. The troops in question were the Daylamīs and probably the Armenians, demanding a restoration of the Armenian dynasty in revenge for its virtual extermination by al-Baṭāʾihī and al-Āmir. The palace was invaded, Hazārmard was decapitated and his head paraded on a lance; two weeks after the murder of al-Āmir, Kutayfāt took power with all the titles of his grandfather and father at the head of both Dawla and Daᶜwa. Whatever ᶜAbd al-Majīd's pretentions to the throne may have been, he was now merely the Walī ᶜAhd al-Muslimīn, the old title of the designated heir which was given to him as the nominal head of state, but one who was neither Caliph nor Imām. Although official documents were issued in his name, conjointly with that of Kutayfāt in his role as Amīr al-Juyūsh, ᶜAbd al-Majīd had in fact been promptly and securely imprisoned in one of the treasuries of the palace. His gaoler was Riḍwān ibn Walakhshī, the senior Amīr, who had thrown in his lot with Kutayfāt in the course of the uprising. Kutayfāt himself was equally prompt in proclaiming the restoration of his own dynasty with a display of generosity calculated to win both loyalty and popularity. Following what was by now a precedent, he removed the wealth and treasures of the palace to the Dār al-Wizāra, after distributing most of what al-Āmir had accumulated in largesse to the people. At the same time, since the price of bread was high, he released the grain from the state granaries, and in particular restored everything that had been confiscated by the hated Ibn Qusā, to general rejoicing, in which his praises were sung and the iniquities of al-Āmir denounced. The military who had brought him to power will necessarily have benefited from his largesse with the customary donative to celebrate the accession of a new ruler; but Kutayfāt made a particular point of rewarding or securing the support of the Ḥujariyya, the elite corps formed by his father, with the grant of *iqṭāᶜāt*. While remaining on the payroll, these now joined the ranks of the *muqṭāᶜūn*, the military tax-farmers created by his grandfather.

Beyond this bid to take back the power and authority of his line, however, lay a much more ambitious determination to free himself from dependence on the dynasty. The title of Walī ᶜAhd al-Muslimīn taken by ᶜAbd al-Majīd, which had traditionally defined the responsibility of the dynasty for keeping the Muslim community in general true to its commitment to Islam, now categorically excluded him from the pretentions of the Fatimids to the Imāmate from which their claim to the Caliphate derived. The Imām was declared to be Muḥammad al-Muntaẓar, the Expected Imām of the Twelver or Imāmī Shīᶜites, for whom the Friday prayer was now said; meanwhile, the coins that were struck in his name declared al-Afḍal Abū ᶜAlī Aḥmad, that is, Kutayfāt, to be his representative. The innovation was not popular; people stayed away from the Friday prayer, while the invocation of the Hidden Imām was declared to be full of mistakes. Nevertheless no one dared protest. The change was given administrative force with a rearrangement of the judiciary. Four *qāḍī*-s were appointed: two Sunnīs (a Shāfiᶜite and a Mālikite); an Ismāᶜīlī; and an Imāmī. Meanwhile, Kutayfāt allowed a new Coptic Patriarch to be consecrated after the office had been vacant for six years. While ᶜAbd al-Majīd's name and title remained on documents that named Kutayfāt as his champion and friend, the eclipse of the Fatimids was not complete, but was certainly foreseeable. Such radical change at home was accompanied by an equally radical change in the stance on holy war. The coronation of Fulk of Anjou as the new King of Jerusalem in September 1131 was the occasion for an Egyptian embassy bringing among its presents an ivory *tau*, or T-shaped cross, which, as a Christian symbol, eventually came to Angers as a sceptre employed in the inauguration of the Counts of Anjou. The offering of such a token would suggest a desire for peace, if not friendship, that may have been prompted by the aggression of Fulk's predecessor Baldwin II.[2] After the fall of Tyre, Ascalon had been attacked in 1125 and its environs subsequently raided, while the city had been granted as a fief to Hugh of Jaffa in the expectation of its eventual fall. But now that this second al-Afḍal was no longer acting for the Imām Caliph, a quite different approach to the world at large is indicated, one that envisaged, among other things, the employment of Christianity to effect a reconciliation with the Franks.

The immediate effect of this revolution in the Yemen is obscured by the retrospective Yemeni tradition, which is concerned with the outcome. But it is clear that from the beginning, al-Sayyida Arwā believed in the succession to the Imāmate of the infant Muḥammad. Thus when the news of the assassination arrived, Muḥammad al-Ḥaydara, the envoy who had brought the *sijill* with the announcement of the birth, is said, in a somewhat garbled but nevertheless plausible tradition, to have preached in the name of this Muḥammad as Imām, ᶜAbd al-Majīd as Walī ᶜAhd al-Muslimīn and Abū ᶜAlī Kutayfāt as Wazīr. The Nizārīs, for their part, seem not to have responded, either at

[2] The episode is recorded by J. Riley-Smith in 'Crusading and the Montlhérys', *The First Crusaders, 1095–1131* (Cambridge, 1997), pp. 180–2.

Alamut or in Syria. At Alamut they were more concerned with their previous capture and sack of Qazvin to the south of Rūdbār, and with the death of Muḥammad Tapar's son Maḥmūd II in Iraq in 1131; in Syria the assassination of the Atabeg Būrī at Damascus in 1131 was a more pressing matter. The consequences, however, at Cairo and elsewhere, had no time to work themselves out, since at the end of 1131 Kutayfāt's revolution was aborted by his murder, not by the Assassins but by the Fatimid establishment. The vast institution that was the palace complex of al-Qāhira was a stumbling block in the way of any attempt to supersede the power and authority of the Fatimids, so firmly was the dynasty entrenched, physically as well as constitutionally, in the government of the state. It had survived the long-standing withdrawal of the Imām Caliph from the personal direction of government, to prove its resilience with the return of al-Āmir to power. Thus it was the palace, in the form of members of al-Āmir's bodyguard, that struck Kutayfāt down in what was now familiar fashion, ambushed as he rode out in procession. ᶜAbd al-Majīd was released from captivity, and acclaimed as Caliph.[3]

The Secession of the Yemen

The first coins of his reign were minted in the name of the Walī ᶜAhd al-Muslimīn, but the pretence of a regency for some infant son and heir to the Imāmate quickly disappeared as ᶜAbd al-Majīd finally took the title of al-Ḥāfiẓ li-Dīn Allāh as Imām and Caliph in his own right. To prove the right in question, the *sijill* that in January 1132 proclaimed his accession not only declared that the Imāmate was like the sun, which had been briefly eclipsed, but had now reappeared in accordance with the divine purpose. It looked to the precedent of the designation of ᶜAlī by his cousin Muḥammad, and to that of Ibn Ilyās by his cousin al-Ḥākim, to explain the break in the direct line of succession as an eventuality foreseen and indeed predicted by the infallible Imāms as a third such designation, one made necessarily though secretly by al-Āmir. As an apology for so irregular a succession, this justification of al-Ḥāfiẓ's accession to the Imāmate and Caliphate for the benefit of the Ismāᶜīlī faithful was generally accepted by the community in Egypt, and was presumably a matter of indifference to the population at large. Outside Egypt, that was no doubt the case with Nubia, but not so in the Yemen. In this last remaining province of the Dawla, the announcement prompted the final break-up of the Ṣulayḥid state as the Zurayᶜids in Aden and the Ḥamdānids in Sanᶜa both recognised al-Ḥāfiẓ, while the Queen, al-Sayyida

[3] For the controversy over his accession and its consequences, see S. M. Stern, 'The succession to the Fatimid Imām al-Āmir, the claims of the later Fatimids to the Imāmate, and the rise of Ṭayyibī Ismailism', *Oriens*, 4 (1951), 193–255.

Arwā, did not. The break-up had been long in the making; the Zurayʾids in particular had grown rich on the trade of Aden, and their ruler Sabaʾ now seized the opportunity to declare his independence as the new Fatimid Dāʿī, a position that was officially conferred upon his son and successor Muḥammad by a delegation from Cairo in 1140.[4] Aden thus became and remained the refashioned Yemeni province of the Dawla at the expense of the original Ṣulayḥid dominion, which effectively ceased to exist at the death of Arwā in 1138. The Ṣulayḥid Daʿwa, on the other hand, founded by Lamak ibn Mālik as a continuation of the Fatimid tradition of learning passed on to him by his mentor al-Shīrāzī, took on a new lease of life as an independent creed in the name of Muḥammad al-Ṭayyib, 'the Good', the infant son of al-Āmir.

Coming some thirty-five years after the Nizārī schism, the secession of this Ṭayyibī Daʿwa from the Imāmate in Cairo reduced the original Fatimid Daʿwa to a Ḥāfiẓī rump. Where the Nizārī schism had come as the climax of Ḥasan-i Ṣabbāḥ's foundation of an independent Ismāʿīlī state under his charismatic direction, however, the hitherto loyal Yemenis were taken by surprise, obliged to establish a foundational narrative of the events surrounding the infant's disappearance, together with a theological explanation. Both turned on the numbers five and seven and the name of Muḥammad, in a manner recalling the tale of the successors of Muḥammad ibn Ismāʿīl in *satr*, concealment, as well as the expectation of his return. Thus al-Āmir in foreknowledge of his death had entrusted his son to the Dāʿī Ibn Madyān together with four, perhaps six, other trustees, who had concealed the child from Kutayfāt. All these were executed for their loyalty; but the child was taken by Ibn Madyān's brother-in-law Abū ʿAlī into *satr*, where he and his descendants have remained against the time of their return. Theologically this withdrawal of the Imāmate into concealment was explicable; in multiples of seven, the child was the third Muḥammad, the fourteenth Imām in succession to Muḥammad ibn Ismāʿīl and the twenty-first from the Prophet himself. As this credo took shape, so did the organisation of the new calling, both established by the Queen before her death in 1138. Her crucial appointment in her capacity as Ḥujja was that of al-Dhuʾayb al-Ḥamdānī, the successor of Lamak ibn Mālik and his son Yaḥyā as the theologians of the Daʿwa, to be al-Dāʿī al-Muṭlaq, the Unconditional Caller, with absolute authority to speak on behalf of the hidden Imām. Succeeded at his death in 1151 by Ibrāhīm al-Ḥāmidī, al-Dhuʾayb was the first of a continuous line of such authorities that has ensured the continued existence of the Ṭayyibī Daʿwa and its community in the Yemen and India to the present day. Meanwhile, the Queen's

[4] Cf. Daftary, *The Ismāʿīlīs. Their History and Doctrines*, 2nd edn, pp. 255–60.

final gesture on behalf of the Daᶜwa was to bequeath her jewellery to the Imām whenever he should appear, while her tomb in the mosque at Dhū Jibla has remained a focal point for the faithful.[5]

The Christian Wazīr

As the faithful were thus parting company from the Imāmate, the episode of al-Kutayfāt had shown that the right of the Caliphate to rule had begun to be challenged. For the moment, however, the problem in Egypt was less one of legitimacy as of government in the aftermath of the crisis. The new factor was the rebelliousness of the soldiery who had brought Kutayfāt to power, and after plundering the *sūq*-s at his accession, now did so again following his murder. His faction did not disappear at his death, and despite the return of authority to the Imāmate and Caliphate, remained in power with the promotion to the Wazīrate of the Armenian Abūʾl-Fatḥ Yānis (Johannes, John). Whether or not he was a Christian, Yānis had begun his career as a *ghulām* of al-Afḍal, rising in the service of his master and of al-Baṭāʾiḥī to the high rank of Ṣāḥib al-Bāb under al-Āmir, the officer who now controlled the public sessions of the Caliph. As Wazīr he took revenge for the killing of Kutayfāt by massacring over half of al-Āmir's old bodyguard, the troop responsible for the murder. But any attempt to consolidate his power at the expense of the Caliph ended with his death at the end of 1132, allegedly poisoned on al-Ḥāfiẓ's orders by the Caliph's physician. As retailed by al-Maqrīzī in the *Ittiᶜāẓ* from divergent accounts, the confused story is of a purge in which the Chief Qāḍī and Chief Dāᶜī was executed, and it may be that Yānis was attempting to follow in the footsteps of Kutayfāt. But if so, like Kutayfāt, he failed to circumvent the palace; and for the next year, al-Ḥāfiẓ undertook to rule himself. Yuhannā ibn Abī Layth, the long-serving colleague of al-Baṭāʾiḥī at the head of the Dīwān al-Taḥqīq since its creation in 1107, was discharged as head of the administration on the grounds that he had been the agent of Kutayfāt's largesse to his circle of supporters. In his place al-Ḥāfiẓ appointed the Sharīf Muᶜtamid al-Dawla, and his brother to be Naqīb, or head of the Ashrāf. This was an evidently political move to enlist the support of the Ashrāf, the influential elite of descendants of the Prophet whose membership was genealogically controlled by their syndic. Al-Ḥāfiẓ's overture to this body of the Fatimids' kith and kin recalled the largely successful attempt of al-Muᶜizz to win them over in Egypt and in Mecca, offset by the hostility of those in Syria and Iraq who had denounced the Fatimids as impostors. In the very different circumstances of the dynasty some 150 years later, coming

[5] Ibid., pp. 261–5.

in particular after the overture of Kutayfāt to the Twelver or Imāmī Shī^c^ites, it signalled an attempt to restore the Caliphate to its place in the world along the lines cultivated by Badr, al-Afḍal and al-Baṭā'iḥī, appealing not only to the Shī^c^ites in general with the cult of the head of Ḥusayn, but to Shī^c^ites and Sunnīs alike with the emphasis on leadership in the holy war. Thus after a quiet period following the fall of Tyre, and the overture of Kutayfāt to Jerusalem, a sortie out of Ascalon in 1132 in support of an opportune rebellion against King Fulk by Hugh, lord of Jaffa, was followed up over the next five years with such vigour that over the years from 1133 to 1142, a ring of new castles were built by the Franks to contain the threat to the vulnerable route between Jaffa and Jerusalem.

It was an offensive that continued even as the regime in Cairo was overtaken by a fresh crisis of the Caliph's own making. In 1134, after the year in which he had dispensed with a Wazīr, al-Ḥāfiẓ sought to consolidate the hold of the dynasty on government by the designation of his eldest son Sulaymān as Walī ^c^Ahd al-Muslimīn with the responsibility of a Wazīr for the administration. This unprecedented step, going far beyond the duties entrusted to Ibn Ilyās by al-Ḥākim, turned to disaster when Sulaymān died after a mere two months, to be succeeded in the post by his brother Ḥaydara. Ḥaydara, however, was promptly ousted by the rebellion of a third brother, Ḥasan, with the support of the Juyūshiyya, that is, the corps of Armenian origin that had sustained the regimes of Badr, the Amīr al-Juyūsh and al-Afḍal, and whose previous rebellion had propelled al-Kutayfāt to power. These defeated the Rayḥāniyya, the Black regiments at Cairo, leaving al-Ḥāfiẓ with no choice but to install Ḥasan as his heir in opposition to himself. After the years in which the Fatimids had, since the time of al-Manṣūr and al-Mu^c^izz, largely been spared the problem of succession by the enforcement of the principle of the Imāmate, most controversially at the deaths of al-Mustanṣir and al-Āmir, the dynasty had finally been overtaken by the rivalries typical of other ruling families. An army of Blacks brought down from Upper Egypt in an attempt to oust him was defeated, but Ḥasan proved to be his own worst enemy. Executions and confiscations rapidly alienated his following, provoking a crisis that was only resolved by the Caliph's capitulation to the demands of a mutinous soldiery. Early in 1135 a revolt of the troops at Cairo drove Ḥasan to flee into the palace, where he was imprisoned by his father while the mutineers demanded his death. Under siege, al-Ḥāfiẓ had him forcibly poisoned, too late for his rescue by the governor of the Gharbiyya, the western Delta, who came up with a muster of the *muqṭa^c^ūn* and Bedouin of the province. The governor in question, Bahrām, was a Christian Armenian of noble family, whose uncle had been the Byzantine governor of Antioch and whose brother Gregorius had been the Armenian Catholicus whose ordination in

Egypt had been approved by Badr in 1087. Arriving as a refugee from some obscure conflict in his homeland, one that may have deprived him of the lordship of the city of Tell Bāshir between Aleppo and Edessa, he had been readily accepted and promoted in the administration up to his present major command. His arrival at Cairo was welcomed by the troops, who had him installed by the Caliph in March 1135 as Wazīr with all the now customary titles of the Amīr al-Juyūsh. His appointment confirmed what the coup of Kutayfāt had demonstrated, that the murders of al-Afḍal and al-Āmir had left the soldiery as the arbiters of power.

Palace and Army in the Twelfth Century

In his *Ṣubḥ al-Aᶜshā*, or Light for the Blind, his treatise on Egyptian administration, the fifteenth-century secretary al-Qalqashandī listed the officers and officials of the Dawla in the twelfth century, from the Men of the Sword to the Men of the Pen. Included with the Men of the Sword were the retainers of the Caliph, beginning with the eunuchs of the Palace, over 1,000 strong, who were called from their uniform al-Muḥannakūn, that is, with the tail of their turban bandaged around their neck and chin in Berber style. After these, some 500 young pages were in attendance on the Caliph, followed by the Ḥujariyya, or Ṣibyān al-Khāṣṣ, the guard created by al-Afḍal, located outside in their barracks. The Palace, however, was no longer entirely self-contained. The office of Ṣāḥib al-Sitr, or Master of the Curtain, at the Caliph's audience was now that of Ṣāḥib al-Bāb, the Door or Gate, no longer held by the head of the Ṣaqāliba, the Slavonic eunuchs, but by an Amīr of the army second in rank only to the Wazīr, and on occasion a Wazīr to come: Yānis, Riḍwān and Ḍirghām. The Amīrs themselves were ranked according to the size of their command, the greatest with golden collars, the next bearing silver batons. The army itself was still of different ethnicities, although on al-Qalqashandī's list the mix had altered: the Kutāma had disappeared while the Kurds had arrived together with the Ghuzz, Turcomans as distinct from the Turkish *ghilmān*; the ᶜAbīd remained, but the Armenians are not mentioned. At the same time the army was divided into corps, not necessarily by race, but named after their founders, most notably the Caliphal Āmiriyya and Ḥāfiẓiyya together with Badr's Juyūshiyya and the Afḍaliyya. The practice was not new – al-Qalqashandī's mention of the Wazīriyya is a reference to the regimental guard of Ibn Killis in the tenth century – but exemplified the restructuring of the army begun by Badr. Thus the Juyūshiyya may have been Blacks, newly recruited and reformed by Badr as an indispensable infantry; the

Rayḥāniyya, whose name was synonymous with the Blacks in the capital in the last years of the dynasty, certainly were. How these various corps related to the *muqṭāʿūn*, the officers and men endowed with tax-farms by Badr and al-Afḍal, is not clear – they are not mentioned by al-Qalqashandī in his list. But it was troops loyal to al- Afḍal who enabled Kutayfāt's coup in 1130, setting off the protracted struggle for power between the Palace and the rival Amīrs that ended with Saladin. In that struggle, in which the Bedouin came to play an increasing part, the Amīrs formed their own bodies of guardsmen and on occasion regiments: Bahrām imported some 2,000 Armenians; Ṭalāʾiʿ ibn Ruzzīk created the Barqiyya, a regiment under the command of Ḍirghām, the Ṣāḥib al-Bāb. This was a combination of power and authority which, after the Palace had contrived the murder of Ṭalāʾiʿ, and his son had been ousted by Shāwar and his Bedouin allies, enabled Ḍirghām to take back the Wazīrate from Shāwar in what proved to be the final act in this internal Egyptian conflict, before the country became a battleground between Jerusalem and Damascus.

Al-Qalqashandī, *Ṣubḥ al-Aʿshā* (Cairo, 1912–38), vol. 3, pp. 480–8; trans. B. Lewis, *Islam from the Prophet Muhammad to the Capture of Constantinople*, 2 vols (New York, 1974), vol. 1, pp. 201–8. For the Juyūshiyya and Rayḥāniyya, cf. Y. Lev, *State and Society in Fatimid Egypt* (Leiden, 1991), pp. 127–8.

Both as an Armenian with strong connections with his homeland and as a Christian, Bahrām was nevertheless well placed to capitalise on a relationship that had developed over the past twenty years, and make a fresh entry for the Fatimids into the complicated politics of the Mediterranean in the form of an alliance with Roger II, the Norman King of Sicily. In looking to Sicily, Bahrām was not only promoting trade with a state that had once been a Fatimid dominion. Roger was an imperialist looking to conquer what remained of the Zirid domain in Ifrīqiya, and at the same time aspiring to take over the Crusader principality of Antioch. In both these designs he relied upon his admiral and minister George of Antioch, a Greek out of the Byzantine administration who may in fact have been an Armenian with connections to Bahrām's family. A talented administrator, George had escaped to Sicily after capture at sea and employment by the Zirids at Mahdiyya, and risen to become the counterpart of Bahrām in the King's service. He was certainly well known in Egypt, becoming the subject of a long and well-informed entry in al-Maqrīzī's biographical *Muqaffā*, which refers to his embassies to Egypt apparently in the time of al-Afḍal and al-Baṭāʾiḥī. He was now lauded in a letter of al-Ḥāfiẓ to Roger, one that makes clear that Bahrām was equally well known and appreciated by Roger. From the letter it is clear that the relationship was based on trade. Under Roger, Sicily had become what it had been in Roman times, a major exporter of wheat, needed by Egypt in years of poor harvests. More to the point, the letter refers to ships belonging to the Caliph, to the King and to George of Antioch, which traded on their behalf, and enjoyed exemptions from the usual import and export duties at Alexandria and Cairo. At the same time, it raised the question of Roger's conquest of the island of Djerba in 1135, the first of his acquisitions of the entire coast of Ifrīqiya from Sousse and al-Mahdiyya to Tripoli over the next fifteen years. A previous unsuccessful attack upon al-Mahdiyya in 1123 had prompted an appeal to Cairo by the Zirid prince Ḥasan, a brief recall of past loyalties that elicited an Egyptian envoy who effected a reconciliation between the two monarchs after the Sicilians withdrew. Continued Fatimid concern with attacks upon Muslim territory is apparent in the case of Djerba. Roger had felt it necessary to excuse himself for this trespass upon the land of Islam on the grounds that the island was a nest of pirates, an excuse that was accepted. Meanwhile, gifts had been exchanged and accepted, among them, at some time, a *miẓalla*, the jewelled parasol under which the Fatimid Caliph rode out. Its reception and employment by Roger is a token of the way in which, from the time of his coronation in 1130, the King had modelled himself upon the Egyptian monarchy in his dress and in his Arabic titles; the documents of his Arabic administration were in the calligraphic style of the Fatimid chancery, taught perhaps by Fatimid scribes; while Egyptian craftsmen and artists were employed in the Fatimid-style art and architecture of his palaces, most notably in the Cappella Palatina, the royal chapel (see Figs 11.1 and 8.1).

Even as this former Fatimid dominion in the Maghrib was falling into Christian hands, the dynasty had made a new acquisition for its empire, symbolised in particular by the *miẓalla* and evidenced by the letter. Part of a serial correspondence, not only was this couched in the elaborate rhymed prose of the Fatimid chancery, addressing the King, the self-styled Malik, from the superior position of one to whom God has granted both this world and the next. Written as it was from such a position, the letter proceeded to accept the apology of Roger's scribe from a fault in his Arabic, which had been pointed out in some previous exchange.[6]

In an age when the tokens of majesty carried such weight, the Caliphate was entitled to lay claim to the Kingdom in this way. But the prospect of a change in relations with the Crusader states came to nothing with Roger's

[6] Cf. J. Johns, *Arabic Administration in Norman Sicily: the Royal* Dīwān (Cambridge, 2002), ch. 10, esp. pp. 258–67.

failure to secure the principality of Antioch, while in Bahrām the alliance lost one of its major advocates. The letter in question was written in 1137, after Bahrām had been ousted by yet another rebellion, explaining his misdeeds to the King, who had written to know why he had gone. Religion had told against him. A Christian as Wazīr was not only unprecedented but shocking. Bahrām's ceremonial functions were taken over by al-Ḥāfiẓ himself and the Chief Qāḍī; but his appointment remained a scandal, aggravated by the arrival of his relatives and Armenian troops from his homeland; his church-building; and the release of 300 Frankish captives imprisoned since their capture in the battles of Ramla. In these circumstances, while Jerusalem remained the enemy, his good relations with Roger may have told against him. Those relations the letter was clearly anxious to preserve; the reason it gave for the Wazīr's downfall was the number of Armenians he had brought to Egypt in an ambitious attempt to seize power. The letter was written after the event, but the accusation that he was attempting a Christian takeover of the state is apparent from the rising that brought him down. In that rising, the factor that had already served to bring Bahrām himself to power came once again into play. This was Badr's division of the provincial government of Egypt into five military provinces. It was as governor of the Gharbiyya, the province of the western Delta, that Bahrām had come to be Wazīr; he had then appointed his brother to be governor of the southern province at Qūṣ. But it was now the turn of the governor he had appointed to his old province to mount a second challenge. At the time of Kutayfāt's coup, in which he had been involved, Riḍwān ibn Walakhshī had been reckoned the greatest of the Amīrs, one who had since succeeded Yānis as Ṣāḥib or Mutawallī al-Bāb before his appointment by Bahrām, in the first place to Ascalon and then to the Gharbiyya. At the beginning of 1137, like Bahrām before him, he recruited an army of Bedouin to advance upon Cairo, this time to overthrow the unbeliever in the cause of Islam. The cause was proclaimed by Qur'āns fixed to their lances. Bahrām's Muslims deserted him, and with his nuclear force of 2,000 Armenians he sailed south to his brother at Qūṣ, while the mob plundered the Dār al-Wizāra and the Armenian quarters outside the Bāb al-Futūḥ. But at Qūṣ, the brother had already been murdered by the townsfolk; Bahrām could not take Aswan and instead went back north to Akhmīm to protest his loyalty to al-Ḥāfiẓ. Whatever he was obliged by the victorious Riḍwān to say about him in the letter to Roger, the Caliph remained well disposed, offering Bahrām the choice of a governorship in the south or that of retirement to a monastery in the vicinity of Akhmīm, the choice he accepted. For al-Ḥāfiẓ, Bahrām and his Christianity was the lesser of two evils; Riḍwān, whom he was obliged to appoint as his successor, promised to be a second Nāṣir al-Dawla,

Figure 11.1 Image of Roger II of Sicily, ceiling of the Cappella Palatina at Palermo. Photo taken in 1989 under the direction of Robert Hillenbrand. Khalili Research Centre, Oxford, image no. ISL.15422. © Barakat Trust and University of Edinburgh.

This image of the Norman King Roger of Sicily depicts him in the same posture as the Caliph in the relief from al-Manṣūriyya, a testimony not only to the survival of a Muslim community under the Normans, but to the close relationship with Fatimid Egypt, whose artists executed the paintings on the ceiling constructed for Roger by Fatimid craftsmen.

threatening to turn the country over, not to Twelver Shīᶜism like Kutayfāt, but to Sunnism.

The Sunnī Wazīr

As Wazīr, Riḍwān inherited the titles of his predecessors as Amīr al-Juyūsh and director of the Qāḍīs and the Dāᶜīs, but with significant alterations. Like Bahrām, he took the new title of *Sayf*, or Sword of Islam, instead of Sword of the Imām; and instead of al-Afḍal's titles of Sharaf al-Aᵓnām and Nāṣir al-Dīn, 'Honour of Mankind and Protector of Religion', substituted that of Nāṣir al-Aᵓnām, or Protector of Mankind. In particular, the title of al-Sayyid al-Ajall al-Afḍal, the Most Mighty and Excellent Lord, which had given al-Afḍal the name by which he is known, mutated into al-Malik al-Afḍal, the Most Excellent King. 'Malik' was the title conferred upon Ṭughril Beg by the ᶜAbbasid Caliph, matching the title of Sultan for the rulers of the Seljuq empire; in a titulature that notably failed to mention the Imām except in the designation of the Wazīr as al-Ḥāfiẓī, it announced Riḍwān's arrival as a monarch in his own right. With Bahrām now in his monastery, his Armenians were disarmed and either settled in Upper Egypt or the western Delta, or were allowed to return to their homeland. In Cairo itself, however, Riḍwān purged the administration of the Christians appointed by Bahrām, some of whom he executed. In the manner of al-Ḥākim, not only did he replace them with Muslims, but as the champion of Islam reintroduced the humiliating obligations upon Christians and Jews to wear distinctive clothing, ride only donkeys, dismount in front of mosques and humbly pay a heavy poll tax at a bench set at head height. Such symbolic treatment did not mean an end to the good relationship that Bahrām had cultivated with Roger II in Sicily, as the letter of al-Ḥāfiẓ makes clear. Riḍwān, however, was evidently responsible for its denunciation of Bahrām as an enemy of the state and its eulogy of himself. Since the letter was written in the name of al-Ḥāfiẓ, it hailed him as the saviour summoned by the Caliph. But the foundation of a Sunnī *madrasa* in Alexandria was a further token of the Islam that had carried him to power, and that in 1138 saw the beginning of what al-Maqrīzī's source for the *Ittiᶜāẓ* called a foolish and reckless attempt to depose al-Ḥāfiẓ as neither Caliph nor Imām.

It was an attempt made in the context of the relationship to Damascus, quiet since the fall of Tyre, but resumed by al-Ḥāfiẓ after the murder of Kutayfāt with the return to raiding out of Ascalon. Correspondence with its Būrid rulers had begun in 1132, in which, to judge from letters sent out by Riḍwān, the Caliphate maintained the lordly stance adopted by al-Afḍal as the prosecutor of the holy war. For Damascus, however, the situation had changed since the death of Ṭughtakīn in 1128 and the assassination in 1132of his son Būrī. As the dynasty fell into the hands of three competing brothers and their rival Amīrs, it was threatened with conquest from the north by a formidable new entrant into the complicated politics of Syria. Zangī, appointed Atabeg of Mosul in 1127, was welcomed into Aleppo in 1128 as the son of Malik Shah's old governor of the city, the *ghulām* Aksunkur, where he confirmed his position by marriage to the daughter of its former Seljuq prince Riḍwān. Not only did this put an end to the long history of battle for Aleppo since the arrival of the Fatimids in Egypt; it turned the city into the capital from which Zangī promptly set out to win a Syrian empire with the annexation of Damascus. He besieged the city unsuccessfully in 1135 and

1139–40, but meanwhile took control of Hamah and Homs in the valley of the Orontes, and eventually Baalbek in the Lebanese Bekaa valley. Against this background Riḍwān not only strengthened the fortifications of Ascalon, but entered into correspondence, again in the name of al-Ḥāfiẓ, with the third Būrid brother, Shams al-Dawla Muḥammad, at Baalbek. Muḥammad had sought a Fatimid alliance in collusion with the Amīr Buzwāj, who had gone to Cairo to offer his services to the Caliphate. Buzwāj, deeply involved in the murderous politics of Damascus, had in 1137 won a victory over the Franks at Tripoli which the letter duly attributed to God and Islam, and by implication to the Caliph as leader of the holy war. A second letter, meanwhile, acknowledged the receipt of a letter from Kumushtakīn, the governor of the southern frontier of the Būrid dominion at Busra and Salkhad, once again offering an alliance with Cairo. As it transpired, this was an alliance concluded not only by Riḍwān but with Riḍwān. The *rapprochement* of al-Afḍal with the Seljuqs of Damascus in the name of the Caliph was about to turn into a recourse for contenders for power in Egypt.

In Cairo, Riḍwān had summoned the Sunnī jurist Ibn ᶜAwf, the Twelver Shīᶜite jurist Ibn Abī Kāmil and the Chief Dāᶜī Ibn Salāma to give an opinion on the deposition of al-Ḥāfiẓ as neither Caliph nor Imām but merely having some other charge. Ibn ᶜAwf, Riḍwān's choice for his *madrasa* at Alexandria, answered cautiously that any deposition had to be in accordance with the law. Ibn Abī Kāmil, on the other hand, answered as might be expected, that al-Ḥāfiẓ was not the Imām and should be deposed; Ibn Salāma, as Chief Dāᶜī, naturally stated that he could not be. News of the consultation duly reached al-Ḥāfiẓ, and as the conflict came into the open with Riḍwān's arrest and execution of members of his entourage, the Caliph sent for Bahrām and lodged him in the palace. In June 1139 matters came to a head when at the Golden Door to the Great Palace opening onto the Bayn al-Qaṣrayn, the main square of al-Qāhira, Riḍwān challenged al-Ḥāfiẓ to his face. With the palace surrounded, his aim was to replace the Caliph with one of his sons. But the palace, with its walls and corps of eunuchs and pages, remained closed, and Riḍwān had mistaken the appetite of army and populace for religious and political revolution. As Chief Dāᶜī, Ibn Salāma repeated the need for designation of the successor to the Imāmate; Al-Ḥāfiẓ had the son killed; and the tables were rapidly turned when at his call a group of the *ṣibyān al-khāṣṣ*, the elite guard created by al-Afḍal, came into the street through the Bāb Zuwayla and began to shout for the Caliph. The whole of al-Qāhira then turned on Riḍwān, driving him to escape the city through the Bāb al-Naṣr, and leave the Dār al-Wizāra to be plundered once again by the mob. Aided by the Bedouin who had first brought him to power, however, he fled through Ascalon to a welcome by Kumushtakīn at Salkhad. From there he returned to

Egypt with a force of Turks, the nucleus of an army of Bedouin with which he advanced on Cairo. But he could not break into al-Qāhira, and was finally routed by the Caliph's men. Like Bahrām and others before him, he retreated into Upper Egypt. There he received al-Ḥāfiẓ's pardon, and came back to internment in the palace, bringing yet another aborted revolution to an end. Bahrām, meanwhile, was not reinstated as Wazīr, but remained as al-Ḥāfiẓ's confidante until his death a year later, at the end of 1140. An old man, possibly in his seventies, he was publicly mourned at a grand Christian funeral by an equally aged Caliph, who after the vicissitudes of the past decade was once again left to take charge of the government.

The Return to Caliphal Rule

No Wazīr was appointed, but the Amīr Salīm ibn Maṣāl, a Berber from Barqa in Cyrenaica with a Berber name of a kind not seen since the Ifrīqiyan days of the dynasty, was vaguely entrusted with the direction of affairs. The management of the administration, however, was returned to the Christian Abū Zakarī, whom Bahrām had appointed to the Dīwān al-Naẓar/ Dīwān al-Taḥqīq in succession to its first head, Yuhannā Ibn Abī Layth, after the interval when it had been awarded to the Sharīf Mu^c^tamid al-Dawla. Abū Zakarī had been dismissed and exiled by Riḍwān, but was now reappointed to the post. As the person in overall charge of the finances, he was then in a position to contract for the revenues of the state, guaranteeing its amount while taking any excess for himself. It was a bid that recalled the excesses of Ibn Qusā, and was equally fatal: failure to deliver led to his dismissal and execution in 1145. The anti-Christian prejudice on which Riḍwān had successfully played was evidenced in the pun on his title of al-Akram, 'Most Noble', which the chroniclers recorded as al-Akhram, 'Slit-nosed', and underlay the appointment of his two Muslim successors. Of these the Qāḍī al-Tinnīsī, glorified with the ^c^Abbasid Caliphal title of al-Muwaffaq, was dismissed in 1147, to be followed by the Qāḍī al-Ṭarābulūsī, reappointed to the position he had held under Riḍwān. Al-Ṭarābulūsī was not simply, like his predecessor, a Muslim head of the administration. Glorified with the second such ^c^Abbasid title of al-Murtaḍā, he was also al-Muḥannak, that is, one entitled to wear the tail of his turban wrapped around his neck, a Berber style which had become the prerogative of the palace eunuchs. In addition to his headship of the financial administration, he likewise became head of the Chancery, with what is perhaps the retrospective title of Bearer of the Inkwell, corresponding to that of Dawādār in the Mamlūk Sultanate. And finally, recalling the way in which the Chief Qāḍī had officiated in place of the Christian Wazīr Bahrām, he attended the Caliph at the Friday prayer and on other ceremonial occasions.

This appropriation by the Caliphate of Riḍwān's Sunnī Muslim cause was the outcome of the crisis that began with the murder of al-Āmir and the coup of Kutayfāt. The Caliphate had survived the challenges to the legitimacy of the dynasty, thanks to the continuing strength of its hold over the patrimonial regime it had created. But the élan of the Daᶜwa which had inspired its creation had largely been lost to the Nizārīs and the Ṭayyibīs, surviving only in the remaining faithful in Egypt and the Yemen; in the lofty tone of the dynasty's leadership in the holy war; and in the rule of succession to the Imāmate and Caliphate. That rule, however, had been severely shaken, in Egypt quite apart from the Yemen, by the succession of al-Ḥāfiẓ, giving rise to challenges from within the family and, more importantly, to challenges to the legitimacy of the Caliphate itself. In defence of his own legitimacy, al-Ḥāfiẓ himself had resorted to the ceremonial of the theatre state, turning the celebration of the Festival of Ghadīr Khumm from an ᶜAlid into a specifically Fatimid occasion.[7] Meanwhile, the successes and ultimate failure of these challenges had depended on the response of a soldiery left by the murder of al-Afḍal without overall leadership, and which in moments of crisis required bribery to rally to the Caliph. Such challenges continued throughout the 1140s. In 1144–5 one Abūʾl-Ḥusayn, a son of al-Mustanṣir, attempted to persuade the Ṣāḥib al-Bāb Khumārtāsh to place him on the throne with himself as Wazīr; Khumārtāsh denounced him, and he was imprisoned. In 1146 the *ghulām* Bakhtiyār, perhaps the governor of Qūṣ, rebelled in Upper Egypt, to be defeated and killed by a force led by a chief of the Berber Lawāta to the west of the Delta. In 1147, however, it was the Lawāta who rebelled at the call of Riḍwān, who had contrived to dig himself a tunnel under the palace wall and escape across the Nile. With the Lawāta and troops still loyal to him he forced his way back into al-Qāhira to besiege the palace; but there he was set upon by the Rayḥāniyya, the Black troops, and finally killed. The Lawāta nevertheless came back in 1148 in support of an alleged son of Nizār coming from the Maghrib, whom they then killed in return for the concession of *iqṭāᶜāt*, the revenues of land in the vicinity of the Delta. And in 1149 the Juyūshiyya and the Rayḥāniyya once again came to blows.

Called in question in this way, the dynasty was nevertheless sustained by the huge vested interest in the regime created by the mechanism of government, through which the wealth of the country circulated in the manner described by Ibn Khaldūn. The employment it provided, the land and offices that it distributed in benefices and tax-farms, the capital these created for investment in industry and trade, made for a prosperity in favour of the status quo. In particular it paid for the army, the prerequisite of a dynasty's

[7] Cf. Sanders, *Ritual, Politics and the City in Fatimid Cairo*, pp. 131–3.

survival, in ways that were described in 1170 for the benefit of Saladin, the last Fatimid Wazīr, by the secretary al-Makhzūmī in his *Minhāj*, or Guide, to the taxation and revenues of Egypt. This account of the fiscal system of Egypt in this late Fatimid period spells out the ways in which the forces, from the household troops to the Bedouin auxiliaries, were paid according to their due. This was a variable amount depending on their rank and on the posting to which they had been assigned. As to the revenues from which these payments were drawn, the *Minhāj* finally clarifies the question of the *iqṭāʿ*/*iqṭāʿāt*. The *iqṭāʿ jayshī* was allocated to an individual soldier of the *jaysh*, the army, whereas a collective *iqṭāʿ* was assigned to each company of Bedouin. In both cases, the *ʿibra*, or portion, of the revenue from the *iqṭāʿ* that was the equivalent of the pay to which the holder was entitled, was both collected and disbursed to the recipient by the state. This was an elaborate process whereby the Dīwān al-Juyūsh, or Ministry of the Army, held the list of *muqṭāʿūn* to be compared with the list of *iqṭāʿāt* held by the Dīwān al-Iqṭāʿāt, and presented to the Dīwān al-Majlis for payment – a particularly sophisticated example of the common practice of allocating specific sources of revenue to specific beneficiaries. Given the turbulence of the times, it is an account of the principle rather than the invariable practice. Nevertheless, the reference to the Bedouin, who had played such a part in the affair of Riḍwān, reveals the extent to which their constant threat to the settled land had earned them incorporation into the armies of the state on a regular basis. As far as the individual *muqṭāʿūn* were concerned, the system did not preclude their residence on the land of their *iqṭāʿāt*, treating these as the profitable investment they had evidently been in the days of al-Afḍal and al-Baṭāʾiḥī. This is clear from the provisions made at this time for the garrison of Ascalon, which rotated every six months. The commander of the relief force, composed of companies of 100 horsemen, went with a register to certify the number of troops on parade, and with a sum of money to pay those who had not yet received their due. If any were absent on their *iqṭāʿāt*, their *nafaqa*, or entitlement, was to be sent to them.[8]

It is not clear how these *muqṭāʿūn*, great and small, stood in relationship to the high command and to the troops stationed at Cairo or in provincial garrisons. Ascalon was exceptional in its role on the frontier with the Kingdom of Jerusalem. Where in the 1130s expeditions out of Ascalon had menaced the Franks, after a final little victory in 1141 the city had been thrown onto the defensive by the cordon of Frankish fortresses built to contain the threat. Thus the provisions for the garrison in the foregoing

[8] See Brett, 'Origins of the Mamluk military system', pp. 48–9.

account were designed to strengthen it for the protection of the Bedouin and others of the vicinity. For their part, the Franks had long coveted the city, and their aggression was the sign of a renewed determination to take it. The predicament in which the city thus found itself was not in isolation, but fell into place in the evolving context of the Frankish-Muslim confrontation in Syria. In 1139, the year in which Riḍwān's attempted coup ended in his failure to win back power with an army of Syrian Turks, Zangī took Baalbek after its governor Muḥammad had succeeded his murdered brother Maḥmūd at Damascus, and advanced to the siege of Damascus itself. There, after the death of Muḥammad in March 1140, the Amīr Unur installed Muḥammad's young son Abaq as his successor, and took charge of the city as Atabeg for the prince. His alliance with King Fulk of Jerusalem obliged Zangī to retreat, and was maintained for the next seven years against the continued threat posed by Zangī to Franks and Damascenes alike. In 1144, however, it was not Damascus that came under siege but Edessa, the capital of the most northerly of the four Frankish states. It was taken, and the principality itself was lost, to the consternation of Christendom. In 1146 Zangī himself turned once again to an assault upon Damascus, but was murdered en route by one of his entourage. Unur at Damascus seized the opportunity to reoccupy Baalbek and recover the allegiance of Homs and Hama, but Zangī's two sons partitioned his dominions between them, the elder taking Mosul and the younger, Nūr al-Dīn Maḥmūd, taking Aleppo, where he rapidly resumed his father's ambitions. In 1147 these took a different turn after the alliance between Jerusalem and Damascus was broken by the Franks, who in response to the overtures of Altuntāsh, the son of Kumushtakīn at Bosra and Salkhad, attempted to annex the two cities while installing Altuntāsh himself as lord of the Hauran to the north. Unur appealed for aid to Nūr al-Dīn, and the Franks retreated. At the same time, seemingly to take advantage of this change in the axis of alliances, al-Ḥāfiẓ sent an embassy to Damascus with appropriate presents. The climax came next year, in 1148, when the Second Crusade, preached by St Bernard of Clairvaux to restore the situation in Syria, advanced upon Damascus and was completely routed. In face of the Crusaders, Unur had finally been driven to ally with Nūr al-Dīn, and next year, in 1149, contributed to Nūr al-Dīn's victory over the Franks in an expedition against Antioch. But after the decade in which he had kept Damascus from its various foes, his death at the end of the year left Nūr al-Dīn to pursue the unification of Muslim Syria under his rule, and to prosecute the holy war upon the Latin states.

At the same time in Egypt, al-Ḥāfiẓ himself died at the end of 1149 at the age of around seventy-five. He had preserved the dynasty from the various threats to its existence, to the extent of recovering for the monarchy the kind of personal control exercised by his predecessor after the lapse of a century since the death of al-Ḥākim. But the cause of the Imāmate as God's authority for the faith had largely been lost to those who had broken with the dynasty over the succession, while that of the Caliphate as God's government of the Dār, the House of Islam, had failed in its reinvention by al-Afḍal as the leadership of the faithful in the holy war. Beyond Egypt and Cyrenaica, the empire had shrunk down to the few who continued to recognise the right of the dynasty – the Ḥamdānids and Zurayᶜids in the Yemen, and the Christian King of Muqurra. The Zurayᶜids at Aden were sufficiently important on the trade route to India to receive an embassy in 1144, while in the West, a commercial treaty was concluded with Roger in 1143 in furtherance of the friendly relationship developed by Bahrām. This apparently continued despite the conquest by Roger of the Ifrīqiyan coast from Tripoli to al-Mahdiyya between 1146 and 1148, putting an end to the Zirid dynasty and any last vestige there may have been of the empire in the Maghrib.[9] The threat of assassination by the Nizārīs had died away after their expulsion from Damascus and surrender of the fortress of Banyas to the Franks; throughout the reign of al-Ḥāfiẓ their energies were devoted to the creation of a lesser Alamut, a mountain state in the Jabal Ansariya west of Homs and Hama on the Orontes, centred on the fortress of Masyāf. Far more sinister as far as the Fatimids were concerned were the designs upon Damascus of Zangī and his son Nūr al-Dīn, his successor at Aleppo, all in the cause of holy war upon the Franks in the name of Sunnī Islam. For the first time since the days of Ṭughril Beg and Alp Arslan, a militant and ideologically driven Seljuq empire was being created in Syria, with consequences for Egypt that played out over the next twenty years.

The Second Murder of a Caliph and the Fall of Ascalon

Over these two decades the Fatimids finally succumbed to a prolonged internal crisis that ran on into the conflict in Syria and turned Egypt into the principal prize in the war between Nūr al-Dīn and the Franks. It began with the accession of al-Ḥāfiẓ's designated son, the seventeen-year-old Ismāᶜīl, with the title of al-Ẓāfir bi-amriʾllāh, Victorious by God's Command. He was thus of an age to take charge of the state, but like al-Ẓāhir in succession to al-Ḥākim, preferred his pleasures to the business of government, and at this critical juncture abandoned the cause of the dynasty that his father had endeavoured to rescue. Power was confided to the elderly Ibn Maṣāl, the

[9] Cf. M. Brett, 'Muslim justice under infidel rule: the Normans in Ifrīqiya, 517–555H/1123–1160 AD', in Brett, *Ibn Khaldun and the Medieval Maghrib*, no. XIII.

Berber Amīr to whom al-Ḥāfiẓ had entrusted some unspecified and otherwise unrecorded oversight of affairs, and who now became Wazīr. In what was almost the customary fashion after the executions of Ibn Qusā and Abū Zakarī, the two al-Anṣāri brothers whom al-Ḥāfiẓ had put in charge of the Dīwān al-Jaysh, or Army Office, were promptly and savagely put to death for having pounced upon, in the words of the chronicler, all the great and the good, right up to the senior eunuchs in attendance on the Caliph; they had, presumably, either held them to strict account or extorted bribes instead. But, like Hazārmard after the murder of al-Āmir, the man who thus stepped forward as Wazīr was straightaway ousted. Ibn Maṣāl survived a rebellion by the Black regiments, but not the revolt of yet another governor of the Gharbiyya, Ibn Sallār. Brought up as a member of the Ḥujāriyya, Ibn Sallār was in alliance with his stepson ᶜAbbās, a grandson of the Zirid Tamīm ibn Muᶜizz at Mahdiyya, who was now governor of Alexandria. At the approach of their combined forces, the new Caliph ordered his new Wazīr to flee, not into the palace like Hazārmard, but away to the Delta to recruit a nomad army of Lawāta and Bedouin.

Meanwhile, the army command in Cairo rallied to Ibn Sallār, and negotiated with the women of the dynasty his appointment in place of Ibn Maṣāl at the beginning of 1150, two months after al-Ḥāfiẓ's death. A month later, as Ibn Maṣāl advanced upon Cairo from the south, he was defeated and killed by ᶜAbbās, and his head paraded through the city. His killing made an enemy of al-Ẓāfir, for whom Ibn Sallār was yet another Sunnī who had set himself up in opposition to the Caliph, and one whom members of the *sibyān al-khāṣṣ*, al-Ẓāfir's bodyguard, conspired to kill. But the conspiracy was betrayed, and almost all of the conspirators were slaughtered. Meanwhile, yet another appointee of al-Ḥāfiẓ was executed: the Qāḍī al-Tinnīsī, who was apparently once again at the head of the ministries.

In the midst of this crisis, the young king of Jerusalem, Baldwin III, seized the opportunity to occupy and begin to reconstruct and fortify the ruined site of Gaza, on the coast to the south of Ascalon. In thus surrounding Ascalon to the south as well as the north and east, aiming to cut off the land approach to the city from Egypt, the purpose was finally to capture the great fortress. Beyond that, a raid upon Farama at the eastern approach to the Delta betokened a future of incursions into Egypt. The response of Ibn Sallār was to seek an alliance with Nūr al-Dīn through the agency of an Arab gentleman and warrior, to quote the title bestowed on Usāma ibn Munqidh by Philip Hitti, the translator of his memoirs.[10] Written in old

[10] Usāma ibn Munqidh, *Kitāb al-I'tibār*, ed. H. Zayn (Beirut, 1988); trans. P. K. Hitti, *Memoirs of an Arab-Syrian Gentleman* (New York, 1927).

age, and in praise of Saladin as his benefactor, these are self-serving, putting a dubious career in as favourable a light as possible as they recount the intrigues and diplomacies of Egyptian and Syrian politics. At the head of his family, the Banū Munqidh, Usāma was lord of Shayzar on the Orontes, a strategic site caught between the Aleppans to the north, the Damascans to the south and, at this juncture, the Nizārīs in the mountains to the west, but as a prime example of the mobility of the warrior elite, preferred to seek his fortune in the service of the various rulers of Damascus and Egypt. Thus he claimed to have been instrumental in the deal whereby Riḍwān had been furnished by the Damascans with a force of Turks to attempt to recover his position at Cairo. In 1144, however, he left Damascus with his family for Egypt, where he was well received, well robed and well housed by al-Ḥāfiẓ, acquiring a substantial *iqṭā*ᶜ and a troop of *mamlūk*-s, as *ghilmān* were called by this time. There, after the death of al-Ḥāfiẓ, he threw in his lot with Ibn Sallār, and in 1151 was despatched on a mission to Nūr al-Dīn at the siege of Damascus as he resumed his father's attempts to take the city. The mission, to invite Nūr al-Dīn to attack Tiberias on the Sea of Galilee while the Egyptian fleet sailed up the coast, was a failure, not because the mule carrying the gold that was part of the present to Nūr al-Dīn bolted off into the Transjordanian desert, but because Nūr al-Dīn was obliged to retreat as the Franks advanced in response to an appeal by the Būrid prince Abaq. This return of Damascus to an alliance with Jerusalem meant that nothing came of the proposed cooperation with the Egyptians. What was once again a powerful Egyptian fleet did indeed sail, after so many years, up the coast as far as Tripoli, successfully raiding the harbours of all the main Frankish ports. But without an attack on the Latin Kingdom by Nūr al-Dīn, there was no strategic gain. Usāma returned to Egypt via Ascalon, where he engaged in skirmishes with the Franks, and where his brother was killed in an attack upon Gaza.

Matters came to a head in 1153 and 1154. In January 1153 Baldwin brought all the forces of Jerusalem to the siege of Ascalon (see Fig. 11.2). On the instructions of Ibn Sallār, ᶜAbbās and his son Naṣr mustered an army at Bilbays to relieve the city. But there the two conspired in collusion with al-Ẓāfir to murder the Wazīr and replace him with ᶜAbbās. Returning to Cairo in April, Naṣr as a member of the family had no difficulty in entering and murdering Ibn Sallār in his sleep, whereupon ᶜAbbās was duly appointed Wazīr by a grateful Caliph. Ascalon, however, was not relieved, although the Egyptian fleet replenished the city in June; and in August it surrendered on terms that allowed the entire population to retire to Egypt, taking with it, among other things, the head of Ḥusayn from its mausoleum. Usāma, now in the confidence both of ᶜAbbās and in particular of his son, then played some devious role in a scheme whereby in April 1154, Naṣr, by now a love of al-Ẓāfir, invited the Caliph to his house and murdered him, throwing the body into a well. In the morning ᶜAbbās, as Wazīr, entered the palace to declare that since the Imām could not be found, his four-year-old son ᶜĪsā was to be Caliph with the regnal title of al-Fāᵓiz, while al-Ẓāfir's two brothers and a nephew were cut down on the spot. It was a slaughter that completely failed in its purpose. The royal women, daughters of al-Ḥāfiẓ in order of seniority, cut off locks of their hair and sent it in an appeal to Ṭalāᵓiᶜ ibn Ruzzīk, the Armenian governor of Ashmunayn and Bahnasā, the central province to the south of Cairo. He responded immediately, fixing the tresses to the lances of his men much as Riḍwān had fixed Qurᵓāns to his spears as a sign of his mission. ᶜAbbās, setting out to meet him, had to fight his way out of al-Qāhira, and finally, in the face of general opposition, turned to flight. Usāma, invited by Ṭalāᵓiᶜ to join him, was compelled to go instead with ᶜAbbās by the seizure of his family. The flight at the end of May, however, was a disaster. Instead of heading back to Alexandria to gather his forces like previous refugees from Cairo, ᶜAbbās followed the example of Riḍwān in making for Damascus. In April, at the same time as the murder of al-Ẓāfir, the city had finally fallen to Nūr al-Dīn, who might be counted on to help with his return. But harassed by the Bedouin, the party was halted by the Franks to the south of the Dead Sea. ᶜAbbās was killed, and Naṣr sold back to al-Qāhira, where he was mutilated and beaten to death with their clogs by the women of the palace. Only Usāma, who had sent his family back to Cairo, managed to reach Damascus.

The Last Great Armenian Wazīr

For the Fatimids, with the Franks in Ascalon, Nūr al-Dīn in Damascus and an infant in al-Qāhira, the events of the year from 1153 to 1154 were climacteric, the culmination of the threat to the dynasty-s position that began with the murder of al-Āmir and now left it fatally undermined and radically exposed. Not only had the dynastic stronghold of the palace complex been breached, but the succession had passed without designation to a child in the care of his aunts. But none of these princesses was a Sitt al-Mulk, a Lady of the Kingdom, capable of taking charge of the government. Instead, al-Sayyida al-Sharīfa, the Noble Lady who was the senior, was the Sitt al-Quṣūr, or Lady of the Palaces. They had come a long way from al-Mahdiyya, eulogised by the Qāḍī al-Nuᶜmān as the citadel in which the daughters of Fāṭima had been preserved from the Dajjāl. Now, in charge of the palace, their enemy became the man they had summoned to their aid as he took power, executing or imprisoning Amīrs and secretaries of the previous regime, including Ibn al-Bawwāb, the head of the administration.

Figure 11.2 Drawing of a battle between Arabs and Franks – siege of Ascalon. Museum number BM1938.3-12.01 © The Trustees of the British Museum.

A rare depiction of an actual event, this drawing of the siege of Ascalon gives an impression of the warfare with the Franks that characterised the twelfth century.

As al-Malik al-Ṣāliḥ, the Virtuous King, in the royal style introduced by Riḍwān into the titulature of the Wazīrate, Ṭalāʾiʿ ibn Ruzzīk was as much a Sultan as al-Afḍal had been in the days of al-Āmir's infancy. He was the son of an Armenian who had arrived with Badr in 1074, and one who, like Kutayfāt, was Shīʿite but not Ismāʿīlī. As such, not only did he build a new mausoleum for the head of Ḥusayn (though in the event it came to rest in the palace),[11] but he also created an endowment, a *waqf*, for the Banū Maʿṣūm, the Iraqi descendants of Mūsā al-Kāẓim, the seventh Imām in the Twelver line of succession, and otherwise subsidised the Ashrāf in the Hijaz and at Najaf in Iraq. Unlike Kutayfāt and Riḍwān, however, he made no attempt to dispose of the dynasty, preferring, like al-Afḍal, to rule on its behalf, maintaining all the ceremonial recreated by al-Ḥāfiẓ.[12] After the murder of its princes, he was indeed its saviour, albeit with a mixed reputation as poet, patron and holy warrior on the one hand, tyrant and usurper

[11] Cf. De Smet, 'La translation du *Raʾs al-Ḥusayn* au Caire fatimide', *Egypt and Syria in the Fatimid, Ayyubid and Mamluk Eras*, II, pp. 39–41.

[12] See above, n. 5.

on the other, all down to what looks like an attempt to return to the glorious days of Badr and al-Afḍal. He faced the usual difficulties. His demands and confiscations followed the example of Ibn Qusā, Abū Zakarī and the Anṣāri brothers as evidence of the problems with the revenue that went back to the days of al Baṭāʾiḥī, to the Afḍalī *rawk* and to the concessions he had made over the tax-farms when he became Wazīr. In 1156 a shortfall of the harvest and a rise in the price of grain compounded the difficulty. Over and above these perennial problems, however, was the heightened cost of the holy war as Ṭalāʾiᶜ resumed the aggressive policy of Ibn Sallār. The fleet was despatched in expeditions up the coast to Tyre in 1155 and to Beirut in 1158, and the army under his lieutenant Ḍirghām against Jerusalem in 1157 and 1158. With these expenses went the weapons and subsidies sent to Nūr al-Dīn in 1158 along with an embassy to secure his alliance. The aim of Ṭalāʾiᶜ was evidently that of al-Afḍal, to win legitimacy for himself in the cause of Islam, but at the same time to guard against the Frankish threat from Ascalon and Gaza. The *sijill* accompanying the embassy has not survived, but its tenor can be guessed from the poems addressed to Nūr al-Dīn which Ṭalāʾiᶜ himself composed and sent via Usāma, who was now in a position at Damascus to act as go-between in the negotiations. As with the pronouncements of al-Afḍal, these poems laid stress upon his dedication to the holy war, as proved by his victories over the Franks by sea and land. But while these victories were cited to demonstrate to Nūr al-Dīn his worth as an ally, it is no longer he who claims the leadership in the war on behalf of the Caliph. It is rather Nūr al-Dīn who is apostrophised as the victor who will defeat the Franks and recover Jerusalem. Usāma in his equally poetic reply is still more explicit, hailing Nūr al-Dīn as the man of destiny who will drive them out of Islam. In the event, the hyperbole was wasted. The embassy went at the wrong time, with Nūr al-Dīn only just back from Aleppo, still recovering from serious illness, worsted in an encounter with the Franks and faced with the imminent invasion of Syria by the Byzantine Emperor. There was no alliance; and when, in 1160, King Baldwin threatened to invade Egypt, he was bought off with a promise of tribute.[13]

At the same time that he was claiming glory for himself in the holy war, Ṭalāʾiᶜ set out to reaffirm what remained of the Fatimid empire and influence in the Red Sea. In 1155 there was received in state in the Golden Hall of the palace, the ambassador of the Sharīf of the Holy Places, the Yemeni jurist ᶜUmāra, to hear his recitation of a laudatory poem. Showered with

[13] For the approach of Ṭalāʾiᶜ to Damascus, see Brett, 'The Fatimids and the Counter-Crusade', in U. Vermeulen and K. D'Hulster (eds), *Egypt and Syria in the Fatimid, Ayyubid and Mamluk Eras*, V (Leuven, 2007), pp. 22–4.

gold by the Wazīr and the Sayyida al-Sharīfa on behalf of the infant Caliph, ᶜUmāra returned to Mecca laden with wealth and with the grain that the governor of Qūṣ had been ordered to supply, together with a letter to the Zurayᶜid prince of Aden containing 3,000 dīnārs in recognition of his loyalty to the Ḥāfiẓī Daᶜwa. ᶜUmāra came back to Egypt in 1157 to settle in Cairo as court poet to Ṭalāʾiᶜ and his successors, writing a history of events in the 1160s as well as a history of the Yemen which is a major contemporary source for the history of the Ṣulayḥids.[14] A Sunnī from one of the heartlands of Ismāᶜīlism, whose attachment to the Fatimid Caliphate cost him his life after Saladin came to power, he illustrates the way in which, over the last thirty years, the doctrinal exclusiveness of the Daᶜwa had for most purposes faded into a more oecumenical Islam in which the original distinction between Muʾminūn and Muslimūn was blurred. Ṭalāʾiᶜ himself, as a Shīᶜite who may have been an ᶜAlawī who gave precedence to ᶜAlī over Muḥammad, not only represented this Islam at the centre of government, but pursued it still further at the death of the epileptic child al-Fāʾiz in 1160. In the absence of a designated successor, he demanded from the Zimām al-Qaṣr, the steward of the palace, the youngest of the princes to be the next Imām Caliph. This was the nine-year-old ᶜAbd Allāh, son of Yūsuf, the murdered brother of al-Ẓāfir, who was enthroned as al-ᶜĀḍid li-Dīn Allāh, the Supporter of God's Religion. The choice of a minor was deliberate, promptly followed by the boy's marriage to the Wazīr's own daughter in an attempt to replicate the marriage of Badr's daughter to Aḥmad, the future al-Mustaᶜlī, and thus to repeat the achievement of Badr and his son in creating a dynasty intimately connected to that of the Imām Caliph. The succession was accordingly celebrated in verse by the poet in Ṭalāʾiᶜ as: 'Two Imāms in the hand of God; a mystery in which one is taken, the other raised up by Him'. Meanwhile, at the practical level, the challenge of Ḥusayn, son of Nizār, who arrived at Barqa from the Maghrib to claim the throne under the title al-Mustanṣir, was swiftly eliminated with his capture and execution.

Had Ṭalāʾiᶜ succeeded in his evident ambition to rule on behalf of the Imām Caliph, both the Dawla and the Daᶜwa might have been relaunched on a further career. But unlike Badr, he could count neither on the loyalty of the palace nor on the absence of serious rivals. Under the princesses the palace was dangerously hostile. Thus in 1158 Ṭalāʾiᶜ arrested Yāqūt, the governor of Qūṣ appointed by ᶜAbbās, who had failed to support him in ousting ᶜAbbās, and who now conspired with the Sayyida, the senior aunt

[14] ᶜUmāra al-Yamanī, *Taʾrīkh al-Yaman*, ed. and trans. H. C. Kay in *Yaman, its Early Mediaeval History* (London, 1892), text, pp. 1–102, trans., pp. 1–137.

of al-Fāʾiz, to revolt and take his place as Wazīr. Yāqūt died in prison later in the year; meanwhile the princess herself, who had plotted to have Ṭalāʾiᶜ killed, was executed along with sundry eunuchs and Ṣaqāliba, leaving the much disturbed infant Caliph in the charge of a second, younger aunt. Given the hostility of his relations with the family, at the accession of al-ᶜĀḍid, Ṭalāʾiᶜ moved to complete his takeover of the Dawla, not with an attempt at reconciliation, but with the removal of the wealth of the palace to his own residence, and with a monopoly on the supply of grain to raise the price. The intention behind both was not simply to meet the general expenses of government and the army in the holy war, but almost certainly to pay for his own government – his household and the wider support he required in the army to secure his position. In this he may have differed from his predecessors only in the ruthlessness with which he built his regime, and which was remarked upon in the chronicles. Thus he had four lieutenants, each with a substantial troop of *ghilmān/mamlūk*-s; an extended family whose members he appointed across the range of government, most notably a brother as governor of the strategically important Sharqiyya, the eastern Delta; and allies including his general Ḍirghām. Various Amīrs were executed or imprisoned, but the veteran Shāwar, a Bedouin Arab who had been a protégé of al-Baṭāʾiḥī and an ally of Riḍwān, was a rival whom he distanced from al-Qāhira by appointing him governor of Upper Egypt at Qūṣ. The palace under the younger princess, now Sitt al-Quṣūr, was another matter. In September 1161 she conspired with the commanders of the Black troops to kill the Wazīr in the corridor leading into the audience hall as he entered for his customary greeting to the Caliph, arranging the matter with the Amīr Ibn Qawwām al-Dawla, the Ṣāḥib al-Bāb. But the affair was bungled. Ṭalāʾiᶜ was mortally wounded, but survived to be carried off to his residence for an eventual state funeral, while the commander of his guard, the Kurdish Amīr Ḥusayn ibn Abī ʾl-Hayjāʾ, set upon the Blacks and killed some fifty of them. The son of Ṭalāʾiᶜ,Ruzzīk, who had been wounded in the attack, sent for the princess and had her strangled with her own veil. Succeeding his father as Wazīr, he made Ibn Abī ʾl-Hayjāʾ his deputy responsible for the business of government, while leaving the youngest princess, protesting her innocence, in charge of the child al-ᶜĀḍid. Ibn Qawwām al-Dawla was duly executed, and all those involved in the murder of his father hunted down. Otherwise he seems, unlike his father, to have aimed at popularity, gaining a reputation for leniency, freeing three of the Amīrs whom his father had imprisoned, despatching the Amīr Muḥammad ibn Shams al-Khilāfa to Mecca with gold and celebrating the wedding of his sister to the Caliph in the Dār, or palace, of the Wizāra. And he made at least one important appointment, having the governor of Alexandria send him the Qāḍī al-Fāḍil to be put in charge of the Dīwān al-Jaysh, the Army Office – important, because al-Fāḍil was to become one of the two major chroniclers of Saladin's achievements

The Intervention of Damascus and Jerusalem

On the other hand, Ruzzīk set out to complete his father's control of the country with the dispossession of Shāwar at Qūṣ, sending Ibn Abīʾl-Hayjāʾ to oust him and replace him with a man of his own. The year 1162 saw Upper Egypt doubly threatened by a Nubian invasion, the first for a century as the King of Muqurra broke his long-standing allegiance to Cairo and attacked Aswan. But Ruzzīk's new governor, Naṣīr al-Dīn, wrote to Shāwar from Akhmīm on the border of his province, resigning his appointment and leaving Shāwar to enter into a rebellion that precipitated the ousting and death of Ruzzīk. With only a small force, Shāwar left Qūṣ for the Wāhāt, the western oases, where he collected a growing army of Bedouin for the advance on Cairo. Whatever popularity Ruzzīk had once enjoyed had been lost by the exactions of the four henchmen he had inherited from his father, in pursuit of the same demand for money. At the news of Shāwar's approach, Ibn Abī ʾl-Hayjāʾ fled to Mecca and eventually to Nubia, where he died, while Ḍirghām, his brothers, his fellow Amīrs and others took their followers over to Shāwar. Ruzzīk himself left Cairo with his *mamlūk*-s and baggage to wander some fifty miles up the Nile to Atfih. There, he and his troop were seized by a Bedouin chief, who handed him over to Shāwar to be killed. Shāwar himself entered al-Qāhira at the beginning of 1163 to be installed as Wazīr with the customary title of Amīr al-Juyūsh.

The downfall of the Banū Ruzzīk was not regretted, but from the point of view of the Fatimids and their mission, Shāwar's triumph put an end to any ideological purpose cultivated on the dynasty's behalf by the Wazīrs of the Sword from Badr al-Mustanṣirī to Ṭalāʾiʿs ibn Ruzzīk and his son. It was, moreover, short-lived, as competition for the Wazīrate degenerated into a simple struggle for power between rival Amīrs. It had been a triumph for the Bedouin, for Shāwar himself as an Arab tribesman by origin, and for those tribesmen who had brought him to power. As the mainstay of his regime, these were richly rewarded with the accumulated wealth of the Banū Ruzzīk, and given free rein to plunder the Ḥawf, the eastern Delta, at the expense of the *muqṭāʿūn* and their estates. Very rapidly, then, the military who had deserted Ruzzīk turned against him, coalescing around Ḍirghām, now Ṣāḥib al-Bāb and commander of the Barqiyya, an elite corps that had been created by Ṭalāʾiʿ. Within six months there was fighting in which two sons of Shāwar may have been killed and a third captured, while Shāwar himself fled away, first to his kinsmen the Banū Manṣūr, and then to Damascus to ask for

Nūr al-Dīn's help. Ḍirghām's victory, meanwhile, was less than complete. Insecure in his position as the new Wazīr, he proceeded to execute some seventy of the Amīrs whom he suspected of plotting the return of Shāwar, and lost any goodwill he had with the capture and crucifixion of the governor of Alexandria. Left with only the personal following on which he could rely, he was thus weakly placed to meet an invasion from Syria should Shāwar gain the support of Nūr al-Dīn. The embassy he sent to Damascus to dissuade Nūr al-Dīn from doing so failed; by April 1164 Nūr al-Dīn had evidently calculated that it was to his advantage to intervene in the affairs of Egypt, whether or not he was persuaded by Shāwar's apparent offer of a third of the country's *kharāj*. Thus he despatched the senior Kurdish Amīr Shīrkūh with a substantial force to reinstate Shāwar, who could expect to raise his own army on his re-entry into Egypt. At the news, Ḍirghām appealed to Amalric, the new King of Jerusalem, but too late for the Franks to muster and come to his aid. An invasion of Egypt which would at the same time forestall its acquisition by Damascus was nevertheless in keeping with their ambitions since the capture of Ascalon and the fortification of Gaza; and Ḍirghām's appeal was the first sign that the squabbling of the Egyptians over the Wazīrate had now gone beyond the internal affairs of the Caliphate. Over the next five or six years, the country was drawn into the conflict between Damascus and Jerusalem as a prize instead of a participant in the holy war.

This radical change in the situation of the dynasty and its state was matched by a shift in the focus of the sources away from the Fatimids towards Saladin, the man who finally won the prize. His fame has ensured that the secondary literature likewise dwells on his career, notably in *Saladin. The Politics of the Holy War*, by Lyons and Jackson.[15] The sources for their account were critically assessed by Holt in his review of the work,[16] and those for his Egyptian career by Lev in his *Saladin in Egypt*.[17] Holt's observation that the picture of Saladin presented by his admirers, as the great champion of Islam in the holy war with the Franks, is at variance with the fact that he spent most of his career at war with other Muslims, does not go quite as far as Ehrenkreutz's portrayal of a ruthless careerist.[18] What is nevertheless clear is the central importance in the sources of a particular admirer, the Qāḍī al-Fāḍil, who passed from Fatimid service into that of Saladin, whom he served

[15] M. C. Lyons and D. E. P. Jackson, *Saladin. The Politics of the Holy War* (Cambridge, 1982).

[16] P. M. Holt, 'Saladin and his admirers: a biographical reassessment', *Bulletin of SOAS*, 46 (1983), 235–9.

[17] Y. Lev, *Saladin in Egypt* (Leiden, 1999).

[18] A. S. Ehrenkreutz, *Saladin* (New York, 1972).

as secretary, administrator and propagandist. His letters have been edited,[19] though his historical work, the *Mutajaddidāt*, is lost except in quotation. His gloss on Saladin's career adds to the contradictions in the account of the last days of the Fatimids, which are difficult to reconstruct in detail if not in outline. It is nevertheless a testimony to the lingering charisma of the dynasty, and to the enduring structure of the regime, that the conflict as it developed in Egypt should have continued the battle for the Wazīrate. In this his first foray, Shīrkūh entered into the country as an adventurer in his own right rather than a simple agent of Nūr al-Dīn. The joint forces of the invaders defeated Ḍirghām's brother Mulham at Bilbays, the outpost that guarded the approach to Cairo from the north-east, before Shāwar went on to occupy Fusṭāṭ, and Ḍirghām himself was killed in flight from al-Qāhira. With Shāwar now reinstated as Wazīr, however, the alliance promptly disintegrated, as Shīrkūh refused to be fobbed off with the sum of 30,000 dīnārs in place of the enormous sum promised to Nūr al-Dīn. Instead, he retired to Bilbays, while it was Shāwar who now wrote for aid to Amalric. The King was now ready to march, and Shīrkūh found himself besieged in Bilbays for some three months until an agreement was reached, the Franks retired and Shīrkūh departed on payment of a further sum of 30,000 dīnārs. For the next two years Shāwar was then free to hunt down his remaining opponents, disposing of the challenge of an obscure rival, Ibn al-Khayyāṭ, and suppressing a rising of the Lawāta and the Arab Bedouin, until at the beginning of 1167 Shīrkūh reappeared in Egypt with an army of his own, reinforced with a contingent supplied by Nūr al-Dīn, and bent on conquest in the name of the ᶜAbbasids. Since the expedition was no secret, Amalric arrived at the same time to ally with Shāwar at Cairo, while Shīrkūh followed the practice of so many invaders and rebels since the days of the Qāᵓim, in camping across the river at Giza. The campaign was complicated: Shīrkūh moved south to the vicinity of Ashmunayn, where he was brought to battle by the pursuing Franks and Egyptians. His victory in the battle, however, was not decisive, and he moved back north to Alexandria, where he was welcomed in a city that had always been a focus of opposition to Cairo. There, his Syrians under the command of his nephew Ṣalāḥ al-Dīn Yūsuf, in other words Saladin, were besieged by the allies, while he himself went back up the Nile as far as Qūṣ. By the end of the summer, with no resolution in sight, it had become clearly to his own advantage and that of the Franks to make peace and leave the country once again in the hands of Shāwar. The final outcome

[19] (al-Qāḍī) al-Fāḍil, *Al-Durr al-naẓīma min tarassul ᶜAbd al-Raḥīm (ibn ᶜAlī al-Baysānī)*, ed. A. Badawi, Cairo, n.d. For his reliability, see, for example, Lev, *Saladin in Egypt*, p. 103.

was thus deferred until the following year, when at the end of 1168 it was Amalric rather than Shīrkūh who was the invader, and Shāwar's appeal was once again to Nūr al-Dīn.

The prompt for the Frankish invasion is uncertain, whether it was a desire to pre-empt a fresh alliance between Cairo and Damascus or to take advantage of Nūr al-Dīn's distractions on his north-eastern frontier, and its objective was equally unclear. But from Ascalon, Amalric advanced to the capture of Bilbays at the beginning of November, burning the city and enslaving its people before moving on to Cairo. At his approach, Shāwar set fire to Fusṭāṭ to deny its capture and use by the Franks as a base for an attack upon al-Qāhira. How much of the city was actually destroyed is unclear; but as the population streamed out towards al-Qāhira, it was plundered by sailors from the fleet and by the Black soldiery. Amalric, however, did not attack, but settled instead for a substantial ransom. A first instalment of some 100,000 dīnārs was paid over immediately, leaving Shāwar to collect the rest while Amalric drew off for some twenty miles in the direction of Bilbays. His invasion, however, had prompted Nūr al-Dīn to muster a force large enough to effect the final conquest of Egypt, with Shīrkūh once again in command at the head of much the largest contingent. Hearing the news of the expedition, in December Amalric withdrew still further to Bilbays, and from there attempted to intercept the Syrians. He failed; Shīrkūh reached the Nile, and Amalric had no option other than retreat from the country at the beginning of January 1169. For Shāwar it was equally the end as his room for manoeuvre was finally closed off, while for the invaders his elimination was required to forestall any further duplicity. Riding out to the Syrian encampment, he was seized by Saladin and put to death. The story that al-ᶜĀḍid himself, now a young man able to exercise what power and authority remained to him, sent his executioners from the palace to demand his head, may have been an excuse on the part of Saladin's chroniclers.[20] Shīrkūh was promptly, and naturally, appointed in his place. Three months later, however, he was dead, of overeating, leaving his men without a leader. In this crisis, in need of a successor to maintain themselves in this foreign land, the Syrians, a miscellany of Turkish and Kurdish contingents each under their own Amīrs, united with one exception behind the relatively junior Saladin, who thus began his historic career as the next and last Fatimid Wazīr.

[20] Cf. Lyons and Jackson, *Saladin*, p. 25.

Saladin and the End of the Dynasty

Almost 100 years after Badr al-Jamālī had arrived in Egypt to rescue the Caliphate from a dire internal and external crisis that had threatened its very existence, a second ambitious adventurer from yet another people on the fringes of empire had come to replicate his achievement in response to yet another appeal for aid. It was a task undertaken once again in the name of the Caliph, as Shīrkūh entered of necessity into the structure of the Egyptian regime in the absence of any legitimacy of his own. That was still more true of the nephew to whom the task was left, a young man of around thirty without his uncle's proven worth as a commander, who needed the Wazīrate to secure not only his power in Egypt but a measure of independence from his suzerain Nūr al-Dīn. For that it was necessary, as it had been for Badr al-Jamālī, to stamp out all internal opposition, and beyond that to repel any further Frankish invasion. The opposition that might have gathered behind Shāwar now centred on the palace in the person of the eunuch Muʾtamin al-Khilāfa, and came into the open in August, when Saladin had him killed as he ventured out of the palace. He had, it seems, conspired with malcontents among the Egyptian Amīrs to invite a further invasion by Amalric, one that would draw Saladin away from al-Qāhira while the city was secured against his return. Al-Qāhira, however, was immediately the scene of a rising by the Blacks, the infantry regiments that over the years had been the guardsmen of the dynasty, and now came out against the foreigner. Joined by other opponents of the new regime, they massed in the square in front of the Great Eastern Palace, fighting for two days with Saladin's forces based around the Dār al-Wizāra to the north. Joined by the Armenian archers on the walls of the palace, they held their ground until al-ᶜĀḍid himself allegedly intervened, letting it be known that he wanted them driven away. Retreating from the Bayn al-Qaṣrayn, they escaped out of the Bāb Zawīla across the Nile to Giza. But there they were followed and more or less wiped out by Saladin's brother Tūrān Shāh, while their quarters in al-Manṣūriyya in the direction of Fusṭāṭ were burnt. The danger from abroad nevertheless remained. Whether or not Muʾtamin had been party to plans for a joint invasion, in October the Byzantine fleet and Amalric's army came to besiege Damietta at the mouth of the Delta's eastern branch of the Nile, a port whose possession would give them a permanent foothold in Egypt. But the allies quarrelled, the attack was not pressed and Saladin had time to despatch the forces required to defend the city and raise the siege in December.

The expedition had cost money, some of it provided by al-ᶜĀḍid, who seems to have come to an understanding with his new Wazīr after the rebellion of the Blacks. As Wazīr, Saladin had no difficulty in taking control of the administration and gaining the cooperation of its officials, most notably the Qāḍī al-Fāḍil, but equally the likes of al-Makhzūmī and Ibn Mammātī, the first of whom was promptly commissioned to provide a description of the financial system and especially of the all-important regime of the *iqṭāʿāt*. As it had been for Badr al-Jamālī, it was of critical importance for him to create his own regime on the strength of a foreign army firmly rooted in the country it had conquered. At the head of his regime he installed his own extended family – an uncle, Shihāb al-Dīn, his brother, Tūrān Shāh, and finally his father, Ayyūb, together with two other brothers, two nephews and a brother-in-law, a family dynasty in the making. Tūrān Shāh in particular was his right-hand man who had driven out and massacred the Blacks, and who in 1171 went up the Nile to deal with Bedouin raiding. Of more fundamental importance for the future was the allocation to his Syrians of *iqṭāʿāt* on much the same terms, it would appear, as those referred to in the dispositions for the garrison of Ascalon in the reign of al-Ḥāfiẓ – payment, that is, of the *muqṭāʿ* by the state at the assessed value of his *iqṭāʿ*, supplemented by the pay and allowances to which he was entitled on campaign, while he himself took care of the cultivation of the estate assigned to him. The systematic adoption and adaptation of this Fatimid practice to the military and political purposes of the new order laid the foundations for the subsequent Mamlūk state in Egypt.

Unlike Badr al-Jamālī, however, Saladin had not come with his uncle to champion the Fatimid Caliphate in opposition to that of the ʿAbbasids and their Seljuq Sultans, or to promote its Shīʿite Daʿwa over and above Sunnī Islam. He was indeed an avatar of the Great Seljuq Sultanate, which had effectively ceased to exist with the death of its Sultan Sanjar in 1157 but had sprouted a series of successors, of whom the Zangids at Mosul and Damascus were those who had taken over its dominions in Syria. And as a henchman of Nūr al-Dīn, Saladin was not only committed to the holy war, but the holy war in the name of the ʿAbbasids and Sunnī Islam. His Wazīrate was a necessary expedient rather than a step towards a monarchy inseparable from the dynasty. While preserving the Caliphate, therefore, not only did his massacre of the Blacks put an end to the power of the palace to intervene in his affairs, but stripped it of all pretentions to religious authority in the state. Thus he dismissed and replaced all Shīʿite *qāḍī*-s with Sunnī Shāfiʿites, and in particular appointed a Shāfiʿite as Chief Qāḍī, thus putting an end to any legacy of the Shīʿite programme of the Banū Ruzzīk. Such measures confirmed the fact that by this time Egypt was predominantly Sunnī, and that the Ismāʿīlī faithful, if not confined to the palace, were inconspicuous. The Ḥāfiẓī Daʿwa was effectively dead, even as the Calling flourished in the Yemen and along the route to India. In Syria the headship of the Nizārīs at Masyāf had been taken in 1162 by Sinān, known to the Franks as the Old Man of the Mountain, whose Assassins came to threaten the life of Saladin himself in his subsequent Syrian campaigns. Most spectacular was the relaunch of the Nizārīs at Alamut by Ḥasan, the grandson of Buzurgumid, who in 1164 proclaimed himself the bringer of the Resurrection and the abolition of the Law, under the name of Ḥasan ᶜalā dhikrihī 'sl-salām, 'on whose name be peace'; in effect, the one in whom the Imāmate of Nizār had been resurrected with a very different message of the Mahdī, a message that harked back to the *ghuluww* once ascribed to the Carmathians, but one that looked forward to a future that has endured to the present day.

In Egypt the end came in 1171, when the order finally came from Nūr al-Dīn to pronounce the *khuṭba*, the address at the Friday prayer, in the name of the ᶜAbbasid Caliph. Perhaps too conveniently, al-ᶜĀḍid fell ill, allowing Saladin to take the momentous step in stages, before and after his death on 13 September. The suspicion remained that out of necessity in the circumstances, he had been murdered.[21] The ending of the Fatimid dynasty was certainly a nervous occasion, for which Saladin took the precaution of a great parade of his troops through al-Qāhira. It called, moreover, for justification. Not only did Saladin attend the funeral; he is said to have told Daᵓūd, the infant son of al-ᶜĀḍid, that as his father had not designated him as his successor in accordance with dynastic principle, he could not inherit, and the line was at an end.[22] It was presumably the argument made in public to explain the demise of a monarchy that had existed for time out of mind. The family itself was left in the palace, to contemplate a possible restoration, but eventually to die out. A plot against Saladin by the Egyptian opposition in 1174 was suppressed; among those executed was the Yemeni ᶜUmāra. Inevitably, sundry pretenders made their appearance, but theirs was a last echo of the call.[23] The great library was dispersed, while the palaces were dismantled and the site built over by the dynasty's Ayyūbid and Mamlūk successors from the thirteenth century onwards. Apart from Badr's great gates and fractions of his wall; the Mosque of al-Azhar; the al-Aqmar Mosque; and the ruins of the Mosque of al-Ḥākim,

[21] Ibid., p. 45, and Lev, *Saladin in Egypt*, p. 83.

[22] Al-Maqrīzī, *Ittiᶜāẓ*, III, p. 347, quoted by Walker, 'Succession to rule in the Shiite Caliphate', in Walker, *Fatimid History and Ismaili Doctrine*, II, p. 48.

[23] Lyons and Jackson, *Saladin*, pp. 66–7; Stern, 'Succession', pp. 211–12; P. Casanova, 'Les derniers Fatimides', *Mémoires de l'Institut français d'archéologie orientale du Caire*, VI (1897), 415–45.

now controversially restored,[24] the Fatimid city has survived only in its plan, in the foundations of subsequent *madrasa*-s and markets, and in the carved woodwork – beams and panels – salvaged and reused elsewhere.[25]

[24] Cf. P. Sanders, 'Bohra architecture and the restoration of Fatimid culture', in Barrucand (ed.), *L'Égypte fatimide*, pp. 159–65.

[25] Cf. N. Hampikian and M. Cyran, 'Recent discoveries concerning the Fatimid palaces uncovered during the conservation works on parts of the Ṣāliḥiyya complex', in Barrucand (ed.), *L'Égypte fatimide*, pp. 649–63.

Conclusion
The Fatimids in Retrospect

'He left a name at which the world grew pale, to point a moral and adorn a tale.' Pope's epithet on the meteoric career of Charles XII of Sweden may apply only by analogy to that of the Fatimids, but points, if not to a moral, to the features and processes of the *longue durée* of mediaeval Islamic history, which entered into the *histoire événementielle* of their dynasty and empire to produce a tale that helped to determine the course of that history. Because the Fatimids failed in their ambition to reconstitute the empire of Islam after its break-up from the eighth century onwards, and at the same time to place its faith under the authority of their Imām, that tale has typically ended in their relegation to the regional histories of North Africa and Egypt, and to that of a sect apart from the great majority of the Muslim community. And it is true that they came too late to reverse the formation of regional states and local dominions, and similarly to prevent the separate development of the schools of the divine law on the authority of their founders. Yet in the course of a career that spanned three centuries, from the world of Late Antiquity to the beginnings of the modern world, the political and religious challenge they offered to the realm of Islam had revolutionary consequences for both its politics and its religion. It was a challenge that succeeded in the first instance because it came as a climax to a long history of religious and political dissent, focused on the claims of the Prophet's descendants to inherit his power and authority, and activated by the appeal of those claims to the margins of society, in particular to tribal peoples on the fringes of the original Arab empire. The monarchy that resulted conformed to the type of its ᶜAbbasid predecessor, and was subject to the same process of institutional development and internal conflict that ultimately proved fatal. But in the middle of the eleventh century its claims to universal dominion provoked a counter-revolution in the form of new empires created by new peoples from outside the old Arab empire, the Turks from central Asia and the Berbers of the western Sahara. Both were religious as well as political reactions to the Fatimid campaign for allegiance, which had provoked a militant Sunnī opposition that went beyond the legalism of the schools with the emphasis placed by al-Ghazālī upon the Qur'ān as a source of illumination, in effect an alternative to the light of the Fatimid Imām. The final twist came at the end of the eleventh century with the arrival of the First Crusade, initially at the invitation of the Byzantine Emperor, to assist his recovery of lands lost to the Seljuq Turks in the course of their westward advance against the Fatimid enemy. By the middle of the twelfth century, that advance had become a counter-Crusade in the name of Sunnism and the ʿAbbasid Caliphate, which came to rest in Egypt with the arrival of Saladin and the final termination of the Fatimid adventure.

Underlying this history is the fraught division within the religions of the Biblical tradition between legalism and messianism that distinguishes Christianity from Talmudic Judaism. In Islam it forms the distinction between Sunnism and Shīʿism that developed out of a quarrel over the succession to the Prophet, one that turned his descendants from Fāṭima and ʿAlī into failed revolutionaries or charismatic holy men. Messianism, the expectation of the coming, or second coming, of an emissary of the deity, destined to appear in the here and now to transform the world, or at the end of time to bring it to a close, entered the equation in the mid-eighth century. The appearance of the Mahdī 150 years later disappointed the expectation of an apocalypse, but exceptionally succeeded in establishing a dynasty destined, by its own account, to conquer and rule the world for God. It did so on the strength of its appeal to a tribal people, one of many such incorporated into the Arab empire by the Arab conquests, but never brought fully under its control. It was an appeal that depended upon their Islamisation, a process that had begun with the Arab conquest, but which almost from the beginning had provoked revolt in the name of the new faith, for the right that it represented against the wrongs that its rulers did. Success in this particular case, as Ibn Khaldūn observed, depended upon the arousal of the *ʿaṣabiyya* or innate solidarity of such a people, and its channelling into a force for world conquest by a messianic preacher of the coming millennium. In North Africa the same phenomenon, the mobilisation of a tribal people for conquest in the name of Islam, was repeated in the eleventh and twelfth centuries by the Almoravids and Almohads, revolutionaries of the same kind though doctrinally different, not simply from the Fatimids but from each other, the one legalistic, the other, once again, messianic.

The rising of the Kutāma at the call of the Fatimid Mahdī may have been one of the series of such risings in North Africa that had begun with the Khārijite rebellions 150 years earlier. But it belonged to a longer and wider phenomenon, a pattern of attempts by such tribal peoples to take over from the empire into which they were marginally incorporated. Thus in the Roman empire of the fourth century, Firmus followed by his brother Gildo, princes of the mountainous Kabylian homeland of the Kutāma, revolted in association with the Donatist opponents of the Catholic Church, in an attempt to make themselves masters of the North African Roman province. And while the Fatimids were coming to power in the Ifrīqiyan avatar of that province, to the east in the old Arab and nominally ᶜAbbasid empire, the Daylamites of the mountains to the south of the Caspian were creating the dominion of the Būyids in Iran and Iraq, while the Kurds of the mountain arc around the plains of Mesopotamia, from the Zagros on the western edge of Iran to the south-eastern edge of Anatolia, produced a series of little dynasties, as did the Bedouin Arabs of the Syrian-Iraqi desert. In the course of the eleventh century these takeovers came to a head as the old Arab empire finally suffered the fate of that of Rome, overrun by such peoples from outside its borders, by Berbers from the Sahara, Turks from Central Asia and the Hilālī Arabs from the western desert of Egypt, while in a different way, the Armenians came to power in Fatimid Egypt.

This takeover of the Arab empire by peoples from inside and outside nevertheless entered into its religious and political mould, one that went back beyond the ᶜAbbasids and Umayyads to the Late Roman empire, and one into which the Fatimids naturally slipped. The elements of both state and monarchy were already in place, both in theory and in practice, to be taken up by the Fatimids in fulfilment of their mission as they rose to power in North Africa and Egypt. The prototype was Byzantium under its Emperors, an autocracy that retained an element of popular election, just as the Caliphate retained the notion of popular leadership, but was otherwise a divinely sanctioned monarchy resident in a vast palace with a household of eunuchs serving not only the family and the ceremonial routine of the court, but also in the administration and the army. Beyond the household was a secretarial and tax-collecting bureaucracy, and an army of guardsmen, regiments and soldiers called up from their land for annual campaigns. The whole of this apparatus rested in its turn upon tax-collection, fundamentally from the land. The right to tax the population was the essential basis of government, creating a state that lived to tax and taxed to live, while at the same time rewarding its rulers with immense wealth in land and other assets.[1] Reproduced under the ᶜAbbasid Caliphate, such a state was inherited by the Fatimids in Egypt, after they had ruled in Ifrīqiya through the extensive delegation of tax-collection to provincial governors. Their monarchy, resting on the principle of designation to the Imāmate, was the supreme example of Caesaropapism, that

1 Cf. J. Herrin, *Byzantium. The Surprising Life of a Medieval Empire* (London, 2007), chs 14, 15, 16.

combination of religious and political authority enjoyed by the Byzantine Emperors, which was diluted in the case of the ᶜAbbasids by the authority of the schoolmen for the divine law, but which in western Europe was claimed by the Papacy, to which the Emperors were in principle subordinated as the Moon to the Sun. The Biblical prototype was Melchizedek, 'King and Priest', a figure who appears not only in Christian but also in Ismāᶜīlī literature.[2] The rise of the Fatimids to power confirmed them in this dual character as the representatives of God on earth, endowing them with a charisma that preserved them as the heads of state in Egypt even as its government passed out of their hands, and their religious authority dwindled down into sectarianism. In other words, they did not simply rule over a Byzantine type of state, but presided over a history described by Ibn Khaldūn on the one hand and Max Weber on the other as typical of a dynastic or patrimonial state, one in which, after the first flush of conquest, the servants took over from the masters to the point at which the dynasty itself came to an end.

Such a typology may seem to fit the Fatimids and their history very well. But to read their history in this way as one of rise, decline and fall is to ignore their positive contribution to state formation in Egypt, which completed the conversion of the country from a provincial backwater under the ᶜAbbasids into a centre of the Islamic and Mediterranean world. It was a conversion that began with the creation of a great patrimonial state, not least through the attraction into its service of Iraqis and others seeking employment after the collapse of the ᶜAbbasid regime, which for almost a century it replaced as the grandest example of Islamic monarchy. That state was most fully realised under the Wazīrs of the Pen in the mid-eleventh century; the subsequent subordination of the Pen to the Sword was a major reform, which although it eventually led to the abolition of the dynasty, was nevertheless responsible for a development of long-term significance, the allocation of the tax farm to the individual warrior as a means of maintaining the army. The *iqṭāᶜ* as a method of providing for the cultivation of the land, the revenues of the state, and the upkeep of the soldiery survived the end of the Fatimids to become the basis of the Mamlūk Sultanate of the later Middle Ages, an equally grand monarchy in which the army was fully integrated into the agricultural economy and the fiscal system.

This peculiarly Egyptian solution to the perennial problem of Kennedy's *ghulām* state, the payment of the troops on which the survival of the regime rested, was symptomatic of a more general militarisation of state and society in the Islamic world, but one that depended upon the cultivation of the

[2] Cf. Brett, *Rise of the Fatimids*, pp. 426–8, 432, 434.

floodplain of the Nile, and upon the system of tax-farming that went back to Roman times. While the cultivation of the floodplain produced the grain that was the staple wealth of the country, it likewise produced the flax, the cotton and the sugarcane that were the raw materials of a manufacturing industry whose products were exported in exchange for the raw materials that Egypt lacked, such as timber and iron. Such trade not only enhanced the prosperity of the country, its state and its rulers, but fed into an intercontinental commerce from the Mediterranean to the Indian Ocean, from Central Asia and from sub-Saharan Africa, for which Egypt was an entrepôt as well as a market. That commerce was fully exploited by the Fatimids and their entourage, who not only bought its commodities but financed it with their investment in its ventures. More important than the vast treasures they accumulated in the palace was the gold coinage made possible by this commerce, for which the consistently fine Fatimid dīnār served in its turn as a standard currency.

The dīnār meanwhile doubled as a symbol of the Fatimid claim to empire, a claim whose fortunes depended upon the realities of the world they set out to win. To use a phrase from the heyday of the British empire, trade followed the flag from Ifrīqiya to Egypt, but thereafter, as the drive to conquer the world from the ᶜAbbasids stalled in Syria, the flag followed trade, or, at least ran out along the lines of travel from end to end of the Islamic world. The reliance of the Holy Places of Mecca and Medina upon Egyptian grain was a principal factor in the recognition of the Fatimids by the Ashrāf who ruled them. Trade and travel up and down the Nile similarly underlay the relationship with the Sudanese kingdom of Muqurra. Beyond Mecca and the Fatimid port of ᶜAydhāb, the Red Sea route to Aden and India extended the relationship to the kingdom of Ethiopia and, more importantly, was vital to the revival of the Daᶜwa in the Yemen and to the creation of an Ismāᶜīlī community and polity whose reach extended out into the Indian Ocean, along the Arabian coast and past the Gulf, as far as Gujerat on the western coast of the peninsula. Back towards Ifrīqiya and Sicily, communication with the Zirids and the Kalbids was maintained along the land and sea routes via Barqa and Alexandria. Away towards Iraq and the Iranian world, the various Seveners were first persuaded of the Fatimid claim, and then organised into a series of Ismāᶜīlī communities under their *duᶜāt*, by correspondence along the well-travelled routes as far as Central Asia and the Punjab. Correspondence was the key, carried by emissaries great and small, in the form of questions and answers to and from the Imām and the Daᶜwa at al-Qāhira, or in that of proclamations and instructions sent out in the name of the Imām-Caliph. Produced by the Fatimid chancery, these *sijillāt* conformed, as their name implies, to a prescriptive type of document going back to Roman origins, and common throughout the Latin, Greek and Arabic worlds. Without this diplomatic lingua franca, through which the authority of the dynasty was conveyed to the recipient, the Fatimid empire could not, or at least would not, have developed and functioned in the way that it did, either as Dawla or as Da^c^wa. And as its creation brought to a head the long-standing conflict between Shī^c^ism and Sunnism, between the claims of the Prophet's descendants to inherit his religious and political authority, and those of the schoolmen to interpret the divine law that legitimised the power of the ruler, so the chain of cause and effect that ensued shaped the course of history in the Mediterranean and Middle East, for better or worse.

With the wisdom of hindsight, what can be said about the outcome of the Mahdī's great adventure? In the Maghrib, the mustering of the Kutāma for the conquest of Ifrīqiya, followed by the abandonment of what had originally been the Byzantine province of Africa to the Zirids, signalled the rise of Berber tribalism under the influence of Islam to become a force not simply for rebellion but for revolution and rule in a land that for centuries had been governed by Romans, Byzantines and Arabs. At the other end of North Africa, in lands that these had never ruled, the force of that tribalism was demonstrated in the conquests of the Almoravids and Almohads, each in its own way a part of the reaction and response to the Fatimid challenge to the world of Islam. Urged on by al-Qāhira, the Banū Hilāl meanwhile precipitated the break-up of Ifrīqiya into a series of city-states, and coupled with the Almoravids, inaugurated the swirl of Berber empire and Arab nomadism that characterised the history of North Africa down to the sixteenth century and ended with the regression of Berber language and culture into the mountains and deserts.[3] In the Mashriq the Fatimid challenge, giving rise directly or indirectly to the similar swirl of Seljuqs and Crusaders, ended with the sweeping up of Egypt into the Ayyubid and eventually Mamlūk empire. In Egypt itself, the factors underlying the prosperity of the Fatimids gave rise to the highly literate society that survived their disappearance to reach a peak in the fifteenth century, when the Fatimid achievement was celebrated by al-Maqrīzī. But at the same time, over the two centuries of their rule in Egypt, the Fatimids presided over a comparable social change with the passage of the country from the heterogeneous society of various Muslims, Christians and Jews that was envisaged in the Amān of Jawhar as coming under the protection of the dynasty, one in which women played a prominent part, into a more homogeneously and consciously Sunnī population. Partly the result of the Sunnī reaction to the Fatimid challenge, this was also the product of the long-term decline of the Coptic community from the majority that may have survived

[3] Cf. M. Brett and E. Fentress, *The Berbers* (Oxford, 1996), chs 3 and 4.

down to the end of the tenth century into the minority that has survived to the present day. This was not simply the result of conversion to Islam, but the probable outcome of a differential birth rate, which may have been crucial as the population as a whole recovered from the *shidda*, or famine, of the years from 1066 to 1073.[4] By contrast, the social and geographical patchwork of Syria, which had brought the Fatimid ambition to conquer Baghdad to a halt, grew still more complicated with the arrival of the Druzes and the Nizārī Assassins, not to speak of the Franks. Down to the arrival of the Crusaders, the native Christians of Palestine and the Lebanon appear to have remained in the majority in the countryside as well as at Jerusalem.[5] The Jews, on the other hand, were driven out by the Crusaders, going, if anywhere, to swell the numbers attracted to Egypt by the Fatimid 'economic miracle'.

In Egypt itself, the Copts continued to flourish in the administration and the Church, largely or wholly reserved occupations that enabled them to resist both the temptation to convert and the periodic hostility of the Muslim population. But as the pomp and circumstance of the dynasty faded away after the murder of al-Āmir in 1130, so an age of cultural splendour came to an end. Its passing was confirmed by the abandonment of al-Qāhira as the seat of government for Saladin's Citadel on a spur of the ridge of the Muqaṭṭam hills, an eyrie overlooking the Fatimid city where the Fatimid palaces were deserted and torn down, their treasures and books confiscated and dispersed. This architectural closure of the Fatimids' political achievement set the seal on the long-drawn-out separation of the Dawla or state ruled by the Fatimid Caliph from the Daᶜwa or mission predicated on the Fatimid Imām, as, one after another, the Druzes, the Nizārīs and the Ṭayyibīs refused to accept the dynastic succession at al-Qāhira. All three reverted to the original concept of an Imām in *ghayba*, 'occultation', or *satr*, 'concealment', to justify a secession which, in the case of the Druzes enabled them to form a refugee community in a Syrian retreat, and, in the case of the Nizārīs and the Ṭayyibīs, enabled them to pursue their own aims in their own countries, while reaching back to Syria and out to India. The doctrine of Ḥasan-i Ṣabbāḥ, that the Imām was to be known by inward contemplation rather than outward signs, found its equivalent in al-Ghazālī's insistence upon meditation on the Qurʾān as the source of spiritual enlightenment, twin concepts at the heart of the mystical tradition culminating in the vision of Ibn al-ʿArabī 100 years later. Otherwise the outcome was sectarianism, on the one hand institutionalised, determined

4 Cf. M. Brett, 'Population and conversion to Islam in Egypt in the medieval period', in U. Vermeulen and J. Van Steenbergen (eds), *Egypt and Syria in the Fatimid, Ayyubid and Mamluk Eras*, IV (Leuven, 2005), pp. 1–32.

5 Cf. M. Gil, *A History of Palestine, 634–1099* (Cambridge, 1992), pp. 171–2, 435–47.

and persistent down to the present day, on the other hand marginalised by the mainstream of Sunnism and Twelver Shīᶜism. It is thus ironic that just as the global demographic growth that began in the nineteenth century has turned the Copts from a community of a few hundred thousand into one of millions,[6] so too the Ismāᶜīlīs, and the Nizārīs in particular, have emerged from obscurity to spread across the world from China to North America. In the process, a new Dār al-Ḥikma has been created in the shape of the Institute of Ismaili Studies in London, one in which modern scholarship is devoted not only to the collection and cataloguing of source material, but to the edition, translation and publication of texts, and to research, not least into the history of the Fatimids, their empire and their cause.[7]

[6] Brett, 'Population and conversion'.

[7] For these post-Fatimid developments, cf. F. Daftary, *The Ismāᶜīlīs. Their History and Doctrines*, 2nd edn, 2007.

Genealogy of Shīʿite Imāms

Muḥammad	
Fāṭima = **ʿAlī I**	
Ḥasan II	**Ḥusayn III**
	ʿAlī Zayn al-ʿĀbidīn IV
	Muḥammad al-Bāqir V
	Jaʿfar al-Ṣādiq VI
Ismāʿīl ʿAbd Allāh	**Mūsā al-Kāẓim VII**
Muḥammad VII	**ʿAlī al-Riḍā VIII**
Expected Mahdī/Messiah of Seveners	**Muḥammad al-Taqī IX** **ʿAlī al-Hādī X**
Ancestor of Fatimids	**Ḥasan al-ʿAskarī XI** **Muḥammad al-Muntaẓar XII**
	Imām in *Ghayba*, Occultation

Genealogy of Fatimids

	Muḥammad ibn Ismāʿīl VII Second Sequence of Imāms	
Caliphate	3 Hidden Imāms, in *Satr*	Imāmate
I	**ʿAbd Allah, al-Mahdī biʾllāh** 910–34	IV
II	**Abūʾl-Qāsim Muḥammad, al-Qāʾim bi-amriʾllāh** 934–46	V
III	Qāsim Others **Ismāʿīl, al-Manṣūr biʾllāh** 946–53	VI
IV	**Maʿadd, al-Muʿizz li-Dīn Allāh** 953–75	VII
V	Tamīm ʿAbd Allah **Nizār, al-ʿAzīz biʾllāh** 975–96	VIII
VI	Sitt al-Mulk **al-Manṣūr, al-Ḥākim bi-amriʾllāh** 996–1021	IX
VII	**ʿAlī, al-Ẓāhir li-Iʿzāz Dīn Allāh** 1021–36	X
VIII	**Maʾadd, al-Mustanṣir biʾllāh** 1036–94	XI
IX	Muḥammad Abūʾl-Ḥusayn ʿAbd Allāh Nizār **Aḥmad, al-Mustaʾlī biʾllāh** 1094–1100	XII
X	**al-Manṣūr, al-Āmir bi-aḥkām Allāh** 1100–30	XIII
XI	**ʿAbd al-Majīd Muḥammad, al-Ḥāfiẓ li-Dīn Allāh** Cousin of **al-Āmir** 1132–49	XIV
	Sulaymān Ḥaydara Ḥasan	
XII	**Ismāʿīl, al-Ẓāfir bi-amriʾllāh** 1149–54	XV

XIII	**ᶜĪsā, al-Fāʾiz bi-naṣriʾllāh** 1154–60	XVI
XIV	**ᶜAbd Allah, al-ᶜĀḍid li-Dīn Allāh** Cousin of **al-Fāᶜiz** 1160–71 Dāʾūd	XVII

Bibliography

Abū Bakr al-Mālikī, *Riyāḍ al-Nufūs*, ed. al-Bakkūsh, 3 vols (Beirut, 1981), vol. 2, pp. 503–6.
Abū'l-Fawāris, Aḥmad ibn Ya'qūb, *Al-Risāla fī'l-imāma*, ed. and trans. S. N. Makarem, *The Political Doctrine of the Ismā'īlīs* (Delmar, NY, 1977).
Abū'l-Makārim Sa'dallah Jirjis, *Ta'rīkh al-kanā'is wa'l-adyira*, attributed to Abū Ṣāliḥ the Armenian, ed. and trans. B. T. A. Evetts, *Churches and Monasteries of Egypt* (Oxford, 1895).
Adams, W. Y., *Nubia. Corridor to Africa* (London and Princeton, NJ, 1977, repr. 1984).
Adra, M. (trans.), *Mount of Knowledge, Sword of Eloquence. The Collected Poems of an Ismaili Muslim Scholar in Fatimid Egypt* (London and New York, 2011).
Anwar, S. and Bacharach, J. L., 'Shī'ism and the early Dinars of the Fāṭimid Imam-caliph al-Mu'izz li-dīn Allāh (341–365/952–975): an analytic overview', *Al-Masāq*, 22 (2010), 259–78.
Assaad, S. A., *The Reign of al-Hakim bi Amr Allah (386/996–411/1021): a Political Study* (Beirut, 1974).
Bacile, R. and McNeil, J. (eds), *Romanesque and the Mediterranean: Points of Contact Across the Latin, Greek and Islamic Worlds c. 1000 to c. 1250* (Leeds, 2016).
Barrucand, M. (ed.), *L'Egypte Fatimide: son art et son histoire* (Paris, 1999).
Bates, M. L., 'Khūrāsānī revolutionaries and al-Mahdī's title', in F. Daftary and J. W. Meri (eds), *Culture and Memory in Medieval Islam* (London and New York, 2003).
Bercher, L. (ed. and trans.), *La Risāla* (Algiers, 1974).
Bianquis, Th., *Damas et la Syrie sous la domination fatimide (969–1076)*, 2 vols (Damascus, 1986, 1989).
Bianquis, Th., 'Al-H'akim bi amr Allah', in Ch.-A. Julien et al. (eds), *Les Africains*, 12 vols (Paris, 1978), vol. 11.
Bierman, I. A., *Writing Signs; the Fatimid Public Text* (Berkeley and Los Angeles, CA, 1998).
Bloom, J. M., *Arts of the City Victorious. Islamic Art and Architecture in Fatimid North Africa and Egypt* (New Haven, CT, 2007).
Bloom, J. M., 'The Mosque of the Qarāfa in Cairo', *Muqarnas*, IV (1987).
Bonner, M. (trans.), *The Empire of the Mahdi* (Leiden, 1996).
Bora, F., 'The Mamluk historiography of the Fatimids recomsidered: Ibn al-Furāt's *Ta'rīkh al-duwal wa'l-mulūk*', DPhil thesis, University of Oxford (2010).
Bosworth, C. E., *The Ghaznavids. Their Empire in Afghanistan and Eastern Iran, 994–1040* (Edinburgh, 1963).

Bosworth, C. E., *The New Islamic Dynasties* (Edinburgh, 1996).
Bosworth, C. E., 'The political and dynastic history of the Iranian world (A.D. 1000–1217)', *The Cambridge History of Iran*, 7 vols (Cambridge, 1968), vol. 5.
Brett, M., 'Ashīr', in K. Fleet, G. Krämer, D. Matringe, J. Nawas and E. Rowson (eds), *Encyclopaedia of Islam*, 3rd edn (available at http://referenceworks.brillonline.com/browse/encyclopaedia-of-islam-3).
Brett, M., 'Ifriqiya as a market for Saharan trade from the tenth to the twelfth century', in M. Brett, *Ibn Khaldun and the Medieval Maghrib*, Variorum Collected Studies Series, no. II (Aldershot, 1999).
Brett, M., 'The Zughba at Tripoli, 429H (1037–8 AD)', Society for Libyan Studies, *Sixth Annual Report* (1974–5), 41–7.
Brett, M., 'The military interest of the battle of Ḥaydarān', in V. J. Parry and M. E. Yapp (eds), *War, Technology and Society in the Middle East* (London, 1975), pp. 78–88.
Brett, M., 'Fatimid historiography: a case study – the quarrel with the Zirids, 1048–58', in M. Brett, *Ibn Khaldun and the Medieval Maghrib*, Variorum Collected Studies Series, no. VIII (Aldershot, 1999).
Brett, M., 'Islam and trade in the *Bilad al-Sudan*', in M. Brett, *Ibn Khaldun and the Medieval Maghrib*, Variorum Collected Studies Series, no. V (Aldershot, 1999).
Brett, M., 'The way of the peasant', *Bulletin of SOAS*, 47 (1984), 44–56.
Brett, M., 'The city-state in mediaeval Ifrīqiya: the case of Tripoli', in M. Brett, *Ibn Khaldun and the Medieval Maghrib*, Variorum Collected Studies Series, no. XIV (Aldershot, 1999).
Brett, M., 'The Islamisation of Morocco from the Arabs to the Almoravids', in M. Brett, *Ibn Khaldun and the Medieval Maghrib*, Variorum Collected Studies Series, no. I (Aldershot, 1999).
Brett, M., 'The flood of the dam and the sons of the new moon', in *Mélanges offerts à Mohamed Talbi à l'occasion de son 70e anniversaire* (Tunis, 1993), pp. 55–67, and in M. Brett, *Ibn Khaldun and the Medieval Maghrib*, Variorum Collected Studies Series, no. IX (Aldershot, 1999).
Brett, M., 'The Mīm, the ᶜAyn, and the making of Ismāʿīlism', *Bulletin of SOAS*, 57 (1994), 25–39, and in M. Brett, *Ibn Khaldūn and the Medieval Maghrib*, Variorum Collected Studies Series, no. III (Aldershot, 1999).
Brett, M., 'The way of the nomad', *Bulletin of SOAS*, 58 (1995), 251–69, and in *Ibn Khaldun and the Medieval Maghrib*, Variorum Collected Studies Series, no. X (Aldershot, 1999).
Brett, M., 'Muslim justice under infidel rule: the Normans in Ifrīqiya, 517–555H/1123–1160 AD', in M. Brett, *Ibn Khaldun and the Medieval Maghrib*, Variorum Collected Studies Series, no. XIII (Aldershot, 1999).
Brett, M., 'The battles of Ramla (1099–1105)', in U. Vermeulen and D. De Smet (eds), *Egypt and Syria in the Fatimid, Ayyubid and Mamluk Eras*, I (Leuven, 1995), pp.17–37.
Brett, M., 'The origins of the Mamlūk military system in the Fatimid period', in U. Vermeulen and D. De Smet (eds), *Egypt and Syria in the Fatimid, Ayyubid and Mamluk Eras,* I (Leuven, 1995), pp. 39–52, at pp. 41–4.
Brett, M. and Fentress, E., *The Berbers* (Oxford, 1996).
Brett, M., 'The execution of al-Yāzūrī', in U. Vermeulen and D. De Smet (eds),

Egypt and Syria in the Fatimid, Ayyubid and Mamluk Eras, II (Leuven, 1998), pp. 15–27.
Brett, M., 'The Lamp of the Almohads. Illumination as a political idea in twelfth-century Morocco', in M. Brett, *Ibn Khaldun and the Medieval Maghrib*, Variorum Collected Studies Series, no. VI (Aldershot, 1999).
Brett, M., *Ibn Khaldun and the Medieval Maghrib*, Variorum Collected Studies Series (Aldershot, 1999).
Brett, M., *The Rise of the Fatimids. The World of the Mediterranean and the Middle East in the Tenth Century* CE (Leiden, 2001).
Brett, M., 'Abbasids, Fatimids and Seljuqs', in D. Luscombe and J. Riley-Smith (eds), *The New Cambridge Medieval History*, 7 vols (Cambridge, 2004), vol. 4, part 2, pp. 675–720.
Brett, M., 'Al-Karāza al-Marqusīya. The Coptic Church in the Fatimid empire', in U. Vermeulen and J. Van Steenbergen (eds), *Egypt and Syria in the Fatimid, Ayyubid and Mamluk Eras*, IV (Leuven, 2005), pp. 33–60.
Brett, M., 'Badr al-Ǧamālī and the Fatimid Renascence', in U. Vermeulen and J. Van Steenbergen (eds), *Egypt and Syria in the Fatimid, Ayyubid and Mamluk Eras*, IV (Leuven, 2005), pp. 61–78.
Brett, M., 'Population and conversion to Islam in Egypt in the Mediaeval period', in U. Vermeulen and J. Van Steenbergen (eds), *Egypt and Syria in the Fatimid, Ayyubid and Mamluk Eras*, IV (Leuven, 2005), pp. 1–32.
Brett, M., 'The Fatimids and the Counter-Crusade, 1099–1171', in U. Vermeulen and K. D'Hulster (eds), *Egypt and Syria in the Fatimid, Ayyubid and Mamluk Eras*, V (Leuven, 2007), pp. 15–25.
Brett, M., 'The poetry of disaster. The tragedy of Qayrawān, 1052–1057CE', in K. D'Hulster and J. Van Steenbergen (eds), *Continuity and Change in the Realms of Islam. Studies in honour of Professor Urbain Vermeulen* (Leuven, 2008), pp. 77–89.
Brett, M., 'The Ifrīqiyan *sijill* of al-Mustanṣir, 445/1053–4', in U. Vermeulen and K. D'Hulster (eds), *Egypt and Syria in the Fatimid, Ayyubid and Mamluk Eras*, VI (Leuven, 2010), pp. 9–16.
Brett, M., 'Egypt', in C. F. Robinson (ed.), *The New Cambridge History of Islam*, 2 vols (Cambridge, 2010), vol. 1, pp. 541–80.
Brett, M., 'The central lands of North Africa and Sicily, until the beginning of the Almohad period', in M. Fierro (ed.), *The New Cambridge History of Islam*, 2 vols (Cambridge, 2010), vol. 2, pp. 48–65.
Brett, M., 'State formation and government', in M. Fierro (ed.), *The New Cambridge History of Islam*, 2 vols (Cambridge, 2010), vol. 2, pp. 549–85.
Brett, M., 'The execution of Ibn Badūs', in U. Vermeulen, K. D'Hulster and J. Van Steenbergen (eds), *Egypt and Syria in the Fatimid, Ayyubid and Mamluk Eras*, VII (Leuven, 2013), pp. 21–9.
Brett, M., 'The Muslim response to the First Crusade', in S. B. Edgington and L. Garcia-Guijarro (eds), *Jerusalem the Golden. The Origins and Impact of the First Crusade* (Turnhout, 2014), pp. 219–34.
Brett, M., 'The diplomacy of empire: Fatimids and Zirids, 990–1062', *Bulletin of SOAS*, 78 (2015), 149–59.
Bryer, D. R. W., 'The origins of the Druze religion', *Der Islam*, 52 (1975), 47–84, 239–262; 53 (1976), 5–27.

Bulliet, R., *Patricians of Nishapur* (Cambridge, 1972).
Cahen, C., *Makhzūmiyyāt. Études sur l'histoire économique et financière de l'Égypte médiévale* (Leiden, 1977).
Calderini, 'Sayyida Raṣad: a royal woman as "Gateway to Power" during the Fatimid era', in U. Vermeulen and K. D'Hulster (eds), *Egypt and Syria in the Fatimid, Ayyubid and Mamluk Eras*, V (Leuven, 2007), pp. 27–36.
The Cambridge History of Egypt, vol. 1, *Islamic Egypt, 640–1517*, ed. C. F. Petry (Cambridge, 1998).
Canard, M., 'L'autobiographie d'un chambellan du Mahdi Obeid-Allah le Fatimide', *Hespéris*, XXXIX (1952), 279–329.
Canard, M., 'Une famille de partisans, puis d'adversaires, des Fatimides en Afrique du Nord', in G. Marçais, *Mélanges d'histoire et d'archéologie de l'Occident musulman*, 2 vols (Algiers, 1957), vol. II, pp. 33–49.
Canard, M., *Vie de l'Ustadh Jawdhar* (Algiers, 1958).
Casanova, P., 'Les derniers Fatimides', *Mémoires de l'Institut français d'archéologie orientale du Caire* (*IFAOC*), VI (1897), 415–45.
Cheddadi, A., *Ibn Khaldūn. Peuples et nations du monde*, 2 vols (Paris, 1986).
Chiarelli, L. C., *A History of Muslim Sicily* (Santa Venera, 2010).
Christie, N., 'Cosmopolitan trade centre or bone of contention? Alexandria and the Crusades, 487–857/1095–1453', *Al-Masāq*, 26 (2014), 49–61.
Colin, G. S. and Lévi-Provençal, É. (eds), *Histoire de l'Afrique du Nord de la conquête au XIe siècle* (Leiden, 1948).
Cooper, R. S. (trans.), *Ibn Mammātī's Rules for the Ministries*, microfilm reprint of PhD dissertation, Berkeley, CA (1973) (Ann Arbor, MI and London, 1979).
Cortese, D. and Calderini, S., *Women and the Fatimids in the World of Islam* (Edinburgh, 2006).
Dachraoui, F., *Le Califat Fatimide au Maghreb (296–365H./909–975 JC. Histoire politique et institutions* (Tunis, 1981).
Daftary, F., *The Assassin Legends. Myths of the Ismāʿīlīs* (London, 1994).
Daftary, F., *The Ismāʿīlīs. Their History and Doctrines*, 2nd edn (Cambridge, 2007).
Daftary, F. and Meri, J. W. (eds), *Culture and Memory in Medieval Islam* (London and New York, 2003).
Darke, H., *The Book of Government, or Rules for Kings* (London, 1960).
De Slane, W. M., *Histoire des Berbères*, 2nd edn, ed. P. Casanova, 4 vols (Paris, 1925).
De Smet, D., 'Les interdictions alimentaires du Calife fatimide al-Ḥākim: Marques de folie ou annonce d'un règne messianique?', in U. Vermeulen and D. De Smet (eds), *Egypt and Syria in the Fatimid, Ayyubid and Mamluk Eras*, I (Leuven, 1995), pp. 53–69.
De Smet, D., 'La translation du *raʾs al-Ḥusayn* au Caire fatimide', in U. Vermeulen and D. De Smet (eds), *Egypt and Syria in the Fatimid, Ayyubid and Mamluk Eras*, II (Leuven, 1998), pp. 29–44.
Den Heijer, J., 'La révolte de l'émir Nāṣir al-Dawla b. Ḥamdān contre le Calife fatimide al-Mustanṣir biʾllāh (première partie)', in U. Vermeulen and K. D'Hulster (eds), *Egypt and Syria in the Fatimid, Ayyubid and Mamluk Eras*, V (Leuven, 2007), pp. 109–19.
Den Heijer, J., 'La révolte de l'émir Nāṣir al-Dawla b. Ḥamdān contre le Calife fatimide al-Mustanṣir biʾllāh (deuxième partie)', in U. Vermeulen and K. D'Hulster

(eds), *Egypt and Syria in the Fatimid,Ayyubid and Mamluk Eras*, VI (Leuven, 2010), pp. 17–25.
Edgington, S. B. and Garcia-Guijarro, L. (eds), *Jerusalem the Golden. The Origins and Impact of the First Crusade* (Turnhout, 2014).
Ehrenkreutz, A. S., *Saladin* (New York, 1972).
Evans-Pritchard, E. E., *The Sanūsī of Cyrenaica* (Oxford, 1949).
Evetts, B. T. A., *Churches and Monasteries of Egypt* (Oxford, 1895).
Evetts, B. T. A. et al., *History of the Coptic Patriarchs of Alexandria*, 3 vols (Paris, 1901; Cairo, 1943–59, 1968–70).
Fierro, M. I., 'On *al-fāṭimī* and *al-fāṭimiyyūn*', *Jerusalem Studies in Arabic and Islam*, XX (1996), 130–61.
Fierro, M. (ed.), *The New Cambridge History of Islam*, 2 vols (Cambridge, 2010).
Fleet, K., Krämer, G., Matringe, D., Nawas, J. and Rowson, E. (eds), *Encyclopaedia of Islam*, 3rd edn (Leiden, 2007–).
Fluck, C. et al. (eds), *Egypt: Faith after the Pharaohs* (London, 2015).
Forsyth, J., *The Byzantine-Arab Chronicle (938–1034) of Yaḥyā b. Saᶜīd al-Anṭākī*, 2 vols (Ann Arbor, MI and London, 1977).
Frenkel, M., 'Medieval Alexandria – life in a port city', *Al-Masāq*, 26 (2014), 5–35.
Fyzee, A. A. A., *Compendium of Fatimid Law* (Simla, 1969).
Garcia-Arenal, M., *Messianism and Puritanical Reform. Mahdis of the Muslim West* (Leiden, 2006).
Geertz, C., *Islam Observed. Religious Development in Morocco and Indonesia* (Chicago, IL and London, 1968).
Gil, M., *A History of Palestine, 634–1099* (Cambridge, 1992).
Goitein, S. D. F., *A Mediterranean Society. The Jewish Communities of the Arab world as Portrayed in the Documents of the Cairo Geniza*, 6 vols (Berkeley and Los Angeles, CA, 1967–93), vol. 1, *Economic Foundations*.
Gottheil, R., 'A distinguished family of Fatimide Cadis (al-Nuᶜman) in the tenth century', *Journal of the American Oriental Society*, 27 (1906), 217–96.
Haji, H., *Founding the Fatimid State. The Rise of an early Islamic Empire* (London, 2006).
Haji, H., *Inside the Immaculate Portal* (London, 2012).
Halm, H., *Kosmologie und Heilslehre der frühen Ismāᶜīlīya* (Wiesbaden, 1978).
Halm, H., 'Der Treuhänder Gottes: die Edikte des Kalifen al-Ḥākim', *Der Islam*, 63 (1986), 11–72.
Halm, H., *Das Reich des Mahdi. Der Aufsteig der Fatimiden* (Munich, 1991), trans. M. Bonner, *The Empire of the Mahdi* (Leiden, 1996).
Halm, H., *The Fatimids and their Traditions of Learning* (London, 1997).
Halm, H., *Die Kalifen von Kairo* (Munich, 2003).
Halm, H., *Kalifen und Assassinen* (Munich, 2013).
Halm, H., 'Le destin de la princesse Sitt al-Mulk', in M. Barrucand (ed.), *L'Égypte fatimide, son art et son histoire* (Paris, 1999), pp. 69–72.
Halm, H., 'Der Tod Ḥamzas, des Begründers des Drusisches Religion', in U. Vermeulen and D. De Smet (eds), *Egypt and Syria in the Fatimid, Ayyubid and Mamluk* Eras, II (Leuven, 1998), pp. 105–13.
Halm, H., 'Der Nubische *baqṭ*', in U. Vermeulen and D. De Smet (eds), *Egypt and Syria in the Fatimid, Ayyubid and Mamluk Eras*, II (Leuven, 1998), pp. 63–103.
Halm, H., 'Badr al-Ǧamālī – Wesir oder Militärdiktator?', in U. Vermeulen and

K. D'Hulster (eds), *Egypt and Syria in the Fatimid, Ayyubid and Mamluk Eras*, V (Leuven, 2007), pp. 121–7.
al-Ḥamdānī, A. H., 'The Sīra of al-Muᵓayyad fiᵓl-Dīn ash-Shīrāzī (London, 1950).
Hamdani, S. A., *Between Revolution and State. The Path to Fatimid Statehood* (London and New York, 2006).
Hamdani, A. and de Blois, F., 'A re-examination of al-Mahdī's letter to the Yemenites on the genealogy of the Fatimid Caliphs', *Journal of the Royal Asiatic Society* (1983), 173–207.
Hampikian, N. and Cyran, M., 'Recent discoveries concerning the Fatimid palaces uncovered during the conservation works on parts of the Ṣāliḥiyya complex', in M. Barrucand (ed.), *L'Égypte fatimide, son art et son histoire* (Paris, 1999), pp. 649–63.
Hartmann, I. M., *The Early Mediaeval State. Byzantium, Italy and the West* (London, 1949).
Ḥasan, Y. F., *The Arabs and the Sudan, from the Seventh to the Sixteenth Century* (Edinburgh, 1967).
Herrin, J., *Byzantium. The Surprising Life of a Medieval Empire* (London, 2007).
Hitti, P. K., *Memoirs of an Arab-Syrian Gentleman* (New York, 1927).
Hitti, P. K., *History of the Arabs. From the Earliest Times to the Present* (London and New York, 1937).
Hodgson, M. G. S., *The Order of Assassins* (The Hague, 1955).
Hodgson, M. G. S., 'Al-Darazī and Ḥamza in the origin of the Druze religion', *Journal of the American Oriental Society*, 82 (1962), 5–20.
Holt, P. M., *The Age of the Crusades, The Near East from the Eleventh Century to 1517* (Harlow, 1986).
Holt, P. M., 'Saladin and his admirers: a biographical reassessment', *Bulletin of SOAS*, 46 (1983), 235–9.
Hunsberger, A. C., *Nasir Khusraw, the Ruby of Badakhshan* (London, 2000).
Ibn al-Haytham, ed. and trans. W. Madelung and P. E. Walker, *The Advent of the Fatimids. A Contemporary Shiᶜi Witness* (London and New York, 2000).
Ibn Abī Zayd al-Qayrawānī, *La Risāla*, ed. and trans. L. Bercher (Algiers, 1974).
Ibn ᶜIdhārī al-Marrākushī, *Kitāb al-bayān al-mughrib*, vol. 1, ed. G. S. Colin and É. Lévi-Provençal, *Histoire de l'Afrique du Nord de la conquête au XIe siècle* (Leiden, 1948).
Ibn al-Furāt, *Taᵓrīkh al-duwal waᵓl-mulūk*; the passages of information not found elsewhere have been edited and translated by F. Bora, 'The Mamluk historiography of the Fatimids reconsidered: Ibn al-Furāt's *Taᵓrīkh al-duwal waᵓl-mulūk*', DPhil thesis, University of Oxford (2010).
Ibn al-Jawzī, *Al-Muntaẓam fīᵓl-taᵓrīkh* (Hyderabad, 1939).
Ibn Khaldūn, *The Muqaddimah*, trans. F. Rosenthal, 2nd edn, 3 vols (New York, 1967, repr. London and Henley, 1986).
Ibn Khaldūn, *Kitāb al-ᶜIbar*, ed. Hūrīnī, 7 vols (Būlāq,1284H/1867).
Ibn Mammātī, *Kitāb qawānīn al-dawāwīn*, ed. A. S. Atiya (Cairo, 1943). English trans. R. S. Cooper, *Ibn Mammātī's Rules for the Ministries*, microfilm reprint of PhD dissertation, Berkeley, CA (1973) (Ann Arbor, MI and London, 1979).
Ibn Muyassar, *Akhbār Miṣr*, extracts made by al-Maqrīzī, ed. A. F. Sayyid, *Choix de passages de la* Chronique d'Égypte *d'Ibn Muyassar* (Paris, 1981).
Ibn al-Qalānisī, *Dhayl taᵓrīkh Dimashq*, ed. H. F. Amedroz (Leiden and London, 1908).

Ibn al-Ṣayrafī, *Al-Ishāra ilā man nāla al-wizāra*, ed. A. Mukhlis (Cairo, 1924); ed. A. F. Sayyid (Cairo, 1990).
Idris, H. R., *La Berbérie orientale sous Zīrīdes*, 2 vols (Paris, 1962).
Idrīs ᶜImād al-Dīn, *ᶜUyūn al-akhbār wa funūn al-āthār*, vols 1–7, ed. Maḥmūd Fakhūrī et al. (Damascus, 2007–12); vol. 5 and part of vol. 6, dealing with the North African period, ed. M. al-Yaᶜlāwī as *Taʾrīkh al-khulafāʾ al-fāṭimiyyūn biʾl-Maghrib* (Beirut, 1985), vol. 7, ed. and summarised A. F. Sayyid with P. E. Walker and M. Pomerantz as *The Fatimids and their Successors in the Yemen* (London, 2003). The section covering the life of al-Muᶜizz has been translated by S. Jiwa, *The Founder of Cairo* (London, 2013).
Ivanow, W., *Ismāʿīlī Tradition Concerning the Rise of the Fatimids* (London, 1942).
Ivanow, W., *Studies in Early Persian Ismailism*, 2nd edn (Bombay, 1955).
Al-Jawdhārī, *Sīrat al-Ustādh Jawdhar*, ed. M. K. Ḥusayn and M. A.-H. Shaʾīra (Cairo, 1954), trans. M. Canard, *Vie de l'Ustadh Jawdhar* (Algiers, 1958), ed. and trans. H. Haji, *Inside the Immaculate Portal* (London, 2012).
Jiwa, S., *Towards a Shiᶜi Mediterranean Empire* (London, 2009).
Jiwa, S., *The Founder of Cairo* (London, 2013).
Johns, J., *Arabic Administration in Norman Sicily: the Royal* Dīwān (Cambridge, 2002).
Johns, J., 'Muslim artists and Christian models in the painted ceilings of the Cappella Palatina', in R. Bacile and J. McNeil (eds), *Romanesque and the Mediterranean: Points of Contact Across the Latin, Greek and Islamic Worlds c. 1000 to c. 1250* (Leeds, 2016).
Julien, Ch.-A. et al. (eds), *Les Africains*, 12 vols (Paris, 1978).
Kay, H. C., *Yaman, its Early Mediaeval History* (London, 1892).
Kennedy. H., *The Prophet and the Age of the Caliphate* (London and New York, 1986).
Khan, G., *Arabic Legal and Administrative Documents in the Cambridge Genizah Collections* (Cambridge, 1993).
Al-Kindī, *Governors and Judges of Egypt*, ed. R. Guest (Leiden and London, 1912).
Kitāb al-kashf, ed. R. Strothmann (London, New York and Bombay, 1952).
Kitāb al-rushd and *Kitāb al-ʿālim*, trans. W. Ivanow, *Studies in Early Persian Ismailism*, 2nd edn (Bombay, 1955), chs 2–4. *Kitāb al-ᶜālim*, ed. and trans. J. W. Morris, *The Master and the Disciple* (London and New York, 2001).
Lalani, A. R., 'A philosophical response from Fatimid Egypt on leadership in Islam', in U. Vermeulen, K. D'Hulster and J. Van Steenbergen (eds), *Egypt and Syria in the Fatimid, Ayyubid and Mamluk Eras*, VII (Leuven, 2013), pp. 115–30.
Lambton, A. K. S., *State and Government in Medieval Islam* (Oxford, 1981).
Lane-Poole, S., *A History of Egypt in the Middle Ages* (London, 1901, 2nd edn 1913, 4th edn 1925, repr. 1968).
Lev, Y., *State and Society in Fatimid Egypt* (Leiden, 1991).
Lev, Y., *Saladin in Egypt* (Leiden, 1999).
Lev, Y., 'Aspects of the Egyptian society in the Fatimid period', in U. Vermeulen and J. Van Steenbergen (eds), *Egypt and Syria in the Fatimid, Ayyubid and Mamluk Eras*, III (Leuven, 2001).
Lewis, B., *The Origins of Ismāʿīlism: a Study of the Historical Background of the Fāṭimid Caliphate* (Cambridge, 1940).
Lewis, B., *The Arabs in History* (London, 1950).

Lewis, B., *The Assassins. A Radical Sect in Islam* (London, 1967).

Lewis, B., *Islam from the Prophet Muhammad to the Capture of Constantinople*, 2 vols (New York, 1974).

Lézine, A., *Mahdiya: recherches d'archéologie islamique* (Paris, 1965).

Lombard, M., *The Golden Age of Islam* (Amsterdam, Oxford and New York, 1975).

Luscombe, D. and Riley-Smith, J. (eds), *The New Cambridge Medieval History*, 7 vols (Cambridge, 2004).

Lyons, M. C. and Jackson, D. E. P., *Saladin. The Politics of the Holy War* (Cambridge, 1982).

Madelung, W., 'Das Imamat in der frühen ismailitischen Lehre', *Der Islam*, XXXVII (1961), 43–135.

Madelung, W. and Walker, P. E., *The Advent of the Fatimids. A Contemporary Shiᶜi Witness* (London and New York, 2000).

Makarem, S. N., ᶜAl-Ḥākim bi-amrillāh's appointment of his successors', *Al-Abhath*, XXIII (1970), 319–24.

Makarem, S. N., *The Political Doctrine of the Ismāᶜīlīs* (Delmar, NY, 1977).

al-Makhzūmī, *Al-Muntaqā min Kitāb al-minhāj fī ᶜilm kharāj Miṣr*, ed. C. Cahen and Y. Raghib (Cairo, 1986).

Mamour, P. H., *Polemics on the Origin of the Fatimi Caliphs* (London, 1934).

al-Maqrīzī, *Ittiᶜāẓ al-hunafāᵓ bi akhbār al-aᵓimma al-fāṭimiyyīn*, 3 vols, ed. J.-D. al-Shayyāl and M. H. M. Aḥmad (Cairo, 1967–73), 4 vols ed. A. F. Sayyid (London, 2010). The section dealing with the conquest of Egypt down to the death of al-Mu'izz has been translated by S. Jiwa, *Towards a Shiᶜi Mediterranean Empire* (London, 2009).

al-Maqrīzī, *Al-Khiṭaṭ* (*Kitāb al-mawāᶜiẓ waᵓl-iᶜtibār fī dhikr al-khiṭāṭ waᵓl-āthār*) (Bulaq, 1853); ed. G. Wiet, first 4 vols only (Cairo, 1911); autograph MS ed. A. F. Sayyid (London, 1416/1995).

al-Maqrīzī, *Kitāb al-muqaffā*, extracts ed. M. Yalaoui (Beirut, 1987).

Marçais, G., *La Berbérie musulmane et l'Orient au Moyen Âge* (Paris, 1946).

Marçais, G., *Mélanges d'histoire et d'archéologie de l'Occident musulman*, 2 vols (Algiers, 1957).

Masqueray, E., *Formation des cités chez les populations sédentaires de l'Algérie. Kabyles du Djurdjura, Chaouia de l'Aouras, Beni Mezab* (Paris, 1886). Repr. with Introduction by F. Colonna (Aix-en-Provence, 1983).

Metcalfe, A., *The Muslims of Medieval Italy* (Edinburgh, 2009).

Mez, A., *The Renaissance of Islam*, trans. S. Kh. Baksh and D. S. Margoliouth (Patna, 1937).

Morris, J. W., *The Master and the Disciple* (London and New York, 2001).

al-Muᵓayyad fīᵓl-Dīn al-Shīrāzī, *Sīrat al-Muᵓayyad fīᵓl-Dīn dāᶜī al-duᶜāt*, ed. M. K. Ḥusayn (Cairo, 1949, repr. Beirut, 1996).

al-Muᵓayyad fīᵓl-Dīn al-Shīrāzī, *Dīwān al-Muᵓayyad fīᵓl-Dīn al-Shīrāzī dāᶜī al-duᶜāt*, ed. M. K. Husayn (Cairo, 1949), trans. M. Adra as *Mount of Knowledge, Sword of Eloquence* (London, 2011).

al-Muqaddasī, *Aḥsan al-taqāsīm fī maᶜrifat al-aqālīm* (Leiden, 1906).

Murray, A. V., *The Crusades: an Encyclopedia*, 4 vols (Santa Barbara, CA, Denver, CO and Oxford, 2006).

al-Musabbiḥī, *Tome quarantième de la Chronique d'Égypte de Musabbiḥī*, 2 vols, ed. A. F. Sayyid in conjunction with Th. Bianquis (Cairo, 1978).

Nāṣir-i Khusraw, *Safar-nāma*, ed. and French trans. *C. Schefer, Sefer Nameh* (Paris, 1881); English trans. W. M. Thackston, Jr, *Naser-e Khosraw's Book of Travels (Safarnama)* (Albany, NY, 1986); biography by A. C. Hunsberger, *Nasir Khusraw, the Ruby of Badakhshan* (London, 2000).
al-Nawbakhtī, *Firaq al-Shīʿa*, ed. H. Ritter, *Die Sekten der Schiʿa* (Istanbul, 1931); trans. M. J. Mashkour, *Les sectes Shiites*, 2nd edn (Tehran, 1980).
al-Naysābūrī, *Ithbāt al-imāma*, ed. and trans. A. Lalani as *Degrees of Excellence. A Fatimid Treatise on Leadership in Islam* (London, 2009).
al-Naysābūrī, *Risāla al-mujāza al-kāfiya fī ādāb al-duʿāt*, ed. and trans. V. Klemm and P. E. Walker as *A Code of Conduct. A Treatise on the Etiquette of the Fatimid Ismaili Mission* (London, 2011).
al-Naysābūrī, *Istitār al-imām*, ed. W. Ivanow in *Bulletin of the Faculty of Arts, University of Egypt*, vol. 4, part 2 (1936), 93–107; trans. W. Ivanow in *Ismāʿīlī Tradition Concerning the Rise of the Fatimids* (London, 1942), pp. 157–83.
Netton, I. R., *Muslim Neoplatonists: an Introduction to the Thought of the Brethren of Purity* (Edinburgh, 1991).
The New Cambridge History of Islam, vol. 1, ed. C. F. Robinson, *The Formation of the Islamic World, Sixth to Eleventh Centuries*; vol. 2, ed. M. Fierro, *The Western Islamic World, Eleventh to Eighteenth Centuries* (Cambridge, 2010).
Nicol, N. D., *A Corpus of Fāṭimid Coins* (Trieste, 2006).
Niẓām al-Mulk, *Siyāsat-nāma*, trans. H. Darke, *The Book of Government, or Rules for Kings* (London, 1960).
Parry, V. J. and Yapp, M. E. (eds), *War, Technology and Society in the Middle East* (London, 1975).
Peacock, A. C. S., *The Great Seljuk Empire* (Edinburgh, 2015).
Poonawala, I. K., 'Al-Qāḍī al-Nuʿmān and Ismaʿili jurisprudence', in F. Daftary (ed.), *Medieval Ismaʿili History and Thought* (Cambridge, 1996), pp. 117–43.
(al-Qāḍī) al-Fāḍil, *Al-Durr al-naẓīma min tarassul ʿAbd al-Raḥīm ibn ʿAlī al-Baysānī*), ed. A. Badawi (Cairo, n.d.).
al-Qāḍī al-Nuʿmān, *Daʿāʾim al-Islām*, ed. A. A. A. Fyzee, 2 vols (Cairo, 1951–61).
al-Qāḍī al-Nuʿmān, *The Book of Faith: Daʿāʾim al-Islam*, section on Imamate, trans. A. A. A. Fyzee (Bombay, 1974).
al-Qāḍī al-Nuʿmān, *Kitāb al-majālis waʾl-musāyarāt*, ed. Ḥ. al-Faqī, I. Shabbūḥ and M. al-Yaʿlāwī (Tunis, 1978); 2nd edn, M. al-Yaʾlawī (Beirut, 1997).
al-Qāḍī al-Nuʿmān, *Iftitāḥ al-daʿwa wa ibtidāʾ al-dawla*, ed. W. el-Qadi (Beirut, 1970), F. Dachraoui (Tunis, 1975); trans. H. Haji as *Founding the Fatimid State. The Rise of an early Islamic Empire* (London, 2006).
al-Qalqashandī, *Ṣubḥ al aʿshā fī ṣināʿat al-inshāʾ* (Cairo, 1912–38).
Rabie, H., *The Financial System of Egypt, A.H. 564–741/A.D. 1169–1341* (London, 1972).
Riley-Smith, J., 'Crusading and the Montlhérys', in J. Riley-Smith, *The First Crusaders, 1095–1131* (Cambridge, 1997), pp. 180–2.
Robinson, C. F. (ed.), *The New Cambridge History of Islam*, 2 vols (Cambridge, 2010).
Rosenthal, F. (trans.), *The Muqaddimah* 2nd edn, 3 vols (New York, 1967, repr. London and Henley, 1986).
Runciman, S., *A History of the Crusades*, 3 vols (Cambridge, 1951).
Sanders, P., *Ritual, Politics and the City in Fatimid Cairo* (Albany, NY, 1994).

Sanders, P., 'Bohra architecture and the restoration of Fatimid culture', in M. Barrucand (ed.), *L'Égypte Fatimide: son art et son histoire* (Paris, 1999), pp. 159–65.
Savage, E., *A Gateway to Hell, a Gateway to Paradise. The North African Response to the Arab Conquest* (Princeton, NJ, 1997).
Sayyid, A. F. (ed.), *Choix de passages de la* Chronique d'Égypte *d'Ibn Muyassar* (Paris, 1981).
Sayyid, A. F., *Al-Dawla al-fāṭimiyya fī Miṣr: tafsīr jadīd/Les Fatimides en Égypte: nouvelle interprétation* (Cairo, 1992).
Sayyid, A. F., *La Capitale d'Égypte jusqu'à l'époque fatimide (al-Qāhira et al-Fustāt): essai de reconstitution topographique* (Beirut and Stuttgart, 1998).
Sayyid, A. F., 'Le grand palais fatimide au Caire', in M. Barrucand (ed.), *L'Égypte Fatimide: son art et son histoire* (Paris, 1999), pp. 117–25.
Sayyid, A. F., with Walker, P. E. and Pomerantz, M., *The Fatimids and their Successors in the Yemen* (London, 2003).
Shaban, M. A., *Islamic History*, 2 vols (Cambridge, 1976), vol. 2.
Al-Sijillāt al-Mustanṣiriyya, ed. A. M. Mājid/Magued (Cairo, 1954), from MS, Library of the School of Oriental and African Studies, London, catalogue no. 27155.
Sīrat Jaᶜfar: text published by W. Ivanow in *Bulletin of the Faculty of Arts of the Egyptian University*, IV (1936), 107–33; trans. in W. Ivanow, *Ismāʿīlī Tradition Concerning the Rise of the Fatimids* (London, 1942), pp. 107–33.
Stern, S. M., *Fāṭimid Decrees* (London, 1964).
Stern, S. M., *Studies in Early Ismāᶜīlism* (Jerusalem and Leiden, 1983).
Stern, S. M., 'The Epistle of the Fatimid Caliph al-Āmir (al-Hidāya al-Āmiriyya) – its date and its purpose', *Journal of the Royal Asiatic Society* (1950), 20–31.
Stern, S. M., 'The Succession to the Fatimid Imam al-Āmir, the claims of the later Fatimids to the Imamate, and the rise of Ṭayyibī Ismailism', *Oriens*, IV (1951), 193–255.
Stern, S. M., 'The early Ismāᶜīlī missionaries in North-West Persia and in Khurāsān and in Transoxania', in S. M. Stern, *Studies in Early Ismāʿīlism* (Jerusalem and Leiden, 1983), pp. 189–233.
al-Ṭabarī, *Kitāb al-rusul waʾl-mulūk*, ed. M. J. de Goeje, *Annales*, 16 vols (Leiden, 1879–1901), trans. *The History of al-Ṭabarī*, ed. E. Yar-Shater, 38 vols (New York, 1985).
Talbi, M., *L'Émirat Aghlabide, 184–296, 800–909. Histoire politique* (Paris, 1966).
Thackston, W. M. Jr, *Naser-e Khosraw's Book of Travels (Safarnama)* (Albany, NY, 1986).
Thomson, K., *Politics and Power in Late Fatimid Egypt. The Reign of Caliph al-Mustansir* (London and New York, 2016).
Trésors fatimides du Caire, Exhibition catalogue, Institut du Monde Arabe (1998).
Turner, B. S., *Weber and Islam* (London, Henley and Boston, MA, 1974).
Udovitch, A. L., 'Fatimid Cairo: crossroads of world trade – from Spain to India', in M. Barrucand (ed.), *L'Égypte fatimide: son art et son histoire* (Paris, 1999), pp. 681–91.
ᶜUmāra al-Yamanī, *Taʾrīkh al-Yaman*, ed. and trans. H. C. Kay, *Yaman, its Early Mediaeval History* (London, 1892).
Usāma ibn Munqidh, *Kitāb al-iᶜtibār*, ed. H. Zayn (Beirut, 1988), trans. P. K. Hitti, *Memoirs of an Arab-Syrian Gentleman* (New York, 1927).

Van Ess, J., *Chiliastiche Erwartungen und die Versuchung der Göttlichkeit: der Kalif al-Ḥākim (386–411H)* (Heidelberg, 1977).
Van Reeth, J. M. F., *Al-Qumāma* et le *Qā'im* de 400H. : le trucage de la lampe sur le tombeau du Christ', in U. Vermeulen and D. De Smet (eds), *Egypt and Syria in the Fatimid, Ayyubid and Mamluk Eras*, II (Leuven, 1998), pp. 171–90.
Vantini, G., *Christianity in the Sudan* (Bologna, 1981).
Vatikiotis, P. J., 'al-Ḥākim bi-Amrillah: the God-King idea realised', *Islamic Culture*, XXIX (1955), 1–18.
Vermeulen, U. et al. (eds), *Egypt and Syria in the Fatimid, Ayyubid and Mamluk Eras*, Proceedings of the International Colloquium (CHESFAME) at the Universities of Leuven and Gent, series 1995 ff. (Leuven, 1995 ff.).
al-Wansharīshī, *Miᶜyār al-muᶜrib*, 13 vols (Rabat, 1981–3).
Walker, P. E., *Exploring an Islamic Empire. Fatimid History and its Sources* (London and New York, 2002).
Walker, P. E., *Early Philosophical Shiism. The Ismaili Neoplatonism of Abū Yaᶜqūb al-Sijistānī* (Cambridge, 1993).
Walker, P. E., *Ḥamīd al-Dīn al-Kirmānī: Ismaili Thought in the Age of al-Ḥākim* (London, 1999).
Walker, P. E., *Caliph of Cairo: al-Ḥākim bi-Amr Allah, 996–1021* (Cairo, 2009).
Walker, P. E., *Fatimid History and Ismaili Doctrine*, Variorum Series (Aldershot, 2008).
Walker, P. E., 'Fatimid institutions of learning', in P. E. Walker, *Fatimid History and Ismaili Doctrine* Variorum Series (Aldershot, 2008).
Walker, P. E., 'Succession to rule in the Shiite caliphate', *Journal of the American Research Center in Egypt*, 32 (1995), 239–64.
Walker, P. E., 'The Ismaili daᶜwa in the reign of the Fatimid caliph al-Ḥākim', in P. E. Walker, *Fatimid History and Ismaili Doctrine* Variorum Series (Aldershot, 2008), vol. II.
Walker, P. E., 'Another family of Fatimid Chief Qāḍīs: the al-Fāriqīs', in P. E. Walker, *Fatimid History and Ismaili Doctrine* Variorum Series (Aldershot, 2008), vol. IV.
Walker, P. E., 'Fatimid Alexandria as an entrepôt in the East-West exchange of Islamic scholarship', *Al-Masāq*, 26 (2014), 36–48.
Wansbrough, J., *Lingua Franca in the Mediterranean* (Richmond, 1996).
Wansbrough, J., 'On recomposing the Islamic history of North Africa', *Journal of the Royal Asiatic Society* (1969), 161–70.
Watson, A. M., *Agricultural Innovation in the Early Islamic World* (Cambridge, 1983).
Wiet, G., 'Matériaux pour un Corpus inscriptionum arabicarum', part 1, Égypte, vol. 2, *Mémoires de l'Institut français d'archéologie du Caire*, 52 (1929–30).
Williams, C., 'The Cult of ᶜAlid saints in the Fatimid monuments of Cairo', *Al-Muqarnas*. I (1983), 37–52; III (1985), 39–60.
Yaḥyā ibn Saᶜīd al-Anṭākī, *Taʾrīkh*, parts 1 and 2 ed. and trans. I. Kratchkovsky and A. Vasiliev, *Patrologia Orientalia*, 18 (1924), 690–833, and 23 (1932), 347–520; part 3, ed. and trans. I. Kratchkovsky, F. Micheau and G. Troupeau, *Patrologia Orientalia*, 47 (1997), 373–559.
Yar-Shater, E. (ed.), *The History of al-Ṭabarī*, 38 vols (New York, 1985).
Yusuf, M. D., Economic Survey of Syria during the Tenth and Eleventh Centuries (Berlin, 1985).

Index of Persons

Note: in all indexes, sub-entries are in chronological and /or topical order

Index of Dynasties, Peoples and Sects

Index of Places

Index of Subjects